D1560116

MEDIEVAL BUDA:
A STUDY OF MUNICIPAL GOVERNMENT
AND JURISDICTION IN THE KINGDOM
OF HUNGARY

MARTYN C. RADY

EAST EUROPEAN MONOGRAPHS, BOULDER
DISTRIBUTED BY COLUMBIA UNIVERSITY PRESS, NEW YORK

1985

EAST EUROPEAN MONOGRAPHS, NO. CLXXXII

The publication of this work was made
possible by generous grants from

THE TWENTY-SEVEN FOUNDATION
and
THE BRITISH ACADEMY

For my Parents

CONTENTS

Acknowledgements   vii
Map: Buda in the Late Middle Ages   viii

1. ÁRPÁD HUNGARY AND ITS FIRST TOWNS
    From Pest to Buda   1
    The Árpad Kingdom   7

2. THE PERIOD OF THE RECTORS
    The Establishment of the Rectorate   23
    The Title of Rector   31
    Family Power   33

3. GOVERNMENT AND *STADTRECHT*
    The Development of Municipal Institutions   39
    Notary and "Place of Authentication"   54

4. ASSOCIATION AND AUTHORITY
    The Burgher Association   69
    Jurisdictional Enclaves   74

5. PATRICIATE AND GOVERNING CLASS
    Wealth and Power   87
    The Separation of Wealth from Power   98
    The 1439 Revolt   105

6. MONARCHY, RIGHTS AND IDEOLOGY
    Municipal Rights   111
    Municipal Ideology   119

7. *PRAESENTIA REGIA* AND TAVERNICAL JURISDICTION
    Justiciar and Tavernicus   127
    Tavernicus and Mother-Town court   141

8.   CONCLUSION   161

APPENDICES

I.   The Pest-Buda Charter of 1244   165
II.   The Judges and Councillors of Medieval Buda   169

Abbreviations Used for Commonly Cited Sources and Archives   177

Notes to Main Text   181
Notes to Appendix II   220
Bibliography   227
Index   247

ACKNOWLEDGEMENTS

This book has its origins in a University of London doctoral thesis completed in 1982 under the supervision of Dr. László Péter and Professor F.R.H. Du Boulay. Subsequent revision of the thesis was greatly assisted by a British Academy exchange-award which enabled me to revisit the Budapest archives during the summer of 1983.

In preparing the findings of my research for publication, I am particularly indebted to the continuing help, encouragement and scholarly example of Dr. Péter, Professor Du Boulay and, in Budapest, Professor András Kubinyi. For the errors and misconceptions which doubtless persist in this work, they must though remain quite blameless.

I gratefully acknowledge the support of the Publications Committee of the School of Slavonic and East European Studies, and subventions in aid of publication from the British Academy and Twenty-Seven Foundation.

To my parents and to Veronica, my wife, I owe special thanks.

August, 1984

London.

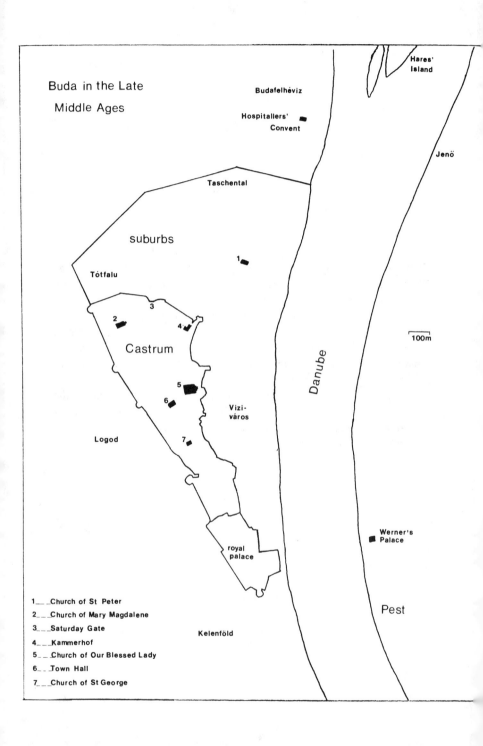

Buda in the Late Middle Ages

Hares' Island

Budafelhéviz

Hospitallers' Convent

Jenö

Taschental

suburbs

Tótfalu

1

3

2

4

Castrum

5

6

Vizi-város

Logod

7

Danube

100m

Werner's Palace

royal palace

Pest

Kelenföld

1___Church of St Peter
2___Church of Mary Magdalene
3___Saturday Gate
4___Kammerhof
5___Church of Our Blessed Lady
6___Town Hall
7___Church of St George

Chapter 1

ÁRPÁD HUNGARY AND ITS FIRST TOWNS

From Pest to Buda

Lying on one of Europe's most important crossroads, the area of modern day Budapest has since early times provided a suitable site for the establishment of large settlements. The fast flowing Danube pursuing through Hungary a southerly course on its way to the Black Sea encounters at this point the westernmost limit of the plain which, through the passes of the Carpathians, connects with the Russian steppe land and Asia. The Danube, no longer impeded by such large islands as lie to its north and south (Szentendre and Csepel Islands) proves here easily navigable. A ready link is, thus, offered between not only "East" and "West" but, more specifically, the Hungarian Lowland (*Alföld*) and the hillier and geographically quite different Transdanubia (*Dunántúl*). Some continuity of settlement in this region is understandable and the successive establishment here of Celtic, Roman, Avar, Slav and Magyar communities can come as little surprise.

Modern Budapest owes its legal origin to the Parliamentary Act of 1872 which for the first time amalgamated the three towns of Óbuda, Buda and Pest. Of these the newcomer is clearly Buda since the sites of the remaining two were both occupied during the Roman period. Óbuda was originally the legionary camp of Roman Aquincum, the sprawling and populous riverside capital of the province of Lower Pannonia; Pest little more than a garrison *castrum* known simply as Contra-Aquincum. With the evacuation of the legions in the fourth century, the life of these two communities came to a gradual end. The dark night of barbarism closed around them, obscuring their past and enhancing their mystery.[1] The early Hungarians who invaded and settled Pannonia at the close of the ninth century thought Óbuda to be nothing less than Attila's erstwhile capital.[2] From this misapprehension derives the town's German name, Etzelburg. Similarly, the old Roman aquaduct was imaginatively mistaken as "the baths of Krimhild."[3] Shortly after the Hungarian invasion, Óbuda's old Roman amphitheatre was occupied by Prince Kurszán of the leading Tarján tribe and, with this, there was forged a close connection between Óbuda and the kingdom's ruling dynasty—the House of Árpád. Its first Christian King, St. Stephen (1000–1038), founded here a collegiate chapter and over the succeeding centuries the town became one of the principal royal residences.[4] The passage of the twelfth century Anonymus Chronicle treating on the discovery of the "city of Attila" by the legendary Prince Árpád and the festivities and decoration that ensued was probably inspired by the building projects undertaken there by King Béla III (1173–1196).[5] Again, it was at Óbuda that the German Emperor, Frederick Barbarossa, jouneying on his way to the Holy Land, hunted and was entertained with great largesse by the Hungarian King.[6] We are told that Béla IV (1235–1270) was accustomed to spend Lent at Óbuda and a later document from 1288 refers to the King's "continual residence" in the town.[7] Around the small haven by the Danube a trading settlement grew up and recent excavations have brought to light not only a hoard of Byzantine coins but also a pair of scales for weighing monies.[8] Clearly, however, the commercial development of Óbuda was greatly hindered by the local chapter house under whose jurisdiction the town fell by royal donation in 1212.[9]

Until the mid-thirteenth century, Óbuda is always referred to in Latin texts as Buda and only with the founding of Buda proper to the south does Óbuda come to acquire the name of *Buda vetus.* The actual origin of the name Buda must remain unclear. A number of explanations have been afforded—that it derives from the Hungarian *bódé* meaning "hut" or the Slavonic *voda,* "water." Most probably, however, Buda was originally a personal name of Turkic origin which at an early stage became associated with the settlement. More is known of the place-name Pest. For Pest means simply "chimney" and, thus, undoubtedly refers to the lime kilns found here in the early Árpád period. The German for Pest is a direct translation of this name—*"Oven"* or *"Ofen"* (later *"Altofen"*).[10]

According to the Anonymus Chronicle, in the mid-tenth century the Hungarian Prince Taksony gave the old and seemingly deserted Roman *castrum* at Pest to the princes of the Muslim Volga Bulgarians.[11] Although this account is quite probably mythical, a Muslim community (but probably of Kaliz origin) was active in Pest as late as the thirteenth century.[12] In 1218 reference is made in a letter of Pope Honorius III to the "Saracens of Pest."[13]

Some historians have attempted to locate this Muslim settlement on the opposite, right bank of the Danube.[14] This would, however, seem unlikely since contemporary writers point to the existence of a pagan cemetery and

"Muslim wells" lying close by to Pest.[15] The desire to shift the Saracens of Pest from east to west across the Danube may be explained by reference to evidence indicating that otherwise this strange group must be presumed dwelling on the same site as a new and quite different people: Germans, whose presence in Pest is quite incontestable.

Precisely when Germans first made their appearance in the Pest region remains unclear. In 1232 a letter issued by Andrew II (1205–35) makes simple mention of "citizens of Pest" and a few years later Werner, "*civis de Oven (i.e.* Pest)," a somewhat disreputable Austrian Knight, had excommunication proceedings taken against him.[16] It has been suggested that this same Werner may have acted in the capacity of a *locator* encharged with the task of establishing in Pest an immigrant community drawn from out of the ranks of his own countrymen.[17] Certainly, both Werner and his immediate offspring enjoyed high rank among the citizenry of the developing town while soon appearing beside him was an evidently not insubstantial German community. In 1240 five Germans of Pest including a certain Master Henry the Bellmaker are known to have leased about 300 acres (200 holds) of vineyards and arable land from two local abbots.[18] A contemporary and well–travelled chronicler confidently described Pest as a *"magna et ditissima Theutonica villa."*[19] No insignificant trading settlement, the town was, furthermore, awarded certain commercial liberties by the monarch and is known to have been in possession of its own civic seal.[20] Materials surviving from this period always designate the inhabitants of Pest "Teutons" or South Germans. In this respect they are distinguished from a smaller and more obscure community of "Saxons" or North Germans who occupied the settlement of *Pest minor* (Kreinfeld, Kelenföld) on the opposite bank of the Danube below the present day Gellért Hill.[21]

During the 1240's Hungary suffered much from the invasion of the Mongols and in this respect the town of Pest proved no exception. "And even though the burghers of Pest hurried to cross the river, the Mongols, nevertheless, surprised them beforehand and those of the burghers who were not drowned in the Danube were put to the sword"—so runs the *Miserable Lament* of the eyewitness Rogerius.[22] Evidently though, there were some survivors and in 1244 Béla IV, anxious to restore the shattered community, awarded them renewed and extended rights since, in his own words, "at the time of the Mongol persecution . . . our citizens of Pest lost the privilege concerning their liberty which had been drawn up and granted to them."[23]

Contemporaries regularly attributed the horrific success of the Mongol invasion to Hungary's lack of local defensive works.[24] Because right up until the close of the thirteenth century the threat of a fresh onslaught from the east was ever present, the monarchy consistently strove to eliminate this strategic deficiency. The town of Pest, unfortified and lying exposed on the edge of the Great Hungarian Plain, was an obvious target for improvement. In a letter of 1255 Béla IV noted that, out of military considerations, "we have taken care to apply our hands efficaciously to the reform, repair, consolidation and strengthening of our kingdom and among those castles *(castra)* consistent with the defence of the realm we have had built a certain *castrum* on the Mount of Pest and filled it with a great multitude of persons."[25]

Importantly though and despite its misleading name, the "Mount of Pest" was not on the left but rather the right bank of the Danube occupying an advantageous hilltop across the river and opposite the older Pest settlement. This eminence, which provided the site for what became the town of Buda, had until the 1240's been only partially inhabited. A portion of the fragmented royal demesne, the hill was crowned by a small castle together with the humble chapel which has become the magnificent Matthias Church of today.[26] A market place and settlement had already developed by the 1240's on the northern end of the hill and below, on its slopes, were the two villages of St. Peter's and Tótfalu.[27] Thus, for the greater part deserted and yet already endowed with what might be developed as an effective military, religious and commercial infrastructure, the Buda hill offered a propitious site in the royal programme of urban and strategic reform.

The building programme undertaken on the hill overlooking the Danube involved, however, more than the simple construction of a walled compound. The area enclosed was substantial and extended in such a way as to incorporate the already existing castle, church and market. In the fifteenth century, the *castrum* was reckoned to accommodate more than 320 dwellings.[28] There is, furthermore, evidence of a system in the new town's groundplan and regularity in the size of the building plots. The paving of streetways was also undertaken at roughly the same time as the walls themselves were constructed.[29] Such features may be taken to indicate that the Buda *castrum* on the "Mount of Pest" was, from the very first, conceived and built to form an urban centre and not simply a defensive stronghold in time of need.

The population of the new town on the Buda hill was varied. Hungarian inhabitants already dwelling on the site were incorporated within the new community while the villages on the hillside were transformed rapidly into town suburbs.[30] Brief references in early documents to a Peter the Hungarian from Tapolca and an Everhard of Ratisbon suggest that some newcomers from quite distant parts took up residence in the town.[31] Undoubtedly though, many of the "great multitude of persons" settled in Buda were the erstwhile inhabitants of Pest. For the new community not only possessed extensive jurisdictional rights over what remained of the former Pest settlement but was considered to hold the same liberties as had been earlier awarded to Pest in the 1244 charter. Motifs, furthermore, of Pest's seal were subsequently incorporated in its own.[32] Indeed, the town, although from its foundation known as Buda, might throughout the medieval period be still referred to as the "*Castrum* of New Pest."[33] Such a form of settlement transferrence involving persons, rights and even nomenclature, although seemingly unique in Hungary, is a not uncommon feature of German municipal development.[34] A further parallel with the German towns has been indicated by Elemér Mályusz who suggests the existence of a Lübeck-style *Unternehmerkonsortium* of leading Pest burghers, among them the family of the Austrian Werner, actively involved as contractors in the commercial enterprise of founding the new town.[35]

The nature of the surviving source material from this period urges a cautious approach towards Mályusz's ambitious proposition. Nevertheless, it may unequivocally be affirmed that, in drawing its inhabitants from Pest, the new town of Buda came like its predecessor to contain a substantial German population. Documents surviving from the half century 1250–1300 include within their texts the names of some forty inhabitants of early Buda. Of these, 23 may be demonstrated on the basis of their personal nomenclature to hold a German ancestry; by contrast, only eleven are of obviously Hungarian stock.[36] More importantly, the earliest magistracy list dating from 1292 suggests that, at the very least, two-thirds of Council places were occupied by immigrant Germans.[37] German ascendancy, already evident at this early stage in the town's history, persevered throughout the medieval period leaving its mark not only on architecture, social divisions and language, but also on the shape gradually assumed by Buda's municipal institutions.

Thus, in the early development of medieval Buda may be seen the emergence of a community which, although having clear antecedents in the region, was in the ethnic character of its dominant class quite distinct from the peoples who, being mainly of Hungarian stock, populated the countryside and world beyond the town. The distinction evident in this regard as existing between town and realm was compounded by Buda's early governmental and jurisdictional organisation. The Pest charter of 1244, subsequently assumed by Buda, entrusted the town with considerable rights of local autonomy. The burghers were allowed their own independent institutions headed by a magistrate appointed by themselves. "And they may elect a mayor of the town *(maiorem ville),* whomsoever they wish, and . . . he shall judge all their secular affairs"— so runs the 1244 charter. Although a different terminology was applied, the same principle was reiterated in 1276 in a charter issued to the town by King Ladislas IV—"This we grant to them: that they shall not be obliged to receive any Judge sent by us but shall assume by free election whomsoever they like as *villicus* and this *villicus* shall annually resign his power into the hands of the citizenry."³⁸ The citizens' right annually to appoint their own chief magistrate was accompanied in the 1244 charter by clauses specifically aimed at limiting the extent to which locally based royal officials might involve themselves in the town's public life. It was, thus, pronounced that the King's Vice-Palatine, lieutenant of the neighbouring Pest county, "might not quarter himself violently upon them nor judge them." Royal moneyers were, likewise, denied access to the town's financial institutions.

The early form of municipal organisation adopted by the new town conformed closely to the principles of local autonomy outlined in the 1244 charter. At the head of the town, as both judge and chief executive, was the *villicus* appointed out of and by the citizenry for a year at a time. Beside him and giving assistance there quickly developed a council of twelve sworn men or *iurati* who were likewise elected officials of the town.³⁹ These thirteen persons were alone responsible for the political, legal and institutional administration of the town. In the daily organisation of Buda no place or opportunity was at this stage afforded to agents of the monarch or the royal administration. Again, since the townsfolk were considered to form a single corporate entity or *universitas*, the *villicus* and his assistants were in judicial actions involving the town held legally to represent the community. Thus, for instance, in the Tárnokvölgy land dispute of the 1260's, in which Buda was involved as a corporate litigant, the town was represented in the proceedings by the *villicus* and *iurati* acting on behalf and in the name of the citizen community.⁴⁰

The autonomous condition assumed by the town in the realm extended, however, beyond simple administrative and legal mechanisms. For quite evidently, and despite the 1244 charter's silence in this matter, Buda was from an early stage empowered with the right to fashion its own legal customs and judicial procedures. No mere collection of bye-laws, this urban *consuetudo*, allegedly determined by the townsfolk themselves, took precedence over the "custom of the realm" as contrastingly observed outside the town's walls. The local law of Buda, although in its details often arcane and subject to arbitrary revision, was later on in the fifteenth century recorded in a private and quite remarkable compilation known as the *Ofner* or Buda *Stadtrecht*.⁴¹

Certainly, both its later development as a capital and the survival of a detailed *Stadtrecht* make medieval Buda quite unique amongst the towns of Hungary. Contrastingly though, as but a cursory glance at towns such as Pozsony, Kassa and Sopron reveals, in other respects Buda's early history suggests little that is at this stage really exceptional. For not just Buda but, indeed, nearly all the towns of Hungary were to varying degrees populated and dominated by powerful German elements whose presence there within them may be traced back to the thirteenth century. Moreover, in the extensive liberties allowed them, these towns all like Buda possessed considerable rights of local autonomy which effectively removed them from the legal and administrative system operating within the realm as a whole. The processes which resulted in the foundation of free German towns in Hungary, and which prompted the arrival in the realm of an alien urban population entrusted with extensive local rights, are complicated and yet closely interrelated. In order to comprehend these developments, crucial to a proper understanding of both the early and subsequent history of medieval Buda, it is necessary to consider the tremendous changes and innovations occurring at this time within the kingdom of Hungary.

The Árpád Kingdom

The grant of municipal autonomy, such as was received by Pest in 1244 and subsequently assumed by the new town of Buda, cannot be considered even in the middle ages an inevitable concomitant of urban development. As the examples of the settlements already existing in the Buda region suggest and as may be more closely perceived elsewhere, some form of town life existed in Hungary well before the thirteenth century. Recent research undertaken by, in particular, György Székely indicates that even after the onset of the barbarian invasions some urban centres established by the Romans continued to enjoy a precarious existence.[42] Topographical and archaeological investigations clearly suggest that, for example, among the ruins of Esztergom, Sopron and Szombathely a shifting population eked out a living throughout even the darkest periods of the first millenium.[43] With the formation of the Hungarian kingdom and the establishment of more secure political and economic conditions, new merchant and manufacturing communities fast developed throughout the length and breadth of the realm. Nor were these settlements merely the rude affairs Bishop Otto of Freising would have us believe.[44] Odo de Deoghilo who traversed the kingdom in the mid-twelfth century noted in regard to one town, Esztergom, that "the riches of many regions are borne by ship to the noble *civitas*."[45] Eastern travellers likewise comment favourably on the early towns of Hungary. Writing at roughly the same time as Odo, the Sicilian geographer, al-Idrisi, declared that the southern town of Bács "is a well-known town and numbered among the great old towns. There are market places, craftsmen and Greek scholars. They have cultivated fields and populous neighbourhoods. As a result of the abundantly available grain, prices here are always cheap." Similar accounts are given by al-Idrisi of Sopron, Keve, Barancs and Nyitra.[46] His contemporary, Abu Hamid, again highly praises the towns of Hungary even comparing them, although with much oriental exaggeration, to Baghdad and Isfahan.[47]

That there should have been some form of town life already in the period preceding the thirteenth century is hardly surprising. The need to exchange and manufacture produce, evident in all but the most primitive societies, surely prompts the formation of trading settlements. The more extensive and varied this activity, the greater and more socially complex the settlement becomes. From early in its history the Hungarian kingdom had possessed an active commercial life. Hungarian merchants trading in metals, slaves and horses were travelling widely throughout central and eastern Europe from as early as the tenth century. During this time and later, Hungarian furs were reaching Amsterdam and Rome where they even trimmed the papal robes.[48] The large quantities of Hungarian coins found in Moravia and Poland, as well as the discovery in Gotland of hoards containing altogether 140,000 coins, attest to a lively trade with northern Europe.[49] Merchants from the west also took advantage of Hungary's latent riches. The visiting German traders who with their cargoes of cloth and linen are such a feature of Hungary's thirteenth century towns are unlikely to represent a new phenomenon. Indeed, the erection of the Vienna staple in 1221 was almost certainly caused by that town's desire to capture for itself the trade already flowing between Hungary and western Europe.[50] Again, from as early as the eleventh century, French, Walloon and Italian merchants, known collectively as *latini,* were trading with Hungary and, evidently preferring bullion to raw materials, making off with so much silver coinage that legislation had to be enacted against them.[51] Numbers of these Latins eventually took up permanent residence in the realm. At the close of the eleventh century the peasant army of Peter the Hermit was afforded assistance by a "town of foreign Franks" near Belgrade.[52] That this was by no means an isolated foreign settlement is suggested by the Byzantine name of *Frankochorion* appended to the Sirmium region.[53] In 1162 craftsmen from Milan, fleeing the destruction wrought there by Frederick Barbarossa, sought refuge in Hungary establishing in the realm their own communities.[54] Large Latin populations later appear during the twelfth century at Székesfehérvár and Esztergom.[55] Smaller native trading and manufacturing communities are likewise evident beside other of the realm's major ecclesiastical centres: at Vác, Veszprém, Csanád, Győr, Pécs and Nyitra.[56]

Quite clearly though, these early trading and manufacturing settlements were towns not of the western but of the oriental genre. With the notable exception of Székesfehérvár, they all simply lacked any right of self-government. No administrative or jurisdictional distinction was made between town and countryside; the residents of both were held directly answerable to the King and his royal servants.[57] In this respect, Hungary's early towns differed markedly from their privileged successors in the thirteenth century. For these communities, as the case of Buda amply demonstrates, possessed considerable rights of local autonomy. Their special legal status was defined by charter and they were entrusted with their own independent judicial and administrative apparatus.

This apparent failure on the part of Hungary's early towns to equip themselves with the right of self-government may only with difficulty be ascribed to their own economic immaturity. For on the evidence of contemporary writers these towns were not insubstantial centres of trade and population. Explanation must be sought elsewhere and in such a quest a passing remark of the twelfth century Abdullah Jakut may prove revealing. For this Arab commentator reported that in Hungary all attempts by the townsfolk to construct city walls were forestalled by nothing less than the fear in which they held the monarch.[58] What Abdullah, thus, suggests is no lack of community sense or aspiration on the part of Hungary's early townsfolk but rather the degree to which their ambitions were checked by the very nature of the kingdom in which they had their place.

The Hungarian kingdom of the early Árpáds was in the nineteenth century described by such historians as Pauler and Marczali in terms of "Asian despotism" and "an autocratic almost despotic power."[59] At this time the monarch possessed an almost unlimited authority. "The will of the prince is held by all as sufficient" wrote Bishop Otto of Freising in his masterful account of the twelfth century kingdom.[60] No mere theoretical claim, the monarchy possessed, moreover, formidable powers in the practical execution of its command and policy. Within the texts of the few surviving decrees and charters, the presence of a pervasive and efficient judicial administration immediately answerable to the monarch is clearly discernible. Most noticeable are the county judges or *bilochi* appointed directly by the King to dispense his justice. These exerted a far reaching authority in the realm. According to the third lawcode of St. Ladislas (1077–1095), they might demand the presence of anyone at their itinerant courts since they were entitled "to send their seals of citation to all."[61] The competence of the *bilochi* was never extended in such a way as to allow them any independence from royal control. The monarch might enter their judicial districts at will and take over from them the adjudication of cases.[62]

Beside the *bilochi* and perhaps later entitled to supervise their activities were local counts into whose areas of jurisdiction the entire realm was divided. Like the *bilochi,* the lieutenants of the counties were agents of the King. Appointed and often rapidly replaced by him, they were largely recruited from amongst the *servi* of the royal household. Outside a judicial function, the counts were charged with the administration of the royal demesne, military preparations and the implementation of the royal command at a local level.[63]

Certainly, from the imperious jurisdiction of the *bilochi* and counts, nobles of the realm early sought their freedom. But far from seeking to distance themselves from the jurisdiction of the Crown, they rather subjected themselves directly to the King and the realm's foremost dignitary, the Palatine. The powers of this figure rapidly increased and in time he came to preside over the kingdom's entire judicial machinery. He might "without exception judge all persons of our realm" pronounced the Golden Bull of 1222.[64] And yet in the more important cases proceeding before him, the Palatine was bound to consult with the King. For it was from the monarch and not, as was later claimed, from the people that the Palatine held his authority. He functioned as the royal *praesentia* and gave out mandates with the King's own seal.

During the eleventh and twelfth centuries, the judicial life of the realm was maintained almost exclusively by *bilochi,* counts and Palatine. As seigneurial courts were virtually unknown, generally all but the most trivial litigation was dealt with by these royal justices. Their power and presence was felt throughout the land and the royal authority reached down through them to the humblest level. As none were deemed exempt from the King or his officials, no opportunity was afforded for the creation of local independent units of justice and organisation.[65]

Fearful of identifying the early Árpád kingdom too closely with eastern societies and, moreover, aware of the very real differences existing between the two, recent historians have sought to avoid such descriptions as might make early Hungary appear nothing more than some form of "Christian coloured Sultanate."[66] The earlier pronouncements of Pauler and Marczali have, thus, been discarded in favour of the term "patrimonial"—a word originally coined by Szekfű in 1912 and still in general circulation.[67] Initially used as a definition of nineteenth century Habsburg monarchy, the word "patrimonial," when applied to the early Árpád kingdom, may at first sight seem misplaced.[68] However, in the context of the eleventh and twelfth centuries it still serves a useful purpose in drawing closer attention to the royal *patrimonium* or private demesne of the Hungarian Kings.

When in 896 the Hungarian tribes occupied the Carpathian basin, the principal tribe of Tarján under the leadership of the legendary Árpád took for itself the central portion of the new state.[69] Over the succeeding years the royal house expanded rapidly its landbase confiscating the properties of rebellious leaders while at the same time occupying both the frontier regions and the unclaimed territories lying between the various tribal settlements. By the reign of St. Stephen (1000–1038) more than two-thirds of the realm lay in royal hands.[70] The close relationship between monarchical authority and the royal *patrimonium* is well illustrated by the increased judicial competence vested in the King's Palatine. Originally this dignitary held only a minor authority which extended but to certain groups of royal servants, the *udvornici,* working on the King's estates. By the close of the eleventh century, however, the Palatine had assumed the character of royal *alter ego.* He was able to modify the judgments of individual *bilochi* and counts and was entrusted with almost supreme jurisdictional powers in the realm.[71] Similar circumstances surround the development of the royal counties. Originally encharged with the administration of the royal demesne, the county lieutenants gradually had the limits of their competence extended so as to embrace almost the entire territory of the realm. The execution of royal authority was, thus, performed by formerly private servants of the monarch whose jurisdictional prerogatives were expanded beyond the royal demesne to encompass the kingdom as a whole.[72]

During the late twelfth and thirteenth centuries the structure and foundation of royal power and authority suffered a major decline as the vast estates of the Árpád Kings were recklessly alienated. Whereas in the past the monarchs had ensured that donations of land would in time revert back to the Crown, now great tracts of royal estate were granted out in perpetuity. Most of these properties passed into the hands of the Church and great magnate families. The former semi-free peasantry who had hitherto worked these lands were converted into a subject feudal class and, with its economic backbone now broken, the royal county system slowly fell into decay. With the erosion of the old commonly held clan properties, the small landowning freemen were likewise squeezed into dependence upon the powerful families.[73]

With its landbase now greatly diminished, the exclusive jurisdictional power of the monarch came to suffer a corresponding decline. Equally, as the great ecclesiastical foundations and magnate families acquired and "feudalised" even larger shares of the redistributed royal demesne so they came to enjoy an enhanced judicial competence. Jurisdictional prerogatives hitherto exercised solely by the monarch and his officials they drew unto themselves. These developments signalled an end for the "patrimonial" kingdom with its aura of despotism and pervasive royal might. Already, by the close of the twelfth century, there had appeared within the kingdom extensive territorial enclaves held by ambitious barons and prelates. In the confines of these estates the monarch and his agents found it increasingly difficult to exert judicial authority and influence; seigneurial courts now occupied the jurisdictional vacuum.[74]

The implications of these changes were well understood by the monarchs of the late twelfth and thirteenth centuries. Innovations were, thus, embarked upon to mitigate their consequences for the exercise of royal power. Although regular attempts were made to win back for the Crown some of the estates previously alienated, increasingly the monarchy sought to rebuild its power on the basis of regalian revenues. Already by the reign of Béla III (1172–1196), profits for the monarch from coinage, tolls and the salt tax exceeded by more than 30,000 silver marks the income obtained from the surviving royal estates. Following the appointment in the early years of the thirteenth century of Dionysius, son of Apod, to high position in the royal financial administration, far-reaching reforms were undertaken to boost yet further the revenues, particularly from coinage, pertaining to the Crown.[75] At the same time, to compensate for the decline of older forms of organisation, a structured judicial bureaucracy was established and, during the reign of Béla III, an efficient Chancellery apparatus installed.[76] The old royal counties, while allowed to fall increasingly under the influence of the local nobility, were yet subtly converted into judicial and administrative instruments of the monarch. Justice was dispensed locally by representatives of the nobility and yet through the agency of the Palatine a firm grip was maintained by the King on county proceedings.[77]

No less significant were the manoeuvres undertaken by the monarchy to prevent the jurisdictional fragmentation of the realm. Appreciating that on the great magnates' estates little possibility remained for the monarchy to regain its hitherto unchallenged jurisdictional position, the Árpád Kings now regularly came to afford a limited legal recognition to the de facto growth of baronial power. Through the granting by charter of an immune status to the lands of the great barons, the monarchy could in accommodating the ambitions of its more powerful subjects preserve some measure of control over their properties and, since this right might be legally revoked, some semblance also of its erstwhile authority. Thus, during the last decades of the twelfth century and more regularly during the thirteenth, privileges were granted out by the Crown affording their recipients exemption from the general rights of legal introitus otherwise claimed by royal officials.[78]

Sensibly reluctant, though, to allow the magnates a free rein to establish petty states of their own, significant restrictions were still imposed by the monarchy on such judicial prerogatives as it granted out. Thus, the charters affording an immune status took care to enunciate the monarch's continued rights within the estates exempted from his immediate competence. Claims of judicial impropriety in a seigneurial court might, hence, be addressed to the monarch and a guilty landowner impeached before the King.[79] Neither were the seigneurial courts allowed to dispose of the crucial right of *ius gladii.* In other words, they simply could not judge and execute those convicted of "greater offences"—murder, assault and robbery. The adjudication of such crimes was reserved for the royal justices of the *curia.* Even the exceptional liberties enjoyed by the Esztergom Chapter on its estates were much circumscribed in this matter.[80] Again, in administrative details the great magnates' rights of territorial immunity were often disregarded. County inquisitions might legally invade their estates and, in prosecuting cases, seigneurial courts were regularly obliged to rely upon local chapter houses which functioned at this time as *loca credibilia* and an integral part of the realm's judicial and administrative apparatus. Royal decrees and "custom of the realm" had, likewise, to be observed within the confines of the great estates.[81]

On the large landed domains, the full or even partial establishment of jurisdictional autonomy proved, thus, hard to achieve. Even the massive rights claimed by the grasping Matthew Csák at the close of the thirteenth century depended much upon his previous appointment to the office of Palatine and his corruption of the local county courts.[82] For, although deprived of that exclusive authority it had hitherto exerted, the Hungarian monarchy even during the tumultuous thirteenth century still possessed tremendous resources and potential. The careful initiatives and limited accommodations of the preceding period ensured that future Kings of Hungary would hold the single and most effective power in the land for a considerable time to come.

In a penetrating analysis of thirteenth century European political literature, Jenő Szűcs has indicated the noticeable change of attitude towards the Hungarians discernible in the works of western writers.[83] Whereas in the eleventh and twelfth centuries the Hungarians were depicted as a wild and alien people, over the succeeding period they become fully accepted within the comity of Christian nations. Szűcs interprets this change of attitude by reference to the appearance in Hungary of those "common denominators" of feudal life as had emerged during the preceding century and have been outlined above. The radical reduction of the royal demesne and patrimonial forms of kingly authority, the appearance of large private estates and the condition of serfdom made it clear to western writers that they were indeed in a culture not markedly different from their own. Possibly, although Szűcs does not mention this, the passage of the various crusades through Hungary may have helped further create a more positive attitude towards the kingdom. Certainly, as Fügedi has argued, it seems to have attracted the attention of travellers to the realm's potential riches and, as a result, over the ensuing period large numbers of Germans settled in Hungary.[84] Primarily farmers, although some as in the case of Pest entered as townsfolk, they occupied the rich lands of Transylvania and the northern Szepesség (Zips). They cleared forests and opened up whole new areas for cultivation. From the reign of Géza II (1141–1162), this immigration was actively encouraged by the monarchy which saw in the German *Ostsiedlung* an opportunity for building up the population of the kingdom and augmenting thereby royal revenues. Lands were accordingly granted out by the Kings to more enterprising magnates on the condition that these estates were worked by persons specially brought in for that purpose. By the thirteenth century there were some 200 German villages in Transylvania and more than sixty in the Szepesség. Extraordinary judicial rights were granted to the new settlers and features of German land-law together with such institutions as the *Schultheiss* made their first appearance within the realm.[85]

By this time two basic conditions had been met for the establishment in Hungary of that type of free German city like Buda which by the close of the thirteenth century would dominate the urban landscape. Firstly, the decline of the patrimonial kingdom and the attendant emergence of seigneurial jurisdiction had provided the necessary political and legal climate within which the towns could be granted their own immune jurisdictional status within the realm. Secondly the attention and interest of the monarchy had been aroused by the German movement eastwards. Exploitation of this new relationship would come to provide opportunities for populating urban centres and thereby forging a municipal and institutional development firmly in the western mould.

Curiously, however, the circumstance which fused together these two otherwise unrelated developments and created therefrom the privileged town of the thirteenth century was no new influential contact with the west. Rather, and the significance of this event has already been made evident in our study of early Pest and Buda, impulse was provided by a direct collision with the dark forces of the east. In the March of 1241 the Mongol armies of Batu Khan broke into Hungary through the Verecke Pass on the north-eastern border of the realm. In the following month, the royal army was routed at Mohi and the eastern part of the country given to plunder and destruction. In the cruel winter of early 1242 the Mongols crossed the frozen Danube and sacked the remaining western regions of the realm. The hunted King, Béla IV, fled despairingly to Croatia while the Austrian armies took advantage of the confusion to invade Hungary from the west. Peace was only restored later in the year when, on the death of the Great Khan Ogotai, Batu withdrew his forces back across the Steppes in the vain hope of winning for himself supreme lordship over the Mongol tribes. The vivid eyewitness account of the Mongol invasion preserved in Rogerius's *Miserable Lament* presents a picture of mindless savagery and calculated destruction.[86] The major centres of the realm were razed and those of their inhabitants not carried off into slavery put to the sword. The invasion combined with the after-effects of disease and famine is reckoned by one historian to have reduced the population by a half.[87]

Already, prior to 1241, Béla IV had adopted a somewhat dilatory programme of fostering the growth of new municipal foundations by the award of town charters. The privileges of Nagyszombat, Krapundorf and Bars date from this earlier period.[88] Now, in the wake of the destruction, this policy was pursued by Béla with a much renewed vigour. Not only were communities such as Pest, Korpona and Zólyom, which had already been awarded charters but suffered the loss of the originals during the invasion, granted fresh and greatly extended rights,[89] but a mass of other towns received for the first time municipal liberties. During the 1240's, Zagreb, Nyitra, Szamobor, Luprecht-háza, Bábaszék and Dobronya were awarded charters.[90] Over the succeeding half-century similar rights were extended to, most importantly, Besztercebá-nya (1255), Komárom (1263), Késmárk (1269), Szatmár (1271), Győr (1271), Sopron (1277), Vasvár (1279), Pozsony (1291) and Eperjes (1299).[91] Particular care was taken to ensure that these newly libertied towns were adequately protected against the possibility of a fresh onslaught from the east.

The actual relationship between the legal foundation of towns and the Mongol invasion has perhaps been overstressed by certain historians who have viewed Béla's policy towards the towns largely in strategic terms and as little more than a military response to the threat of renewed attack. But, as we have seen, in the period already preceding the 1240's, royal charters had been awarded to urban settlements. Indeed, the liberties held by the mainly Latin townsfolk of Székesfehérvár owe their origin to a privilege granted their community as early as the reign of Stephen III (1162–72).[92] This document came, furthermore, to serve very much as a model for those charters issued to towns in the second half of the thirteenth century. The foundation and encouragement of urban centres held obvious attractions for the monarchy and the existence of a favourable royal policy towards the towns in the period prior to the 1240's must come as no surprise. With the decline of the royal *patrimonium* old domainal forms of revenue had been lost to the monarchy and the struggle with the baronage become all the more debilitating. By encouraging municipal growth, the commercial life of the realm would considerably benefit. Some awareness of the relationship between these two factors is clear in the towns' royal charters wherein much space is devoted to outlining the commercial liberties to be enjoyed by the various communities. The fostering of trade would in its turn much assist the monarchy in its endeavours to switch its revenue base from land to regalian rights. For almost bound to follow was an increased income both from the tolls levied on merchants and from the *lucrum camerae* tax which closely depended on coinage circulation and was rapidly becoming the monarch's single most important source of cash revenue. Furthermore, although whether the monarchs ever thought of this is unclear, by encouraging the development of a flourishing burgher class a political counterweight to the nobility ready to support the King militarily and financially would also be brought into play.

Nevertheless, until the 1240's the Kings of Hungary were reluctant to give their full undivided attention to municipal development. Alternative, more traditional programmes were pursued beside the more innovatory town policy to the obvious detriment of the latter. Hence, Béla IV, while giving some encouragement to the development of the realm's towns, still during the years preceding the Mongol invasion sought in vain to restore the shattered and moribund framework of the royal county network.[93] Plans to revive this old and outdated form of patrimonial administration were, thus, entertained even while the first steps towards founding a monarchical power firmly based on the concept of regalian rights were being made. The Mongol destruction of the realm and the blow this had upon what was left of the royal county system simply put an end to indecision. Inspired by the *tabula rasa* the invasion had provided, Béla came now to discard former policies and devote himself almost exclusively to the problems of municipal development.

A clear indication of the degree to which any plans for reviving the old patrimonial form of state organisation were now subordinated to the new needs of the towns is given in the privileges awarded to Sopron and Győr. In both these cases, villages of kingly servants or *udvornici,* who had hitherto played an important role in working the old demesne lands, were absorbed by the new foundations and their members afforded burgher status.[94]

The examples of Sopron and Győr suggest, however, a particular difficulty experienced by the towns of the thirteenth century. Although royal charters were largely bestowed on already nascent settlements, an often considerable population influx was necessary if these foundations were ever to achieve a lasting and truly urban character. This simple fact was recognised in the arengas of the various town charters which all stressed the close relationship between the foundation of a town and the need for a sufficient number of inhabitants to make the project viable.[95] The incorporation of existing villages within the new town was an expedient which hastened the gradual immigration of peasants from the countryside. This demographic shift was to continue for much of the middle ages for in east-central Europe generally no great limitations were imposed on the free movement of peasantry.[96] In Hungary, royal statutes further ensured that seigneurial controls did not significantly interfere with the population drift.[97] Clearly though, human reservoirs within the realm were limited and much depleted as a result of the Mongol invasion. Just as his predecessors had sought to open up new tracts of agricultural land for exploitation by encouraging the settlement of German farmers, now Béla himself resorted to foreign colonisation as a rapid and effective means of populating the towns. Accordingly, the middle years of the thirteenth century witnessed the onset of a second wave of immigration into the realm as the newly chartered towns of Hungary were occupied and directed by specially introduced foreign elements.[98]

The early history of Kassa well illustrates the scale of this movement. Hitherto but a small village occupied by a mixed Hungarian and Latin population, from the middle years of the thirteenth century Kassa was progressively taken over by German immigrants. The identity of some 63 inhabitants is known from the period 1261–1332 and of these 48 are of clear German ancestry. Their names dominate also the surviving Council lists.[99] A similar picture emerges from Brassó, Pozsony (Pressburg, modern-day Bratislava), Sopron and Székesfehérvár. At Vác and Visegrád German communities were established beside existing native settlements and peculiar *doppelstädte* thereby created. Entirely new German urban centres were established in the rich mining lands of the north.[100] The origin of the town-dwellers is reflected in the terminology applied to them. At first they were known not as "citizens" or *cives,* since in the thirteenth century this carried an association with the old royal county network, but as "guests" or *hospites.*[101] Although this term was quite readily applied to Hungarians who moved to the towns, it evidently owed its origin to the foreign immigrant character of the urban population.[102] Later, with the regular appearance of the term *civis, hospes* assumed an alternative meaning designating an inhabitant of an unprivileged market town or an inferior townsman who had not acquired the special status of citizen.[103]

It was the successfully implemented decision to fill the towns with German immigrants and not simply rely on the native population that finally forced the monarchy to concede to the urban centres the extensive liberties of the thirteenth century of which the Pest 1244 charter is but one example. Certainly, with the decline of the old form of patrimonial kingship and the development of the notion of jurisdictional immunity, the realm was now placed in a better position to accommodate the presence within itself of local autonomous units. Again, with the "westernisation" of Hungary, apparent even to contemporaries, the kingdom was likely to prove more receptive to externally derived concepts of municipal independence. But, in pursuing a town programme dependent upon the arrival of a foreign burgher class, a new and sudden urgency was born.

In Árpád Hungary, a close relationship is often evident between foreign immigration and the grant of an immune status of which the town charter is the most extreme manifestation. The very first Hungarian privilege of immunity—the bizarre and quite exceptional Pannonhalma charter awarded by St. Stephen in 1001—was granted to a monastery of Italian monks;[104] the right to a unique judicial system and their own laws to Hungary's German farmers. Again, during the twelfth century, special privileges were granted to the Cistercian foundations by simple virtue of their foreign character.[105] The earliest Hungarian town charter which was awarded to Székesfehérvár by Stephen III (1162–1172) and permitted the election of a town *villicus* with a competence extending over all civil, criminal and financial actions, must likewise be considered a direct product of the earlier establishment in the town of a large and flourishing Latin merchant community. In the following century, special rights conceding far-reaching legal and administrative exemptions were allowed the wild Cuman tribesman who had settled in the realm fleeing from the Mongols.[106] In all these instances the relationship between foreign immigration and the grant of immunity status may be easily explained. For a diversity of reasons the monarchy was anxious to encourage outsiders to the realm and prepared for this end to make concessions. Quite clearly, the newcomers would wish to preserve as much of their old way of life as was possible. Rather than be subject to strangely speaking officials and a differing legal system, they naturally preferred to continue living under their own laws and to remain subject to their own judges. In order to provide these circumstances, special rights had needs be granted them which had, effectively, to take them outside the realm's normal administrative and judicial machinery.

This simple causal relationship lies at the very heart of our understanding of thirteenth century urban development in Hungary. In order to encourage German settlers to the realm's towns, rights of local autonomy such as were enjoyed by citizens in the west had also to be granted them. The point is clearly recognised in a number of charters and perhaps most strikingly in the later Zólyomlipcse privilege of 1330. Here the Angevin King of Hungary, Charles Robert (1308–42) expressed his desire to award the town "the prerogatives of liberty in the pattern of our other German towns in order that to a further degree the number of our guests dwelling in the town shall be augmented."[107]

Although examples of textual borrowing are hard to find and regular allowance had to be made for local practices, the principles and rights contained in the town charters of the thirteenth century conform closely to those found in privileges earlier issued to the politically less constrained towns of Germany and the west. Major concessions were, accordingly, awarded to the immigrants much in excess of anything hitherto granted out by a Hungarian monarch. As in the case of Pest, the form of government and jurisdictional rights vested in the kingdom's townsfolk took them right outside the administrative and judicial machinery otherwise evident in the realm. Almost universally, they were allowed the right annually to elect their own judges and councillors: *iudices* or *villici* and *iurati.* In the majority of cases the competence of the magistracies extended to all actions involving the earthly lives of their towns' inhabitants. Clauses contained in the charters provided for the complete exclusion of all other officials, locally or royally appointed, from the administrative and judicial life of the community. The Nyitra privilege of 1248 makes these points clearly: "The *villicus* who is for a period appointed from their number shall together with twelve sworn men *(iurati)* judge and duly bring to the conclusion all matters—financial, civil and criminal . . . Neither shall the citizens of Nyitra be impleaded before any outside judges, the Palatine or local counts."[108] The Besztercebánya privilege of 1255 is equally emphatic: "The citizens shall elect with the counsel and consent of the community a *villicus* who will hold office for a year and judge all their cases. They cannot be made to appear before any other judge in any suit whatsoever."[109]

In obvious and necessary imitation of earlier prerogatives awarded in Germany, the extensive jurisdictional rights allowed the Hungarian towns encompassed also the privilege of *ius gladii.*[110] As we have noticed, this liberty was not during the thirteenth century allowed even the most independent baronial lordships. Still, as early as 1238, the Nagyszombat council held the "power of decapitation and inflicting any other penalty."[111] The 1244 Körmend charter similarly noted that, "If a thief be found amongst them (i.e. the burghers) whose crime extends to objects above the value of 60 Friesach denars he shall be sent to the gallows."[112] Only exceptionally were some towns denied full rights of *ius gladii* and obliged to present serious maldoers to the local royal courts or, like Visegrád, compelled to have sentence of death confirmed by a high dignitary of the realm.[113]

Beyond this and closely related to the right of self-government was the award of *ius statuendi* through which individual towns of the realm were allowed to fashion and develop their own customary procedures and legal principles for determining justice.[114] This right had long been allowed the more advanced towns in the west. Indeed, as early as the first half of the twelfth century, the Count of Flanders had allowed the burghers of Bruges to "correct their customary laws from day to day and improve them according to the needs of time and station."[115] Although in the charters granted to the Hungarian towns this concept is never accorded such full expression, it still remains a recurrent and underlying theme in many texts. Thus, for instance, the Pozsony charter of 1291 notes that, "If any excesses emerge or occur in the town or its lands, the judge and sworn men shall dispense to the plaintiff the customary and usual justice just as the custom of the town demands of them."[116] Already by the third quarter of the thirteenth century, one North Hungarian town had produced its own, sadly all too brief, compendium of municipal law.[117]

The extent to which rights earlier allowed western communities influenced the liberties granted to the Hungarian towns is evident even within the more detailed provisions of the thirteenth century charters and, more specifically, within the privileges afforded Pest and Buda. The limited *praescriptio* contained therein, outlining the period after which a burgher was deemed fully and incontestably in possession of his estate, derived from provisions earlier laid down in Germany and running quite contrary to the principles of Hungarian land-law.[118] The mechanisms discussed for providing for the family of a murderer echo rights earlier granted out to Austrian towns.[119] Significantly also, the prohibition of the duel, contained in a considerable number of charters of the thirteenth century, must be reckoned an indubitable borrowing from practices observed within the towns of the Empire. For, indeed, at the time the Hungarian town charters were drawn up, the duel as a judicial procedure was still in its infancy.[120]

The processes which prompted the legal establishment of towns in Hungary and defined the early organisation of medieval Buda were, thus, the product of a subtle amalgam of pressures. Certainly, well before the thirteenth century towns existed in Hungary. But set in the patrimonial kingdom of the Árpád Kings they lacked any right of self-government and local jurisdiction. Only with the decline of kingly "despotism" and the attendant erosion of ancient forms of royal revenue emerged the necessary conditions and impetus for the foundation of free cities in the realm. During the thirteenth century and in response to changes affecting the kingdom's political climate, the monarchy actively sought for the first time to encourage the development of the realm's towns. It arranged for their military defence and, by taking advantage of the German *Ostsiedlung,* encouraged their settlement by a foreign population. But in order to attract westerners to the kingdom, considerable rights of urban autonomy such as were already enjoyed in the west had needs be transferred to the new towns. This is plainly evident in both the general principles and details enunciated in the towns' early charters.

The developments outlined above suggest, however, a significant twist in our interpretation of the early history of medieval Buda, and indeed, of town life generally in thirteenth century Hungary. Medieval Buda was, as we have seen, a free German city. It held the right of self-government and of local jurisdiction. It was dominated and populated by German burgher groups. Yet these two elements prove closely interrelated. For the town was free because it was German and, arguably also, German only because it was free. Population and rights—the one depended upon the other. And yet, in the neatness of this historical equation, one fundamental discrepancy remains. For, however much the realm may have adjusted to accommodate a town life in the western mould, the character and extent of autonomy granted Buda and the towns of Hungary was yet essentially determined by circumstances unparalleled in and quite outside the realm's historical experience. German rights and freedoms had, in effect, to be transferred to communities which, if containing substantial German elements in their population, were established in the altogether very different kingdom of Hungary. The easy and straightforward maintenance and development of these rights could, thus, be by no means assured.

Chapter 2

THE PERIOD OF THE RECTORS

The Establishment of the Rectorate

The rights granted to the Hungarian towns were remarkable. Liberties which had over a long period to be squeezed and cajoled from reluctant princes and bishops by the townsfolk of the west were awarded in their entirety to the realm's nascent urban communities. Self-sufficient in their legal and governmental institutions, the towns of Hungary were almost completely removed from the judicial apparatus of the realm. Permitted, moreover, to found their own laws and practices, the towns through this developed their own special *consuetudines* which at variance with the custom of the realm further emphasised the distinctiveness of their legal status.

Yet the neat separation of town from realm reflected in the terms of the towns' charters proved hard to maintain. Granted not in recognition of a political *fait accompli* but rather as an innovation of royal policy, many newly established communities found it hard to preserve their independence in the face of the encroachments made on their rights by local landowning families. Often lacking a solid economic foundation capable of reinforcing their immunity rights, some were reduced within a short period to little more than villages dependent on a local lord.[1] Again, since it was calculated royal policy and not a forceful burgher class which had taken the initiative in legally establishing the individual towns of the realm, so the monarch might feel more freely disposed to rearrange and alter policy decisions to the seeming detriment of the townsfolk. Such occurred within but a few years of its foundation in thirteenth century Buda.

The Pest charter of 1244, subsequently assumed by Buda (and for that reason it shall hereafter be known as the Buda charter), allowed for the free election of a town *maior* or *villicus* by the citizens: "They may elect a mayor of the town, whomsoever they wish, and once elected shall present him to us. He shall judge all their secular affairs." In accordance with the terms of this charter we may find Peter, *villicus* of Buda and son of the Austrian knight, Werner of Pest, functioning during the 1260's as headman of the town. He seems firm in his authority, taking on in the name of the town some local nobility and disputing their rightful possession of properties south of Buda, at Tárnokvölgy.[2] But shortly after, Peter was evidently ousted from authority and in his stead appear a succession of dignitaries holding the unfamiliar title of Rector.

The functions of the Buda *villicus* as both Town Judge and representative of the community were taken over by this new official. Just as the *villicus* Peter had earlier represented Buda in the dispute over Tárnokvölgy, so the Rectors Walter and Werner were both closely involved in the legal confrontation between the town and the archbishopric of Esztergom. When this dispute reached a high point in 1289, with Buda itself being placed under an interdict, it was the Rector Werner together with certain *iurati* who was excommunicated.[3] Furthermore, the role of individual Rectors in judging cases brought before them provides sure proof that their additional title of *iudex*, which in an urban context was synonymous with *villicus*, was not an empty one.[4]

However, one should not imagine that the title of Rector was but a local variant of *villicus*. No elected official, the Rector was quite plainly a royal appointee. Hence the German knight, Charles of Óbuda, who in 1276 assumed the Rectorate, was "judge on behalf of our Lord King in Buda."[5] Johann, Rector in the first part of the fourteenth century, was specifically referred to as a "deputy" of King Charles Robert.[6] When in 1301 Wenzel of Bohemia occupied Buda he took prisoner the Rector Ladislas, imposing his own supporter, Petermann, as "Rector and Judge."[7] Further evidence that these town dignitaries were royally appointed, as opposed to elected by the citizens, is provided by the examples of the first two Rectors of Buda: Henry Preussel and the Ban Mykud.

Henry Preussel was an Austrian knight who, having played some part in the troubles which beset the Duchy in the period following the extinction of the Babenberg line, entered the service of Béla IV, became a favourite of the Queen and obtained the County of Bars.[8] When the long expected war between Béla and his son broke out in summer of 1264, Preussel, as part of an attempt to secure the strategically important town of Buda, was invested with the Rectoral office.[9] His selection for this role was quite possibly prompted by the presence in the town of Greyf, a relative from Vienna and prominent member of the town.[10] However, at the battle of Isaszeg, fought some miles to the east of Buda, the army of Béla was defeated and Preussel slain by the hand of the Ban Mykud. Buda was thereupon occupied by the forces of Béla's son,

Stephen, and this same Mykud assumed the now vacant office of Rector.[11] By the terms of the ensuing peace, Buda fell again under Béla's control and Mykud quit the scene (c. 1267), to be rewarded later by Stephen with extensive holdings in Transylvania.[12]

Clearly, then, the Rector was the royally appointed *iudex* of Buda and in the first instance the motives behind the appointments of Preussel and Mykud may appear to lie in the necessities brought upon by civil war. Certainly such circumstances as are occasioned by conflict in a state may well provoke changes within that state's established framework of law and rights. However, the necessities of war which may be taken to explain the elevation of Preussel and Mykud had largely ceased to exist by 1268. In apparent confirmation of this, headship of the town was now temporarily reassumed by Peter acting in the capacity of "former *villicus.*"[13] And yet at this very point, when indeed we might expect the peculiar Rectoral office to have been altogether abolished in favour of a return to the elected *villicus* system, another Rector, Walter, Count of Komárom, was installed by Béla over the town.[14] With this appointment the Rectoral office took on a new form. No longer did it exist as but a product of specific emergencies occurring within the mid-1260's. Rather, through the appointment of Walter in 1268, the Rectorate assumed the character of a more enduring institution—an institution which was to continue for some further eighty years, in apparent contradiction not only to the town's charter, which was even confirmed in 1276,[15] but to the whole principle of municipal autonomy being extended over this period to other Hungarian towns.

Despite the publication of some admirable source editions illustrating the early history of medieval Buda,[16] documentary materials for the period of the Rectors remain scarce. Since those that survive are primarily concerned with litigation, they tend by their very nature to emphasise the Rector's judicial function. Clearly, however, the Rectors of Buda performed additional functions within the town, the importance of which cannot be disregarded.

It is significant that, besides being Count of Komárom, the Rector Walter was from 1268 to 1276 also an official of the Treasury: a *Comes Camerae* or *Camerarius.*[17] The Count of the Camera or Chamberlain was the principal administrator of a royal mint. It was his responsibility to supervise the weight, content and distribution of the coins produced there as also to pass judgment in disputes involving the minters under his charge.[18] Despite the frequent leasing out of this office, the monarchy remained particularly anxious to ensure a full control over appointments to the office of Chamberlain. Hence when in 1231 Andrew II reissued the Golden Bull of nine years previous, the clause "Counts of the Camera, moneyers, salt and tribute collectors shall be nobles of the kingdom" was struck out with only the provision forbidding the appointment of "Jews and Ishmaelites" remaining.[19] Nor is this surprising since the exercise of the royal prerogative over the minting of coins was not only a highly important source of revenue,[20] but also necessary for the preservation of economic stability within the realm. In recognition of this, the monetary reforms of 1323, inaugurated by King Charles Robert and following hard upon the suppression of the anarchy which had greeted his accession, were undertaken "in order to restore the pristine status of our realm."[21] The financial reorganisation of the Angevin period, inaugurated in these measures, had the effect of undermining in no small way the principle of judicial autonomy within certain towns. Chamberlains were not only given authority to judge false coiners "both in towns and in villages" but were on occasions even imposed as the heads of town magistracies.[22]

In the fourteenth century, therefore, in direct relationship to the monetary reforms of the Angevin period, close links are evident between the office of Chamberlain and restrictions placed upon the exercise of certain municipal rights. But in the century preceding these reforms, during the reign of Béla IV and indeed in those very years during which the office of Rector first emerged in Buda, there was undertaken a reform of the minting system which was in certain respects to have as equally significant consequences as those of the Angevin period. It is precisely within this framework that any explanation as to the appointment of Walter in 1268 and continuation of the Rectorate must be sought.

The need for reform of the country's coinage and, moreover, of the minting system as a whole had long been pressing.[23] An annual event from the reign of Béla II (1131–41), the highly lucrative process of coinage reissue and debasement was accelerated during the first decades of the thirteenth century. By 1222 it had become alarming enough for the nobility to compel—in vain as it turned out—Andrew II to affirm that, "our new coinage shall be respected throughout the year, from Easter to Easter, and denars such as there are shall be of the same fineness as in the time of King Béla."[24] To the continuing decline in the value of Hungarian coinage may be largely ascribed the influx of foreign coins into the kingdom: of, in particular, the Friesach and, from the middle of the century, the Viennese denar.[25] Whereas in the past Hungarian coins had been a common unit of currency in Central Europe, roles became increasingly reversed with the native currency being steadily replaced by the foreign.[26] Of the fifty-seven coins found in a hoard in Örkénypuszta and dating from around 1235–40, only six are of Hungarian origin and even these are low value bracteates.[27] Partly as an attempt to prevent large sections of the realm becoming, in effect, foreign "coinage provinces," during the course of the thirteenth century a stronger currency was introduced and new mints established at Csanád (until 1241), Sirmium, Buda and in the Croatian Banate. Although all these functioned as offshoots of the mint at Esztergom, their organisation remained irregular.[28] The Sirmium mint was administered, like that at Esztergom, by chamberlains: more specifically, "by our camerers of Sirmium, namely Leopold and his colleagues."[29] In the case of the Croatian mint or *Camera beyond-the-Drava*, however, authority over its operation lay in the hands of the Ban and Bishop of Zagreb.[30] The Bishop's hold on the mint, however, seems to have been the stronger and at some point between 1256 and 1260 the *camera* was moved to Zagreb.[31] The Buda *camera*, established at a later date than the Croatian, always remained particularly closely connected to that at Esztergom. Indeed, according to a royal charter of 1255 it was operated by "our craftsmen of Esztergom who at the time of new money work in a factory."[32] But, in contrast to both Sirmium and Zagreb, immediate responsibility for the mint lay in the hands of the town *villicus*, Peter.[33]

Although they must be regarded very much in the light of his general reorganisation of the realm, the cameral reforms of the last years of Béla's reign seem to have been initiated by the investiture of the Queen with authority over the royal mint at Sirmium.[34] The motives behind this extraordinary action remain unclear and certainly the possibility of a generous impulse cannot be excluded. However, it is more probable that the alteration in the mint's status was precipitated by the claims of Béla's rebellious son, Stephen, asserted in respect of his title *iunior rex*.[35] In any event, the action seems to have drawn Béla's attention to the irregularities existing within the whole framework of the royal minting system. Accordingly, in the space of the next three years, administrative reforms of far-reaching import designed to eradicate these discrepancies were embarked upon in both the Buda and Zagreb mints. Although no change in their status occurred, the actual internal organisation of these two *camerae* was brought into line with the system already existing at Sirmium and Esztergom. Henceforward, chamberlains were to be the officials solely responsible for the operation of the kingdom's mints.

Archynus and Walter, the two officials charged respectively with authority over the Zagreb and Buda mints, had until the time of their appointments been leading chamberlains at Esztergom. As early as 1249, Archynus was recorded as "a wealthy man, Count of the Camera, a Venetian, now citizen of Esztergom."[36] The title of *comes camerae* seems, however, to have been bestowed on Walter only in 1265 and was probably not unrelated to his acquisition of the County of Komárom, with which the cameral administration had previously been closely connected.[37] But, as a deliberate attempt towards the enhancement of their authority as chamberlains, the actual appointments of

Walter and Archynus to Buda and Zagreb involved the suspension in these two towns of the system allowing for the free election of a Town Judge and the consequent absorption of the latter into the cameral office. This policy held obvious attractions for the monarchy. In order to preserve the spirit of urban immunity right, Buda's charter had greatly limited the degree to which outsiders might perform the crucial task of coinage recall and reissue. As the 1244 charter pronounced, officials entrusted with this task "shall not stand with their moneyers among them but a trusty man of the town shall join with them who shall vigilantly and diligently administer the reception of the royal coinage." Thus, the proper exchange of money, upon which depended not only a sizeable proportion of royal revenue but also the successful introduction of a stronger coinage, was to be administered by an official over whose appointment the monarch had no obvious influence.

Certainly, Béla could simply have ignored this section of Buda's charter and installed in the town his own official as money-changer *(cambsor regius)*. But such could hardly resolve the fundamental problems involved. For in the very performance of this task, such an official would be almost totally dependent upon not only the goodwill and support of the Council but also and more importantly upon the magistracy's legal rights of judicial enforcement. A close awareness of this problem is clearly reflected in royal letters of the fourteenth century which frequently stress the important role played by town councils in the proper fulfilment of monetary programmes.[38] Quite possibly, the appointment of the *villicus* Peter to headship of Buda's minting organisation represents an early attempt to obviate this difficulty. Clearly insufficient though, for it allowed the king no right of preferment to the mint in Buda, this policy was soon discarded in favour of the reverse. In both Buda and Zagreb, town government was, effectively, absorbed into the minting organisation. In Buda, this radical experiment was to meet with a measure of success and through it to develop the system of the Rectorate. In Zagreb, the attempt was to fail quite dismally.

As with Buda, the town of Zagreb owed its establishment to Béla IV. Its location and construction was to a large degree determined by strategic considerations. The town's first royal charter, bestowed in 1242, records the King's wish "to found a free city and call there *hospites* to strengthen and fortify that part of the realm."[39] The provisions concerning municipal government, as laid down in the charter of 1242, differed little from those granted to other Hungarian towns. The citizens had the right "to elect whomsoever they wish as Judge of the town, to present him to us and change him annually according to their wish."

The appointment of the Chamberlain Archynus as Town Judge in 1266 was a direct breach of the right of free election. The citizens reacted almost immediately, petitioning the king.[40] Béla, fearing disaffection, recognised that in appointing Archynus as judge he had infringed the townfolk's liberties. Offering the excuse of ignorance, implausible as his present Chancellor was a former Bishop of Zagreb, Béla accordingly confirmed the citizens' right to elect annually whomsoever they wished as "podestà or judge."[41] Thereupon, the royal privileges given to the town in 1242 were reissued with the provision concerning the election of a Town Judge remaining unmodified.[42] Archynus appears now to have left Zagreb re-emerging in 1269 back at Esztergom as a member of the municipal council and subsequently chief magistrate.[43]

In Zagreb, the royal imposition of Archynus in the bifurcate role of Chamberlain and Judge of the town failed as a result of local opposition. However, the events of 1266 were to make a lasting impression on the financial administration in the town. Prior to this date, no chamberlains had held office in respect to the Zagreb mint. For the latter lay under the jurisdiction of the local Bishop and Ban. But, after 1266 cameral organisation in Zagreb became the preserve of the chamberlains. In 1270 a certain Grenchol was recorded as *Comes Camerae Zagrebiensis.*[44] This office, like so many others elsewhere, would appear to have fallen into the hands of the town's leading citizens being held, in the early 1290's, by a burgher of Zagreb called Markulin.[45]

In Buda, the attempt towards a combination of cameral and judicial functions proved more lasting. Materials from the period of Walter's Rectorate (1268–76) show Walter as acting still in the capacity of a *comes camerae* while, as may be ascertained from an undated document of the reign of Ladislas IV (1272–1290), simultaneously holding the office of Count of Komárom.[46] That as Rector he performed certain judicial functions is also evident. In 1268, the year in which he is first credited with the title of Rector, Walter may be seen adjudicating together with the twelve sworn men of the town in the dispute raging at that time between the local chapter and the boatmen of Pest.[47] It is unlikely, however, that Walter's cameral duties were confined just to Buda. The connection between the Esztergom and Buda mints was always close. Both were treated in the Angevin period as very much a single unit. Nicolas of Szatmár, whose close involvement in the cameral reorganisation of that period is evident from the *proemium* of the 1345 decree, was in 1342 chamberlain of both the Buda and Esztergom *camerae* while in the following year these two mints were placed under the jurisdiction of a certain Master Hypolitus.[48] It is possible, moreover, that this double jurisdiction was also exercised to a lesser degree in the 1270's by Michael, referred to then as a "Count of the Camera of the Lord King." Michael's primary function would, however, appear to relate to the Esztergom mint.[49] Walter, on the other hand, by holding the office of Town Judge, must clearly have had the Buda mint as his main responsibility. Since the judicial office, as more fully outlined in later documents, was evidently a rather time-consuming one, assisting Walter in the performance of his cameral duties was a certain Perchin, also a chamberlain.[50]

Ultimately, however, the attempt made in Buda towards a reinforcement of the cameral office through its association with a judicial authority was to fail as much there as it had in Zagreb. In the case of Zagreb, the townsfolk by their opposition to the installation of Archynus and insistence upon the provisions of the 1242 charter put an end to the experiment. In Buda, the increasing influence exercised, as we shall see, by the town patriciate on appointments to the office of Rector similarly brought about the abandonment of the system inaugurated by Béla IV. The chamberlains carried too great a responsibility for their office to be haphazardly conferred by the monarch on to town *iudices* over whose appointment he held in reality very little control.

At what point the combination of cameral and judicial offices was finally dissolved in Buda is unclear. Following the assassination of Walter in 1276 and the crisis thereby produced, the Rectorate was assumed by a local man, Charles, who was apparently not a chamberlain.[51] In contrast his successor, Hench, first mentioned as holding the office of Rector in 1279, was the scion of a provincial landowning family and in 1268 is recorded as purchasing estates near Radna in Transylvania.[52] It is very possible that this same Hench is identifiable with a chamberlain of that name referred to in a contemporary (but undated) document.[53] Some caution must, however, be observed in regard to this identification. The name Hench is not uncommon being a variant of the German Heinrich. Furthermore, it may be that the *Comes Camerae* Hench is identifiable rather with a "Comes Hench" mentioned in 1282 together with Archynus as a *iuratus* of Esztergom.[54] Traces, though, of the old association of cameral and judicial function are still evident to a minor degree in the fourteenth century. Petermann, appointed Judge by Wenzel of Bohemia, was the son of the Buda *examinator* of minted coins, Kunc Prenner.[55] Again, towards the middle of that century, certain cameral offices, including the highest in the land, were held by one of the Buda *iurati*, Lorand.[56]

But such traces should be regarded as largely coincidental and more a reflection of growing burgher involvement in the kingdom's financial administration. Essentially, it must be admitted that the practice of combining cameral and judicial functions had come to an end in Buda, if not by 1276, then by 1288, with the conclusion of Hench's term as Rector. Yet in the first instance it was this association of functions which provided the basis for the continuation of the Rectorate beyond 1268: an event which must be seen as part of a greater scheme of cameral reform undertaken by Béla IV and affecting municipal institutions not just in Buda but in Zagreb as well. It is perhaps worth noting at this point that the Rectors of 1265, Preussel and Mykud, may themselves have also performed certain cameral duties. Neither are recorded as chamberlains and their appointments must be seen primarily within a military perspective. However, in so far as the office of *villicus* was absorbed into that of Rector and since, furthermore, we know that the *villicus* Peter acted also in the mint as *villicus fabrorum,* it does not seem unreasonable to suggest that both Preussel and Mykud may have possessed also certain cameral responsibilities.[57]

The Title of Rector

In any attempt to unravel the office of Buda Rector, some interest must be shown in the actual shades of meaning implicit within the title itself. In such an analysis, caution should of course be especially displayed for terminology may vary considerably according to time and place. The application of the term *jobag,* which at the beginning of the thirteenth century had indicated a member of the upper nobility and yet by 1300 become synonymous with serf, is a fine example of this phenomenon. Since, however, in contrast to that of *jobag,* examples of the title of Rector in urban usage are scanty in thirteenth and fourteenth century Hungary, it may be illuminating to consider briefly the term as employed in the towns of neighbouring Germany. Nor is the basis for such a comparison groundless. As we have seen, medieval Buda was in many respects not at all dissimilar to a small German town. Its legal and institutional character was greatly influenced by the towns of the west while Buda's leading citizens were largely of German extraction. Again, of the Rectors of medieval Buda, only the Ban Mykud of the native Kökényes-Rénold clan was not of German origin.

Attention has been drawn to the fact that in certain German towns the term Rector was used to describe a *iudex* appointed either by the townsfolk or, in certain cases, by the Emperor himself.[58] In Freiburg, the advocate elected by the citizens with imperial confirmation was known by the title of "Rector of the Citizens." Again, in the privileges given by Frederick II to the town of Lübeck mention is made of a *"rector ab imperio statuetur."* Further examples of the Rector title being employed in similar contexts may be cited from the charters of Osnabrück (1171) and Berne (1218) respectively.[59] The term, however, appears to lack precision even within a specifically urban context, designating in Strassburg no more than the town *iurati*.[60] Austria was a part of the Empire closely associated at this time with Buda. During the second half of the thirteenth century, merchants from Vienna were regular visitors to the new town.[61] Moreover, the *villicus* Peter, the Rector Preussel and the citizen Greyf are all known to have enjoyed close family connections with the Duchy. However, in Austria the title of Rector was employed in a context quite different from that of *iudex*. The administrative reforms undertaken by Ottokar of Bohemia in the 1270's had led to the creation in Austria of a new functionary: the *Rector officiorum*.[62] The first holders of this office, Gozzo of Krems and Paltram of Vienna, jointly administered *"omnia officia per Austriam,"* effectively controlling thereby the entire fiscal administration of the Duchy.[63] Both Gozzo and Paltram were, furthermore, chamberlains in Austria as was Jacob of Hoya, similarly recorded in 1283 as a *rector officiorum*.[64] Whether these figures obtained the title of Rector by virtue of an enhanced cameral status remains unclear. It is well to remember that the scope of the Rectoral office in Austria was largely determined by earlier developments occurring within the originally non-financial office of the *Landschreiber* and that also the powers of the Austrian chamberlains were at this time much wider than those of their Hungarian counterparts.[65] Nevertheless, during the period of Angevin rule in Hungary, a certain association is apparent between the title of Rector and the cameral office. Chamberlains appointed over mining communities were on occasions given that title. In 1344 reference is made to a certain "Master Marin, Count of our Camera at Szomolnok, *urburarius* and Rector of our town of Telukybánya."[66]

As an alternative explanation, György Györffy has suggested a possible analogy between the terms Rector and Castellan.[67] His interpretation is largely based upon the reference in 1315 to the head of the royal castle in Óbuda as *"rector vel conservator domus."*[68] In the case of Óbuda, though, examples of such a terminological correlation are confined to this one instance. However, further evidence does exist to lend support to Györffy's thesis. In 1321 members of the Rátold family, in a letter of confirmation, referred to one of their castles as lying under the immediate jurisdiction of "rectors" while, a few years previous, in Esztergom mention is made of a *"Castellanus seu Rector castri strigoniensis."*[69]

Although unlike Preussel and Mykud the Rectors appointed after 1268 in Buda were not foremostly warriors, it is certainly possible that these Rectors continued to hold some military authority within the town. In 1329 the town magistracy referred in a letter to Johann as *"noster Rector Capitaneusque in medio nostri constitutus."*[70] The term *capitaneus,* although suggesting a military function, is nevertheless imprecise. Yet it would seem quite possible that the Rectors may have acted more in the capacity of royal castellans. A later chronicle refers to the Rector Petermann as "prefect" of town and "citadel" *(arx).*[71]

Certainly, the evidence for a connection in Buda between the offices of Rector and Castellan remains slight. Still, the possibility of such a link existing is in no way undermined but rather endorsed by the cameral function originally pertaining to the Rectoral office. In Buda there were two castles both in existence by the mid-thirteenth century. The castle set at the southern end of the town was to assume a major importance as a result of its rebuilding during the Angevin period. Originally however, it most probably belonged to the Queen who held as a domainal estate a portion of the settlement of *Pest minor* or Kelenföld (Kreinfeld) at its foot.[72] The castle at the northern corner of the town (on the site of the present 9 Mihály Táncsics Street) which was constructed before the Mongol invasion almost certainly represents the site of the King's *curia.* Significantly, it seems to have been here that the royal mint also functioned. Besides *magna curia* this building was known as the *domus regia:* a term regularly employed at this time to designate a minting house.[73] German texts similarly mention a mint or *kammerhof* existing on the same site as the castle and note the residence here in the early fourteenth century of Wenzel, King of Bohemia.[74] Although the *curia* was alienated in 1382, the fifteenth century Buda *Stradtrecht* reveals the royal mint as still standing close by this site.[75] Indeed, as late as the seventeenth century, the building on this spot was referred to both as *magna curia* and *Kammerhof.*[76]

Any connection between the actual town administration headed until 1346 by the Rector and the office of Castellan seems, though, to have disappeared in the course of the second half of the fourteenth century. In 1355–56 the office of "Master of the Gatekeepers and of the Castle of Buda" was held by a certain Thomas who plainly had no connection with the town magistracy,[77] while in the privileges given to the town by Sigismund the office of Castellan was quite distinctly separated from any municipal office.[78] But, in any event, even assuming that all the Rectors of Buda held authority as Castellans in the town, which is by no means clear, from 1268 this authority must be considered as developing out of the Rectoral office as opposed to providing the basis and reason for it in the first place.

Family Power

It was the programme of cameral reform initiated by Béla IV, rather than any strategic consideration, that lay behind the appointment of the Chamberlain Walter to the office of Rector in 1268. However, as we have seen, this association of judicial and cameral functions had clearly ceased by at the very latest 1288, with the conclusion of Hench's term as Rector. Yet royally appointed Rectors continued to exercise a judicial authority over the town for a further sixty years: until 1346. In addition, the continued existence of the Buda Rectorate as, what appears, an institutional anachronism becomes all the more puzzling in the light of the townsfolk's apparent acquiescence to this irregularity cutting across the whole notion of municipal autonomy—a condition usually fiercely defended by urban communities.

In Zagreb, Béla IV's attempt to impose his own nominee, Archynus, at the head of the town magistracy survived only a few months being thwarted by local opposition. Indeed, a century and a half previous, in one of the earliest encounters between a Hungarian monarch and developed urban communities, the Dalmatian towns had reacted in more violent vein to King Koloman's attack upon their municipal right of self-government.[79] In contrast, the leading citizens of Buda reacted in an entirely different manner to the royal imposition of a Town Judge and to Buda's apparent loss of liberty. It is precisely within the context of this reaction that the explanation for the problematic continuation of the Rectorate must be sought. For the powerful urban patriciate of Buda ultimately came to regard the Rectorate as an office which they could use to their own advantage and as a means of strengthening both their position and hold upon the town.

During the middle years of the thirteenth century, the most powerful family in Buda was that of the Werners. The family owed its origin to an Austrian knight of that name who was later to win much notoriety as a result of his appropriation of monastic estates in the Duchy.[80] Settling in Pest around 1230, this Werner built for himself a palace beside the town in which he acted as head of the nascent German community. His son was almost certainly that Peter who, in the years before the establishment of the Rectorate, held the office of Buda *villicus*.[81] In terms of status and authority within the town, this family would seem to have suffered not inconsiderably as a result of the imposition of the Rectoral system, losing its pre-eminence among the townsfolk and virtually disappearing from the records of this period.

Even though Walter may possibly have acquired citizenship of the town shortly before his appointment as Rector, he remained in the eyes of the Buda townsfolk an outsider whose true allegiance belonged to a rival landowning class.[82] In 1276, eight years after Walter's installation, the crisis came to a head. Walter was assassinated by Werner and his son Ladislas, the immediate descendants of the *villicus* Peter.[83] Ladislas IV responded at once to the emergency, reaffirming the citizens' right to elect their own judge: "This we grant to them: that they shall not be obliged to receive any judge sent by us but shall assume by free election whomsoever they like as *villicus* and this *villicus* shall annually resign his power into the hands of the citizenry."[84] Ladislas however, perhaps viewing with reluctance the imminent demise of the cameral-judicial system established by his grandfather, began once the initial crisis had passed to undermine this latest provision. After the space of a few months he appointed as Rector Charles of Óbuda reaffirming thereby the Rectoral system through an appointment unlikely to arouse much opposition in the town. For Charles, besides being a local man, had been an associate of the *villicus* Peter and formerly a member of the town council.[85] Since Charles's immediate successor, Hench, was quite possibly himself a chamberlain, Ladislas's bid to maintain Béla IV's institutional arrangement within the town may well be considered successful.

The disorder of the last decades of the thirteenth century provided the opportunity for members of the Werner family to regain their lost ascendancy within the town. From 1288 to 1319 the Rectorate lay largely in their hands being held in turn by Werner and Ladislas, murderers of the Rector Walter and son and grandson respectively of the *villicus* Peter. Thus besides becoming the preserve of a single family, the Rectorate was gradually assuming during this period the character of a hereditary office. Even after the death without heir of Ladislas in 1319 and the consequent elevation to the Rectoral office of another of the town's citizens, Johann,[86] this aspect of the office persisted. On Johann's death in 1336, his son Nicolas assumed the title of Rector.[87]

The families of both the Rectors Werner and Johann were, furthermore, closely connected by bonds of marriage to other of the town's leading burgher families. Such not only consolidated the position of the individual Rectors and reduced faction-fighting but also ensured that power within the town was continually vested in the hands of a single social group. Werner and his son Ladislas are known to have been interrelated with at least three of those families whose members may regularly be found on the surviving council lists.[88] Likewise, Johann and his son Nicolas forged links with notable burgher households like the Ulving, Weidner and Tilmann.[89] In 1337 almost a half of council places were occupied by relatives of the Rector Nicolas.[90]

Of all the Rectors of medieval Buda, it was Johann, father of Nicolas, who wielded the greatest authority. A powerful citizen in his own right, he owned extensive properties around Buda in the counties of Pest, Tolna, Veszprém and Fejér.[91] Always a firm supporter of King Charles Robert, he was also Castellan of Óvár and Count of Moson.[92] It is an illustration of his loyalty that in 1324 Johann took a leading part "in the attack on the castle of Tolna which was held by enemies of our Royal Majesty." Having suffered on his master's behalf a near fatal wound in the assault, Johann was rewarded for his services with the nearby Simontornya Castle and surrounding estates.[93] In the document recording the exchange in 1329 of one of these properties, mention is again made of the laudable actions performed by Johann in the name of the King.[94]

The closeness of Johann's relationship to the monarch was, however, by no means unique among Buda's Rectors. Walter was evidently a trusted subject of both King Béla and Ladislas IV while the Rector Werner felt close enough to the monarch to be able to petition him on behalf of some nobles accused of treason.[95] In the civil war of the early fourteenth century, Werner's son, Ladislas, similarly acted in a manner guaranteed to win later royal favour.

In 1301 Wenzel of Bohemia occupied Buda as the first step in his proposed subjugation of Hungary made on behalf of his son, Ladislas, claimant to the throne. Although Buda's citizenry largely supported the Bohemian party, the Rector Ladislas was evidently loyal to the rival Angevin cause.[96] Accordingly, he was seized by the invaders and later, in 1304, brought back with them as a captive upon their return to Bohemia. In his stead, as Rector of Buda, was now appointed Petermann, a supporter of the Bohemian King and citizen of the town. During his Rectorate, the clergy of Buda took the remarkable action of excommunicating the Pope and Hungarian episcopate largely on account of their failure to support the Bohemian claimants.[97] Despite the withdrawal of the Bohemian garrison and the appearance in the town of Otto of Bavaria, a third contender for the Crown, Petermann remained Town Judge. Quite possibly, Otto may have entertained the idea of replacing Petermann with Andrew, son of the murdered Rector Walter and now a citizen of Esztergom. For in 1306 and in an obvious attempt to win his support, Otto returned to Andrew his family's estates on the nearby Csepel Isle previously confiscated by Werner, father of the now imprisoned Rector Ladislas.[98]

Buda's opposition to the candidacy of Charles Robert proved but of short duration. Released in 1307 after almost three years captivity, the deposed Rector Ladislas re-entered his home town at dead of night and fell upon "his adversaries and betrayers." Petermann only narrowly escaped the wrath of his attacker, fleeing the town in a state of undress. Ladislas thereupon reassumed the Rectoral title while the "perfidious priests" of the town were duly despatched to the Archbishop of Esztergom for punishment.[99] Two years later, Ladislas was included among the "magnificent and noble men" present at Charles Robert's 1309 coronation. For his good deeds he was invested by the new King with the estates of the vanquished Petermann.[100]

Although actual nomination to the Rectoral office was determined largely by family connection, the monarch in so far as he possessed a *de iure* right of appointment could still exert, should the need arise, a stronger control over what was fast becoming the foremost town of the realm. What is more, the actual authority wielded by the Rectors, both within and without the town, together with the *fidelitas* they generally displayed towards the monarchy, influenced to no little degree royal policy towards the town's institutional structure. It was hardly in the interests of the Hungarian Kings to abolish the Rectoral system created by Béla IV. For in so doing they might risk antagonising the holders of the office and through them the distinguished families of the town upon whose very support these same monarchs had at times to rely. In effect, then, a most peculiar situation developed. Elsewhere, a monarch was generally unable to impose his own nominee as chief magistrate for fear of exciting the wrath of the community. In Buda, however, this very same fear dictated the continuation of a system which, at least theoretically, allowed for such impositions to be made.

The anomalous position of the Buda Rectorate became all the more apparent in the course of the fourteenth century. From the very middle of the thirteenth century, and increasingly thereafter, the privileges of Buda came to provide a pattern for royal charters donated to other Hungarian towns. In 1317, for instance, the townsfolk of Sopron were given by King Charles Robert "the prerogatives of liberty which our faithful citizens of Székesfehérvár and Buda obtained from our predecessors."[101] A few years later, a similar formula was applied to the town of Maros with the exception being that now all reference to Székesfehérvár was omitted.[102] Buda's charter now alone provided the touchstone for urban liberty. That the Hungarian monarchs were quite aware of the content of Buda's original charters is suggested not only by the above instances but also by the personal inspection of the town's liberties made in 1343 by King Louis only shortly after his accession.[103]

Furthermore, the practice of imposing Rectors in Buda never worked to the total exclusion of the electoral principle behind other appointments to the town magistracy. There is no indication in any of the records of the period to suggest that the twelve *iurati* of the Buda Council were, like the Rector, royally appointed. In fact, the reverse seems more likely. In 1287 Ladislas IV in a letter to the town, while referring to the Rector as *"pro tempore constituto,"* applied no such definition to the councillors.[104] The town of Pest, lying as it did in a somewhat confused legal relationship with Buda, seems to have chosen its own magistrate while recognising the Rector as possessing certain rights as a *villicus*.[105] Whether, in fact, these rights allowed the Rector to control the choice of magistrate is uncertain. Still, it is interesting to note that during the Rectorate of Johann the office of *iudex* in Pest was held by one of his relatives.[106]

During the first half of the fourteenth century, a series of changes occurred within the structure of the Buda *iurati*, inaugurated through the development of a process which allowed for one of their number to act as a judicial deputy to the Rector. The earlier phases of this development remain unclear as do the actual terms of the Deputy's appointment. By the last years of Johann's Rectorate, however, the system appears to have become fully established. In 1329, Tilmann, a prominent citizen of the town and son-in-law of Johann, was recorded as *"Iudex Castri Novi Montis Pestiensis,"* ratifying in conjunction with the eleven sworn men of the Council the donation of a vineyard made by the Rector.[107] A few years later, in witnessing a similar transaction together with the Rector and the other *iurati,* this same Tilmann was formally accorded the title of *vice-iudex.*[108] By 1342 the practice of appointing a *iuratus* to act simultaneously as the town's Deputy Judge had been clearly replaced by a system giving this office its own special identity quite distinct from that of *iuratus.*[109] A new judicial office was thereby created which, set between that of Rector and *iuratus* and taking upon itself a share of the judicial business originally falling to the Rector, was thereby to provide a firmer institutional basis for the eventual return from a Rectoral to electoral form of municipal government in Buda.

In 1346 (possibly 1347) and probably as a result of the plague, the Rector Nicolas, son of Johann, died. The office of Rector, long apparent as a glaring anomaly with no sanction in law and, since the emergence of the Deputy Judge's office, increasingly little significance, passed away with him. With the election in 1346–1347 (the precise date is unclear) of the long serving *iuratus* Lorand as Town Judge, the citizens regained that right and *libertas* which, although legally allowed them in 1244, had through the Rectoral system been effectively denied them for some eighty years.[110]

The long duration of the Rectoral period contrasts markedly with the painlessness of its death. The system created by Béla and maintained by his successors left in its wake no lasting impression on town institutions. Even the office of Deputy Judge slipped into the past. Buda seems soon to have reverted back to its earlier form of governmental life with little difficulty or administrative upheaval. Perhaps this is a reflection on the surviving source materials which in their dryness conceal the real vigour of change. Yet, by any measure, the age of the Rectors is more than a bald institutional curiosity. For it anticipates developments which in differing and more subtle forms, but for this no less striking in their import for the principle and practice of town autonomy, were to reemerge during a later period.

Chapter 3

GOVERNMENT AND *STADTRECHT*

The Development of Municipal Institutions

By 1347 the Rectoral period had come to a close and the chief magistrate of the town become once again an elected official. Yet after the Rectors, this figure never reassumed the title of *villicus,* as formerly used by his elected thirteenth century counterparts. Henceforward, he was to be known as the *Richter* or *iudex* of the town—a title indeed used on occasions by the Rectors themselves. Just as the terminology of government underwent alteration, so, likewise, the organisation of government experienced fresh change and development. Even during the Rectoral period, new administrative departments came to be founded in Buda and the Council of twelve sworn men of the town finds first mention during the Rectorate of Walter. While this institution probably owes its origin to an earlier date, the succeeding years under the Rectors came to define more closely the role assumed by its members in the municipal government and judiciary. Again, in 1316, reference first occurs to a Town Notary: an official in charge of the written business of the Council.[1] The foundation and development of new municipal departments was to continue throughout the fourteenth and fifteenth centuries and thereby was created a complexity of interlocking town institutions and offices. The character of Buda's governmental and judicial organisation was, however, influenced and moulded by a variety of different factors and pressures. Of these the most obvious is the sheer force of expediency arising out of the problems of urban growth.

Within a few years of Buda's foundation, mention is made of the existence of churches serving the largely Hungarian population living in the town suburbs. The first of these churches, Mary Magdalen's, was situated towards the northwest corner of the *castrum* where its tower is still visible to this day.

The second, St. Peter's, lay some few hundred yards outside the town walls at the meeting place of the present day Csalogány and Medve Streets.[2] From the mid-thirteenth century until 1440, these two foundations were busily involved in litigation with the parish church of Our Blessed Lady (the present-day Matthias Church or *Mátyástemplom*) situated in the very heart of the walled *castrum* area. The dispute ranged around the payment of symbolic fees by the two churches to Our Blessed Lady's and the demand that they be accorded similar status as parish churches with their own defined boundaries. For, while the two churches exercised a parochial authority, their competence was conceived to extend not over a defined geographical area but over certain categories of person. Accordingly, they were ranked as but *filiae* of Our Blessed Lady's and snubbed by contemporaries as being only inferior chapels.[3] The principal parish church of Our Blessed Lady counted as the German church of the town and its priest was, according to the terms of the town's 1244 charter, elected by the citizenry. But, because there were many "who did not understand the German tongue which the aforesaid priests publicly speak," the two other churches had been designated for the use of Buda's Hungarian population and the right of advowson was exercised by their respective Hungarian congregations.[4] It is almost certain that the foundation of Mary Magdalene's predates the establishment of the town of Buda. Most probably, the church served a small indigenous settlement on the northern part of the Buda hill which was subsequently incorporated within the new community. St. Peter's, likewise, although dating only from the 1250's, seems in its turn to have provided for the spiritual needs of an older village ranged along the site of a Roman road. A market continued to be held here until well into the fifteenth century.[5] The inclusion of these earlier settlements within the parish organisation of the town—a process evidently complete by the mid-thirteenth century—was paralleled by the extension of the magistracy's jurisdiction over the inhabitants of these two areas. Much later, during the second half of the fourteenth century, a new wall was built enclosing those suburbs of the town already mentioned together with the entire area lying between the *castrum* and the Danube (the Viziváros).[6]

At the same time, the actual number of persons living within the *castrum* was increasing. Around St. George's Place and the market square by Our Blessed Lady's, the construction of new houses was proceeding apace. Throughout the same period, wooden buildings were being gradually replaced by stone houses.[7] Foreign merchants and members of the nobility were fast attracted to the flourishing community. Any estimate of the actual size of Buda's population during the medieval period must remain little more than speculation. Some limits to conjecture are, however, imposed by the fortunate survival of a house list dating from 1437. For, in this year, the legate Martin Berruer reported to the Council of Basle on the logistics involved in the planned prorogation of the Church Council to Buda. His report, while noting that there was a "generous provision" of grain and victuals in Buda, concerned itself mainly with details of accommodation available.[8]

Berruer's report sought to break down the statistical information into four sections according to what the author saw as the four quarters of the town. Unfortunately, his divisions seem to have been largely arbitrary although recent research tends to suggest that the first two sections most probably refer in fact to the *castrum* area, the remainder to the suburbs outside the *castrum* walls.[9] Thus, within the central walled portion of the town were 322 houses— seemingly substantial buildings each with one or more cellars. Each house would appear to comprise about 8-9 rooms of reasonable size known as *aestuaria, camerae* and *testudines*. Contrastingly, the houses in the suburbs lacked foundations as solid as those of their counterparts in the *castrum*. Only 95 of the 645 houses appear to have been equipped with cellars. Again, but four rooms was the average for each of the suburb houses. This contrast between *castrum* and suburbs is reflected also in house prices. The cost of a well appointed house in the central more fashionable part of Buda might run to many thousands of florins. Contrastingly, a property in the suburbs could be purchased for but a score.[10] Not surprisingly, it was here that the majority of artisans lived and the suburbs formed the industrial nucleus of the community.[11] The application of a general multiplier, as favoured by Szűcs,[12] to the problem of Buda's population in the mid-fifteenth century is, therefore, fraught with considerable difficulties. Moreover, it is evident that within individual localities, considerable discrepancies might arise in the type of accommodation available. Many of the houses in the *castrum* enclosed a double plot. Others were divided into two or into flats with further dwellings available in a central courtyard.[13] Again, even within the ramshackle suburbs, great palaces were built, some of which even survive to this day (e.g. 3 Corvin Place). In Tótfalu and the nearby suburb of Taschental, prominent members of the town citizenry owned small farms and orchards.[14] Beyond this, one may presume that a large shifting population of day-labourers periodically made their way into Buda, particularly during late summer when the vines were harvested.[15] Suffice it to say that statistics available from the mid-nineteenth century when analysed and applied to Berruer's report tend to suggest that the Buda *castrum* and suburbs may together have held as many as 15,000 persons.[16] This figure approximates Kubinyi's research based upon wine-tithe lists extant from the early sixteenth century which indicate a population of some 12,500–15,000 persons.[17] Such, indeed, would seem a more reasonable conjecture than

Szűcs's estimate of about 8,000 persons—a figure which relegates Buda to little more than the status of an *oppidum*.[18]

Commerce was the lifeblood of the town and provided the material support for Buda's substantial population. The 1244 charter and a subsequent privilege of 1255 refer to the existence of two markets: the *cottidianum* or daily market, and the *sollempne* by which may be understood the weekly market. The former seems soon to have been abolished, while the latter is probably identifiable with the Saturday market to which reference is first made in 1322 and which was held on the square by Mary Magdalen's (the present day Kapisztrán and Vienna Gate Squares).[19] The Saturday market evidently soon came to lose its importance and by the early fifteenth century had been reduced to but a few stalls actually within the portals of what is now the Vienna Gate, then, not surprisingly, known as the Saturday Gate.[20] Around Mary Magdalen's a weekly market continued to be held, but only on Fridays. Every Wednesday, a further market was held on the square by Our Blessed Lady's with stalls extending down Apothecaries' Row (now Tárnok Street) to St. George's Place, where Louis the Great founded a church to serve those attending the sales.[21] The Buda town customary makes it clear that this was the principal weekly market in the town. When the Friday market coincided with a festival day or Christmas, then the site of the market was transferred down the road from Mary Magdalen's to Our Blessed Lady's. Outside the *castrum,* in the suburbs, two further weekly markets were held: the one at St. Peter's and the other at Zeisselpüchel, the actual location of which remains unclear.[22] Both neighbouring Óbuda and Pest, likewise, had their own weekly markets.[23]

Besides these weekly markets, two yearly fairs were held for the exclusive benefit of foreign merchants visiting the town. Native traders were expressly denied the right to sell their wares at these two events.[24] The fairs lasted a fortnight each and were held in May and September respectively. The town customary referred to the sites of the two markets as being located at *Anger* and *Aigen.*[25] Aigen probably corresponds to the settlement of Budafelhéviz, north of the town.[26] Thus, it would appear, one of the fairs was held actually outside the suburb walls and the effective jurisdiction of the Town Council. The Anger fair is probably identifiable with the yearly market mentioned in a privilege bestowed on the town in 1287 by Ladislas IV. Although the term Anger is strange, this fair would appear to have been held on the site of the German Wednesday market by the Church of Our Blessed Lady.[27] Pest, likewise, enjoyed two yearly fairs which, according to Hans Paumgartner, had proved by the early sixteenth century to be "generally better than those held at Buda."[28]

Now Béla IV's charter of 1244 had bestowed upon the town full rights of judicial immunity and self-government. The many needs of the community were, thus, to be served specifically by municipal institutions. No recourse might be had or remedy sought from royal government or those agencies serving the countryside around the town. For such a resort could but contradict the town's liberty and peculiar status within the realm. The 1244 charter had, however, empowered but one figure, the *villicus,* with the entire governmental and judicial organisation of the town. Obviously insufficient, the charters bestowed on other towns of the realm provided for the establishment of a Council of sworn men working in conjunction with the chief magistrate. As we have seen, Buda itself came to adopt this institution. But even so, the vast amount of business arising out of such a large community with so active a trading life called for the establishment of new municipal departments. Accordingly, proper arrangements had to be made for tax collection and citizens drafted in to perform this task. Again, despite the three days of the week upon which the Judge and twelve *iurati* met in their capacity as the town's magistrates, the weight of litigation demanded the foundation of new judicial forums. Hence, a court for smaller financial disputes was instituted and, in the suburbs, prosecutors' offices established. While the major decisions on trade, tariffs and prices were determined by the Council, the day-to-day commercial life of the community was regulated by a formidable array of market officials and trade inspectors. Constables, night watchmen, messengers and the grim figure of the hangman: all were likewise in the employ of the town.[29]

Much of our information about the judicial and governmental organisation of Buda during the late medieval period is derived from the town's customary or *Stadtrecht.* This is indeed a remarkable source and the first substantial collection of customary law to survive from the Hungarian middle ages. Written in middle German, it includes within it not only what the author viewed as the customary law and procedure within the town but also the texts of the various privileges bestowed on Buda by the Kings of Hungary. The three surviving copies of the customary each run to 75, 83 and 88 folios apiece, and the most recent critical edition[30] comprises altogether some 175 pages of text—445 chapters in all not including the Prologue. Unfortunately, the original is no longer extant, a loss which complicates any analysis of the actual stages involved in the customary's composition.[31]

Nevertheless, it is possible to ascertain that the *Stadtrecht* underwent three distinct phases of compilation. After the moral exhortations of the prologue and a table of contents, in his very first chapter, the author declares: "And this book is divided into three parts after the three estates or divisions *(standt oderr wesen)* of mankind: the high, the middling and the lowly. To the first belong the high laws *(obristen rechten)* of the King, the barons and also the nobility of . . . Hungary; thereafter, those of the Judge and sworn men or Council of Buda Town; lastly, those of the persons possessed of land and of the craftsmen and also of all types of persons in the community." This plan, the original scheme of the *Stadtrecht,* was pursued up until Chapter 158 although the logic of the divisions soon came in part to break down. Chapters 3–19 concerned the town's relations with the King, royal family and magnates. However, in discussing the payment of taxes to the monarch, the author felt it necessary to go off at a tangent and pronounce upon the principles of tax collection in the town (ch 11–15). Chapters 20–64 were concerned with the various municipal offices and the correct procedure for elections and appointments. Thereafter, the author devoted the following ninety-four sections to laws regarding trade, foreign merchants, market days, guild organisation and practices.

Hereafter, however, a certain confusion entered into the original plan. In attempting to discuss the actual status and laws governing "the persons possessed of land," the author found himself increasingly embroiled in the complicated procedures governing oath-taking, inheritance, securities on debt and the criminal law in so far as it affected housebreaking (ch 159–64). These matters the author had hitherto successfully managed to avoid. The *Stadtrecht,* thus, assumed a new direction and one which evidently demanded greater elaboration. Whether the author gave up his enterprise at this point and the lengthy second part (ch 165–403) is the work of a later writer must remain unclear. Since, however, what follows is both stylistically and linguistically very close to the first part, we may perhaps presume that the author simply suspended the project for a time to carry out further researches. Evidently, these researches took some time and, in the intervening period, certain municipal departments had undergone a process of reorganisation. The author's studies brought him also fresh information and insight on the workings of town offices and institutions which he had either already discussed or overlooked when writing the first part. Accordingly, the continuation assumed the character of a veritable hotch-potch with details of criminal and civil law mixed in with fresh or repetitious observation on the "three estates" of persons. The third section of the customary, comprising Chapters 404–440, simply records new trading and commercial regulations drawn up at a session of the Town Council in 1421 and these in places contradict sections of the preceding two parts. The four final chapters clearly represent additions appended much later, during the early years of the sixteenth century, and are not relevant to this enquiry.

Because in the seventy-seventh chapter and, thus, within the first part of the work, sections of the text are derived from the *Decretum Minus* of 1405,[32] this year may be postulated as the *terminus post quem* for the first two parts of the *Stradtrecht*. Again, since the third part consists of regulations made in 1421, one may presume that this year represents the final date upon which the first two sections of the customary could have been compiled. Thus, it would seem, the vast bulk of material treating on the town's government, judiciary, internal administration and law is derived from the sixteen years between 1405 and 1421. Most probably, the original text of the first two parts was, in fact, drawn up during the second decade of the fifteenth century, since the customary's discussion of Tavernical jurisdiction indicates a maturity of development which it is difficult to credit to the years immediately succeeding 1405.[33]

Beyond this, however, it is evident that the *Stradtrecht* was itself subject to a revision occurring most probably during the course of the 1420's. Chapters 107, 111, 112 refer directly to "the ordinance imposed by the Judge and Council at the behest of the King upon the butchers, fishermen and fishmongers" of the town. The terms of this ordinance, according to the *Stadtrecht,* embodied two principles: that the fishermen might freely sell whatever they managed to catch, whilst their rivals, the fishmongers, might deal in imported fish cargoes. These regulations derive, without question, from a Council ruling of 1424, made at the request of Sigismund, the aim of which was to remedy the quarrels among the various trades "long vented out among the stalls and tables of the market place." The terms of the Council's decision, preserved in the transcript of a patent of that year,[34] correspond exactly with the principles outlined in the town customary. Nevertheless, since contradictions and general muddle persist within the final version of the *Stadtrecht* and, indeed, in many places, a chapter title is given with no succeeding text, one may assume that any later revision was but minor in its application. Certainly, no attempt was made to have the *Stadtrecht* conform to the sweeping constitutional changes which overtook the town in 1439.[35]

The actual authorship of the *Stadtrecht* must remain unclear. The close of the first chapter contains a special request to the reader, "And pray to God for me especially, saying these words: Please Remember Johann for Evermore." The inclusion of this passage has certainly guaranteed that Johann be, if not remembered, then certainly a source for conjecture. The tiresome omission of the surname makes his identity almost impossible to ascertain even more so since Johann was a particularly popular name in medieval Buda. The circumstances, however, under which his name appears, suggest that the mysterious Johann was writing with an audience in mind. But even if originally only a private compilation, the existence of three surviving copies indicates that by the close of the medieval period, the *Stadtrecht* was more widely disseminated. Clearly our Johann was a knowledgeable person. He had access to the town archives where he inspected the various liberties bestowed on Buda as well as the town books. He was, however, neither a member of the Town Council, nor, as has been suggested, the town's Notary. For he makes a number of important omissions when describing the activities of the Council, while, at the same time, ignoring certain judicial procedures regularly outlined in letters drawn up by the Notary and his office. Besides exhibiting an otherwise wide understanding of Buda's legal traditions, the author also displays a considerable knowledge of German law codes, whole sections of which were included within the text. The diverse character of the material from which the *Stadtrecht* drew is indicated by its author in the opening lines of the first chapter: "Here is the Law Book written after the laws of Buda Town and it contains, in a few places, Magdeburg Law and it is written on the basis of all judgments pronounced and after good praiseworthy custom *(nach allen ausgesprochen urtaillen und nach gueterr löblicher gewonhait)* and generally after the privileges with which the same Buda town was founded and given rights and freedoms by the many Kings and Princes of the lands of Hungary. . . ."

Examining the text of the *Stadtrecht* in detail, it is quite clear that often substantial sections were lifted *verbatim* from Magdeburg Law. Thus, in discussing the summoning of burghers to attend deliberations of the Council, the *Stadtrecht* borrowed directly:

Stadtrecht, ch 159	Magdeburg Law, Art 1.
Der zu dem purg ding nicht kümbt, so man dy glogken lewt, derr verrleust VI den. Wirt ym aber das purgerr ding gekundiget und kumbt er nicht, er verleust V schilling.	*Swer so zu deme burdinge nicht en cumet, so man die glocke lutet, der wettet sechs pfenninge. Wirt im daz burding gecundeget, her wettet vunf schillinge.[36]*

similarly in the *Stadtrecht's* definition of what counted as "inherited" property:

Stadtrecht, ch 162	Magdeburg Law, Art 108
Mit welichem guet der man stirbt, das haisset alles erb.	*Mit swelcheme gute der man erstirbet, daz heizet allez erb.[37]*

Copies of Magdeburg Law are known to have been available in Hungary during the medieval period: in Eperjes and in the Saxon towns of Transylvania.[38] Indeed, it is not impossible that, during the later middle ages, actions were even appealed from certain Transylvanian towns to the Magdeburg mother-town court in northern Germany.[39] But, besides Magdeburg Law, other legal codes were also in circulation. The seventeenth century Count Frankenstein reported the existence of a late medieval Nuremberg law code, probably the *Reformatio Norimbergensis,* in the Council House at Szeben.[40] Another Transylvanian town is reliably reported to have had in its possession a volume of Eike von Repgow's *Sachsenspiegel.*[41] Hence, it is not altogether surprising that besides Magdeburg Law a variety of other legal compendia came to the attention of the *Stadtrecht's* author and that sections of the *Sachsenspiegel, Schwabenspiegel* and Viennese Town Law came also to be incorporated word for word within the customary. The discussion of the Cardinal Virtues and the little poem addressed to the Town Judge in the Prologue: both again have their parallels in the contemporary literature of the period. A popular German proverb, "One man's rede is but half a rede, the other side should be heard," also found inclusion.[42]

This plagiarism on the part of the author, Johann, seemingly contradicts his claim, made in the first part of the *Stadtrecht,* that the work conformed to the "good praiseworthy custom" followed in Buda. Accordingly, the veracity of the author and, thus, the authenticity of the whole customary becomes thrown into question. However, further analysis only serves to vindicate Johann. All in all, there are some eight chapters of the *Stadtrecht,* the contents of which derive *verbatim* from earlier legal codes. Three of these chapters (ch 374, 375, 376) occur side by side within the second part of the Stadtrecht.[43] The texts of two of these chapters (374, 376) were themselves subject to interpolations and additions by the author which suggests an attempt to modify the content of the borrowed passages to fit the actual customary usage adhered to within Buda. Moreover, in the case of Chapter 376, the borrowed text appears also to correspond to practices observed, if not within Buda, then certainly in Pozsony.[44] More significantly, the remaining five derivative passages of the *Stadtrecht* (ch 159, 161, 162, 163 and 164)[45] all fall within that section of the work which, as we have seen, forms the link between the first and second parts and which represents the author's attempt to write on a subject about which, at the time, he was less well apprised. The direct plagiarism of the author is, thus, confined really to this one small section of the *Stadtrecht* and suggests a temporary expedient, perhaps anticipated by the author at the outset of the work, but one, nevertheless, to which his own integrity soon placed a halt.

Relković, in her discussion of the relationship between the *Stadtrecht* and other contemporary legal codes, has noted the many places in which the procedures and laws outlined by the Buda customary conform closely to practices observed elsewhere.[46] It would, of course, be difficult to maintain that the majority of those passages borrowed *verbatim* from earlier legal codes mirror the true customary law of the town. Conversely however, there seems no reason to suppose that the judicial and legal principles outlined in the *Stadtrecht,* simply because they correspond to customary usages elsewhere, do not truly reflect the practices observed within Buda. Buda was a community dominated by a large ruling class of German burghers. These persons hailed from and maintained contact with a great variety of other towns both within and without the realm. The customs of Buda, thus, never developed within a vacuum—as a series of responses influenced alone by the immediate needs of the community. Rather, the town's customary law was itself conceived and fashioned within the framework of traditions and moral attitudes common to a far wider, European *Städtewesen.*

Thus, in its concept of the pledge taken out on a loan, the customs of Buda accepted the crucial German legal conception that the value of the loan should be equal to the value of the pledge. Should the pledge be worth more or less than the loan, then, with the pledge sold off, any difference was to be met by either creditor or debtor, whosoever was the beneficiary.[47] This idea, quite fundamental to mercantile activity and the fostering of greater confidence in the business of commercial credit, depended upon the proper and impartial evaluation of securities offered to guarantee a loan. Procedures for this, namely the estimation of the collateral's worth and the repayment of any difference in value with the loan, as they are outlined in the *Stadtrecht,* may be supported by charter material and other quite independent sources.[48] The loss of the town books, however, makes it impossible to verify in the same way such details of criminal law and procedure as are preserved within the Buda customary. However, the very full records surviving from fifteenth century Pozsony suggest that practices described in the *Stadtrecht* and closely resembling those observed in Germany were at least carried out in this town.[49]

The various governmental departments and offices of the town, to which the *Stadtrecht* accords a fairly full treatment, have obvious parallels with institutions established in other Hungarian towns or in more distant German communities. Again, the characteristics of these institutions, as they are described by the Buda customary, may largely be corroborated within the quite independently surviving source material. Evidently, the judicial and governmental organisation of Buda developed in very much the same way as the laws and customs of the town. Both were influenced by wider traditions and notions implicit within European town life as a whole. The problems occasioned by urban growth and for which solutions were sought were hardly unique to Buda. Likewise, the principles of government and judicial immunity were fundamental concepts determining municipal development throughout Europe. Thus, it was possible also for institutions and procedures which seemed successful elsewhere to be directly borrowed and adapted to fit the requirements of the town.[50]

The principal figure within Buda, whose title appears at the head of every charter issued by the town and to whom all royal mandates and requests were mainly directed, was the Judge. It was he who headed Buda's governmental and judicial apparatus and who acted as the foremost representative of the community in official functions. An elected dignitary, he held office for a year at a time after which period he was obliged to seek re-election. Certainly, the *Stadtrecht* makes much of the Judge's role within the community, likening him to "the King in the affairs of the townsfolk."[51] To him it addresses a little poem in the Prologue emphasising the many qualities which he should possess. Evidently however, this concern with the character of the town's supreme office and dignitary reflects not so much any real authority wielded by this figure, as rather the principles of good government which his very being was held to signify.[52] While, in practice, the Judge's superior status and obligatory prior experience of municipal office may have given him the opportunity to press his own decisions and personality upon Council proceedings, in both a governmental and judicial capacity his authority remained in theory exceedingly limited. He appointed the Town Judge of the Monies who in the absence of the Judge performed as his deputy. Again, since the Judge of the Monies was according to the *Stadtrecht* appointed from out of the ranks of the twelve sworn men, the Judge might of his own accord co-opt a citizen of the town to fill this vacancy.[53] The Judge was responsible for prisoners placed in the town gaol, for hoisting the flag and directing the setting up of stalls on market days.[54] But in litigation proceeding before the Council, he might only act in conjunction with the other sworn men and, indeed, his presence may not even have been regarded necessary in the hearing of cases. Although the Judge was held personally responsible for all decisions and verdicts, judgments of the magistracy were never made in his name alone, but rather in the name of the Council and town as a whole.[55]

Georg Von Below has remarked that in the medieval German towns, "The Judge . . . did not speak the law, but only directed the proceedings and passed sentence."[56] In principle, the law was determined by the citizenry themselves and, partly for this reason judgments given out in patent letter form by the Buda magistracy associated all decisions with the collective will of the people.[57] In Pozsony, the Judge might ask the advice of simple burghers "about the Law."[58] In Buda, similar requests for advice in judicial matters from persons outside the magistracy are not unknown and, in general

discussions involving important business of the community, the presence of
guild masters and other notables might be demanded.[59] Generally though, the
law of the town was determined by the twelve sworn men of the Council who,
like the Judge, were elected annually on St George's Day (April 23).[60] The
fourteenth century formulary, the *Ars Notarialis,* referred to the *iurati* of a
town as *assessores*—persons empowered with the duty of discerning the law
and its relationship to individual judicial actions.[61] According to the *Stadtrecht,* the presence of all twelve sworn men was not necessary for the prosecution of justice. A *quorum* of six was quite sufficient. Judicial sessions of the
Council met on three days of week: Monday, Wednesday and Friday. Again,
on Thursday and Saturday, the Council assembled to discuss the business of
the town. All such meetings were held in the Town Hall overlooking the
market place and the Church of Our Blessed Lady.[62]

The Council was entrusted with all decisions affecting the life of the community, with the financial organisation of the town and public works. In the
interest of the citizenry, the Council involved itself in a wide range of commercial and economic activity. It initiated measures to prevent the hoarding of
goods by traders and closely regulated the minimum quantities of commodities to be purchased by foreign merchants.[63] Most probably, the Council
also fixed prices. Thus, when in 1522, in a bid to control inflation, Louis II
attempted to enforce price controls throughout the realm he still invested the
Town Council with the right to determine more closely such provisions as he
himself had enacted.[64] Again, in order to encourage day-labourers to work in
the vineyards at harvest time, the Council guaranteed the payment of their
wages. It authorised special watchmen to guard the vines and forbade the
citizenry to employ others in this capacity lest competition for jobs "reduce
the wages of the community's official watchmen."[65] Presumably, the Council
appointed the town's minor functionaries as seems certainly to have been the
case with the three prosecutors in the suburbs. It was the task of the prosecutors to assess the quality of claims initiated by members of the populace living
in the suburbs and direct, as they saw fit, actions to the Town Council for
adjudication. They themselves might hold no court nor levy any fines.[66]

The Judge and Council received no fixed payment for their onerous duties
although a portion of the fines taken at judicial sessions passed into their
hands. Also, they were held exempt from certain tax payments.[67] Control over
the trading life of the town clearly provided, however, an excellent means for
protecting and advancing their own commercial prosperity. The opportunities
for financial manipulation were many and the revolt in 1402 was seemingly
directed against abuses in the system of tax collection. In Kassa, during the
early sixteenth century, town monies were diverted towards the funding of a

merchant enterprise founded by certain councillors acting in a private capacity.[68]

Individual members of the Buda Council might be employed within a variety of public functions. During the yearly fairs, two of their number officiated as special market judges. Later, in the sixteenth century, this duty was entrusted to officials specifically appointed for this purpose.[69] Again, in judicial matters individual *iurati* might be despatched on inquisitions within the town to inspect for instance the damage done by straying cattle.[70]

According to the *Stadtrecht*, the citizens of Pest were obliged to choose their own Town Judge from out of the ranks of the Buda *iurati*. Most probably however, this system had been long discarded by Pest in favour of greater autonomy and the author of the *Stadtrecht* simply sought to endorse claims still raised in this matter by the Buda Council. Certainly, the *Stadtrecht* devotes no adequate discussion to how was to be filled the vacancy among the twelve councillors occasioned by the departure of one of their number.[71]

A frequent task of the town *iurati* was the installation of members of the populace into what were usually donated properties within the town. This legal process, based upon procedures widely adopted throughout the realm, was designed so that those who entertained doubts about the new owner's right to the property might make their objections known to members of the magistracy and so initiate a judicial enquiry. The installation, to which regular reference is made in the charters bestowed by the Council, was in a document of the mid-fourteenth century designated an integral part of the town's customary procedure.[72] Significantly, however, the *Stadtrecht* never alludes to this practice, nor indeed to the frequent use of individual town *iurati* in summoning or as arbitrators in litigation.[73] Other features of the Council's activity, as for instance details of their internal business arrangements, are either omitted or given but a summary treatment. Hence, despite the *Stadtrecht's* silence in this matter, the hours of the day during which the Council convened in its judicial capacity had been regulated at an early date and incorporated within the wide notion of town custom.[74] More importantly, no discussion is afforded in the *Stadtrecht* of the actual procedures involved in the introduction of civil litigation to the Council's attention. This is indeed surprising for, already during the early years of the fifteenth century, notarial marks referring to such procedures were being regularly attached to charters issued by the Council. The most common of these, the *relatio* mark, appears normally above the text of the charter and associates with it the names of one or two *iurati* of the Council.[75] In its place is alternatively found the mark "Commission of the Lord Judge and Lords Iurati" or, as a variant, "On the Mandate of the Lords in Council."[76] Both these marks correspond closely to

forms employed within the royal administration, about which we know far
more.[77] On this basis, the *Commission* mark may be presumed to signify that a
litigant had brought his case directly before the Council for adjudication and
the Council directly authorised the drawing up of a patent. As in the royal
Chancellery, the *relatio* mark was most likely included in a charter when an
approach was made first to individual *iurati* who themselves introduced the
matter to the Council and on the completion of discussions ensured that a
patent was duly issued. Some indication of this is preserved in a charter of
1471 issued on a *relatio* of Matthias Vitripar, *iuratus*. This letter concerns the
donation of a house in the *castrum* made by the Bishop of Veszprém—a
property which the Bishop had originally acquired from the *iuratus* Matthias
himself. Seemingly, in wishing to have his donation confirmed in written
form, the illustrious prelate had approached a member of the Council already
known to him and with whom he had earlier enjoyed business dealings.[78] But,
in the absence of corroborative information in the *Stadtrecht,* any assumptions
in this matter must remain little more than enlightened speculation. It is,
however, precisely such minor but often irritating omissions as these which
tend to suggest that the writer of the *Stadtrecht* was himself less aware of the
day-to-day details of business undertaken by the Council and, thus, it would
seem unlikely that he ever held membership of this body.

The Judge of the town had the right to appoint a Judge of the Monies
(Geldrichter) from out of the ranks of the twelve *iurati* and, thereafter, co-opt
a member of the citizenry to fill the vacancy occasioned by this appointment.[79] Quite clearly, the office of Judge of the Monies was founded to
relieve the magistracy of some of the less important business hitherto passing
before it. The Judge of the Monies held a court on the same days of the week
as the magistracy at which he judged disputes involving small sums of money
up to the value of forty florins. A special session of his court was also
convened on a Saturday on which day were heard pleas of the women
townsfolk. Appeals from the court of the Judge of the Monies might be
moved before the Town Council. A Vice-Judge of the Monies was weekly
sent round the town to seek out those owing debts to others. Beyond this, the
Judge of the Monies was deemed also to represent in his absence the Judge of
the town although whether this entitled him to take the chair in judicial
sessions of the Council remains unclear.[80] The later *Laws and Customs of the
Seven Towns,* which were drawn up with Buda serving very much as a model
for customary procedure, while noting the separate court held by the Judge of
the Monies, nevertheless, accorded to this dignitary the right to participate at
sessions of the Council when more "arduous" cases were being tried. At such

times, the Judge of the Monies sat directly at the right hand of the Judge of the town.[81]

All these institutions and the range of activities undertaken by them closely resemble those evident in other Hungarian and German towns. A Judge and Council of Twelve holding full executive and judicial authority within the community is a common feature of many medieval German towns as well as the Hungarian towns as a whole.[82] Apparently simple expedients such as the establishment of a separate office of Judge of the Monies may still be compared with the developments surrounding the office of burgomaster in such other towns as Pozsony and Sopron.[83] The very fact that through the later *Laws and Customs of the Seven Towns* other burgher communities of the realm could at least consider basing their administrative and legal system on a scheme so closely related to Buda's only further highlights the close resemblance between Buda's governmental and judicial organisation and that instituted elsewhere.[84]

Nevertheless, specific pressures and rivalries within the town exercised their own effect upon the development of municipal institutions. While certain governmental and judicial agencies of the town may, thus, be easily compared with those operating in towns elsewhere, forces more keenly felt in Buda contributed also in determining the shape and character of its institutions. The desire of the dominant German burgher class to maintain its powerful position within the community meant that special measures had to be enacted to exclude Hungarians from town offices.[85] Such, however, had little immediate effect upon the development of municipal institutions influencing largely the electoral process. The intermingling of general governmental forms with more specific pressures finds best expression in the context of the Outer Council.

The Outer Council owed its origin to the Buda revolt in 1402 led by certain guildsmen of the town. The privilege given out by Sigismund upon the suppression of the uprising in 1403 indicates that the course of the revolt was marked by a conspiracy, a fraudulent election and the subsequent establishment of an Outer Council of twenty-four persons.[86] The detailed discussion in the privilege concerning how the town was in future to regulate the collection of the royal and municipal taxes suggests that the revolt may have been inspired by a sense of grievance in this matter. Both in Sopron and Pozsony, the previous establishment of an Outer Council had, likewise, been accompanied by protests of malpractice in the system of municipal tax collection.[87] Almost certainly, earlier developments in these towns influenced the establishment of Buda's own Council of Twenty-Four. Although Sigismund, in his privilege, specifically ordered the immediate abolition of Buda's Outer Council, nevertheless, means were provided within the charter whereby this organ might effectively be reinstituted. For the privilege noted that, henceforward, tax payments were to be assessed and raised by "trusty and suitable persons elected for this purpose by the community." Only thereafter were the taxes to be handed over to certain *iurati* of the town. The sums due to the King were to be delivered to the royal Treasurer and an invoice correctly obtained. The remainder was to be used for the benefit of the town.

The *Stadtrecht* gives a detailed description, in both the first and second parts of the work, of how Buda's tax collection system actually operated in practice.[88] Quite clearly, the Council felt the existence of an elected body empowered with the rights of tax collection to be a threat to its own authority and, thus, sought to reduce this institution's independent powers. In the first part of the customary, a council of twenty-four, strikingly identical in number to that established during the revolt, is mentioned in the context of personal tax assessment made on the basis of property held by the individual. Quite clearly however, this was a body chosen not by the community but the "inner" Town Council itself. Again, the actual task of tax collection was entrusted not to members of the Outer Council, but rather to persons held answerable to the Judge and Council alone. In the interval between the compilation of the first and second parts of the *Stadtrecht*, the Outer Council had largely ceased to exist. A portion of the tax assessment, where it related to vineyards, was undertaken by a *iuratus* and a citizen of the town especially appointed for that purpose. Otherwise, the assessment and collection was performed by the Town Council with the assistance of but "twelve or fourteen trusty men" of the community.

Although violent events surround its foundation the history of the Outer Council suggests how an institution seemingly based upon precedents existing elsewhere might yet come to be distorted and the scope of its activities reduced as a result of pressures and rivalry within the town's governmental organisation. Moreover, the contradictory effect of Sigismund's privilege upon this body indicates the extent to which external forces might be brought to bear upon the character of municipal institutions. In the case of the Town Notary and his office, the effect of such pressures was far more subtle and, accordingly, all the more pervasive.

Notary and "Place of Authentication"

The Town Notary, *Stadtschreiber* or Town Scribe was appointed by the Judge and Council of Buda and, like his masters, held office for a year at a time. The *Stadtrecht* includes, beside those of the Judge and sworn men of the town, the resignation speech which the Notary was himself to deliver before the assembled populace at the close of his term of office.[89] Reference is first made in 1316 to a town scribe of Buda, Johann Kantus *protonotarius*.[90] Johann's title suggests that already by the early fourteenth century a notarial department made up of more than one scribe had come into existence within the town. Individual sections of the *Stadtrecht* confirm that, indeed, a number of scribes were in the municipal employ including, amongst them, a special secretary to the Judge.[91] The later *Laws and Customs of the Seven Towns* mention also a notary attached to the office of Judge of the Monies.[92]

The Town Notary was the official entrusted with the written business of government. Details of judicial actions taken before the Council were entered by him into the town books and he drew up at least a part of those documents relating to individual tax assessment. Between the Notary of Buda and his counterparts in other Hungarian towns, there was maintained a lively correspondence out of which developed a primitive news service.[93] Documents relating to legal actions were entrusted to his care and, evidently as a result, the Council came greatly to rely upon the good organisation of his office in the prosecution of judicial business. In 1511, the death of the Town Notary followed immediately by the death of his executor threw the Council into a state of confusion. The Council was obliged to explain to the royal Tavernicus that certain letters despatched by him to the town had since been mislaid and request him, accordingly, to forgive the somewhat unusual procedures which as a result they were forced to adopt.[94] The central role of the Notary in the municipal administration and the havoc that could be wrought by his untimely death find reflection in the *Stadtrecht.* For the latter, in an extraordinary passage, records the procedure to be followed in the event of the Town Notary's sudden departure from this life. The Judge should immediately seize control of the town books and two sworn men of the Council "take hold of, and at speed, a wise and experienced scribe" to fill this crucial vacancy.[95] In no other part of the customary are the practices to be followed upon the death of a town official given such treatment.

Just as the Town Notary assumed a central position within the administrative organisation of medieval Buda, so his office also lies very much as the centre of our understanding of the town's governmental and judicial life. For much of the surviving charter material is the product of his office and, thus, the medium through which we view the town, its laws and government. Even the *Stadtrecht* itself was, albeit in a different way, greatly influenced by the practices of record keeping observed by Buda's Notaries.

Details of litigation passing before the Council were all entered by the notary into a "Special Register" or notebook. In this, he recorded "all cases as they proceeded and were determined by the law, after the accusation and retort as well as the pronouncement and judgment of the court." In this same work, the Town Scribe also took note of such letters as he himself wrote out at the request of various parties in an action.[96] The practice of keeping a scribal notebook is affirmed by the mid-fourteenth century formulary, the *Ars Notarialis.*[97] This work, however, allows for a far simpler procedure of record-keeping than that outlined in the *Stadtrecht.* Quite clearly, the details of cases kept in the notebook could not themselves be later invoked as legal evidence in subsequent litigation. The *Ars Notarialis* regarded the charter as the sole truly valid legal instrument. Hence, from his notebook, the Notary together with the Judge and Council was in a quiet place and preferably not a tavern (since *"Ebrietas frangit quidquid sapientia tangit"!*) to transcribe on to letters-patent full details of all civil actions as had proceeded before the Council. Beside the charter, however, the Buda *Stadtrecht* postulated the Town Book: "The town shall have a particularly important book . . . to act as its Town Book in which the scribe shall note in a quite orderly fashion the argument and content of all letters which have been sealed under the town seal and given out over land, legacies and other important matters."[98] In a number of places, the *Stadtrecht* seems to contradict the assertion that only letters given out under the town seal be recorded within the Town Book. Details of major criminal cases and the recantations of heretics and sorcerers would appear, likewise, to be here included.[99] A similar organisation of the Town Book was adopted in Pozsony and some of the North Hungarian mining towns and is noticeable also among the earlier records kept by certain German towns in the twelfth century.[100] Possibly though, the term "Town Book" *(statpuech)* which the author of the customary treats as quite synonymous with "Town Ground Book" *(statgrundpuech)* was a collective title used to cover a wide variety of differing categories of material separately organised. Such a generic use of the term would again appear common in parts of Germany.[101] On the other hand, though, the author of the *Stadtrecht* clearly differentiates between *"statpuech"* and *"echtpuech" (Achtbuch)*—the special book containing the names of those outlawed and exiled from the town.[102] On this basis, one might expect a slightly more discriminate terminology.

The entering of materials into the Town Book was strictly regulated. New entries might be made only in the presence of two or three men of the Council specially despatched by the Judge to oversee the Notary's work. For, entries in the Town Book, unlike those in the scribe's notebook, were accorded the character of fully legal instruments. They were, in the words of the *Stadtrecht,* "to be believed as much as are letters of the town sealed with the town's own seal." Indeed, so continues the *Stadtrecht,* in the event of a party in an action losing a charter issued by the Council, a replacement might be easily arranged by recourse to the Town Book.[103] This notion of the legal authenticity of all entries made in the Town Book is reflected also in certain procedures employed during sessions of the Tavernical court. Here, extracts from the Town Books of both Buda and Pest were submitted as legal evidence with no doubt as to their veracity being ever entertained.[104] Moreover, in 1459 during the course of a land dispute being heard by the royal Council and involving both members of the nobility and properties within Buda, the King himself requested the town to forward to the Chancellery details of a land transaction "which, as is your custom, you have written in the Book of your town of Buda."[105]

Although this basic legal idea was common among the towns of Germany, the acceptance of the Town Book's claim to authenticity by institutions of the royal administration must in part be explained by the spread of similar practices to other judicial agencies of the realm. Contracts between private persons which were drawn up before a monastic chapter were frequently copied out in full into books specially reserved for that purpose. This practice, evident during even the Árpád period, came to be generally observed by the fifteenth century and replaced the chirograph as the traditional means of record-keeping. The transcript of a charter preserved in a monastic or convent register was employed as an exemplar from which subsequent copies might be taken.[106] Again, from as early as 1331, reference occurs to the use of registers preserved in the royal Chancellery. The copies of charters entered here had the character of fully legal documents. From them new charters might be transcribed and forgeries determined.[107] By the mid-fourteenth century, individual dignitaries of the realm likewise kept their own registers.[108] By contrast, record-keeping in the counties appears underdeveloped and, indeed, until the sixteenth century, few counties had even their own scribes. Mostly, such notaries as appear were simply the often illiterate servants of the local lord. Although from as early as the first half of the fourteenth century records of civil and criminal processes might be kept, the actual registering of documents was haphazard and often substituted by the clumsy expedient of unsealed copies made on loose membranes. In any case, since even the sealed charters given out by the county courts were not held to be valid legal instruments, such register entries as existed must have been effectively worthless.[109]

The Town Book, however, is distinguished from these registers in one crucial respect. The register contained a full transcript of the charter. The Town Book, in contrast, was mainly concerned with but the bare essentials of a judicial action. Certainly, as the *Protocollum Actionale* from fifteenth century Pozsony and the later surviving sixteenth century transcripts of entries from the Buda Town Book reveal, the records of individual cases might be given in some detail.[110] But, by contrast, the Town Book from fourteenth century Besztercebánya displays a remarkable conciseness. In land sales, it merely notes the names of buyer and seller, the property involved and the sum of money exchanged.[111] Most probably, during the fifteenth century, the Buda Town Book erred similarly on the side of conciseness. For the *Stadtrecht* noted that, in the drawing up of replacement charters, written afresh and based upon the contents of the Town Book, often the latter proved insufficient and it was necessary to consult "other town letters."[112] One example from the early fifteenth century suggests that in practice when a patent was reissued in privilege form, a procedure which called for the text of the original to be repeated *verbatim,* the transcript was made only from the patent and no immediate recourse was had to the Town Book.[113]

The Town Book, thus, consisted of a series of entries and not full transcripts. In this respect, it resembles closely the book-keeping practices observed in the towns of Germany as opposed to those employed in the monastic chapters and royal Chancellery. Almost certainly, the author of the *Stadtrecht* based his documentary researches primarily upon the scribal notebooks and the Town Books. These, after all, were the principal municipal records and only a little native charter-material could have been available in the town archives. Indications that it was this source which the author actually consulted are hinted at within the *Stadtrecht* itself. ". . . And it (i.e. the *Stadtrecht*) is written on the basis of all judgments pronounced . . ." *("nach allen ausgesprochen urtaillen")*—so runs the very first chapter of the customary. An almost identical phraseology is employed in the section on the town scribe's notebook; this was "to be written after the pronouncement and judgment of the court" *("nach ausspruch und urtail des gerichts").*[114] Now because the scribal notebook and Town Book contained only brief entries and not full transcripts, use of these materials may explain why it was that the author of the *Stadtrecht* failed to note certain civil procedures generally recorded in the charters themselves. For in giving but a brief record of a land transaction in the Town Book or alternatively inserting only short notes in his notebook, the town scribe most probably omitted reference to certain procedures otherwise outlined in the charters. The author of the *Stadtrecht,* in relying upon the notebook and Town Book, remained thus ignorant of various aspects of municipal process law.

Hungarian land-law recognised that, in the alienation either by sale or gift of estates originally inherited as opposed to bought by or donated to the seller, the consent of relatives and especially male children was a necessary concomitant.[115] The charters given out by ecclesiastical chapters and other "places of authentication" noted that this consent had been previously procured. The formula "with the counsel and permission of his relatives having been obtained" is a common feature of charters of this kind. The notion of consent, characteristic of feudal societies in general, was designed so as to prevent the wholesale partition and alienation of estates.[116] In Hungary, concepts of clan ownership may also have played a part in the formulation of this principle.[117] In Buda, likewise, a number of charters recording alienations of property similarly include the consent formula. Such is indeed surprising since in medieval towns generally the family unit tended soon to lose its socio-legal significance and the easy transfer of property become a prerequisite for mercantile activity. But, within the charters issued by the Buda Council, the consent formula was by no means employed in an arbitrary or indiscriminate fashion. Occasionally the property involved is specifically referred to as having actually been inherited by the seller.[118] Again, the later *Laws and Customs of the Seven Towns* clearly state that relatives should be consulted prior to the alienation of inherited estates.[119] The *Stadtrecht,* however, makes no mention of consent of relatives playing any active role in the process leading to the sale or donation of properties.

Possibly, the author was himself muddled over the terms of municipal land law and in his confusion felt it was best to write as little as possible. Certainly, he seems remarkably vague over the tricky question of whether or not a burgher might freely dispose of property by will.[120] Contrastingly though, some detailed knowledge of wifely property or *morgengab* law is evident.[121] Most probably, however, the author was simply unaware of the principle of consent. The briefness of the entries made into the Town Book, from which the author is likely to have derived much of his information, most probably precluded any reference to consent having been obtained. Again, as a procedure initiated privately and outside the courtroom, no reference to it may have been made in the scribal notebook. By contrast, procedures more publicly adopted to ensure generally that the sale of inherited property was pursued in a legal fashion (namely the proclamation from the balcony of the Town Hall on three consecutive Sundays) together with an elucidation of the types of person who might approach the Council in respect to an illicit sale do find some discussion in the *Stadtrecht* although no explanation of the principles behind these occurrences is ever afforded.[122]

Again, in Hungarian land-law, the seller of property frequently bound himself in the contract of sale "to defend and uphold" the purchaser "with his own labours and expenses." By this undertaking, it was understood that in any future legal action directed against the purchaser's rights to the property presently being negotiated, the seller and, thus, former owner would appear in court and assume the role of defendant. Therefore, instead of those of the present owner, the previous owner's rightful claims to the property in question came under examination. If the previous owner successfully established that the property had indeed been rightfully held by him, then the claims of the present owner were assumed upheld. But, should the previous owner lose the case or not bother to appear in court in the first place, the lands were granted to the plaintiff and the previous owner obliged to award the dispossessed owner lands to the same value as those forfeited.[123] This principle known as the *evictio* or *expeditio* was widely employed in one form or another throughout much of medieval Europe. It is closely related to the warranty in England and may be observed operating also in Austria and parts of Germany.[124] From the mid-thirteenth century onwards, it is a common feature of those charters used to authenticate land transactions in the Hungarian countryside.[125] Within less than seventy years, it came to be included also within all charters treating on property contracts issued by the Buda Town Council.[126]

Like the consent of relatives formula, the *evictio* finds no mention in the *Stadtrecht*. Possibly, the formula was omitted from entries made in the Town Book and, accordingly, the author of the *Stadtrecht* was ignorant of its usage. However, had this principle been ever employed in actions taken before the Council, of which we have no evidence, and the owner of a disputed estate actually had recourse to *evictio* procedure, then one might expect some record to have been entered in the scribal notebook or Town Book and, thus, for at least a garbled account of the procedure involved to be recorded in the *Stadtrecht*. Alternatively, it may be that the *evictio* was a procedure only very rarely invoked. In Pozsony, where a modified form of this procedure was seemingly in employ, recourse to the *evictio* might only be had within the limited period of the *praescriptio*.[127] For, in the towns of Hungary, ownership of property was incontestable with a year having elapsed from the date of purchase. Contrastingly, with country estates, the *praescriptio* period was normally thirty-two years.[128] Accordingly, in the towns the number of objections to the sale of town properties and, thus, the circumstances under which recourse to *evictio* procedure might be had, came correspondingly to be limited. Again, since all objections to the sale of town properties had to be moved as rapidly as possible, it could be that the *evictio* came somehow to be incorporated within those procedures adopted generally to ensure that land purchases were conducted in a rightful manner.

Even so, a number of doubts must be raised as to whether the *evictio* clause, so regularly found in the charters issued by the Buda Council, had any real significance at all. The *evictio* formula when included in documents drawn up by other judicial agencies in the realm was often accompanied by a statement outlining exactly what lands the seller would grant the purchaser in the event of forfeiture.[129] The inclusion of such a statement firmly reveals that in such circumstances the *evictio* formula had a concrete application and meaningful legal consequences. Now, in the charters issued by the Buda Council, this additional statement is, to the present author's knowledge, applied only on one occasion: in 1403. But here, the purchasers involved were Nicolas of Gara, the Palatine, and his brother, the Count of Temes. Quite clearly, these great lords would wish for such procedures to be enunciated in regard to the sale as were usual outside the town. The Council merely concurred with their wishes.[130]

There is furthermore much to suggest that the *evictio* was a formula which ran against certain notions implicit within Buda's customary law. For the *Stadtrecht* suggests that in the purchase of town properties the buyer himself was obliged to ensure that the lands transacted were not the subject of a dispute. A land transaction involving disputed properties rendered the purchaser liable not only to loss of the properties involved but also to payment of a substantial fine.[131] Thus, it would seem, in land transactions, the risk firmly lay with the purchaser and few obligations were imposed upon the seller. This principle obviously contradicts the fundamental notion underlying the *evictio*.

Arguably, the *evictio* clause represents no more than a meaningless formula simply inserted in town letters to make these conform to usages current elsewhere. If such, indeed, is the origin of the *evictio* then its inclusion in the charters issued by the Buda Council may most directly be associated with the work of the Town Notary. For it was he who, as we have seen, was responsible for the drawing up of letters given out under the town seal.

The *Stadtrecht* declared that the Town Notary should be a man of clear German ancestry. Evidently, though, he rarely was. Good professional notaries were a commodity very much in demand. For most institutions it proved generally difficult enough to find Hungarian scribes, let alone German ones.[132] Again, seemingly absent from the Hungarian towns were any families whose members over a long period successively filled the ranks of the municipal notariate.[133] The towns of Hungary were, thus, obliged to recruit notaries from outside their own populace[134] and in this respect Buda was seemingly no exception.

The names of four Town Notaries survive. Of these, Johann Kantus was of Hungarian noble lineage, Wenceslas obviously no German and George of Szeben, apparently again, neither a German nor originally from Buda.[135] Only Christian Bauman, Notary in 1429, was of clear German stock and even he hailed from distant Kolozsvár.[136] In neighbouring Pest, the Town Notary for a time was Johann of Magh, famous for his late fifteenth century formulary, a man who had previously worked as a scribe in the Óbuda chapter and thereafter occupied high rank within the royal Chancellery.[137]

The career of Johann of Magh suggests that Town Notaries were recruited from the ranks of those who had previously worked in the ecclesiastical chapters and royal government. Most of these persons had undergone their training in the chapter schools and, indeed, both the mid-fourteenth century *Ars Notarialis* as well as Magh's later formulary include large sections for the benefit of students subsequently to be employed in the service of town government.[138] Almost certainly, Buda's municipal notariate were drawn from the chapter schools, a point which must in part explain the close similarity between the charters given out by the town and those issued by other judicial and governmental agencies of the realm.

The charters of Buda may be divided into three separate categories of letter: the privilege, patent and closed. All three classes were normally written in Latin, although a few in German, mainly closed letters, have survived. These three classes conform exactly to the divisions employed generally throughout the realm and, moreover, their language and phraseology closely correspond to usages current outside the town. Again, the chirograph form of letter-patent and varieties of seal employed tend to make the charters of Buda appear largely unexceptional. However, this close conformity between the charters of Buda and those issued out elsewhere may very well have been forced on the letters of the town by its own imported notariate. For indeed, as the *Ars Notarialis* explains, prudent Town Notaries were expected to avoid "defective forms" and advised to adhere to common usages writing out letters according to rules laid down in their chosen text-books.[139]

Such an interpretation may very well account for the inclusion of the *evictio* formula in Buda's charters. It may, moreover, afford some explanation for the anomalous clauses treating upon seal usage found also in town letters.

According to the practices of the time, all civil contracts undertaken by private parties were deemed of a legal character only when recorded on a sealed charter issued by a recognised "place of authentication." Normally religious houses, although dignitaries of the realm acted also in this capacity, these "places of authentication" or *loca credibilia* drew up the relevant deeds and appended their own authenticating seals. Beyond this, they might rewrite charters or reissue patents in privilege form.[140] Certain activities of the Buda Council and, indeed, of other municipal councils in the realm bear a close resemblance to the practices of the *loca credibilia.* Details of private transactions were taken before the Council and, thereafter, recorded in charter form. Moreover, records of transactions involving lands even outside the town and made between persons who were neither citizens nor members of the populace were again authenticated by town charter and seal.[141] Hence, the Buda Council would appear to act as "place of authentication" and to be generally recognised as such by both burghers and countryfolk alike. The principal feature distinguishing the privilege from the patent letter was the seal. Privileges issued out by the *loca credibilia* had to them appended a hanging double seal. Patents, drawn up in a more concise language than privileges, were authenticated with only a seal impression made in wax on the dorse. A contract written up in privilege form was deemed to have a permanent legal validity for the double hanging seal was held to confer an "authentic" legal status. But, contrastingly, a patent with only an impressed seal was an instrument of a more limited credibility. A year after the original draft of the charter, the legal rights and obligations expressed in a patent letter were held to be quite void. But, within this period, the holder of the patent was entitled to have his letter rewritten in privilege form. Documents recording land sales, transactions and donations were normally first recorded in a patent letter. Thereafter, if no objections to the contract were raised, a privilege was issued guaranteeing a permanent legal validity. Regularly, on patent letters there was included at the end of the text an undertaking that the issuing agency would, if requested, subsequently draw up the letter in privilege form: *"Presentes autem quandocunque nobis fuerint reportatae, eas nostro faciemus privilegio confirmari."* Privileges, in their turn, had in place of this clause the *corroboratio* formula attesting to the permanent legal validity of the letter and its contents: *"In cuius rei memoriam perpetuamque firmitatem ad instanciam et peticionem parcium presentes concessimus litteras sigilli nostri, munimine roboratas."* [142]

From the late thirteenth century, Buda was in possession of two seals. The first was a double seal, bearing on one side the royal coat-of-arms and on the other three towers and a gateway—the characteristic symbol of a town. This seal was appended to privileges issued out by the Town Council. On the dorse of patents was impressed a smaller one-sided seal upon which were embossed those motifs evident on the obverse and reverse of the double or greater seal.[143] It is quite remarkable that, from such an early date, a town such as Buda should have been in possession of two separate seals. For this is a development normally associated with the fifteenth century.[144] On both privileges and patents issued by the Buda Council may be observed those two formulae either promising the subsequent reissue of the patent in privilege form or alternatively attesting to the permanence of the terms announced in the privilege itself. Thus, the notion of the patent letter's inferior status and of its limited legal character was enshrined within the text of every charter issued out by the Buda Town Council.

Clearly however, the majority of persons requesting the Buda Council to confirm land transactions felt that a patent here issued had a full legal validity for all time and was in no way an inferior instrument. For examples of privileges issued to confirm and replace a patent remain remarkably rare. Thus, despite the large number of patents surviving from the period 1346–84, only some seven privileges are extant.[145] In the twenty years between 1387 and 1406, some thirty-one patents issued by the Buda Council have survived but, contrastingly, only three privileges.[146] Neither is it possible to explain such a curious phenomenon by reference to the vagaries of documentary survival. For, generally, one might expect the more important privileges to have been more rigorously guarded over the ages than patents and, thus, now to exist in greater quantities. Again, it is evident that the Council itself did not regard the legal validity of a patent to have expired after the period of a year. For in 1378, 1392 and 1396 the Council reissued in privilege form patent letters given out in fact a number of years earlier.[147] Indeed, in a quite remarkable about-turn, in 1412 a patent was even used to confirm a privilege actually issued some forty years previously.[148] Kubinyi has sought to explain this peculiar development by reference to the growth in usage of the lesser seal which he regards in time as having conferred upon this seal an authenticity which came to outweigh the otherwise limited legal character of the patent. Accordingly, the privilege with its hanging double seal came to be used by the town "only in the most important matters."[149] Certainly frequent use of a seal might come to confer authenticity upon that instrument. For, to a degree, authenticity was itself deemed the counterpart of visual recognition. On the other hand, it must be remarked that while in the privileges to which it was appended Buda's double seal is often designated "authentic," no such terminology is ever applied to the lesser, impressed seal.[150]

Kubinyi's view that privileges were only conferred in respect to more important matters may perhaps find some limited support in the *Stadtrecht*. For the *Stadtrecht* regarded the greater, double seal as employed only on *hantfesten,* by which it understood those charters recording not so much contracts between individuals as rather liberties pertaining to institutions.[151] Certainly, although the guilds of tanners and tailors were content with mere letters patent, the rights awarded to the Butchers' Guild in 1481 were drawn up in privilege form by the Buda Council.[152] Nevertheless though, and with due respect to Professor Kubinyi, closer examination of the actual terms under which individual privileges were granted out suggests a quite different explanation to that of degrees of importance.

From the second half of the fourteenth century, privileges to confirm land transactions were only issued out in regard either to estates held by burghers in the countryside around the town or alternatively to high dignitaries of the realm who were not themselves of citizen status. Neither is this really surprising. For such persons were most likely to be involved in litigation taken before courts other than Buda's. Alternatively, they might wish to exchange their properties with persons who were themselves neither citizens nor inhabitants of Buda. Well might the Buda Council or its townsfolk regard a patent as a sufficient guarantee of ownership but other courts or persons might not be so disposed.[153]

Buda's own acceptance of the patent letter's full legal validity must be held to owe its origin to the differing laws and customs of the town. For in Buda there was simply no need for acquirers of property to have their ownership affirmed by privilege after the lapse of a year. As we have seen, unlike estates held in the countryside, the ownership of town properties was incontestable upon the expiry of the yearly *praescriptio* period. Thus, after a year no circumstances would normally arise under which a burgher might be required to show evidence of rightful possession. Again, even if the provenance of the patent he produced as proof of ownership was held in doubt, recourse to the Town Book might be made and the authenticity of the instrument there determined. For, as the *Stadtrecht* pronounced, entries made into this work had the same legal validity "as . . . letters of the town sealed with the town's own seal."[154]

Notions, therefore, of the patent letter's inferior status to the privilege were, in practice, only entertained in exceptional circumstances. For burghers buying properties within the town, a patent was a quite adequate legal record. The town charters clearly erred in attributing to the patent a limited legal validity, for, as such, were disregarded the special practices commonly observed by both the townsfolk and the Council itself. For this error, the town's imported Notaries must be accorded a substantial share of the blame. In drawing up the town's charters, they failed to allow for Buda's differing usages. Instead of adopting a more pertinent seal formula, the Notaries simply adhered to meaningless clauses in their attempt to avoid "defective forms" and have the town's charters conform to the more acceptable usages of the *loca credibilia.*

The activities of the Town Notary and his office illustrate in microcosm a particular difficulty facing the town's government and judiciary. Specific administrative arrangements and practices had developed within the town and been integrated within a legal framework peculiar to the town alone. Yet, at the same time, usages and customs observed more generally within the realm and yet quite foreign to the town's life as a whole might still be superimposed. In the case of the town's charters, this dichotomy remained unresolved. But such confusion is exceptional for, in other respects, Buda was well able to adapt its institutions to fit both the requirements of the town and, at the same time, conditions and pressures imposed from outside. Already, it has been noted how Buda's Town Council undertook the function of a "place of authentication," performing activities normally associated with institutions in the Hungarian countryside. However, the *loca credibilia* functioned as far more than just charter-issuing agencies.

On a mandate from the King, Chancellery or high dignitary of the realm, the *loca credibilia* might issue summonses or perform inquisitions and installations. Objections over the terms of land transactions might be brought before a "place of authentication" and from here initiated the relevant procedures leading to an action being brought before a court of the realm. Witnesses might be saved the bother of attending court by making their evidence known in a deposition drawn up in a *locus credibile*.[155] Certainly, many of these functions were practised by the Buda Council. But obviously, simply because the magistracy was empowered with a full judicial authority, a number of these procedures never came to be practised. The Council came, thus, largely to deal with *relationes* or mandates, as opposed to *litterae*—the instruments despatched to a court of the realm to initiate legal actions. For as all cases arising within the town were largely dealt with by the magistracy itself, recourse to a court of the realm proved both unnecessary and unwelcome. But, on occasions, a royal mandate might evidently be despatched to the town requesting the Council to investigate by inquisition the property rights of an individual. Thus, in 1397, Sigismund requested the Buda Council to enquire as to whether one nobleman of the town had illegally seized and occupied the properties belonging to another. Presumably employing the Town Book, the magistracy were able to locate the previous owners and oblige them to make depositions which were subsequently included in a prompt reply to the King.[156] With the exception of the Town Council, no judicial institution was permitted to perform inquisitions within Buda. As the *Stadtrecht* asserts, any letters empowering judicial agencies from outside the town with inquisitorial powers were held to be invalid.[157]

A principal task undertaken by the *loca credibilia* was the installation or *statutio* of an owner to his newly acquired property. Originally applied only to those in receipt of royal donations but gradually extended to include all sales and exchanges of land, this process was normally initiated by either royal mandate or a *relatio* despatched from the office of one of the realm's high dignitaries. An ecclesiastical chapter operating as a *locus credibile* was ordered to send forth one of its number to the property presently being transacted. The cleric was accompanied by a *homo regius,* usually a reluctant member of the nobility delegated to undertake this task. Upon reaching the estate, the two officials called together the neighbours and asked of them whether there was any reason why the new owner should not be admitted to his property. After remaining in the locality for three days, the delegates retired and protestors were allowed a fortnight in which to make known to the chapter any objections they might entertain. Thereafter, the new owner was entitled to assume full possession of the property and a patent to this effect was issued.[158]

Likewise, in Buda, and usually on a royal mandate, were performed also installations to donated properties. Because of the immediacy of the Council, it was probably not necessary for the appointed delegates to remain in the proximity of the property involved for the customary three days. As seems to have been the case in other towns of the realm, all protests might be addressed from the first day directly to the magistracy.[159] However, at no time were clerics or *homines regii* ever entitled to install persons to properties in Buda. This procedure was performed only by sworn men of the town who undertook their task at the Council's behest and reported back to this body once the installation had been completed.[160] Even when in 1346 and in a quite extraordinary incident, the Queen appointed a citizen and a nobleman to install a court official to his house in the town, the two delegates took care to notify the Council that none had opposed the installation and that it had been wholly performed *"iuxta dicte civitatis libertatem."*[161] Likewise in the fifteenth century and for a similar perhaps unwitting disregard for municipal rights, the delegates involved were obliged to work out with the Council a satisfactory formula to conceal their infringement of urban liberties.[162] Evidently then and as these two incidents suggest, the town's special judicial status within the realm demanded respect. As a result, procedures had to be employed which varied with those practices observed elsewhere. Persons from the countryside and outside the limits of council jurisdiction were rigorously excluded from any share in installation procedure. Any contravention of this principle demanded a formal explanation to the Council to the effect that no assault had been intended on the town's privileged status within the realm. Certainly then, the Buda Town Council may be viewed as operating very much in the same way as a *locus credibile,* undertaking on a mandate judicial tasks normally associated with this institution. However notions of self-government and judicial immunity came to modify traditional practices more widely observed and procedures were accordingly adjusted to satisfy both the town and the governmental agencies of the realm.

The function of the Buda Council as a "place of authentication" and the contrasting procedures adopted within the town in the fulfilment of this role may perhaps provide an indication of certain broad principles underlying the development of municipal institutions. Expediency, influences from other towns, internal rivalries and outside pressures all played an important part in shaping the character of the town's offices and departments. Yet, whatever forms of organisation were adopted, all came, nevertheless, to be incorporated and defined within the overall notion that the burgher community should be self-governing and entrusted with its own judiciary. The organisation of the town had advanced far beyond the simple structures proposed in the charters of the thirteenth century. But still, in accordance with the principles expressed in these charters, Buda remained a distinct governmental and judicial unit within the realm. Its own judges, councillors and officials dominated every aspect of the town's public life.

Chapter 4

ASSOCIATION AND AUTHORITY

The Burgher Association

The structure and organisation of Buda's government and judiciary were in their development subject to a variety of pressures and influences. Traditions common to many European towns mingled and became blended together with forces peculiar to Hungary alone. Beyond this, certain activities and customs unique to Buda exercised their own effect upon the general character of municipal government. The constitutional development of Buda thus took place within an atmosphere of contrasting and often conflicting forces. It was the combination of these elements which was to lend the town its own distinctive governmental organisation and flavour to its judicial life. The way in which Buda's government came to develop bears in many respects a close resemblance to the pronouncements of the early sixteenth century jurist, Stephen Werbőczy.[1]

In Werbőczy's opinion, each town represented a *pluralitas:* an amalgam of persons, each quite different and with his own individual background and way of life. Furthermore, every town was a unique combination of walls, buildings and streetways. Differing legal traditions and geographical location amongst the towns of the realm likewise contributed to diversity. Conversely, however, every free town of the realm was a *unitas civium:* a community whose members being of equal rank enjoyed the same privileges and obligations. This feature, being fundamental to all towns, made possible Werbőczy's general treatment of their institutions and status within the realm. But, as Werbőczy suggests, the notion of *unitas* acted also as the bond which welded together the amorphous *pluralitas* evident within each town and so forged therefrom the *communitas* itself.

Significantly, therefore, in his discussion of those pressures influencing municipal development, Werbőczy largely ignores the immunity. For him,

69

the principal defining force which pulled together the diversity of pressures and responses and which forced the *pluralitas* to coalesce was nothing less than an underlying notion of *communitas* or *unitas civium*.

Werbőczy's interpretation adds accordingly a new aspect to our understanding of Buda and the medieval town in general. Hitherto, we have largely attempted to interpret governmental and judicial organisation by reference to the immunity: a status bestowed upon the town from above, by royal grant of charter. But, in contrast, Werbőczy draws attention to the *unitas civium* and understands this concept to be the mainspring of the town's governmental and judicial life. Such an approach makes necessary some elucidation of the fundamental idea of the citizen association.

The towns of medieval Christendom owed their legal origin to the *coniuratio* or *Eidgenossenschaft*. In purely chronological terms the emergence of these unions succeeded the actual establishment of groups of persons living side by side in emergent urban settlements.[2] The *coniuratio* was frequently inspired by a legal need. Often involved in litigation with local lords, the townsfolk bound themselves together in a *universitas* through the agency of which they might the more easily prosecute their legal claims. Such a development was by no means confined to urban centres. In Hungary, serfs and countryfolk likewise formed themselves into associations when involved in judicial actions.[3] But what characterises the associations of townsfolk is the endurance of their *universitas* and the significance which membership of this institution came to assume. Precisely because the townsfolk's struggle against seigneurial lordship was often protracted and compounded by a desire to free themselves from any form of jurisdictional subordination, so their associations assumed a distinct character of their own. Through the burgher oath, the townsman entered into membership of a citizen brotherhood which recognised few responsibilities and duties other than those owed to fellow members. Former status and obligations counted as nought. Before the law of the town, all citizens were of equal status. In the words of the scribe of Eperjes, they were alike "in the payment of their penalties and in their wergild."[4] Moreover, as Ebel has shown,[5] membership of the association of townsfolk assumed the form of a contract. For through this membership, the townsman chose no longer to live by the law of the land, but instead voluntarily submitted to a new law determined by himself and his fellows. By extension, in Buda, through mere residence in the town, the newcomer was deemed willingly to have entered into "union with the citizens of the same." In return for the benefits of town life, he was obliged to obey and respect the various laws and liberties of the community—whether he liked them or not.[6] In time, an elevated and mature burgher consciousness was to express itself in the formulation of town customaries. These collections of law, allegedly determined and approved by the association of town citizens, contained principles which flatly overrode land-law and established criteria for judgments and procedures peculiar to the individual burgher associations. Such is, indeed, evident within the Buda *Stradtrecht.* This body of law, likened to nothing less than the Will of God, was in the words of its author the embodiment of "Law amended and made new." It was, moreover, a "Willkür," a term regularly applied throughout German-speaking Europe to indicate *Verwillkürung*— that process whereby the member of the burgher association voluntarily submitted himself to the law and direction of the sworn brotherhood.[7]

Certainly, in Hungary, the bestowal of municipal privileges and liberties was regularly employed to create or hasten the growth of a town and, within such circumstances, an association of citizens might almost unnaturally be pressed into existence. But, more usually, in Europe, the privilege succeeded the actual establishment of the burgher association. Again, in the words of Gierke, "The association, like the individual exists whether the state recognises it or not. Like that of the individual, its legal subjectivity requires recognition by state law, but the underlying personality of the association is no more created by state or law than is the personality of the individual. The role of the state and state law is merely declarative, not creative."[8] Thus, in legal terms, the privilege acted not as the force which brought into being the burgher association but rather the medium through which the association achieved formal recognition.

The privilege established the sworn association on a more secure legal footing. By affording recognition to the association and admitting the right to legal representation and a seal, the town acquired in law the character of a juristic person. And so out of the burgher association was born the burgher corporation. Importantly also, the privilege defined the status held by the citizen association within the realm as a whole and enunciated, at least in part, the relations henceforth to be observed between the association and those persons existing outside its membership. Such was, in effect, the origin of the immunity: a legal right dependent upon charter and restricting the degree to which outside governmental and judicial agencies might interfere in the life of the town. The grant of immune status thus depended upon the prior existence of the burgher association and was ultimately bound up with the state's formal recognition of the same. In the development of the town as a legal entity, the *prima causa* was neither privilege nor immunity but rather the forging of the association—the *communitas* or *unitas civium* itself.

Since the notion of the burgher association was transferred in an already mature form to the kingdom of Hungary, certain features surrounding the early development of this idea came to be lost. Procedures associated with the initial *coniuratio* phase—namely, collective oath-taking—never made an appearance. Still, nevertheless, the idea of the burgher oath remained. In Sopron, a newcomer wishing to assume the rank of citizen was obliged to swear that he would remain "true, worthy and obedient to the Hungarian King and his successors and to the Burgomaster, Judge and Council." He solemnly vowed to obey the laws and customs of the town "in all points and articles."[9] Likewise, in Bártfa, whosoever wished to be taken up into the body of the citizenry had first to promise due obedience to the "Laws and praiseworthy Customs of this town." Only then was his name attached to the list of those newly acquiring citizenship right.[10] Similar *matricula neocivium* survive from fifteenth century Pozsony, Kassa, Körmöcbánya, Besztercebánya, Trencsén and Eperjes.[11] In Buda, likewise, a newcomer without property in the town was obliged to swear that he, like his fellows, would perform all necessary services and pay the proper taxes.[12] Thus, through the very assumption of citizen status, the individual undertook by oath to perform his contractual obligations and bound himself to the law of the citizen association of which he now became a part. The tendency towards sworn union manifested itself also within the town's supreme governing body. For, as Planitz has argued, the actual institution of the *iurati civitatis* demonstrates the continuing "strength of the idea of the sworn association within the ranks of the townsfolk."[13]

It remained common for newly-appointed members of Town Councils to swear before the assembled citizenries an oath of office. This procedure was likewise adopted in medieval Buda. On election day and in front of the Town Hall, the Judge, Council members and Notary solemnly vowed to remain true to the law and to administer it fairly and without impartiality. They promised to show due allegiance to King, Crown, baronage and citizenry and to act in all things with a view to the common good.[14] Within the citizenry corporation there thus came into being an association of sworn men or *iurati* bound by oaths of office to the body of the townsfolk itself.

The bond existing, however, between citizenry and Council penetrated far deeper than the formal expressions of an oath of office. The burgher association occupied a place within the broad spectrum of popular associations all of which tended towards the realisation of what Ullmann has termed "the ascending theory of government."[15] Like the burgher association, the power wielded by the Council did not owe its creation to royal privilege; this only recognized and gave greater definition to an already existing phenomenon. Rather, the Council's power derived from the collective will of the citizenry itself. It rested upon a delegated authority, received from below and ordained for the purpose of ministering to the "common good"—the *gemain nutz* of the *Stadtrecht.*[16]

References to the popular origin of governmental and judicial power within Buda occur in the texts of every patent issued by the town magistracy. For judgments and confirmations were made not just in the name of the Council, but also in that of the citizenry *universitas:* "*Nos N. Judex Castri Novi Montis Pestiensis* (alternatively *Civitatis Budensis) Jurati ac universi cives de eodem memorie commendamus, quod etc.*" Again, the symbol of judicial power, the white staff, was on election day discarded by the outgoing Judge and laid on the ground betwixt himself and the assembled citizenry. The power hitherto exercised by the Judge was thereby visibly returned to the townsfolk from whom it was derived.[17] Indeed, this same notion is reflected also in Ladislas IV's privilege to Buda, given in 1276. In reaffirming the citizens' right to elect their own chief magistrate, Ladislas noted that this dignitary should annually "resign his power into the hands of the citizenry."[18]

As the examples of the staff of office and the 1276 privilege suggest, the election process itself crucially symbolised those concepts of governmental power and authority dominant within the town. Neither of course is this surprising. As Erler has shown, the townsman was a basically down-to-earth creature who interpreted such notions as contractual rights and responsibilities in terms little more elevated than those of tax obligation.[19] Election day was, likewise, an easily comprehensible manifestation of a scheme of government and order to the principles of which the citizen subscribed but only dimly understood. Particularly also, in the gathering of the citizenry for the purpose of electing their masters, there occurred a positive affirmation of citizenship right and a renewed awareness of the bond which linked together the individual members of the burgher community.

Although power was vested in the Town Council by the burgher association, the actual area over which this power was wielded was not confined solely to the body of the citizenry. The charters bestowed on the various towns of Hungary accorded recognition to the burgher association and awarded the right of self-government and an independent judiciary. But the terms under which this immune status was afforded suggests that notions previously applied to the landed immunities now became likewise incorporated within the overall idea of municipal liberty. For the sphere of the Council's jurisdiction came also to embrace a territorial conception and, thereby, to extend beyond the ranks of the citizenry to, indeed, all persons living within the physical confines of the town.

Jurisdictional Enclaves

Amongst the population of medieval Buda, there existed an evidently large group of freemen who never acquired burgher status. These were mainly members of the poorer classes who, being propertiless, found it not easy to acquire the right of citizenship. To their ranks were added such alien residents as Italians and merchant adventurers from the Orient. Because these persons belonged to neither a privileged nor a servile class, the magistracy was able to extend its jurisdiction over them with little opposition or real difficulty. Any immigration into the towns of serfs still owing legal obligations or duties as yet unfulfilled to their masters was strictly prohibited both by royal statute and municipal law.[20]

But besides these groups of freemen bereft of legal status, there remained the privileged classes of nobility and priesthood. Relations between the Council and resident nobility of the town long remained a contentious issue. Both Hungarian customary law and specific royal pronouncements affirmed that in disputes involving properties within the town, nobles were obliged to proceed before the Council and not seek out any of the central courts of the realm. Such, of course, only made sense in view of the town's established role as a "place of authentication" and the fact that all property was held in Buda under the terms of the town's own customary law. Criminal actions committed by nobles within the confines of Buda were similarly deemed to fall beneath the Council's jurisdiction. However, this last principle, as most firmly enunciated in the royal decree of 1405, came to be hedged about with contradictory judgments and limitations. A nobleman could not, for instance, be arrested as a "notorious maldoer" but only seized in the actual act of committing a crime. Furthermore, if the Council executed a nobleman unjustly, the Judge and *iurati* were held themselves liable to the death penalty. In practice then, the nobility's right to be impleaded only before the highest courts of the land remained in criminal cases largely intact.[21]

In contrast to those of the nobility, the legal rights of the priesthood suffered a drastic curtailment—a process which may be partially understood in the context of a general erosion of their status within the realm as a whole.[22] In Buda, the claims advanced by the priesthood in regard to probate and the administering of wills were refuted by the *Stadtrecht.*[23] Clerical procedures posed an obvious threat to the well organised system of municipal record-keeping. As it was necessary for the details of land transactions including wills to be registered in the Town Book,[24] recourse to agencies other than the Council could only prove detrimental to the completeness of the municipal records. Again, since the Council was considered a "place of authentication," there was simply no need to involve the priesthood in the drawing up of wills. For a burgher to do so would signify contempt for the special status of the town as a *locus credibile*. Likewise, the priesthood's claim to act on behalf of widows and orphans was denied and this duty fastened upon the burgher community as a whole.[25] More significant to the theme of this chapter, the priestly right to be impleaded only before church courts came itself to be undermined. Outside the towns, landowners vigorously upheld the *a priori* judicial rights of their own seigneural courts against any counterclaims raised in actions involving priests by the consistory courts.[26] Certainly, within medieval Buda, the church courts were still able to exercise some jurisdictional rights even as late as the last decade of the fourteenth century. In November 1395 the Rector of St. Andrew's at Sasad slew with a hatchet a German hay merchant in nearby Buda. Despite the fact that the murder had occurred within the town and, thus, within the limits of the Town Council's jurisdiction, the action against the priest was heard by the Esztergom consistory court alone. Possibly because the case against the priest was so good, with him quite unable to offer any satisfactory defence save that his victim should have summoned a doctor before he died, the Town Council felt that the matter would be best left in the hands of the ecclesiastical authorities.[27] Evidently though, by the second half of the fifteenth century, the powers of the church courts within the towns of the realm had been largely curtailed. As King Matthias explained in a letter to the Pest magistracy in 1481, municipal liberties were in no way to be overridden by the church courts. All actions conjointly involving citizenry and priesthood were to be the subject of normal municipal procedure.[28]

Problems of jurisdictional demarcation were, however, encountered by the Buda Council not only in its dealings with nobility and priesthood. For actually dwelling within the town were privileged associations and organisations which like the burgher association itself had been endowed with an immune status. In this regard, the peculiar position held by the royal chamberlains has already been noted,[29] and besides them may of course be added the Jews. Associations of such persons might be found in other towns of the realm and, accordingly, this circumstance cannot be considered a phenomenon confined to Buda alone. But in Buda, the actual relations exercised between the burgher association and the other associations and organisations of persons dwelling within the town assume a fresh significance. For the number of non-citizen associations was not limited to chamberlains and Jews but came to include two new groups as well: those of the Danube sailors and fishermen.

The royal chamberlains together with the minters and craftsmen who laboured beneath them in workshops set in the very centre of the town were exempt from the jurisdiction of Buda's municipal Council. The special status of the chamberlain organisation is clearly enunciated in the texts of the fourteenth century royal privileges outlining the conditions under which the royal mints were to be administered: "As the ancient liberty of our mint chambers requires, so we declare, that no one at all, of whatever rank he be, shall presume to bring before his judgment the officials and servants of our mint chamber, but they shall be judged by our Chamberlain. If the Chamberlain fail to do justice to any party, then our Tavernicus shall judge them."[30] The chamberlain or cameral organisation, thus, represented a small enclave of persons holding an immune status and placed entirely outside the orbit of the Town Council's jurisdiction.[31]

However, the judicial immunity vested with the chamberlain organisation seems within a short space of time to have been circumvented as new powers were acquired over the royal minters by the Town Council. In a letter treating upon the royal mint at Buda, King Louis in 1343 declared that the jurisdiction of the royal chamberlains extended only to actions "touching upon the matter of the mint."[32] Evidently, the Town Council now possessed some judicial rights in the personal affairs of the royal minters. Although Sigismund was some sixty years later to reaffirm that members of the cameral organisation were to be entirely exempt from judgments given out by any persons other than their own ordinaries,[33] this attempt to redress the balance proved seemingly ineffective. The Buda *Stradtrecht,* which includes a summary of Sigismund's decree, quite ignored the provisions treating upon the minters' immunity. Instead, it merely repeated the terms of Louis' letter of 1343 permitting the jurisdiction of the chamberlains to extend only to "the business of the mint and coin." In all other matters the minters were bound "to adhere to the law of the town."[34] Generally the impression received from the *Stradrecht* is that the status of the chamberlain organisation had been downgraded and reduced to little more than the position of a craft guild within the town. Significantly also, the important task of assaying the quality of coinage issued by the mint was, according to the *Stradtrecht,* to be performed by none other than a citizen of the town.[35] This development foreshadowed a gradual insinuation of the Council's jurisdiction into even the business of the royal mint—a process which appears to have been completed by, at the latest, 1430.[36] Not only, therefore, had the members of the chamberlain organisation been brought under the Council's overall jurisdiction but also the internal activities of the mint had become subject to municipal supervision.

Obviously the gradual erosion of the minters' immune status within Buda may be partly explained in broad terms of a conflict with the judicial rights pertaining to the Council and the eventual triumph of the town over what was, in effect, a jurisdictional anomaly. Again, since the coin in circulation within the town affected the commercial life of the community, some attempt by the Council to increase its measure of control over this medium is hardly unexpected. The background, however, against which this development occurred and the means whereby the Council's triumph was secured remains significant. Because the royal chamberlains were regularly recruited from the ranks of the citizenry itself,[37] the extension of jurisdictional authority over these persons by the town magistracy came to be greatly facilitated. In this respect, there is a clear parallel with the decline of the independent judicial status afforded to the combinations of minters in the medieval German towns. Here similarly, an association of citizen and *Hausgenosse* status largely came to undermine a hitherto privileged legal position.[38] But, beyond this, there remained the sheer problem of enforcement. In the reissue of coinage and in the various attempts to restrict the circulation of old monies, the minters depended upon the goodwill and powers of the Town Council. This is made clear in the provisions of royal decrees which repeatedly stressed that it was the duty of Town Councils to seize the goods of merchants dealing in bad money and to ensure that practical arrangements were made for the periodic exchanges of coin.[39] Forced, thus, into a dependence upon the Council's powers of enforcement, there came only to be hastened that process culminating finally in the subordination of the minting organisation to the municipal government. A reliance upon the magistracy's powers of enforcement held important implications also for the Danube sailors.

Riversides witnessed often during the middle ages the early formation of associations of persons entrusted with peculiar status. On the banks of the Seine at Paris there might be found the ancient *collegium* of boatmen.[40] Bestowed in 1106 on the fishermen of Worms was one of the earliest privileges accorded to a craftguild in the whole of Europe.[41] In this respect, the Danube around Buda proved no exception. Here, from the mid-thirteenth century onwards, references occur to "confraternities" of sailors organised, like the town itself, under their own *villici* or *iudices*.[42] Originally these sailors formed part of a royal *clicium* centred around Óbuda. They were servants of the King, known variously as *conditionarii, cliciarii* or *libertini*,[43] who during the early Árpád period provided for the needs of the monarch and his itinerant court. As such, they all ranked as members of a servile class collectively referred to as *udvornici*.[44] Although the actual judicial organisation to which these *udvornici* were subject appears rather confused, it would seem probable that as a whole they were subordinated to the jurisdiction of the Palatine.[45] As his name suggests, this dignitary acted originally as a kind of royal "major-domo" or "Mayor of the Palace." But because the number of *udvornici* was scattered throughout the realm, a system of local organisation came to develop centred upon, although by no means exclusively, the *comites curiales*. In the case of the sailors of Óbuda, the curial count to whom they remained subject was the Castellan of Óbuda.[46]

In the locality of Óbuda, there were three principal ports served by the royal sailors: at Pest and Jenő on the left bank of the Danube and, on the right, at Budafelhéviz (the "forum Geyzae"). Later, after the foundation of Buda, a fourth port was established on the river bank by the eastern suburb of the town (the Viziváros).[47] The Danube sailors not only provided transport for the provisioning of the palace at Óbuda but acted also as ferrymen taking charge of goods crossing the river. The most important crossing-point was the reach of water stretching between Pest and Budafelhéviz. By both these points, there soon came into being two small markets and, quite possibly, it is to one of these that the charter of 1244 alludes in its reference to a *forum cottidianum*. However, well before the foundation of Buda, dues hitherto pertaining to the King and deriving from the sailors' activities as ferrymen had already been granted out. For, in 1148, Géza II had given over to the Buda Chapter (located at Óbuda) the tolls of the markets at Budafelhéviz and the port of Pest together with a portion of the passage money taken by the sailors.[48]

Already by the thirteenth century, the *udvornici* organisation as a whole had entered upon a period of decay. The institution of the *comites curiales* was squeezed out by the emergent county system while, together with the royal lands on which they worked, many *udvornici* were alienated by the Crown.[49] The development of a more advanced economy and a commercial life further contributed to render unnecessary this primitive form of provisioning.[50] Groups of kingly *udvornici* like the Ruthenes of Oroszfalva in Nógrád county or the royal cooks of Nagyszakácsi and Vid were, thus, able to elevate themselves into the ranks of the petty nobility.[51] Here an obvious parallel may be found in the history of the German *ministeriales* class.

The *clicium* centred around the castle at Óbuda proved no exception to the general decline. In 1267 the sailor community at Jenő was handed over to the convent of nuns dwelling on the nearby Hares' Island (the present day Margitsziget),[52] while later another group of royal servants hitherto dwelling in Óbuda, the King's Falconers, were sent away and the buildings which they had formerly occupied given to the local Chapter.[53] In 1343, even the old castle itself was given up by King Louis and bestowed upon the Queen Mother.[54] The authority of the Castellans came thus to be further diminished. In 1355, Louis arranged for the market dues payable at Budafelhéviz to be surrendered by the Buda Chapter to the Castellan in exchange for royal lands in Somogy and Zala counties.[55] Although these revenues were still being paid to the Queen through her Castellan in 1367, during the succeeding period the Chapter came quite illegally to reacquire them. The rights of the Castellan were conveniently forgotten.[56]

Evidently, the jurisdictional authority to which the Danube sailors had been originally subject came to lose effective control. Contrastingly though, the special status held by these royal *conditionarii* never came to be eroded. Nor, indeed, did the sailors ever suffer the dismantling of their *confraternitas* organisation.[57] The sailors of Pest, who worked also the port at Budafelhéviz, remained subject to the jurisdiction of their own judges.[58] However, since actions were almost exclusively raised against the body of Pest sailors as a whole, immediate problems of jurisdiction soon occurred. Theoretically, such cases should have been heard by the Castellan of Óbuda under whose authority the *confraternitas* lay. However, the power of this figure had been much reduced. Furthermore, in 1343, the Castellan had become an agent of the Queen Mother while, indeed, the sailors continued to function as kingly servants.

From the middle of the thirteenth century, the sailors of Pest were involved in lengthy litigation with the Buda Chapter. The sailors simply refused to pay over the portion of passage money owed to the canons by virtue of Géza II's privilege. In their battle against the Chapter, the sailors often resorted to violence and deceit. Nor is this really surprising for some four hundred florins a year were at stake.[59]

Since the sailors lived for the most part in Pest, the canons proceeded at first before the Buda Town Council for remedy of their grievances. Certainly, the Council had no real right to judge servants of the King. But in the absence of any effective exercise of authority by the Óbuda Castellan, the Buda Town Council represented a convenient forum; Pest was at this time still within the limits of the Buda magistracy's overall jurisdiction. The Town Council led by the Rector Walter found in favour of the Chapter and a subsequent attempt to have this verdict reversed by the Archbishop of Esztergom proved, needless to say, unsuccessful.[60] Four years later, the King accused the sailors of mendaciously tricking him by having him earlier confirm a liberty which forbade the Chapter from exacting a portion of the passage dues.[61]

Previous endeavours having proved fruitless, the sailors now sought to buttress their claims on the town's charter of 1244. In an extraordinary about-face, the Council rallied to their support declaring that the liberties of the community prohibited the collection of tolls from the citizens of Buda.[62] Quite clearly, the Danube sailors had never held citizen status and, as such, the intervention of the Council is unlikely to have been inspired by considerations of municipal liberty. Rather, the Council's support was probably engaged as a consequence of the general worsening of the town's relations with the Chapter[63] and motivated also by a very real fear that the canons' demands for a portion of the passage dues could only raise the cost for merchants of using the Danube ferry at Buda. The Town Council, thus, assisted the sailors in their struggle and took no action even when violence was employed against the outraged canons.[64]

As a result of the assistance given by the town to the royal pretender, Ladislas, rival of the ecclesiastically supported Charles Robert, further strains were imposed on Buda's relations with the Church. In 1301, employing the continued harassment of the Chapter as an excuse, the Pope slapped an interdict on the politically defiant Council and townsfolk of Buda.[65] In return and with the open connivance of the citizenry, "false and disobedient" priests in the town boldly excommunicated the Pope, Hungarian episcopacy and, for good measure, all members of religious orders in the realm.[66] These heady days soon gave way to more sober reflections. With the return from captivity of the Rector Ladislas, loyal to the now established Angevin party, a resolution of outstanding difficulties with the Esztergom Chapter was embarked upon. In the interest of better relations with the Church, the Council abandoned the sailors. The policy now pursued by the Council was, quite simply, to relieve itself as expeditiously as was possible from the problems occasioned by the sailors' activities and their peculiar jurisdictional position. Difficulties brought about by the sailors were, henceforward, left to the responsibility of neighbouring Pest's own Town Council. Again, in 1336, the Buda Council actively opposed the continued existence of the small port situated on the edge of the Viziváros suburb. The Judge, sworn men and leading citizens of the town declared before the King that this haven had been established quite illegally and they supported demands for its immediate closure.[67]

The conclusion of Buda's involvement with the Danube sailors afforded, however, no solution to the pressing problems surrounding their passage dues and legal status. The community of sailors now dwelling almost exclusively in Pest continued to remain a distinct jurisdictional unit within the town while the dispute with the Buda Chapter raged unabated. The nearby Town Council proved as before the only effective local authority with the necessary powers of coercion. Paradoxically though, no judicial action against the sailors could proceed through the Pest magistracy. For in law, the town might exercise no jurisdictional rights over these royal servants. Accordingly, a compromise solution was reached. In 1326, the Pest Council's right of enforcement was formally recognized by the King.[68] Hereafter, however, the right of judgment became regularly exercised by one of the principal royal ordinaries: the Tavernicus.[69] In this way, the unique jurisdictional status of the Danube sailors was reaffirmed while the more practical task of enforcing judgments was left in the hands of the local magistracy.

Had a community of sailors continued dwelling in Buda then perhaps in time they, like the royal minters, might have lost their special status and become fully subject to the jurisdiction of the Town Council. In this respect, it is perhaps interesting to notice that already by the time of their expulsion, the sailors' organisation in Buda appears somewhat weak in form. Although still functioning as a royal *cellacio,* the community of sailors was represented not by an appointed *iudex* but simply by one of their number acting as a special delegate.[70] Additional support for this supposition may be found in the history of another group of royal servants dwelling in Buda: the Danube fishermen.

Although, like the Danube sailors, the fishermen belonged to the class of royal *udvornici,* they were most probably subject originally not to the Óbuda Castellan but the King's Seneschal.[71] With the decline of the *udvornici* system, the royal fishermen found themselves also left stranded in a problematic jurisdictional position. By the fourteenth century, however, the town of Buda had grown up around their own little community. The fishermen, thus, found themselves living in the suburbs by the river, possibly, as has been suggested, in the neighbourhood of the present day Fisher Street (*Halász utca*).[72] Not surprisingly, the Town Council soon acquired certain powers in enforcing judgments affecting these royal servants. In 1336, Charles Robert ordered the Buda Council to prevent the fishermen from molesting the private fish pools on the opposite bank of the Danube.[73] The Council together with the Tavernicus and Castellan of Buda was, likewise, requested in 1405 to ensure that the terms of a royal judgment affecting the fishermen was fully observed.[74] Hereafter, the jurisdictional rights of the Council came increasingly to be extended over the community of fishermen. In 1424, when the dispute between the fishermen and butchers of Buda was directed to Sigismund for adjudication, the matter was referred back to the Town Council for final judgment.[75] By this time, the fishermen's status as servants of the King seems to have been largely forgotten and municipal regulations were even applied to their business activities.[76]

Throughout the medieval period, the unique status and position held by the Jews remained firmly fixed in the minds of populace and government. Here were a group of persons who wore a distinctive dress, adhered to their own religious principles and in their official business wrote both backwards and in strange characters. Their New Testament role in the slaying of Christ was never effaced from memory and for this deed the Jews suffered both vilification and actual physical violence.[77] The otherwise restrained language of the

Buda *Stadtrecht* lapsed even into insult and abuse when treating upon the presence of this small minority within the town.[78] Fearful of local antagonism, Hungarian Jewry looked towards the monarchy for support.

The rights of the Jewish community in the realm were first accorded a full recognition in the privilege granted by Béla IV in 1251.[79] Although largely derived from the Bull given in 1244 by Duke Frederick of Babenberg to the Jews of Austria,[80] the 1251 privilege, nevertheless, indicates the close association forged from an early date between the King and his alien subjects. Regularly, on the accession of a new monarch, leaders of the Jewish community requested the full confirmation of this charter.[81] In return for receiving some measure of royal protection, Hungarian Jewry paid to the Treasury a special tax known as the *census iudeorum*.[82] Their continued presence in the kingdom depended upon royal favour while their possessions might be distrained by the King at will.[83] The monarch further exercised the right to release from their legal obligations those persons owing money to Jews.[84] Possibly, it was the combination of these conditions which lay behind the early reference to the idea that the Jews were in some way a part of the royal *camera*.[85] Mention, however, of this peculiar status never occurs in the thirteenth and fourteenth centuries outside the privilege of 1251. Accordingly perhaps, the term may have been regardlessly borrowed from the text of Duke Frederick's Bull of 1244. Certainly there is no indication to suggest that the Jews were in any way jurisdictionally subject to the royal Treasury or, alternatively, a judicial part of the Chamberlain organisation.[86]

In their mutual dealings, the Jews were subject to the jurisdiction of their own courts. These were arranged locally and administered by rabbis and leading members of their community. Judgments were fashioned in accordance with Old Testament precepts and oaths made on the Torah or by the ring on the synagogue's door.[87] In tricky religious questions, the advice of foreign Jewish theologians might be also taken into account.[88] When a Jewish court or *Beth-Din* functioned in a town, then often party to the discussions was a Christian official: the Judge of the Jews. Appointed by either the King or a superior Judge of All Jews in the Realm, this figure was usually a leading citizen of the town. Besides his involvement in litigation the Judge of the Jews also administered a special prison, confirmed land transactions and liaised between King, townsfolk and the local Jewry.[89]

As indeed the institution of a town-based Judge of the Jews suggests, the majority of Jews in the realm dwelt in the urban centres. For the Jew, an involvement in agricultural activity proved hard since the laws of the realm had of old forbidden him to employ Christian workmen. However, in the towns, the Jews found themselves excluded from the craft guilds and, later, measures were enacted to prevent them from indulging in any form of artisan or commercial occupation.[90] Such circumstances only made the practice of usury more attractive, for this pursuit was denied to all except those who did not profess the Christian religion. Involving themselves in this form of entrepreneurial activity, the Jews found themselves frequently liable to legal action. When disputes occurred between persons subject to different jurisdictional authorities, it was customary procedure for the plaintiff to take his case before the court of the defendant *(Actor sequitur forum rei)*. A similar system operated also in legal actions initiated by Jews.[91] Thus, for instance, in 1350, Solomon Longus, Jew of Buda, referred his complaint against a certain serf to whom he had lent money to the village court of the serf's headman.[92] Again in 1426, the Jews of Sopron took their complaint against one of that town's citizenry to the Sopron Council and the case quite evidently followed regular municipal procedure.[93] However, an inevitable problem emerged in those actions wherein the Jew was defendant. Clearly, that a Christian plaintiff should be humbly compelled to present his suit before a Jewish court was entirely out of the question. Thus, whereas Duke Frederick's earlier Bull had declared that actions initiated by a Christian against a Jew should be taken before the latter's court, this article was amended by Béla IV. The competence of the *Beth-Din* extended only to actions wherein both parties were of the Jewish faith. All other matters were subject to the jurisdiction of the Town Council.[94] Additional evidence for this unusual procedure is provided in the Law Code treating on the Jews of Pozsony. According to this work, a Christian might certainly bring an action against a Jew before the *Beth-Din*. But should either party feel dissatisfied with the procedural law there followed, then the action might be moved directly before the municipal Council for adjudication.[95]

The new authority gained by the Town Councils grew, however, not merely out of a concern to protect the Christian from any judicial submission to a tribunal composed of infidels. As is indicated by both the Buda *Stradtrecht* and the surviving registers from Pozsony and Sopron, the records of loans and debts were kept by the municipal Councils.[96] In the case of Buda, the necessary details of these transactions were entered into the Notary's Town Book. Accordingly, when disputes occurred, it was only natural that the judicial agency most fully aware of the circumstances under which the loan had been originally negotiated should come to be also the most closely involved. Again, as with sailors, fishermen and royal minters, the local Council's power of enforcement was the most efficacious. In recognition of this, the actual business of collecting the Jewish tax and exacting fines was, until the end of the fifteenth century, left largely in the hands of the municipal Councils.[97]

The competence of the town magistracies did not, however, extend to actions initiated against Jews by the members of the nobility. Generally, such cases were heard from the last quarter of the fourteenth century until the middle of the next century by the royally appointed Judge of All Jews in the Realm. This dignity was usually bestowed on the principal ordinaries of the realm: the Justiciar, Tavernicus, Treasurer or Palatine. As with the local, town-based Judges of the Jews, these figures also undertook functions other than the purely judicial. They ensured that royal decisions affecting the Jews were correctly administered and officiated in other, more complex, negotiations.[98] Thus, for example, in 1381, the Tavernicus and Judge of All Jews, Thomas (Temlin) of St. George, was called upon by the Queen to resolve the problem of some securities given to a Viennese Jew by Johann Hoffar, citizen of Buda. The Jew had, allegedly, taken charge of the burgher's property without actually giving him the requested loan. Thereafter, he had quit Hungary for Vienna refusing to return since, in his opinion, there was a plot afoot to have him murdered. Some diplomatic negotiations with Albert, Duke of Austria, were evidently necessary and, thus, the matter was entrusted to the Judge of All Jews.[99]

From the middle of the fifteenth century, the institution of Judge of All Jews was abolished and, henceforward, his functions were assumed by the Tavernicus. Before him were on occasions also initiated actions brought by Jews against members of the nobility.[100] Quite possibly, this arrangement was convenient for both parties involved in the suit. Usury was a practice not recognised by the law of the realm and many agreements were, thus, conducted informally and on the basis of trust.[101] Ironically, it was in the Christian man's dealings with the infidel that the commitments of honour and duty acquired real significance. Thus, when in 1511 the magnate Gabriel Csák borrowed two hundred florins from the Jewess Melamen of Buda, he agreed that failure to abide by his part of the bargain would indicate a disregard for "faith and humanity" and that henceforward he would not be fit company for "honest and upright" men.[102] In certain cases also, the noble debtor had evidently no right to put up his landed properties as security. For, unless he had himself acquired the properties by his own endeavours, the consent of relatives was a necessary commitment to any alienation.[103] Under such circumstances, it is not surprising that recourse to equity procedure might on occasions be had. For only through equity could the traditions and encumbrances of the Hungarian common law be successfully circumvented and a truly just solution be found to resolve disputes involving trust and obligations unrecognised in law.[104] Probably at first, equity judgments were only given out by the King and, as such, originated from his *plenitudo potestatis* and function as the *lex animata*.[105] Already however, by the close of the thirteenth century, it was possible for judges acting on a royal mandate to adjudicate according to the principles of equity.[106] By the fifteenth century, the right to *absoluta potentia* had not only been secured by the Palatine but also by the royal Tavernicus. It was, thus, convenient for members of both nobility and Jewry to proceed before the high courts of the land for the resolution of their disputes and not have their actions subject to the clumsy procedures and principles adhered to in the local forums and Town Councils. The close contact maintained between the Tavernicus and the towns of the realm, wherein the Jews were mainly resident, led to his court being especially favoured by litigants.[107]

Certainly then, the Jews remained a distinct legal unit within the town and in their relations with the nobility procedures were elaborated which quite disregarded the authority of the municipal Council. Importantly though, from the thirteenth century onwards, the Council had acquired a competence over actions conjointly involving citizens and Jews. Thus, even though town Jewry remained jurisdictionally outside the limits of the Council's authority, measures were enacted which only came to enhance the actual powers of this institution.

By the early fifteenth century, it would thus seem that in Buda the burgher association had acquired a new strength and cohesion. The association had with the award of a town charter achieved state recognition and been endowed with a corporate status. Thereafter, in a slow process, the peculiar jurisdictional enclaves within the town had been steadily eroded. The chamberlain organisation together with that of the royal fishermen had been absorbed by the town. The problems occasioned by the royal sailors had been successfully resolved by shifting the burden of their presence to Pest. Only the Jews had succeeded in preserving their special identity and privileges. But, even so, these had been amended in such a way as to reduce unnecessary conflict with the Council and the Christian townsfolk. With this one exception, it would hence appear that the contradictions formerly implicit within the notion of *civitas* had been largely resolved. The idea of the town as a geographical entity became reconciled with the notion that the town represented also a specific legal and jurisdictional phenomenon. Within the physical confines of the town, the sole association was the association of burghers and the one jurisdictional authority the Council holding its power by delegation from that association.

By the early fifteenth century and the years of the *Stadrecht's* compilation, it would, thus, seem that the era of the Rectors, when the claims of town autonomy had been so easily set aside by the monarch, was but a temporary aberration signifying very little. The town, in keeping with the principles of its charter and despite the application of a medley of compelling influences and pressures, had developed its own independent governmental and jurisdictional organisation institutionally quite distinct from the world beyond its walls. Furthermore, the notion of immune status which formally recognised the legal separateness of town and realm had been so reinforced as to embrace a territorial principle. Yet, at this very time, when the successful maintenance of the idea of municipal autonomy as set down in the town's earliest charter seems assured, strange developments begin to emerge within the social organisation of the town's governing class. As a consequence of influences applied from without, a classic pattern of social order evident in almost every medieval European community appears in Buda quite inexorably to break down. This departure in its turn heralded and facilitated a succession of new developments which in their significance contrast markedly with the successes of the preceding century.

Chapter 5

PATRICIATE AND GOVERNING CLASS

Wealth and Power

The scribe of the German town of Ulm, Felix Fabri, writing in the latter part of the fifteenth century noted how country folk having left the provinces might enter the towns, "make money out of trade or the crafts and at length enter into the order of the noble citizenry," that class of town councillors whom Felix defines as being "the principal persons in the town . . . whom we can call senators, magistrates, the highest, the best, the most powerful and the greatest by reason of their birth."[1] This entry of newly-rich burghers into positions of authority within the medieval town and, conversely, the declining role in town government accorded to those whose fortunes had diminished, is a frequent phenomenon. In such North German towns as Stralsund and Hamburg it encouraged regular changes and renewals among the urban patriciate class. The great families could maintain their position for only two or three generations at a time and in their wake came new families in time themselves to be replaced. In Augsburg, as late as the 1530's, representatives of, among others, the great merchant families of Haller and Paumgartner who had earlier settled in the town were formally admitted into the ranks of those families entrusted with the municipal government. Their coats-of-arms were solemnly recorded in the contemporary town histories.[2] Similar tendencies are evident even in Nuremberg, whose council-dominating families generally reveal an almost extraordinary endurance. Here, nevertheless, between 1330 and 1520 about a half of the old families suffered replacement.[3]

In the absence of legal constraints on social mobility, such as were later exercised in the early modern period, the newly rich were regularly able to advance to positions of power within the medieval town. Nor indeed is this surprising. As Brunner-Schubert has argued in her study of the Regensburg Runtinger family,[4] it proved by no means disadvantageous for the established patrician groups to admit to the Council new and successful entrepreneurs. Their advice and often superior knowledge might prove distinctly beneficial both to their colleagues and to the town as a whole. Certainly at times family oligarchies, jealous of their privileges, attempted to exclude wealthy newcomers from their ranks. But such resistance proved normally of short duration. Often enlisting the support of other groups within the town, the newcomers were able, sometimes literally, to force their entry to the centre of municipal power.

Once having achieved a position of authority in the town, the successful newcomer was well able to reinforce his family and business connections. Access to the deliberations of the Council and the town's exclusive drinking clubs and societies yielded him useful trading insights and contacts. Marriage into a more established patrician family provided fresh resources for his commercial enterprises as well as support in times of hardship. In the medieval German town, wealth and power were mutually indivisible. Thus, in the elevated language of one historian, the *divites* of the community were at one and the same time synonymous with the town *potentes*.[5]

Within the German towns of Hungary, a similar identification between rich and powerful burghers is also evident. On the basis of those tax returns and Council lists which survive from the second quarter of the fifteenth century for the town of Pozsony, Szűcs has demonstrated that the wealthier citizens of the town dominated also the municipal Council. Of the recorded fifteen wealthiest burghers in Sopron in 1459, eleven held council places and, amongst these, the *bürgermeister* Leonard Ainweg was the second richest citizen.[6] The absence of comparable statistical information for Buda puts any analysis of this town's patriciate on far less firm ground. Generally though, until the opening of the fifteenth century, the social basis of the town's government appears to exhibit tendencies of no great peculiarity. Throughout this earlier period, the traditional *potentes-divites* order was preserved with only some minor modifications in evidence.

Of course, the simple identification of wealth with power within the medieval town does not necessarily mean that every wealthy burgher involved himself in town government. Thus, for instance, in Buda, Johann Ellenpek, a prosperous merchant and generous benefactor, appears to have played no part in municipal government.[7] Challenged by such failings in public spirit, the Buda *Stadtrecht* pronounced that, in the event of a burgher refusing on three separate occasions to assume a place within the Council, a penalty of one year's banishment was to be enforced.[8] Again, since in Buda the partial semblance of democracy was at least preserved until the 1440's, the electorate's prejudices might upset the fulfilment of individual ambitions.

Of course, any election proceeding by acclamation rather than ballot is liable to be a shambling affair and one wherein a sufficiently unscrupulous candidate may deftly overcome the wishes of the majority. Nevertheless, it may be significant that the wealthy Francis Bernhard, despite his clear assumption of citizen status and otherwise eager involvement in municipal administration, was never as far as we know returned to the Council. Quite possibly, it was not so much his technically disqualifying Italian ancestry that prevented him from assuming office but rather his reputation for corruption and questionable business dealings.[9]

The ruling élites within the town of medieval Germany were often known by contemporaries as the *Geschlechter:* the families or dynasties. The idea of the citizen-dynasty was a highly developed one and came later to form in some towns the touchstone for representation within the Council. The Nuremberg citizen, Ulman Stromer, in his *Little Book* written at the close of the fourteenth century, noted with pride his distinguished ancestry and the many links which his family had forged through intermarriage with the other leading families of the town.[10] In Hungary, while the fifteenth century generally saw a marked absence of this type of "family power," the earlier period of the thirteenth and fourteenth centuries displays certain characteristics similar to those evident elsewhere. Already in an earlier chapter we have remarked upon the almost hereditary character of the Rectoral office in Buda. Likewise, in contemporary Nagyszombat, the government of the town lay in the hands of the three Megerdorfer brothers, Kunc, Conrad and Peter, who succeeded one another in holding the supreme judicial office.[11] In Pozsony for much of the later thirteenth and fourteenth centuries the two families of Jacob achieved a similar domination within the Council.[12]

As soon as representation on the Town Council becomes conceived of within the unit of the burgher family, however, any too rigorously applied an identification on our part of the rich with the powerful proves no longer possible. For one wealthy scion of a family might forsake public life in the knowledge that his own interests and the interests of the family as a whole were preserved by relatives more mindful of their duties. Such a tendency is clearly evident within fourteenth century Buda.

The burgher Kunc who acted as Deputy Judge during the Rectoral period had two sons. To the elder, Rubin, he left his estates while the younger son, Johann, who seems to have acquired at some point possessions of his own, assumed his father's role within town government. Johann's son and grandson continued to hold high office within Buda, while the other branch of the family kept to their estates. In this they seem to have been curiously inept, being obliged finally to sell out to their relatives.[13] A similar avoidance of office is possibly evident also in branches of the Tilmann and Lorand families. Long gaps, however, in the Council lists at this point make any clear analysis impossible. Further to this theme, a study of the Ulving and, again, Lorand families indicates that the avoidance of office could work vertically as opposed to laterally with the entry of a second generation into the Council only occurring upon the retirement of the first.[14]

The various members of the Kunc, Lorand and Ulving families dominate the list of Buda's judges for the second half of the fourteenth century. Michael of the Kunc family held the title of *iudex* on five occasions. The name of Lorand appears seven times, while representatives of the Ulving family altogether acted as Town Judges on eight separate occasions. During both this half-century and the earlier Rectoral period, members of these same families assumed also a prominent position within the ranks of the *iurati*, occupying between 1317 and 1370 roughly one-fifth of Council places. A long participation in the Buda Town Council extending over a number of generations was by no means confined to these three burgher dynasties. For, like the Tilmann, other families are in evidence whose members while rarely reaching the rank of Judge are regularly to be found on the surviving Council lists. Of these lesser families the most significant are the Megerdorfer, Pern-hauser, de Eger, de Győr, Rabensteiner and Hailmann. Altogether, over a half of those burghers known to hold office between 1317 and 1370 stem from the top ten citizen families of fourteenth century Buda.

Between these Council families bonds of marriage developed similar to those maintained earlier during the Rectoral period. Already related through the family of the Rector Johann to the Ulving, the Tilmann dynasty forged marriage bonds with the de Eger.[15] Later members of the Ulving family established marriage links with the Lorand.[16] But at no time did the structure of citizen marriage allow the formation of any closed *connubium.* Rather, for prosperous newcomers it was always possible to wed into the more estab-lished family lines and thus secure promotion within the Council.[17] The development of personal bonds between the various citizen families well explains the relative stability in government enjoyed by Buda during the fourteenth century. At no time does evidence of faction–fighting between the various dynasties emerge. Buda, was thus thankfully spared such warring between rival *generationes* with all the attendant riot, throat-cutting and arson as so troubled contemporary Kolozsvár.[18]

Importantly also, this monopoly of power by but a handful of interrelated Council families contributed to a continuity of purpose in town government. As son succeeded father on the Council, so tested technique and the wisdom of experience was passed on to the new generation. The development and preservation of the institutions of town government over this period, the maintenance and extension of the immunity idea, cannot be deemed entirely the result of some ineluctable working out of the urban *coniuratio* concept with all of its attendant ramifications. Due attention must be paid to the great, long-serving burgher dynasties whose members through the Council directed and dominated the activities of government and judiciary.

Although it is not possible to quantify their wealth with any precision, members of the town's prominent citizen families appear to have commanded substantial resources. Frequent references in charters attest to their financial and landed interests as well as their often considerable generosity.[19] Members of the Ulving, Lorand and de Eger families were able to effect large purchases of property and frequently loan substantial sums of money to nobility and clergy.[20] As Otto Brunner has demonstrated for fourteenth–century Vienna, the granting of credit by burghers was often allied to their holding of financially significant Crown offices.[21] So in Buda, prominent burghers regularly secured for themselves appointments in the realm's financial administration and undertook the leasing of Crown revenues, particularly within the minting organisation. In 1344, Lorand was head of the kingdom's mints and *examinator auri* at Buda.[22] In other years he functioned also as a royal chamberlain. Ulving (I) held similar office during the 1330's as indeed later did Ladislas Ulving's father-in-law, the *iuratus* Frederick Chratzer.[23] Another member of the Ulving family, Nicolas, was during the 1340's involved in the lucrative collection of the royal thirtieth toll (the *tricesima*).[24] The occupation of burghers in financial organisation extended also to the business of the Church. During the 1320's and 1330's Johann de Eger acted as a papal tithe collector, performing a task later to be undertaken by Italian financiers.[25] Ulving (I) most probably acted in the same capacity; certainly tithe collectors are known to have met for business in his Buda house.[26] Among the prominent burghers of contemporary Pozsony, a similar interest in royal and ecclesiastical finance is evident.[27] But whereas in Pozsony, burgher wealth was frequently augmented by the acquisition of annuities, in fourteenth century Buda this phenomenon appears relatively restricted.[28] Possibly this omission reflects the limitations of the surviving source material for the Buda *Stadtrecht* certainly includes some detailed discussion on the purchase and solution of annuity rights.[29] Nevertheless, the seeming failure of Buda's leading citizen families to invest in rentage must qualify any discussion of their role in medieval finance. Attention may thus be drawn away from their involvement in the "money-market" to what instead was almost certainly the major source of their wealth and revenues: their private estates.

Around the town and deep in the heart of the surrounding countryside, great tracts of land including both vineyards and serf villages lay in the hands of Buda's leading citizen families. The Lorand occupied extensive possessions in neighbouring Pest county of which their Harkyán estate alone commanded a value of one-and-a-half thousand florins.[30] Ulving (I) was the proud owner of manors near Buda, at Horhi, Tárnok and Szenterzsébet, while his son-in-law, Nicolas, evidently finding lands of his own, entered into a possession dispute with the magnate Losonczi family.[31] Likewise, members of the Til-mann dynasty acquired estates in Tolna and Fejér counties, these being augmented in 1338 by Jacob de Eger's donation of Régenszenttamás.[32] Family estates were, moreover, regularly supplemented by properties mortgaged by the monarch as well as impoverished members of the nobility.[33] Neither does it seem likely that the involvement of these burghers with large estates was the product solely of their role as financial agents. Certainly, the Italian merchants resident in the town seem to have viewed land acquisition as a means of capital surety; estates were but objects to be sold off in times of hardship. Outside the towns, nobility might lease out portions of their proper-ties in return for yearly money rents.[34] Contrastingly however, the burghers of fourteenth century Buda show few of these tendencies. Estates were passed on from father to son and in the event of death without heir might even be taken over by colaterally related citizen families.[35] An interest in land determined principally by agricultural considerations explains, furthermore, the willing-ness of Buda's burghers even to rent country properties, purchase ploughland and either lease or buy corn mills particularly to the north of the town, at Felhéviz.[36]

In certain respects, Buda's dominant citizen class appears to exhibit attitudes towards rural landholding not too dissimilar to those analysed by Pfeiffer in Silesian Wroclaw.[37] Although Pfeiffer's study has received some recent criticism,[38] his description of an entrepreneurial burgher élite deeply involved in the development and capital improvement of land suggests possible parallels with Buda. This analogy is particularly evident in the case of one of the lesser families of Buda whose members, while never achieving the rank of Town Judge, nevertheless exercised a continual presence within the council. The Megerdorfer family, originally from Nagyszombat, had success-fully petitioned the king in 1268 to give them some lands near that town which had lain empty and unpopulated for some twenty years, since, in fact, the Mongol invasion. Subsequently, members of the family moved to Buda where, from the second decade of the fourteenth century, they acted as town councillors. But only in 1340 were the family's Nagyszombat possessions finally sold off to some local nobility. By this time, the estates appear to have been well developed and with a value of 200 marks.[39]

The managerial skills of citizen landholders were widely recognised and, accordingly, burghers of Buda were employed by local bodies outside the town to renovate estates. In 1345, the nunnery of Hares' Island gave over for twenty years to Jacob de Eger, *iuratus* of Buda, a once populous but by then abandoned property in Fejér county. For this, Jacob paid only a nominal fee, but agreed to transform the estate into a profitable concern by "adorning it with persons."[40] In 1407 the Buda Chapter gave over for five years to leading citizens of the town a large estate with all its serfs, vineyards, cultivated and uncultivated lands. In return for a portion of the revenues, the citizens were obliged "to care for, improve and put to use" the capabilities of the property.[41]

The enterprise of citizen landholders might, however, be more meanly exploited. During the 1360's, Nicolas of Pest arranged with the monastery of St. Benedict's-by-Gron to rent for three years a property in Csongrád county. For this he paid an annual fee of sixteen marks. The terms of the lease allowed him to make such improvements to the estate as he thought fit and during his tenancy the value of the property evidently increased substantially. Accordingly, when on the expiry of the three years, Nicolas sought to renew the lease, he discovered that the rent had been raised by more than a third—a preposterous situation and one indeed impossible under town law.[42]

The entrepreneurial talent of Buda's fourteenth century patriciate seldom seems to have expressed itself in trade. Only very rarely does evidence of commercial involvement emerge and then, more often than not, in relation to estate produce: wine, oil or cattle.[43] While certainly imbued with strong, proud notions of civic service, Buda's leading burghers seem, nonetheless, in many of their activities to be almost indistinguishable from the provincial nobility. Sometimes they even held noble status; more commonly they would assume the title of *Comes,* itself reminiscent of the feudal world outside the town.[44] In Buda, as indeed elsewhere, they built towers for themselves or acquired palaces in the surrounding countryside.[45] Peculiarly hybrid creatures, they contracted marriages not just with other burgher households but with scions of the nobility as well.[46] The life of the royal court at Visegrád exerted its own social attractions and in Buda, as in Pozsony, a leading burgher came to provide a suitable husband for one of King Charles Robert's discarded mistresses.[47] The Queen on several occasions petitioned and requested the Pope's permission for prominent citizens of Buda to go on pilgrimage to the Holy Land—evidence in itself that the horizon of these citizens was in no way bound by any narrow parochialism.[48] In time, descendants of the great *Ritterbürger* families, so long involved in the world beyond the town, finally came to seal their bonds with the countryside. Many quit Buda altogether to embrace the life of rural gentlefolk.[49] Within this predominantly land-orientated and agricultural framework, fluctuations within a family or individual's wealth were far less than in those communities where fortunes depended more upon the success of merchant ventures. Accordingly, changes in Council membership and the declining or advancing role of persons amongst the town *potentes* tend to reflect more the influences of mortality and "feudalisation."

Hence the appointment of Lorand to the rank of Town Judge in 1346 was only possible with the extinction of the old Rectoral family of Johann and Nicolas. The emergence of Ulving and his offspring to a position of power within the Town Council depended much upon the failings of the Kunc line and the gradual "feudalisation" of the Lorand. In their turn, the Ulvings themselves came to be increasingly preoccupied with the world beyond Buda, squabbling with and then finally passing into the nobility.[50]

The Ulvings really represent the last of Buda's great fourteenth century landed patrician families. The persons who succeeded them as Judges in the Town Council, while belonging themselves to such long serving families as the Rabensteiner and Pernhauser, seem to have possessed no great wealth of their own. Beyond the isolated vineyard, few assets are visible.[51] Unable to achieve any real position of dominance they soon disappear altogether from the town and perhaps the realm as a whole. By the last decades of the fourteenth century, the social structure of Buda's town government was undergoing rapid change. New burghers with no known previous involvement in either town government or even the town itself were able to make a speedy entry into the Council. In 1377, Johann Gleczel, a newcomer, probably from the northern mining towns of Slovakia,[52] acted as town *iudex*. He appears in the same capacity in both 1388 and 1392 while in other years officiating as a Council member. Similar circumstances surround the careers of the Judges Lawrence, known only as the son of Chamar, and Hertlin. Nor does this development appear confined to Buda alone or, for that matter, the towns of Hungary. In Pozsony, towards the end of the fourteenth century, the great families of Jacob lost their preeminence within the Council and were replaced by a succession of short-lived burgher familes.[53] The title of Judge was assumed in Kolozsvár by newcomers with no known antecendents in the town while in Vienna the old *Erbbürger* were replaced by fast-moving merchant groups.[54]

These changing circumstances may largely be explained by shifting economic conditions. During this period the price of agricultural commodities such as grain was steadily falling. Only on the larger estates where a conversion to more profitable forms of demesne exploitation, such as cattle rearing, was possible could a landed family hope to preserve its wealth.[55] At the same time, the opportunity to extend estates was being eroded as a result of land starvation. This situation was exacerbated in Buda by the encroachments of ecclesiastical corporations and the Rozgonyi magnate family.[56] Again, viticulture was for all but a few insufficient to provide a steady income and even then, particularly at harvest time, required a massive capital expenditure.[57] In Buda, where only a low-quality sulphurous wine was produced, competition was intense. Subsequently, a ban on imported wines was imposed although this was probably ineffective.[58]

Equally, however, the effects of increased long-distance trade were beginning to be felt. German merchants were selling off the cloth surplus of the west to Hungary and the other land of east-central Europe. In exchange they were exporting furs, wax and metals both precious and otherwise. The surviving, worm-eaten fragments of the Schürstab trading book amply reveal the extent to which already by the 1370's Hungarian cargoes were reaching Nuremberg, Cologne and northern Italy.[59] This development had been actively encouraged by Hungary's fourteenth-century Anjou kings. In 1335–6 Charles Robert as part of his attempt to break the Viennese staple and construct new trading connections which bypassed the Habsburg lands, had concluded a commercial alliance with the Bohemian king, John of Luxemburg. A relaxation of toll dues was shortly afterwards awarded to Bohemian, Swabian, Rhenish and Flemish merchants.[60] Twenty years later, Volfram Stromer, a leading Nuremberg trader, obtained privileges for himself and his colleagues. These privileges were subsequently ratified on a number of occasions.[61] Accordingly, the Hungarian market was flooded by different varieties of German, Flemish and English cloth, while furs and metals poured westwards. In England, the Duchy of Lancaster accounts record the various types of Hungarian pelt available,[62] while one political poem refers to the high quality of Hungarian silver.[63]

Nor surprisingly, foreign traders and representatives of the new commercial wealth began to take a seat on the Buda Town Council. Earlier a distinct Viennese orientation had been in evidence among Buda's leading burgher families. The Ulving, Chratzer, Rabensteiner and Pernhauser were all connected through family or business with citizens of Vienna.[64] But now, in their place, came South Germans and, in particular, Nurembergers: long-distance merchants from that town which had so rapidly eclipsed Vienna in commercial importance. Berchtold Kraft, a partner in one of Europe's major trading companies (Kraft-von Locheim-Stark-Tracht-Weissenburger), based at Nuremberg and with business connections in east-central Europe, Italy and Spain, acted as a town *iuratus* in 1392, subsequently dying in Buda.[65] In 1398, Hans Groland, an associate of the Stromer, held similar office as indeed earlier did a probable fellow Nuremberger, Johann Greczinger.[66] Peter Rauczan, whose family was closely related to that of the Nuremberg Neidung, was Judge in 1403 and 1404.[67] These men and others like them had a clear interest in obtaining the right of citizenship within the town. For as such, they might enjoy the special toll privileges awarded to Buda's merchants. Petty restrictions and limitations on minimum quantities bought and sold might be circumvented; legal problems occasioned by the association of foreign and native merchants successfully be avoided.[68] The interest of the new commercial class in Buda's municipal government sprang from similar considerations. For the Town Council possessed the at least *de facto* right to fix prices and modify even such royal legislation as touched on commercial affairs.[69] Assets which burghers had invested in the town might likewise be protected and the produce of their vineyards defended against competition. Equally important although less obvious benefits might accrue through the realm's "old boy" network of town councillors. In February 1422, for instance, Buda's Judge, Gaspar Bernhart, wrote to the Sopron magistracy with the request that it so arrange the transport of his Venice-bound cargoes as to avoid the King's border toll collectors. He promised that, should the need arise, he himself was ready to return the favour.[70]

The newly arrived burgher families had none of the deep involvement over a long period with the town which the great patrician families of the fourteenth century had exhibited. Like Hans Groland, they might return westwards after a few years, once their initial interest in the town had been satisfied. As with the Greczinger family, times of hardship might provide also a good motive for departure.[71] The brief involvement of these families in the town may explain again in part the decline in rural landholding. A family or burgher who might move off at rapid notice was unlikely to sink capital or seek additional revenues through the clumsy expedient of land. Where commercial interests were involved a ready outlet for excess wealth was provided either through reinvestment or a diversification of commercial or financial interests. Again, in the case of the long-distance merchant partnerships, any excess of credit in their Buda accounts might be redressed by the simple expedient of despatching monies westward.[72] A short-lived and often mercenary involvement in town government fostered the temptation to embezzle. Both Sopron and Pozsony witnessed an unrest among the non-governing classes which was itself the direct product of the misappropriations of town revenues by Council members.[73] In Buda, although the circumstances are less precise, a revolt in 1402–3 and the subsequent instatement of an illegal Town Council appears to have been motivated by fraudulent tax collection. Certainly, both the royal charter issued at the time of the revolt's suppression and the town customary compiled shortly afterwards devote considerable space to the regulation of taxation procedure.

Primary agents in this revolt were two guildsmen: a butcher and a furrier. Accordingly, certain historians have attempted to see in the events of 1402–3 an incipient class conflict.[74] Certainly, the late fourteenth and early fifteenth centuries form that period in Hungary's history when there emerge the first guilds and labour organisations. Again, with an increase in the fur trade and a probable expansion of Buda's meat-consuming population, the furriers and butchers may be viewed as upwardly mobile social groups whose advancement to positions of authority in the town had been blocked by an antagonistic merchant class. Nonetheless, it must be remarked that a butcher and a furrier seem unlikely bed-fellows in any class movement. The furriers belonged to a wealthy craft whose members regularly lodged in the more fashionable quarters of the town.[75] Already, from the 1370's, a certain Jacob Longus *pellifex* may be found acting as a town councillor. The butchers by contrast occupied a humbler position dwelling below the furriers in the poorer town suburbs. Here they gave their name to a street in the locality—the *platea carnificum*.[76] Only infrequently did any of them achieve the rank of *iuratus*. More significantly, it should be noted that Buda's leading guild families tend to demonstrate an endurance within the town which contrasts markedly with the short life-span of the merchant families. Throughout the fifteenth century, for instance, the Butcher's Guild was dominated by the Aldoth family.[77] Later the guilds both in Buda and elsewhere were to introduce restrictive measures intended to perpetuate a family power within the various crafts.[78] The conflict of 1402–3 may thus reflect in part a contradiction between the short and long-term interests of the various groups within the town. But, in any event, the revolt had made obvious the guildsmen's power. Subsequently a proportion, perhaps as high as a third, of Council places came to be occupied by craftsmen, generally from the wealthier guilds of grocers, goldsmiths and furriers. Sometime before 1420 (the date is unclear), a cloth-trimmer was appointed to the rank of Town Judge.

The emergence of guildsmen within the Council is, however, conceivable only within the context of Buda's declining commercial importance. The cornerstone of the town's trading life was its staple right. This privilege which the town had enjoyed since the thirteenth century provided for the compulsory unloading and sale of all goods passing through the town. During the second half of the fourteenth century similar privileges were awarded to Kassa and Brassó.[79] At the same time indications appear that Buda's staple was being circumvented either illegally or, in the case of merchants from Szeben and later Kolozsvár, with specific authority having been obtained from the King.[80] Excessive tolls on the Danube discouraged Viennese merchants from pressing as far downstream as Buda. As it was, the incidence of brigandage within Hungary appears relatively high and frequent references to robber bands of nobles suggests that the low *homagium* payable by the murderer of a merchant contributed to rural violence.[81] Now however, new political pressures were applied which left these same merchants liable to arrest and, thus, militated against all but the shortest journeys into the Hungarian hinterland.[82] By the opening years of the fifteenth century, Buda's commercial fate had been sealed. For at this point Sigismund granted staple rights to the western border towns of the realm, Sopron and Pozsony, while finally revoking in 1405 the Buda staple itself.[83] Thus, the major commercial families of the realm, in particular the Gutgesell, Gailsam and Poll, came to found their merchant enterprises in Pozsony. Only their factors operated in Buda, there maintaining the interests of their firms in an increasingly reduced market.[84] The involvement of such notable persons as Hans Groland or Berchtold Kraft in Buda's government came to a close. The merchants who replaced them on the Council, despite some connection with such centres as Vienna or the north Italian towns,[85] never seem to have engaged in any significant commercial undertakings. The only exception was the Colognese Jacob von dem Pach, a cloth merchant with contacts in both Vienna and the Rhineland, who acted as a town *iuratus* in 1429.[86] Diminished wealth, moreover, worked against the establishment of long-lived burgher dynasties. The majority of the town's office-holding merchant families entered and left Buda within the span of a single generation, perhaps to seek a more profitable location for their business enterprises.

However, indications remain that a small but wealthy burgher élite was at this same time developing within the town, a group which played no part in municipal government but whose members nevertheless intermarried and formed ultimately amongst themselves a patriciate of sorts shunning responsibilities within the Council.

The Separation of Wealth from Power

A major distorting force within Buda affecting the traditional *potentes-divites* structure of government had its origin in the peculiar position which the town held during much of the fifteenth century. For most of the preceding period the court had been settled at Visegrád, a small town some twenty miles to the north of Buda. While Buda during this period was frequently used for ceremonial purposes such as the reception of the Byzantine emperor, John V Palaeologus, in 1366, full establishment of the court there was delayed until the first decade of the following century. Thereafter, Buda became the principal royal residence and centre of the realm's administration. The chronicler Bonfini noted that, "Before Sigismund's time nothing worth mentioning was built in Buda castle." But during the subsequent period, as recent excavations have revealed, an extensive rebuilding of the royal palace at Buda was undertaken.[87] In the meantime, the old royal residence at Visegrád was allowed to fall into disrepair.[88] The organs of government had become firmly fixed in Buda.

Conversely, however, the town no longer held any significant commercial position within the realm. The centre for burgher wealth and aspirations had passed elsewhere. Certainly, the very settlement of the court at Buda offered some minor compensations. The nobility, royal family and numerous minor court officials provided a ready market for loans or a trade in fine cloth and jewellery.[89] However, it is evident that the court might yet exert an attraction beyond the purely commercial.

The importance of patronage was well noted by contemporaries. One fourteenth century Italian romance illustrates this point simply although perhaps in rather fabulous terms. In the hope of making their fortune, two Italians ventured abroad to the Kingdom of the Hungarians. Footsore, they arrived at last in Buda where they wandered the streets. By chance, they encountered a helpful fellow who it later transpired was none other than great King Louis himself. From this point onwards, needless to say, there was no looking back. Success and prosperity surrounded the future careers of both Italians.[90]

Such good fortune was of course exceptional. For the majority a harder struggle was necessary before the fruits of royal or court patronage came to be won. The attention of the realm's high dignitaries might be obtained, however, in a variety of ways—within the ecclesiastical promotion structure for instance. An alternative channel lay through membership of the Buda Council. As a result of Buda's declining commercial importance, a career in town government had been made possible for persons with relatively little wealth. The departure of the great fourteenth century *Geschlechter* and the short-lived involvement of the new merchant families provided an easier access into town government for rootless newcomers. Once a position of importance had been secured, the possibilities of transfer to the royal administration with all its rewards became greatly enhanced. Whether such a hope guided persons when they first sought municipal office remains unclear. Evidently though, a number of successful Town Judges ceased their involvement with municipal government upon an entry to the favours of the court. But, at the same time, they continued to hold the rank of town citizen while displaying no diminished interest in other town affairs.

Johann Siebenlinder, Town Judge in 1410, 1411 and 1414 was a newcomer. He seems to have involved himself in trade with the north dealing in commodities which he subsequently despatched westwards to Pozsony.[91] Probable commercial connections with Vienna are suggested by both his own and his daughter's marriages to prominent burgher families of that town.[92] Together with other citizens Siebenlinder acted also as a contractor on some estates not far from Buda.[93] But in 1415 he was appointed to a court office, collector of the royal marten furs, and his involvement with town government immediately came to a close.[94] In later years he was a royal toll collector and the Castellan of Óbuda. The Queen employed him as a financial agent to repay some debts she owed in Vienna.[95] Towards the end of his life, Siebenlinder was invested with the important office of Chamberlain to the mining districts of northern Hungary. His notable services to the monarchy resulted in several grants of land.[96] Shortly after Siebenlinder's death his widow was recorded as among those in attendance at the birth of the Emperor Albert's son, Ladislas.[97] Throughout his life Siebenlinder remained a citizen of Buda and for him this proved no empty title. He rented estates beside the town, was involved in commercial undertakings with fellow burghers and operated as an importer of quality wines.[98]

A similar career is evident in the case of the burgher Michael Nadler, the son of a former town *iuratus* and himself Judge on six occasions. By 1434, the last year in which he officiated in the Council, Michael had risen to the rank of Chamberlain of the royal mint at Buda.[99] Thereafter, while maintaining a house and family in the town, he held a series of court appointments. Principal amongst these was collector of the imperial Jewish tax, a task which took him abroad to various distant parts of Europe.[100] In 1440 royal jewels worth one and a half thousand gold gulders were placed in his care and he was charged with their safe passage to Vienna.[101] It is perhaps a measure of his importance that, in the affair of Michael's wrongfully seized estates in Fejér county, the Hungarian Diet itself intervened on his behalf.[102]

Assisting Michael Nadler in one of his missions at the royal behest was a Hungarian called Ladislas Farkas.[103] The career of this former draper of Buda follows in many respects the distinctive pattern already displayed by Siebenlinder and Nadler. Because of his native ancestry though, Ladislas had first to secure the acceptance of Buda's ruling German minority. This he achieved by an illustrious marriage to the daughter of a Nuremberg family.[104] During the disorders of the late 1430's, Ladislas rose to a position of power in the town holding judicial office on at least two separate occasions. Thereafter he entered the royal administration and, despite his active support for the losing side in the civil war of the 1440's, subsequently came to command both high rank and exceptional riches. But despite the pretensions of nobility, Ladislas Farkas remained, and was as such addressed until his death, a citizen of Buda. It was from here he arranged his many business transactions and administered his far-flung estates. And indeed it was in Buda that he died, in January 1457, "with the light in his hand."[105] Other burgher careers from this period and later attest again to the same trend. The former *potentes* of the town were quitting the Council and acquiring wealth through a connection with the court. At the same time they continued as burghers of the town closely involved in the life of the community.

There is, however, a deeper aspect of this development and one which is highlighted in part by certain features of Johann Siebenlinder's career. For Johann towards the end of his life enjoyed by virtue of his role as chamberlain a close involvement with the Hungarian mining industry. Whether he was in fact actually involved in the metals trade remains unclear. Certainly though, business and family connections with the South German merchant firm of Wendelstein and the Pozsony Gailsam may be seen as pointing in this direction.[106]

An interest in metals was by no means confined to Johann Siebenlinder alone. For the North Hungarian metal trade acted as a major lure for the German merchants of this period. The great Nuremburg families of Schürstab, Eisvogel and Stromer dealt in Hungarian silver during the fourteenth century while merchants from Aachen traded their cloth in the markets of Hungary in exchange for the rich silver-bearing copper of its mines.[107] Neither of course is this surprising. Precious metals were in constant demand throughout Europe at this time. Copper, likewise, even without its silver content, was a highly prized commodity. Its value was steadily increasing in response to the developing South German metal industry and the growing demands of the Antwerp and Aachen brass foundries.[108] Even as early as 1306, Hungarian copper was being exported northwards through Poland to the Baltic where merchants of the Hansa made arrangements for its final sale.[109] So great indeed was the attraction of metals for the German firms that quite long-lived partnerships were founded which specialised only in this commodity. The production of Hungarian copper rose, thus, to meet the new market demand and the realm's mining industry experienced rapid growth.[110]

Money was to be made in metals and yet, despite this, the business of mining itself remained both risky and unattractive. Certainly, some great Nuremberg industrialists and financiers, Ulrich Eisvogel and Lutz Steinlinger for example, directly funded and involved themselves in Hungarian mining enterprises.[111] But the technology, while advanced, could in no way prevent either a physical or financial ruin. For, as shafts were sunk below the water-table the dangers of flooding and firedamp correspondingly increased. Edward Browne, a seventeenth century English traveller with an interest in mining, described how in 1642 an entire 1000 yard long gallery at Körmöcbánya caught fire "by the carelessness of a boy wiping the snuff of a lamp upon the wood." Fifty men were smothered in the conflagration and "they were all taken out except one, who was found to be dissolved by the sharp waters of the mine." Similar more laconic accounts survive for the medieval period.[112] Again, mining remained a highly speculative profession. Stephen Jung spent an entire fortune trying to win success in the copper mines of Besztercebánya. Finally bankrupt he was obliged to sell up in order to pay off his creditors. Eventually he wandered over to Germany where, according to legend, he ended his days begging for bread—a sad case but by no means unique.[113]

In contrast, the actual transporting and, more particularly, the processing of metals remained highly lucrative and certainly less fraught with difficulties. One Nuremberg merchant in the 1520's acquired from Bohemia a load of argentiferous copper which after refinement produced a quantity of silver worth more than forty times the original cost of the purchase.[114] Likewise and despite the intense business competition, profits of 10-20% were obtained by the foundries working the sixteenth century Saxon Mansfeld copper field.[115] The profits to be made from the refinement of copper were, during the fifteenth century, probably yet greater. For prospectors were then less apprised of the techniques of assaying and might, thus, remain ignorant of the true value of the ore they sold off for processing.

But an entry into this the more profitable side of the Hungarian metals trade was subject to restrictions other than purely market in origin. In Hungary, a trade in raw gold and silver was forbidden as such metals were part of a royal monopoly and might only be negotiated in the form of coinage. Copper, unfortunately for Hungary, while it might be broken down from the slurry in which it was originally found and so reduced to "black copper" could not be adequately refined and its precious silver "impurities" channelled off. For this process, the liquation *(seiger)* technique, remained a closely guarded secret, known only to the Medici and a few German industrialists.[116]

The actual acquisition of unrefined copper ore became steadily harder during the late fourteenth century. Royal controls similar to those imposed on gold and silver came increasingly to be employed.[117] Previously merchants had attempted to gain supplies either directly or, through the *verleger* system, by an investment in mining enterprises.[118] But by 1405 such immediate nego-tiations with the source of supply were prohibited. All copper had to be sold off by prospectors to the royal chamberlains of the mines. They alone might arrange for its final sale.[119] Accordingly, mine owners confronted by a state monopoly of their retail outlets inveigled themselves into the royal chamberlain organisation. Not surprisingly also, the German metal merchants pursued a rival interest in this branch of the Hungarian administration.

Already in 1398, Ulrich Kammerer, a partner in one of central Europe's greatest firms of metal merchants (Ammann-Kammerer-Seiler-Grau), had advanced to the rank of Chamberlain in Hungary.[120] Since some "free" copper, not yet subject to a royal monopoly, was still available to his competitors, he supplemented his position by acquiring the office of toll collector. His manifold abuses were a frequent lament among contemporaries.[121] One of Ulrich's associates, Peter Reichel, obtained likewise the rank of chamberlain during the 1420's. Operating closely in conjunction with Lutz Steinlinger and the mining proprietor, Johann Valbrecht of Thorn, it was probably Peter Reichel's task to arrange the transport of cargoes of Hungarian copper bound for Nuremberg and eventual refinement.[122] Some business links between Reichel, the Stromer and Koler are also evident.[123] Beyond these two figures, nearly all of central Europe's best-known firms of metal merchants may be found variously represented amongst the chamberlains of Hungary's northern mining towns: the Ebner, Flextorfer-Kegler-Zenner (through the agency of Mark of Nuremberg), the Ramenstein, Kammermeister, the Lemmel, through the Lemmel the Imhoff and, although this is more speculative, through the Chamberlain Henry Munich, the great South German firm of Wendelstein.[124]

Within the copper trade though, citizenship of one of North Hungary's rough and drunken mining towns conferred little advantage. The Chamberlains by the very virtue of their position were able to achieve a dominance in these communities sufficient to make membership of a Town Council unnecessary. Peter Reichel was thus in the 1420's able to impose his own nominee at the head of the Körmöcbánya magistracy. The objections of the citizenry were directed only at the unsuitability of his choice.[125] Again, since copper was usually exported immediately out of the country, in an opposite direction to the commercial centre of Pozsony, any attempt to win influence within this town was largely superfluous.[126] On the other hand, Buda, both traditionally and subsequently as the centre of government, acted very much as the hub of the chamberlain organisation. It is not surprising then that Buda witnessed the arrival of some of these copper merchants and administrators. The Chamberlains Ulrich Kammerer, Peter Reichel and Henry Munich all made their homes within Buda and settled their families within the town.[127] Here they endeavoured to win royal support in their merchant enterprises and intrigues. All were men of quite exceptional wealth. Peter Reichel and his family owned great estates both in Hungary and Germany.[128] In his turn, Henry Munich held lands in the north and with his profits from the copper trade set up a credit business in Vienna.[129] Ulrich Kammerer, besides paying for a son at university, acted together with the Medici as a principal financier of Rupert of the Palatinate's Italian campaign.[130] Considering the international character of their business and political operations, it is hardly surprising that none of these men played any visible role in town government. For them it was, quite simply, an irrelevant activity; their commercial interests and aspirations were directed elsewhere.

Among Buda's copper trading families, there soon developed close interrelationships through marriage. This network came to extend also to those former Town Council members who had entered the royal service and while remaining active citizens of Buda had forsaken town office. Thus, Ulrich Kammerer's daughter married a Nuremberg merchant, Ulrich Vorchtel, who between 1406 and 1410 had represented the metal interests of the Stromer in Buda. The two daughters of this marriage wedded respectively the copper merchant Peter Reichel and the former Judge, thereafter royal official, Ladislas Farkas.[131] Again, the daughter of Johann Siebenlinder married the Chamberlain Henry Munich.[132] Although some commercial rivalry is evident between Munich and Reichel,[133] members of this entire group were, nonetheless, closely bound together by reason of their business activities. Ladislas Farkas and Michael Nadler both operated on behalf of the Queen in Vienna. Here they established contact with Henry Haiden, Johann Siebenlinder's son-in-law.[134] In the text of the same royal pardon afforded them in 1443 occur the names of Ladislas Farkas, Henry Munich and a member of the Koler family which itself enjoyed business links with Peter Reichel.[135]

Business and family contacts fostered also a social cohesiveness which achieved expression in Buda's German *Corpus Christi* Brotherhood. Although the actual membership of this exclusive society is difficult to determine, its close involvement with the great metal merchants of Buda is readily apparent. Thus, in her will, Ulrich Kammerer's granddaughter, the wife of Ladislas Farkas, left to the Brotherhood annuities she had acquired in Nuremberg. These were still being paid as late as the sixteenth century.[136] By then, however, the great metal merchants had left Buda and the Brotherhood become closely associated with the remnant of the town's ruling German class.[137]

Among the towns of Germany, urban unrest and disaffection is often interpreted by reference to a disturbance of the traditional *potentes-divites* order. In towns such as Lübeck and Cologne, for instance, the ruling burgher dynasties obtained formidable prerogatives in the holding of Council places. Establishing an inwardly-looking social caste and maintaining their own exclusive clubs, the great families sought to deny a share in town government to the representatives of new wealth. Unable to effect an entry to the centre of municipal power and, moreover, with the medieval town constitution lacking any device for redress other than persuasion, new and politically disadvantaged groups of *divites* were forced to compel change through the only alternative of an uprising.[138] In Buda a peculiar variant to this theme is clearly demonstrable.

For much of the first half of the fifteenth century and as a direct result of Buda's commercial decline, the town's *potentes* consisted in the main of poorer trading elements: the guildsmen and short-lived merchant families. Their brief involvement in the town militated against the establishment there of close family bonds and burgher dynasties in the old fourteenth century mould. Quite outside their number, the town's *divites* formed a distinct network of their own. They enjoyed mutual business and social interests. Their families intermarried. But although long resident in the town, their fortunes could little profit from any involvement in the Council. In their quest for continued influence at the court, these persons had either left or from the first ignored the narrow parochialism and limited commercial benefits of town government.

Buda faced, therefore, an almost unique situation. In Germany the *potentes-divites* order of government was often threatened by the establishment of closely knit oligarchies opposed to the introduction of the newly-rich to their number. As a consequence came conflict, crisis and change within the Council. By contrast, in Buda power was held by a humbler, fast-moving citizenry. Remaining aloof from the Council was the interwoven network of the town's *divites*—an almost hidden patriciate reluctant to involve itself in Buda's public life. This disturbance of the established *potentes-divites* order had, however, the consequence not of impeding social movement but rather of over-exaggerating it. With the *divites* absent from the Council, the entry there of persons of not only relatively little wealth and connection but also, as it turned out, undesirable nationality was greatly facilitated. The implications of this development, finally sealed in bloodshed, were to have a profound effect upon both the character and concept of town government in Buda.

The 1439 Revolt

The leading families in Buda, discussed so far, were all German. Not surprisingly though, the town had also a sizeable Hungarian population. Hungarians belonged in the main, although by no means exclusively, to the lower classes, living outside the walls in the ramshackle suburbs.[139] Their entry into the Council was restricted. According to the Buda town customary, only two Hungarians at a time might act as *iurati*. They could never achieve the rank of Town Judge or Judge of the Monies.[140] Generally, on the surviving fourteenth century Council lists, the bottom two, perhaps three, places seem to be held by persons whose names indicate a Hungarian origin. Promotion higher up the list appears dependent upon intermarriage with more established German elements. Nor were the Hungarian majority able to exercise any significant influence in elections to the Council and, thus, secure the appointment of councillors favourably disposed towards themselves. For the right to participate in elections depended upon the previous acquisition of citizenship—a condition which might only be bestowed on the wealthier property owners.[141]

By the third decade of the fifteenth century, however, the traditional dominance of the Germans within the town was undergoing a noticeable decline. Of the twelve councillors in 1429, five were clearly Hungarians. The Judge for that year, "Little" Heinrich (Hyko) seems also to have thought it expedient to change his name from Wolfgang to the Magyar equivalent of Farkas. Subsequently the Judge in 1435, Peter Onwein, was to do very much the same, assuming the Hungarian name of Bornemisza.[142]

Quite clearly a number of factors may have influenced this development. The Hungarian court and the growth of higher education establishments in the town encouraged the arrival of a new native intellectual and administrative class willing to involve itself in town government. Their very residence in the town may possibly have affected the composition of the electorate. The nobility, householders in the town, may also have taken up the cause of the disadvantaged and pressed changes upon the Council.[143] But at the same time the fragmented character of German government cannot really be overlooked. During the fourteenth century, the very wealth of the town's prominent citizen families had reinforced German dominance in the Council and ensured that, in accordance with the terms of the *Stadtrecht,* the poorer Hungarians enjoyed a largely insignificant role in government. But now, as Hungarians emerged through the crafts to wealth or alternatively immigrated into the town with riches already secured, they found themselves possessed of a financial status equal to that of the established *potentes.* The riches acquired by the Hungarian goldsmith, Peter Borgyas, or members of the town's de Bathe family far exceeded the wealth of many of their German contemporaries in the Council.[144] Beyond the economic, however, the social base itself of German government was enfeebled. Again in marked contrast to the fourteenth century, the town now lacked any enduring Council families who could lend municipal government a semblance of continuity, whose expertise and influence might be employed to bolster German interests. Instead the Council was dominated by short-lived merchant families and humbler artisan elements. Confronted by a fearful but, nonetheless, disunited and relatively impoverished German governing class, better-off Hungarians were successfully able to effect a gradual entry into the Council.

By the late 1430's relations between the two nationalities in the realm, Hungarians and Germans, had greatly deteriorated. Reports sent home by visiting German merchants refer to a growing animosity which had been fuelled by the election of Albert, the Habsburg King of Hungary, to the imperial dignity in 1438. "One may well say that the Hungarians hate the Germans and Bohemians more than ever," wrote Walther von Schwarzemberg to the Frankfurt Town Council. His colleague, Henry Wisse, expressed similar views.[145] Neither were their fears unfounded. The Diet of 1439 drastically curtailed the further holding of Crown offices by extranei. Enforcement was immediate and within a month many Germans had forfeited their jobs to Hungarians.[146]

This antagonism had already found its way into the realm's capital. In 1436 George the Deacon, an administrator and popular Hungarian attorney, was preaching openly against German domination in Buda's ecclesiastical life and condemning the luxuries of the Corpus Christi German merchant society.[147] Although the town was quiet enough for Sigismund to make arrangements for the prorogation of the Council of Basle to Buda, intrigues surrounding the leadership of an incipient Hungarian faction were evidently in progress.[148] Alarmed by these developments and the growing influence of Hungarians on the Council the Germans appear to have embarked upon a series of countermeasures. In an attempt to cut their losses they secured the election of the Hungarian Ladislas Farkas: a patrician whose business and family connections made him sympathetic to themselves and their interests. But this proved of little avail and in 1439 a more drastic policy was adopted. According to one account, the leader of the Hungarian faction, Johann the Silversmith, was secretly lured to the Town Hall, tortured, murdered and thrown in the Danube.[149] This means of disposal of the corpse proved, needless to say, singularly inadequate. Johann's body was discovered on the riverbank by his supporters and an apparently spontaneous uprising followed in the town. German shops and merchants were plundered, peasantry joined in the looting and the royal treasury was sacked. The "quisling" Ladislas Farkas was forced to flee to the royal palace. Here behind bolted doors, the King despairingly watched the progress of the revolt. Although the rioters were eventually dispersed and Ladislas returned to power some far-reaching compromise between the two warring nationalities in the town had clearly become necessary.

Negotiations between representatives of the two communities were entered into almost immediately and certainly completed by April 1440. Assisting the parties in the solution of their difficulties were the various prelates, magnates and nobles of the royal council. The discussions were wide ranging and representatives of the German minority were obliged to concede many points. Parish boundaries within the town were clearly delineated and the jurisdictional rights of the Germans' Church of Our Blessed Lady curtailed. The filial status of the Hungarians' churches, Mary Magdalen's and St. Peter's, was revoked and the payment of symbolic fees by their priests to the Germans' church discontinued. Instead, the two Hungarian churches were now accorded a status equal to that of Our Blessed Lady's and awarded their own independent parishes within the town.[150]

Concepts of parity between the town's two "communities," as they were known, similarly underlay discussions on the future character of Buda's municipal government. Neither is this surprising. For although the Germans were a minority group within the town, still, as one contemporary French traveller remarked, much of the town's commerce and manufacturing skill rested firmly in their hands.[151] Inferior numerical status was thus compensated for by their crucial role in the town's economic life. Accordingly it was determined that every year the twelve Council places would henceforward be equally divided between Hungarians and Germans, while the supreme judicial office would alternate with a Hungarian one year and a German the next.

If, during the actual violence of the revolt itself, control of the Hungarian party had, as various chroniclers suggest, become assumed by *lumpenproletariat* groups, this development should be interpreted as but a transitory phase depending upon the heat of the moment. For otherwise, leadership of the Hungarian faction was consecutively vested in an intellectual, a silversmith and, subsequent to the revolt, a resident member of the lesser nobility (Dionysius de Kopách). Council lists from both before and after the uprising further indicate that over this period Hungarian representatives consisted of the better-off craftsmen, *litterati* and former noblemen. Again, among the supporters of George the Deacon may be numbered at least three nobles, two apothecaries, a grocer and a saddler.[152] The interests of this group stood appreciably far closer to the contemporary German councillors than to the urban poor who had played such a conspicuous part in the 1439 revolt. The increased "politicisation" of the "mob" expressed not simply in 1439 but in later years as well, suggested moreover a dangerous development.[153] The Hungarian leadership delighting like its German counterpart in such appellations as "wealthy," "circumspect" and "prudent" was understandably concerned lest any of its newly acquired power slip into the hands of its erstwhile supporters: the foolish poor. Again, since these persons had, after all, ransacked German shops, any advancement of their condition could only have been inimical to the German party in the discussions. These considerations underlay the future arrangement of municipal elections.

The constitutional crisis provoked by the 1439 revolt was by no means the first experienced by medieval Buda. During the thirteenth and fourteenth centuries the institution of royally appointed Rectors had deeply struck at the fundamental notion of municipal liberty and the immune status held by the town within the realm. The Rectoral period is itself illustrative. Then, the town's principal citizen families rather than oppose the Rectoral system had willingly acquiesced to its infringement of urban rights. For through the royal appointment of Rectors drawn from out of their number, their continued dominance in the town was assured. Finding much useful support in the Rectors and anxious not to antagonise the leading families, the King was reluctant to abolish the institution even though it had outlived the purpose for which it had been initially intended. Some ninety years after the formal abolition of the Rectoral system, Buda's leading German and Hungarian citizens similarly taking advantage of a somewhat confused situation found an opportunity also for maintaining their power in the town.

In view of social and economic disparities, it would have been difficult so to arrange electoral procedures as to accord with the notion of the Hungarian community possessing an equal constitutional status to the German. Evidently though, with the right to participate in elections dependent upon a property qualification which thereby ensured German dominance of the electorate and, thus, the regular return of prominent German citizens, some change in procedures was clearly necessary. But to establish parity within the electoral body, wealth would have to be replaced by nationality as the criterion for determining suitable electors. There was little way this could numerically be achieved without at the same time increasing the election-day power of the town's poorer elements. But in view of the close social and economic kinship existing between the actual leadership of the town's two communities, an accommodation pleasing to both parties in the discussions could be achieved, political power be restrained from any too great a slide down the social scale and thorny electoral problems circumvented. Hence it was determined that in future there would be, quite simply, no more public elections. A hundred persons of Germans and Hungarians in equal numbers would be selected, not by the citizenry *universitas,* but instead by the retiring Council. This specially appointed electoral college would alone decide the membership of the new incoming Council.[154] Such a development was to exercise a profound effect upon not only the constitutional organisation of late fifteenth century Buda but also notions implicit within the associative idea.

Chapter 6

MONARCHY, RIGHTS AND IDEOLOGY

Municipal Rights

In his famous Nuremberg *Weltchronik,* Hartmann Schedel includes a late fifteenth century woodcut of contemporary Buda.[1] Looking across the Danube from the Pest side and near the site of the present day Academy of Sciences, the illustrator directs our gaze through time to the skyline of Buda's *castrum* area. From the centre of Buda and surmounted by a cross rises the spire of Our Blessed Lady's, the German parish church of the town. To the right is the splendid nave and tower of the rival Mary Magdalen's. Set below lie the squat roofs and gables of the burghers' own houses. But no symbol of civic pride, it is the royal palace bedecked with its many vanes and turrets which commands the horizon and occupies almost a half of the picture. With its walls and fortifications reaching down to the shores of the Danube, the palace's high Stephen Tower still climbs majestically to the uppermost border of the woodcut. Beneath, the palace's crenellated battlements press into the burghers' quarters, overpowering and drawing attention away from the narrow perspectives of the streetways. These artistic imbalances correspond closely with social and political realities. In this respect, Schedel's illustration unwittingly symbolises fundamental inequalities apparent also in Buda's relationship to the monarchy. During the course of the fifteenth century, these, in becoming particularly evident, conferred a new measure of fragility upon the established patterns of town life.

Already in the preceding chapter, we have noted the lure exercised in Buda by the royal court. The potent influences of royal patronage had the effect of forcing apart the traditional alliance of wealth and power earlier apparent amongst the town's ruling class. Partly as a result of this was provoked a revolt and, through the constitutional innovations which followed, Hungarians assumed parity with Germans in municipal government. Certainly, the Germans resident in Buda lost in the process little of their economic supremacy; indeed, if anything, over the succeeding period the disproportionate distribution of urban wealth shifted even further in their favour. During the second half of the fifteenth century, Buda's commercial position within the realm much improved. In the Austrian monetary crisis of the time, both Pozsony and Sopron were hard affected while in 1483 King Matthias (Corvinus) Hunyadi, by revoking the Viennese and Pozsony staples, reopened a direct route between Buda and the towns of southern Germany.[2] Over the ensuing forty years the proportion of Hungary's export trade passing through Buda doubled. Branches of the Great Ravensburg Company and of the Fugger and Welser banks were established in the capital. At the same time, the commercial prosperity of Pest, fast becoming the realm's most important centre for the cattle trade, spilled over on to its neighbour.[3] In the wake of this recovery came a new class of wealthy German merchants anxious to take advantage of the town's commercial potential. During the 1470's there settled in Buda members of the Nuremberg trading families of Mühlstein and Haller and of the Austrian Pemfflinger and Forster. The next decade witnessed in its turn the arrival of the Nuremberg Mulner and Pozsony Gailsam. Besides these may be reckoned also a host of lesser families from the west: the Meixner, Dax, Harber and Stenczel. With the more established elements in the town and, of course, amongst themselves, the newcomers contracted marriage and business bonds.[4] The constitutional arrangements inaugurated in 1439–40 ensured, moreover, that these Germans might exercise a formidable presence within the Council. But, their riches notwithstanding, the Germans' erstwhile political ascendancy was never regained and, thus, they were forced to share office with Hungarians whose inferior business contacts afforded them a reduced prosperity. In this way, the separation of wealth from power earlier evident in the town's history was largely maintained right through until the sixteenth century. Indeed, it was only in the years immediately following the battle of Mohács in 1526 that this fundamental dichotomy in the town's social organisation found resolution. For with the Turkish onslaught and the outbreak of civil war, Buda's German citizenry forsook the town looking for safety and stability elsewhere. In 1529, whether by a dreadful misunderstanding or with the connivance of King John Zápolyai is unclear, the last remnant of Germans dwelling in the town was slaughtered by a Turkish band. Hereafter, until the town's final absorption into the Ottoman empire in 1541, the government of Buda lay firmly in Hungarian hands.[5]

Although right up until the time of their departure, Buda's Germans continued to shun family contacts with the rural world, such feelings of distinctiveness were rarely entertained by their Hungarian contemporaries in the

Council. Even more so than the great *Ritterbürger* families of the fourteenth century, Buda's leading Hungarian citizens regularly intermarried with the nobility, both lesser and baronial. Some of their number even held a noble ancestry. Stephen de Mykola, for instance, Judge on four occasions, was descended from a small noble family holding estates in Fejér county. The Judges Lawrence *Litteratus* de Bayon and Johann de Attád likewise enjoyed noble status as did the *iurati* Clement Berki, Valentine Themeskezy and George Kömlődy, *pistor semellarum.* Besides these may be added also the noble families of Iváncsi and Patócsi whose members, although belonging to the Hungarian patriciate, never attained rank in the Council.[6] The increasing involvement of Buda's Hungarians in the cattle trade fostered also close links with noble estate holders.[7]

These contacts with the lesser nobility, traditional supporters of the King, generated amongst the Hungarian patriciate a clear sympathy for the monarchy and royal ambitions. In recognition of this, the Hungarian Dionysius of Buda was appointed in 1464 to an office closely associated with King Matthias's centralisation of judicial procedures—justice of the royal "personal presence" *(személynök).* Of patrician origin and recorded as a *iuratus* in 1462, this Dionysius is most readily identifiable with the Dionysius of Székesfehérvár who was Judge of Buda in 1456.[8] Significantly also, in 1473 Matthias elevated Stephen Ermen, a leading Hungarian citizen and Judge on three occasions, to the rank of Castle Bailiff in Buda. The jurisdiction of the Bailiff regularly at this time trespassed into the town at the expense of Council authority. Supervising the administration of the vast Hunyadi estates and the king's private demesne, very much the backbone of royal authority, the Bailiffs were otherwise without exception recruited from amongst the monarch's own most trusted supporters. Evidently, Ermen was considered firm in his loyalty to the monarch and, indeed, quite ready to assume an office which might put him at odds with the Council.[9]

Increased susceptibility to royal influence occurred at a time when throughout the realm monarchical authority was on a rapid ascendant.[10] The young and dynamic Hunyadi monarchy, having forced the disintegration of the old baronial leagues which had so troubled the preceding period, vigorously set about reinforcing its newly acquired wealth and power. Earlier on in the fifteenth century, the monarchy had sought to maintain authority by actively collaborating with the baronage. Respecting and augmenting magnate rights, the Kings had vainly reduced themselves to *primi inter pares* in the pursuit of "consensus politics." Contrastingly, under the Hunyadis royal policy was primarily directed at removing long established baronial prerogatives and, as in military organisation, at securing a power-base and administration quite free from the constraints imposed by a fractious magnate class. In this programme the support of the Diet was readily secured. Accordingly, for the first time, the Chancellery apparatus was removed from the restrictions of baronial control and officials appointed by the monarch assumed a greater role in its administration.[11] Likewise, the powers of the court of the royal "personal presence" were greatly augmented and, as this institution came to incorporate the court of the "special presence," so it assumed a major significance in the judicial life of the realm.[12] The administration of the court of the "personal presence" was directly subject to monarchical supervision and, as in the Chancellery, loyal secretaries of the King were entrusted with its proper functioning. Appeal procedures for the transmission of cases from the usually magnate-dominated courts of the Palatine and Justiciar to the "personal presence" were greatly simplified and became quite regular as this court adjudicated all year round and not simply at the octaves.[13] Precisely because the courts of the Palatine and Justiciar were closely bound up with noble, seigneurial and county jurisdiction, so through the "personal presence" the monarch was able to exert his influence more forcibly on a local level. Appeals might indeed proceed here directly from the county courts thus bypassing altogether the great ordinaries of the realm.[14] More regularly though, appeals from the counties passed for adjudication immediately before the court of the central royal *curia,* the *tabula regia judiciaria.* At this court the King himself was present in person and evidently able to wield a formidable influence. Otherwise, membership of the *tabula regia* was increasingly dominated by representatives of the lesser nobility appointed by the Diet as a counterweight to baronial power.[15]

Not simply content with a centralisation of judicial procedures, Matthias Hunyadi sought also to extend the competence of the county courts. Through the links forged between the county courts and central royal judiciary, the prerogatives of those forums over which the monarch exercised immediate influence were, thus, greatly expanded. As part of this policy, the nobility dwelling on the large landed estates had the immune character of their judicial status radically redressed. For the first time, they were held subordinate to the jurisdiction of the county courts. Privileges, moreover, granting landowners and serfs an exemption from these local forums were, in their entirety, "revoked, struck through and considered to hold neither power nor validity."[16] At the same time, the opportunities available to the great magnates of the realm to exercise a control over the operation of the county courts were removed and the process whereby local officials were appointed by the *universitas* of county nobility given direct encouragement by the King.[17]

Even though the six million acres of the Hunyadi patrimony afforded Matthias a financial self-sufficiency equalled only by that of the early Árpád kings, innovations aimed at bolstering royal revenues were still embarked upon. To this end, the support of the Diet was earned. In 1478 and in a remarkable "self-denying" ordinance, the Diet even permitted the monarch to raise extraordinary royal taxes without any reference to itself.[18] Nonetheless, in other financial matters, there was displayed the same disregard for established rights as characterises also Matthias's reform of judicial procedures. A new impost, the *tributum fisci regalis,* was instituted to replace existing taxation systems. Applied as a tax on households and not simply groundplots, yet collected from peasants and nobility without any reference to earlier won exemptions, the levy of the *tributum* excited a revolt which only with difficulty was suppressed.[19]

Royal indifference for established rights spilled over into the affairs of the townsfolk. Certainly, in contrast to developments occurring at this time in the countryside, no calculated assault on municipal freedoms was intended. Unlike the barons, the urban communities represented little threat to the monarchy. Generally, they remained aloof from the realm's opposition movements. When drawn into political struggles, the towns largely sided with the Crown offering military and financial support when requested. Indeed, for both town troops and credit Matthias and his successors were at times grateful.[20] Programmes directed at reducing municipal autonomy were in the political context of the period largely unnecessary. Nonetheless, the towns proved unable to withstand altogether the effects brought about by an upsurge in royal authority. Household officials rendered newly powerful by the King might overstep the limits of their competence in a manner injurious to town freedoms. Such clearly happened in Debrecen and Pozsony and in both cases a redress of grievances had needs be sought from the Crown.[21] More particularly though, the monarch in the pursuit of other interests might choose to ignore such town rights as impeded the proper fulfillment of his objectives. Although these interests were largely financial, jurisdictional prerogatives of Town Councils might as a consequence suffer redress. This development is, unsurprisingly, most marked in the context of Town Jewry. For, despite the rights entrusted municipal Councils in the adjudication and treatment of Jews, considerable irregularities here persisted. In cases conjointly involving Jews and nobility, the jurisdictional competence of the Judge of All Jews was involved. Moreover, Jews continued paying special taxes of their own to the monarch. Never fully integrated within the ambit of municipal jurisdiction, the Jews' final removal from the competence of the Town Councils and subordination to agents of the monarch was greatly facilitated.

During the second half of the fifteenth century the status of the realm's Jews noticeably underwent sharper clarification. For the first time, charters repeatedly stressed the position of the Jews as but a part of the royal *camera*.[22] Chancellery marks on these same instruments suggest that a keener interest in Jewish affairs was displayed by household officials otherwise closely involved in the administration of the royal fisc.[23] Procedural revisions affecting Jewish jurisdiction developed in accompaniment. Earlier, all actions conjointly involving Jews and citizens had passed directly before the Town Councils for adjudication. Now, however, differing judicial methods were employed and former Council prerogatives ignored. Thus, while actions initiated by Jews against Christian citizens continued to be taken before the town authorities, cases wherein the Jew himself was defendant were in 1499 removed completely from municipal jurisdiction. Hereafter, Jews might be prosecuted only in the presence of the Buda Castellan, appointed by the King. Appeals from his court were to be directed to the royal Tavernicus.[24]

This circumscription of jurisdictional rights formerly vested in Town Councils largely reflects the impact of changes made in regard to Jewish tax collection. In the past, Town Councils had alone administered the raising from Jewish townspeople of the special royal tax, the *census iudeorum*. In the performance of this task Councils were even permitted to distrain the property of reluctant Jewish taxpayers.[25] Matthias, however, as part of a more general attempt to centralise the collection of royal revenues, greatly modified established procedures. The post of Prefect of the Jews was instituted and this figure entrusted alone with the assessment and collection of all Jewish taxes.[26] Peculiar discrepancies in the Treasury accounts for this period suggest that these monies were for the most part paid directly to the King's Bailiff so bypassing the more baronially controlled Treasury apparatus.[27] After the establishment of the Prefecture, Town Councils played only a minor role in the raising of the Jewish tax simply assisting, when called upon, the Prefect in the completion of his duties.[28] It seems, moreover, probable that around this time also the obligation of Jewish residents to pay additional property taxes to the municipal authorities was limited by royal decree.[29] Both legally and financially the Jews were, thus, put outside the ambit of municipal jurisdiction. This development affected in particular fifteenth century Buda in which was concentrated much of the realm's Jewish population.[30]

During the sixteenth century, as the new Jagiello monarchy, which in 1490 replaced that of the Hunyadis, found itself increasingly subject to financial constraints, so it became tempting to encroach yet further into the towns privileged taxation system. Throughout the medieval period municipal Councils had alone possessed the right to raise taxes from their respective citizenries.

Revenues due to the monarch were collected by town officials and tithe payments delivered in a lump sum to local ecclesiastical lords. Already weakened, however, by developments in the collection of Jewish taxes, during the early sixteenth century the prerogatives of the Councils in the whole area of municipal taxation came yet further to be diminished. In 1521 a Diet held near Buda proclaimed at the royal behest the levy of a new impost to be raised not simply on the basis of landed wealth, but including also a tax on drink, beasts of burden, artisan workshops, merchant incomes, even, as it turned out, millstones and fishing nets. The collection of this tax was entrusted to representatives of the estates appointed by the Diet. Their competence was not restricted to the countryside but extended also to the privileged urban communities. Protests were duly lodged by the already financially hard-hit Councils but seemingly to little avail. When in 1523 the new taxation system was suspended, the explanation given was not one of jurisdictional impropriety but rather of widespread corruption.[31]

Interests other than financial ones might also cause urban liberties to be set aside. During the Jagiello period, as the monarchy sought the renewed support of the Diet, concessions at the expense of town rights had regularly to be made in order to placate the nobility.[32] The conflict between royal objectives and established municipal freedoms reached, however, quite unprecendented heights in late fifteenth century Buda. During a period when little consideration was paid to local rights, the proximity of the palace, in which Matthias and his successors were long resident, afforded Buda a particular vulnerability.[33] This might at times touch seemingly absurd proportions. Thus, for instance, in 1478 Matthias found himself much irritated by the general shabbiness of the town. In his displeasure, he immediately threatened a confiscation of all citizen properties left in a condition of disrepair.[34] No trivial instance, the heavy penalty threatened by the King lay in direct contravention of the town's earliest charter. Still beyond this, as other local rights came into conflict with the royal will, so no less than almost a half of those clauses which had been written into the 1244 charter and held relevance in the context of this later period were, in their turn, subjected to royal abuse. In 1468 the town's freedom from the obligation of quartering distinguished visitors was called into question.[35] Again, in 1492, and in an early attempt to buy their support, King Vlászló II freed the nobility resident in Buda from the duty of paying taxes to the Council.[36] Later on, in the sixteenth century, Louis II despatched his own servants and *homines regii* to inspect cloth prices in the town and invested these officials with the right to arrest citizen profiteers.[37]

Royal disregard for municipal freedoms might, however, be conducted on a more enduring level than these four isolated examples suggest. The right of the citizenry to elect its own priest, the incumbent of Our Blessed Lady's, had been bestowed by royal charter during the thirteenth century. Although in effect, appointment to this office was according to the *Stadtrecht,* made by the Council, the wishes of the townsfolk had needs be taken into consideration. From the middle of the fifteenth century, however, the King himself secured a major influence over appointments. Vacancies were filled by agents of the royal court who found financial support in the handsome revenues pertaining to this priestly office.[38] In 1454, the Vice-Chancellor of Hungary, Nicolas Varius, was town priest of Buda.[39] He was succeeded a few years later by Ladislas V's Austrian Chancellor, Stephen Aloch.[40] Between 1467 and 1490 Buda's parish priest was no less a person than King Matthias's favourite astrologer, the theologian Martin of Ilkusch.[41] Nor should these instances of disregard for Buda's rights be conceived of as but casual or accidental errors on the part of the King. Quite clearly, as Matthias's Chancellor Gabriel explained in a quite formidable statement of royal prerogatives, the monarch felt himself entitled, when the need arose, to override the *ius* of Buda town.[42] Indeed, by this term may be understood not simply the provisions of the town's charter, but also of customary law itself.[43]

Certainly, the indifference shown for the rights contained in Buda's 1244 charter hardly inflicted significant damage to the town's institutional life. In its relationship to the citizenry, the prerogatives of the Council suffered little redress. Likewise, no lasting inroads were made into the independent governmental and judicial life of the town. To a degree, this is unremarkable. Even towns which lost their free status during the fifteenth century and underwent mediatisation often maintained the form and institutions of government they had acquired during the preceding period. Their new relationship to a local landowner was simply expressed in the payment to him of certain feudal revenues and in the direction to his court of actions appealed from the municipal Council. Nevertheless though and as we shall see, the encroachment of royal power in Buda might yet exercise a profound effect upon deeper historical developments.

During the fourteenth century, the Council had increased its jurisdictional competence over the smaller independent organisations existing within the physical confines of the town. The extent of Council authority had, thus, become coterminous with the actual geographical bounds of medieval Buda. As both a legal and territorial entity, the *civitas* was united with a single immune identity under the jurisdiction of the Council. But, during the second half of the fifteenth century, as royal authority encroached further into the town, this earlier development was strikingly reversed.

By the early fifteenth century the Buda fishermen dwelling in the riverside Viziváros suburb had become jurisdictionally subordinate to the Town Council. Although perhaps they still continued to provide the royal court occasionally with produce,[44] in all other respects they had been relegated to little more than the level of a craft guild. During the later fifteenth century, however, in a quite remarkable development, memory of the fishermen's erstwhile condition was recalled and their status as royal *conditionarii* newly affirmed. Here some parallel with changes affecting the status of the town's Jews may be drawn. Thus, in 1474, a charter issued by King Matthias refers to the fishers of the Buda suburb as pertaining *"ad nostrum regale pallacium."* A letter of the same year speaks, likewise, of the *"piscatorum regalium."*[45] Addressed to, among others, the Castle Bailiff of Buda, this letter suggests that it was to his authority that the fishermen were made subject. At this time, many surviving groups of *conditionarii* within the realm were being made subordinate to the Bailiff.[46] Moreover, the fishermen's special relationship to the royal palace, as pronounced upon in the 1474 charter, together with the role they played in satisfying the court's huge demand for fish, further suggest close contacts with the Bailiff.[47] Almost certainly, as was the case with the sailors of Pest, the Bailiff exercised a judicial authority over the fishermen.[48] Thus, once more they became legally exempt from the jurisdiction of the Town Council. It was, moreover, usual at this time for groups of *conditionarii* subject to the Castle Bailiff to pay their taxes to the monarch directly through this official. Less than the royal *census* imposed on the townsfolk and collected by the Council, it was of clear advantage to the fishermen to have payments levied on them no longer by the town but rather by the Bailiff.[49]

During the second half of the fifteenth century, the exercise of monarchical power, thus, not only caused basic principles enshrined in the town's charter to be set aside. Evidently, with the expansion of royal authority, a detrimental effect was exercised also upon earlier processes associated with the fuller development of the jurisdictional notion of urban immune status. Nevertheless, the monarchy proved by no means a force gradually encroaching into the town at the expense of Council authority. For in the ideological sphere royal prestige acted not so much as a constraint but rather as a focus to municipal aspirations. In this development, particular conceptual problems introduced by the 1439–40 innovations in town government exercised a significant influence.

Municipal Ideology

Already, during the early decades of the century, basic conceptions influencing the overall notion of the burgher association were suffering alteration and redefinition. The traditional bond between the citizens and their magistracy became threatened as, betwixt these two bodies, new associations interposed themselves. As a result, the established lines of power and authority in the town were much disturbed. The presence of any association existing amongst the citizenry and within the fabric of the burgher association itself was recognised as a menace by the author of the *Stadtrecht*. Such associations fundamentally denied the contractual principles upon which the idea of citizenship rested. For, through membership of any additional body, the citizen recognised new responsibilities and duties which could in time only conflict with the obligations he owed to the burgher association as a whole. Hence, in the *Stadtrecht*, the categorical prohibition of any "brotherhood . . . combination . . . or assembly" followed directly upon a pronouncement of those terms under which citizenship right might be obtained.[50] Membership, thus, of any additional associative organisation represented a denial of the citizen's obligations owed to the burgher association, of which also he was a member.

The tendency of citizens to found amongst themselves new unions and associations could not, however, be restricted. Thus, although principally a religious society and social club, the *Corpus Christi* Brotherhood possessed its own seal and held the status of a corporation.[51] The craft guilds, despite having no seals of their own, enjoyed, likewise, a full corporate identity. They were able to acquire their own properties and administer their own finances. Like the town itself, the guilds were administered by elected masters acting in the name of the union as a whole. The collective will of the guild might also extend to the institution of bye-laws and regulations treating upon the conditions under which the individual was not only to exercise his craft but even to order his own private life.[52]

The increasing economic power gained by the guilds combined with the regular advancement of their members to high office within the town won for these associations a new political significance. According to the *Stadtrecht*, guild masters were to be consulted in all major decisions affecting the life of the community.[53] In 1421, it is recorded in the *Stadtrecht* that guildsmen participated in deliberations with the Council leading to the promulgation of commercial legislation.[54] The new role assumed by the guilds in the political life of the town achieved further recognition in the procedures followed on election day. Like the town councillors, it was on 23 April that the guild masters were elected by the craftsmen. Together with the appointed Judge and sworn men of the town, the new masters vowed before the assembled populace to minister to the needs of both the guildsmen and the community of townsfolk.[55]

These developments suggest that Buda's constitution was during the early decades of the fifteenth century advancing very much in the direction of what has been recently termed the "corporate federation."[56] The shape of municipal government was experiencing a transformation as additional powers were vested in the smaller unions existing within the wider framework of the burgher association. The later *Laws and Customs of the Seven Towns,* in the drafting of which Buda's own constitutional arrangements exercised a powerful influence, suggest a possible culmination to this process. Here the crucial right of the citizen to participate in Council elections was abrogated. Instead, guild masters now came exclusively to exercise this privilege.[57] Again, in 1488, when the leading burghers of Kolozsvár approached the Buda Council for a written outline of the town's constitution for themselves to follow, there was suggested a similar displacement in municipal elections of the citizens by the corporations of craftsmen.[58]

The gradual movement towards a constitution based upon the principles of corporate federation was disturbed by the 1439 revolt and the reforms of town government which closely followed. In attempting to maintain social harmony within the town, the already weakened notion of *unitas civium,* upon which the associative idea rested, had now almost entirely to be abandoned. Thus, in place of a single burgher *communitas,* the presence of two distinct *communitates,* out of which Hungarian and German councillors were to be equally chosen, was formally admitted.[59] Certainly, in so far as the Council remained a single administrative organ and was still held legally to represent the townsfolk *universitas,* some semblance of burgher unity was preserved. But the new system of appointing councillors with its division of Council and electoral college on national lines gave in this ideologically crucial matter institutional recognition to the now plural character of the burgher association. Significantly also, as the councillors sought to perpetuate their own power within the town, new "electoral" procedures had to be introduced which ignored the citizenry altogether. Membership of the electoral college, the Committee of One Hundred, was determined by the outgoing Council. This body alone was entrusted with the right to determine the succeeding Judge and *iurati.*

Such a system of appointments fundamentally disturbed the principles upon which the authority of the Council rested. Election day and the assembling of the burghers to choose their magistrates was abolished and, therewith, the visible link formerly binding the Council to the conceptual source of its power, the citizenry, was severed. Certainly, a constitution based fully upon the notion of corporate federation would likewise have dealt a death-blow to the old electoral process. However, in such a constitution, the old lines of power were not so much torn up as sublimated. Guild membership was dependent upon the former acquisition of citizenship right. The guild held a corporate identity and its masters were elected by the craftsmen. Even though probably only a portion of the citizenry could have been also guild members, through the masters' election of a Council some vestige of the old bond linking government and citizenry might have been preserved.

In contrast, the system established in 1439–40 held no such redeeming qualities. Certainly, the term *communitas* was applied to the two national groups in Buda as well as the Committee of One Hundred itself. These *communitates,* however, entirely lacked any corporate structure. Outside their function in appointing a Council, they remained only fictional bodies not having any independent legal existence of their own. Membership of the Committee rested alone upon the favour of the outgoing Council and the principal criterion for selection was clearly not citizenship but nationality. Indeed, as the outline of Buda's constitution given in 1488 to Kolozsvár suggests, members of the Committee of One Hundred might themselves be mere *incolae:* residents of the town not even holding citizen status.[60]

Consequentially, the authority wielded by the Council could no longer be considered to derive from the burgher association. In Ladislas IV's privilege of 1276, the principle had been enunciated that every year the Judge "resigned his power into the hands of the citizenry." By the third quarter of the fifteenth century, however, this notion had undergone a clear transformation and, in seeming parody, it was declared that governmental power was merely "resigned into the hands of the Committee of One Hundred."[61] In recognition of this new ideological deficiency, the *intitulatio* formula on patents issued by the Council suffered alteration. From the early fourteenth century, the Judge and Council had on all patent letters associated their writ with the collective will of the people—hence the formula *"Nos. N. Judex Castri Novi Montis Pestiensis/*alternatively *civitatis Budensis/Jurati ac universi cives de eodem memorie commendamus, quod etc."* Strikingly from the middle years of the fifteenth century reference to the *"universi cives"* becomes omitted entirely from the *intitulatio.* Patents were hereafter issued solely in the name of the Judge and sworn men—*"Nos N. Judex Juratique cives Novi Montis Pestiensis memorie commendamus, quod etc."* [62]

This evident lack of source for the Council's authority in Buda was compounded by new developments in the wider field of political ideology. In 1440, for the first time, substance was given to the old claim raised by the estates of the realm that they held the right to elect their own monarch. The untimely death of the heirless Albert of Habsburg provided the circumstances whereby the Hungarian Diet was able to choose its own monarch—the Polish

King, Wladislas III (Wladislas or Vlászló I of Hungary). Hereafter, the Diet's claim to be able to select its own monarch irrespective of *a priori* hereditary claims became the more entrenched finding further expression in the 1458 election of Matthias Hunyadi. Again, political literature reflecting the populist principles of Roman Law entered not only the realm but the towns of Hungary. In Pozsony, Kassa, Eperjes, Bártfa and Nagyszombat, copies of Raymundus Parthenopeius's *Summa Legum* made their appearance.[63] In Buda, likewise, this work became also available. In 1489, the merchant and town councillor, Nicolas Ebendorffer, transcribed the *Summa Legum* for the benefit of himself and his sons. Quite probably it was Ebendorffer's intention that this work be widely disseminated. For that purpose he appended two important statutes treating upon the operation of the Tavernical Court and even modified place-names in the text to make the work more agreeable to a Hungarian audience.[64] The principal feature of the *Summa Legum* is the emphasis it places upon the popular origin of governmental authority. Power was vested in both legislative and executive organs in order that the common good might be maintained. In this respect, Parthenopeius rejected the Thomist perspective of his former mentor, Aegidius Colonna, who had held that a centralisation of authority was part of the natural order.[65]

Political developments outside the town and the appearance of the *Summa Legum* within only served further to accentuate the ideological deficiencies inherent in the new constitution. The Council, plainly no longer viewing itself as vested with an authority deriving from the citizen body, had needs justify the power it wielded within the town. Already, as the remarks of the Chancellor Gabriel make clear, the monarch felt in Buda well empowered with the legal right to erase the principles of town *ius* and, in his own interests, to circumscribe popularly defined customary laws. The visible encroachments of royal authority underwrit these theoretical powers claimed by the monarch. Not surprisingly then, in a seeming endorsement of royal might, the Council increasingly sought to legitimise its authority by reference to the King.

The *Laws and Customs of the Seven Towns* well reveal the depth to which the idea had penetrated that the source of governmental authority in Buda lay no longer with the citizenry but rather with the monarch. Town government was held to possess no special quality of its own save that some electoral process was allowed by generous concession of the King. The appointment of magistrates was only permitted by dint of royal charter; hence as an act it was held irredeemably bound up with the person of His Majesty. More significantly, the judicial authority of the Council was considered to derive exclusively from the monarch. In contrast to the older notion that the Council adjudicated in the name of the citizen community, the principle was firmly expounded that all judgments were administered "on behalf of and in place of His Majesty."[66] Seemingly then, not only was the associative idea greatly undercut in fifteenth century Buda but dispensed with entirely as the conceptual source of Council power. In its place, notions of royal authority were advanced to justify the town's departure from an "ascending" theory of government.

Developments in Buda during the second half of the fifteenth century echo social trends evident earlier in the town's history. Then, amongst the town's patriciate, the wealthy were drawn through the system of royal patronage away from the ranks of the Council *potentes*. Thus, as a direct result of influences brought to bear by the monarchy, social patterns established during the fourteenth century fell into abeyance. In the wake of this followed a revolt which, in its turn, made necessary some reform of town government. Deficiencies inherent in the new constitution and the gradual abrogation of the associative principle argued though for alterations in the notion of Council power. Here, once again, royal prestige and might exercised a potent influence overturning accepted notions of Council power. In this respect, the upsurge in royal authority which characterises the Hunyadi period and particularly affected the legal rights of medieval Buda was made manifest in municipal ideology.

Nonetheless, the troubles experienced by fifteenth century Buda cannot be chronologically isolated and interpreted simply in the context of the peculiar conditions imposed on this period by internal social pressures and a sudden expansion of royal power. Rather, these developments reflect back on the town and, repeating one of the lessons of the Rectoral period, suggest once again that the structure of municipal autonomy built up over the preceding century was of a fragile character. As in the thirteenth century, so in the fifteenth, the monarch evidently felt well able to override the town's chartered rights and subordinate these to his own interests. Moreover, basic principles involving the associative idea and popular notions of Council authority, seemingly fundamental to medieval town life, could yet be jettisoned in Buda. In place of these and in response to new political forces touching the town, notions of royal authority were invoked to fill the ideological vacuum. Well might, therefore, Buda's privilege and institutional arrangements argue for a divorce of town from realm. Contrastingly though, it would seem that such a formal separation of the two organisms proved hard to maintain. Evidently, the sheer scope and magnificence of royal authority, symbolised in the Schedel woodcut, could cut through existing barriers and in so doing upset the humbler independent life of the town.

It is during the thirteenth and late fifteenth centuries that a basic imbalance in the town's relations to the monarch registers itself most dramatically. A display of royal disregard for Buda's established freedoms is clearly manifested in both periods. But, even if the most obvious, these developments are by no means exceptional, indicating but temporary collisions between, on the one hand, the reality of royal power and, on the other, the principle of urban independence. For throughout the intervening period and beyond, agents of the monarch were in his name steadily involving themselves in the activity of municipal jurisdiction. Actually welcomed at times by the townsfolk, as the limits of their competence came to be closely defined, so a formal bond was established linking together the otherwise unrelated royal and municipal administrations. Highly significant for the history of medieval Buda, it is a study of the King's Tavernicus, the most important agent of royal power on a municipal level, which proves also the most revealing. Detailed discussion of his court brings more sharply into relief those contradictions, already suggested in this chapter, which remained inherent not only within the governmental and jurisdictional history of medieval Buda, but of Hungary's towns as a whole.

Chapter 7

PRAESENTIA REGIA AND TAVERNICAL JURISDICTION

Justiciar and Tavernicus

In 1333 the burgher Kunclin, a prominent member of Buda's patrician family of Kunc, bought from his cousin, Jacob, a plenteous estate to the north-west of the town.[1] A fine property and well drained, it was liberally bestowed with gardens, vineyards and arable land. None objected to the new owner's rights of purchase and documents attesting to the legality of Kunclin's possession were drawn up by both the Buda Council and the nearby Hospitaller convent at Felhéviz. Set nearby their own lands, the Hospitallers soon cast envious eyes on Kunclin's prosperous estate. In 1343 claims were raised against him and according to "custom of the realm" *recaptivatio* procedures embarked upon.[2] Kunclin was formally reintroduced to his possession and an objection forthwith lodged by the Hospitallers. The Buda Chapter which had overseen the *statutio* despatched the matter for adjudication before the "royal presence" *(praesentia regia)*. Here the case was taken up by the King's Tavernicus or, to give him his full title, *Magister Tavernicorum*—at that time Thomas, Count of Szepes and Újvár. But he, "having seen the letters drawn up and concerning the liberty of the aforesaid town of Buda," handed back the case to the Buda Council. No doubt, Thomas' attention had been directed to the clause in the 1244 charter asserting that the town magistrate should adjudicate in all of the burghers' "secular affairs" and in accordance with this principle set aside his own rights of judgment in the matter.

On March 12, 1343, Geubul *Litteratus* acting on behalf of the Hospitallers presented himself before the Town Council. The defendant, Kunclin, was also in attendance. As attorney, Geubul offered in support of the plaintiffs' claim three privileges all of which were transcripts. Not surprisingly, in view of the problem of widespread forgery, Kunclin demanded that the originals be shown for inspection. The action was accordingly prorogued and after much

127

bother the first day of July set for the resumption of the case. At this juncture and at the apparent request of the Hospitallers, the King in advance ordered an inquisition to be undertaken on the morning of that day. The results were to be relayed to the Council in the afternoon and on their basis a judgment fashioned. The Hospitallers, however, quite failed to notify the town of these new arrangements. Thus, on July 1, Kunclin and the Council spent a frustrating morning in session vainly awaiting the arrival of the plaintiffs who, for their part, thought that proceedings were to begin in the afternoon. At last Kunclin rose up, accusing the Hospitallers of neglect and contumacy. He demanded an immediate judgment given out "as was the customary law of the town" before the session closed for the day at lunchtime. After briefly conferring, the Council ruled that in the absence of the Hospitallers, their attorneys and any explanatory notes, the case was by default awarded to Kunclin and his defence considered upheld. Perpetual silence was now imposed on the seemingly disrespectful plaintiffs.

Shortly afterwards however, the Council and townsfolk were apprised of the real reasons lying behind the Hospitallers' absence. Clearly, now doubts might be raised about the validity of the verdict and pressure be exerted to have the case reopened. Moreover, since the text of the royal letter originally sent to the Hospitallers had assumed that the Council held sessions during the afternoon, which it did not, some royal disregard for town *consuetudo* was imagined by the anxious burghers. Matters reached a head on 5 July. King Louis returning from a hunt entered the town and the citizenry pressed for an audience. Their leaders declared that it was one of Buda's basic liberties that those summoned before the Council should appear and exhibit any documents pertinent to their case before midday. Failure to observe this principle could, so they said, result in a party losing his case. Louis, much embarrassed, admitted that he had unwittingly contravened town custom and put both parties in an awkward situation. However, he noted that the Hospitallers had signally failed to inform the town of his request for an afternoon session and, thus, apportioned to them a sizeable share of the blame. Nevertheless, so as to resolve the matter once and for all and ensure the town was conserved in its liberties, the King redirected the case back to the Tavernicus for final adjudication. By this time, however, the Hospitallers, realising the inadequacies of their claim and smarting under Louis's criticism, had come into private agreement with Kunclin. They withdrew their plaint altogether in exchange for a reassessment of their tithe rights.

Although in the course of this dispute, the royal Tavernicus was only involved on two brief occasions, the Hospitallers' action against Kunclin well illustrates those types of action arising out of the more problematic areas of municipal jurisdiction which were in time to pass with increasing regularity before his court. The neat separation of town from realm outlined by the foundation charters and pursued in the development of municipal institutions proved, as this instance makes clear, impossible to maintain on an everyday level. Besides Kunclin, many other burghers held estates outside the town and, likewise, clergy and nobility owned extensive properties within. Between the town and the countryside, the passage of goods and persons also presented obvious jurisdictional difficulties. Serfs, moreover, drifted into Buda and the other towns of the realm, drawn by the *Stadtluft* of freedom. Regularly, their outraged masters declared them to have been seized by the townsfolk and demanded immediate redress.[3]

In such cases, clear lines of jurisdictional demarcation were plainly necessary and yet strangely lacking. Even the most basic geographical notions set to define the limits of the Town Councils' authority remained questionable. Thus, for instance, Szomolnokbánya's claim that both its citizenry and Council enjoyed rights within a territory extending up to two miles beyond the city walls, "as is the custom in other towns," was rejected by local nobles much aggrieved at this extension of town rights at their own expense.[4] Equally illustrative is the confusing sequence of events in the Kunclin case outlined above. Initially the case was opened according to custom of the realm in a procedure which suggests that both parties felt the affair to lie outside the bounds of municipal law and jurisdiction. Yet after first proceeding to the *curia,* the matter was transmitted to the Council since this organ was considered on the basis of the 1244 charter to hold *a priori* rights of adjudication. But at this point no further action should technically have been possible. Kunclin had held his estate uncontested for ten years; the town's privilege provided for a *praescriptio* period of only one year after which time a burgher might possess a property "in peace and quiet without objection."[5]

Regularly, in matters wherein individual citizens were plaintiffs and the problems of jurisdictional demarcation less intense, recourse might be had to the accepted procedure of *actor sequitur forum rei*—the common sense dictum normally applied in cases where conflicts of judicial competence were involved.[6] Thus, for instance, in 1394 two *hospites* of Buda directed their complaint against the Castellan of Sempte before the defendant's master, the Count of Pozsony. Again, in 1438 the county court of Bodrog judged in the matter of the unlawful possession of a horse, seized by a local serf and belonging to Gaspar, citizen of Pest. As we have already seen, similar procedures were embarked upon in actions initiated by Jews against Christians.[7] However, in cases wherein citizens were by contrast themselves defendants the standard form of *actor sequitur* proved less easy to apply—even though town charters had repeatedly stressed that citizens might only be impleaded before municipal Councils.[8] For, and this held particular significance in criminal cases, the giving of evidence by outsiders at sessions of town courts was seriously restricted by the urban charters. As is enunciated in Buda's 1244 privilege, the testimony of witnesses was only deemed acceptable in the event of the witness being himself of the rank of citizen. This was not, as at first might seem, an attempt to disadvantage outsiders in the prosecution of their claims. Rather it was a recognition of the problem of status which could seriously affect such notions as the quality of evidence being given.[9] Standard expedients such as the duel were, moreover, quite forbidden in the towns.[10] Just as the provisions of the town charters had facilitated the introduction of customary procedures, so local *consuetudo* itself prompted further difficulties. Although by no means devised to cause injury to parties from without the town, the differing and often arcane procedures followed in the towns might leave outsiders unaware of their legal rights and obligations—as indeed the Hospitallers found to their cost.

As developments within this dispute suggest, notions of town custom and liberty might easily cause the town as a single corporate unit to be drawn into an action originally only involving individual members of the citizenry. In fourteenth-century Pozsony, the arrest of the local garrison for rape and speedy execution of some of their number rapidly resulted in a legal enquiry into the terms of the town's charter with the Council assuming therein the role of defendant.[11] The hanging by the town of Bars of a gang of local brigands, foolish enough to have paraded themselves in the clothes of their victims, likewise provoked an indictment against the Council and citizenry together with a full examination of the *"lex privilegiata ipsius civitatis"* by which the townsfolk sought to justify their use of the death penalty.[12] The early circumstances surrounding the establishment of Hungary's towns added further complications. Founded on the top of existing legal rights and privileges pertaining to older institutions, aggressively defending their newly won *libertas* and immune jurisdictional character, the towns found themselves increasingly involved as corporate entities in litigation. Clear procedures for the resolution of these types of dispute were never enunciated in the majority of charters. Indeed, in the case of Buda, certain chartered rights awarded the town by the monarch only made more pressing the need for some form of jurisdictional mechanism through which indictments might be laid against the Council and citizen *universitas.*

Thus, an undated privilege preserved in a late fifteenth century transcript but probably owing its origin to the thirteenth century allowed the town the right not only to arrest criminals found within the precincts of the town but, moreover, to seize malefactors dwelling "outside our territory," quite ignoring, therefore, the *a priori* jurisdictional claims of other bodies.[13] Similar rights were awarded the northern town of Eperjes.[14] Hence in 1339 and in accordance with this principle, Jacob, son of Nicolas, acting on behalf of the Buda Council, broke into a local abbey vineyard and for various unspecified offences arrested and carried off a serf who had been working there. The serf's master, the abbot of St. Benedict's-by-Gron, complained bitterly to the King of this action and proceedings against the town were embarked upon. For the abbot, by virtue of his lordly status, viewed himself as possessing the principal rights of judgment in the matter and resented Buda's violent, if theoretically permissable, intrusion into these rights—not to mention his vineyard.[15]

Certainly, in the resolution of disputes involving towns as corporate units in litigation, approaches might at times be made to the agencies of county justice. In 1406 at a *congregatio* held in Abaújvár and Sáros counties the Judge of Szeben appeared raising on behalf of his town a complaint against some local landowners.[16] Nevertheless, such instances are but rare events. The townsfolk bore a not unnatural mistrust of the county tribunals, largely opposing any attempts at citation before them or, as in the case of the burghers of Székesfehérvár called before the county court of Komárom, altogether refusing to recognise the county authority.[17] Occasionally involved in this area of litigation were the local ecclesiastical chapters acting in the purely *ad hoc* capacity of arbitrators.[18]

The infrequency, though, with which cases involving towns as corporate units actually proceeded before these local organs reflects their general ineffectiveness. Mistrusted by the townsfolk with whom they invariably had a conflict of interests, the local tribunals were, furthermore, ill equipped for this sort of litigation. They were largely unable to oblige the attendance of the individual parties involved in an action. The competence of a county court ran at best no further than the borders of that county and its writ held no force in a town.[19] In the absence of specific royal mandates an effective judicial operation was denied the religious houses. Moreover, it proved difficult for these bodies to enforce their decisions unless both parties had prior to judgment paid a substantial cash *vinculum* which might be forfeited in the event of contumacy.[20] Arbitration was then, in the words of Buda's *Stadtrecht,* only effective "among good people," freely disposed towards "a friendly judgment."[21]

The inadequacies of the local forums only made an approach to the royal *curia* more attractive. Of this development (the younger) Szentpétery has written, "To whom, then, could the townsman turn? Who recognised his customary law and might be hoped to offer goodwill? The burgher class had mostly been established by the King; he had given and confirmed their privileges and taken the citizenry under his special protection. The burghers, thus, turned to the King for remedy. For it was he in particular who was the highest judge and source of law in the land."[22] Certainly, Szentpétery's rhetoric may be deemed to find some support in the approach made by the citizens of Buda to King Louis returning from his hunt in 1343. Nonetheless, the rarity with which the townsfolk actually succeeded in having their plaint heard by the King in person suggests more complex forces at work. By the fourteenth century a well functioning administrative machine operating in the name of the monarch had developed in the kingdom. This was maintained even in the grimmest days of the succeeding period lending thereby the semblance of authority to princes who personally might hold little real power of their own. High judges of the *curia* took charge of all the realm's most important judicial business, hearing appeals from the seigneurial and county courts and administering their decisions and commands through the local *loca credibilia*. In contrast to the humbler forums, justices of the *curia* were through their rights of summons able to fine and pass sentence in default of attendance and coerce to their courts not only countryfolk but townsmen as well—despite the protestations of various Councils that such rights were contrary to their towns' liberties.[23] Judgments given out and foolishly ignored might, moreover, be enforced by the application of physical pressures. In December 1403, in support of a royal decision forbidding the continued existence of an illegal Town Council in Buda, troops from the palace garrison were seemingly deployed.[24] Thus, with no other satisfactory recourse available, the townsfolk were inevitably sucked into the powerful and effective central judicial organisation of the realm. Long established procedures were accordingly applied to the trickier areas of municipal jurisdiction and problematic cases directed before the "royal presence" or *praesentia regia.*

Following the early separation of the Palatine's office from the *curia* and his assumption of the role of royal representative at a county level, the Justiciar, or, to give him his proper title, the *Iudex Curiae,* emerged as the principal court official acting in a *praesentia regia* capacity. *"Ad praesentiam regiam seu iudicis curiae suae"* ran the contemporary phraseology. The Justiciar operated *"(regis) tribunalis apice"* and in 1327 this official reckoned his position to be that of the greatest of the ordinaries of the land.[25] As late as 1390 by which time the overall authority of the Justiciar had suffered some decline, the competence of his jurisdiction was still defined on the basis of customary procedure as embracing all cases brought before the royal person.[26] Since this declaration was itself the product of a case involving the Justiciar, Emerich Bubek, and the burghers of Kassa, it seems evident that the *praesen-*

tia regia authority of the Justiciar extended to the townsfolk as well. Moreover, a letter written by the Esztergom Primatial Chapter and sent to the Bishop of Győr in 1325 complaining of the general misbehaviour of the local citizens noted the close legal relationship which existed between the townsmen, King and Justiciar.[27] That these were no mere empty legal formulae may be adduced from a succession of case histories wherein the Justiciar may be seen to act in the affairs of the townsfolk as the *praesentia regia,* passing judgment *verbo regio.*[28] Not surprisingly, therefore, as the pre-eminent court official acting in a *praesentia regia* capacity, it was the Justiciar who during the period of reform in the 1370's was by implication to adopt the title *Iudex universarum civitatum Hungariae.*[29]

However, the pre-eminence of the Justiciar in disputes involving the towns and passing before the "royal presence" was to a large degree illusory. For there emerged from an early stage a tendency for those cases which involved the townsfolk and were brought to the *curia* for adjudication to be despatched not before the Justiciar, but a lesser court official: the Tavernicus. In this development, the case *Hospitallers v. Kunclin* represents an early but by no means exceptional example.[30] This tendency was, moreover, to receive some indirect sanction in a number of charters granted to towns during the fourteenth century. Hence, in impeachment procedure, the community might direct a case to either the "royal presence" or Tavernicus. In this respect, the formula *"in praesentiam regiam vel Magistri Tavernicorum"* replaced the older clause found on such documents as Buda's 1244 charter, *"coram illo, cui duxerimus committendum."*[31] Statutory approval of these new developments reached a high point in 1405 when in the *Decretum Minus* of that year Sigismund laid down that the Tavernicus be regarded as the principal royal official responsible for actions arising out of the realm's towns.[32]

The decree of 1405, by its formal separation of the Tavernical office from the royal *curia* and creation of a separate structure for municipal pleas, may be considered as largely bringing to a close the significance of *praesentia regia* jurisdiction in so far as it affected the kingdom's towns.[33] However, well before this date, it is evident that the Tavernicus possessed a *praesentia regia* authority in municipal affairs which put him on an equal level to the Justiciar.[34] When, therefore, the Hospitallers' dispute with Kunclin was first directed to the royal *curia,* the affair passed immediately into the hands of the Tavernicus. Indeed, the transmission formula employed within the text of these proceedings, *"ad regiam presenciam . . . in causam attraxisset,"* was itself a direct borrowing from the legal phraseology normally found in documents issued by the Justiciar.[35] Seemingly so great was the identification of Tavernicus with "royal presence" that one testimonial relating to the case was even to confuse Tavernicus with King, attributing to the latter actions which the former had really undertaken.[36] Similar circumstances surround a whole series of actions arising out of the towns which destined for the "royal presence" were immediately taken up by the Tavernicus.[37] On this basis, it would appear that the Tavernicus operated as an authority parallel to the Justiciar in such affairs as proceeded *praesentia regia* and touched upon the affairs of the townsfolk. Indeed, this parallel status on occasions even appears to extend itself to that of superiority. In 1357 King Louis declared that the townsfolk of Varasd had the right of being summoned before none other than the Tavernicus—"as is the case with other towns of the realm."[38]

The fourteenth century, then, witnessed a peculiar shift in the application of *praesentia regia* procedures as far as it involved the townsfolk, with a less important court functionary, the Tavernicus, assuming and, as it turned out, eventually displacing the traditional role of the Justiciar. Certainly, the more general circumstances in which this shift occurred may greatly assist our understanding of it. The fourteenth century represented a period of great turmoil within the *curia:* a product largely of a vast increase in the number of cases proceeding before it. The Angevin centralisation process of the fourteenth century, most strikingly apparent in the return of the Palatine to the court, gave a hitherto unknown authority to the royal *curia.* This authority was exaggerated through a decline in the number of those ecclesiastical bodies which as *loca credibilia* might authenticate documents and contracts and by the corresponding assumption of this role by the *curia.*[39] Landowners tended more and more to bring their property disputes to the *curia* for checking against forgery and towards the close of the century it was laid down that all matters concerning the possessions of nobles be adjudicated there.[40]

Fresh expedients were sought out to relieve these new pressures. These, in their turn, prompted far reaching changes. The century saw a vast increase in the number of lesser officials, notaries and secretaries attached to the individual judges at the court. The Chancellery assumed, originally on a special mandate, an authority in *praesentia regia* matters that was towards the century's close to establish it as one of the realm's principal *praesentia regia* forums. In the area of municipal jurisdiction, newly founded towns were placed under the judicial sway of a mother town and ordered to direct certain cases to the latter.[41]

Against this changing framework of jurisdictional relationships, it is necessary also to note a general lack of clarity in the actual application of this crucial term, *praesentia regia.* It is clearly erroneous to view, as did certain of the older Hungarian historians, *praesentia regia* authority as the sole preserve of the Justiciar.[42] On the basis of what we have already seen, the Tavernicus possessed a *praesentia regia* authority as indeed did a number of other officials operating within the *curia*. The term *praesentia regia* was itself a vague one and towards the end of the century was in part superseded by the more specific formulae, *specialis praesentia* and *personalis praesentia:* two terms which through the various branches of the Chancellery were to introduce a more coherent and defined system of jurisdiction than the older *praesentia regia* formula could alone.[43]

Who exactly possessed an authority to judge in municipal affairs remained correspondingly unclear and this lack of clarity found particular expression in the case held during the May of 1347 involving the burghers of Esztergom and their local chapter. For the matter was heard at the request of the Queen by a number of major temporal and ecclesiastical dignitaries as well as "other nobles of the kingdom specially convoked for this purpose" of which six by their own authority were to issue patents in favour of these much troubled canons.[44]

Lack of close definition provided, thus, a clear way along which another official could emerge as a parallel and later even superior authority to the Justiciar in municipal *praesentia regia* cases. Yet it remains important to ask actually why the official selected for this role should be the Tavernicus as opposed to, for instance, the Chancellor or, for that matter, the royal *scansor* who might on a royal mandate be clearly endowed with some minor jurisdiction in municipal affairs.[45]

The development of Tavernical jurisdiction can only be understood by reference to judicial mechanisms within the realm's administrative apparatus. Certainly, at times circumstances could be irregular and petitioners address their plaints directly to the monarch or his foremost justices.[46] Nonetheless, the view entertained by Bertényi that parties in an action could generally exercise some determining influence in the choice of their judge is misplaced.[47] Normally, as the 1343 Kunclin case suggests, the basic administration of such disputes as involved townsfolk lay in the hands of the local *loca credibilia* and Chancellery. It was to the *loca credibilia* that protests initiating proceedings were formally made, recorded on special *litterae* and addressed simply to the "royal presence." Hereafter and with these having arrived at the *curia,* details of the individual cases were examined by the Chancellery notaries and on the basis of their contents entrusted by these persons to whomsoever they considered to be the relevant judge. A request was then relayed back to the pertinent *locus credibile* stating that it should inform all parties of exactly when and where their case was to be heard.[48]

More than any other official in the royal *curia* it was the Tavernicus who had from an early stage been most closely involved in the affairs of the towns.

Originally, up until the first half of the thirteenth century, the Tavernicus had acted as the head of a network of lesser *tavernici*, royal servants of the *conditionarii* class, whose function it was to provide for the more personal needs of the monarch.[49] His authority extended also to the municipally based cameral and mining organisation.[50] During the course of the thirteenth century, this competence was steadily expanded to take in the field of taxation in general.[51] Such activities brought the Tavernicus into close contact with the townsfolk. Indeed, so great was this, that as early as 1244 the Buda charter specifically limited the degree to which the Tavernicus could operate amongst them by placing a restriction on his personal rights of entry into the town.[52] But the account books of other towns attest to the Tavernicus's presence within them and the various costs necessary for his provision and entertainment. His messengers and officials, moreover, passed regularly amongst them.[53] In recognition of this close involvement, the Tavernicus was occasionally entrusted by the monarch with special rights in certain towns—as for instance in regard to the sailors of Pest, the execution of offenders in Visegrád and, in the case of one small community, even with the appointment of the Town Judge.[54]

From around 1330, since from then on his seals of office were held in the Visegrád *curia*,[55] the Tavernicus was on his peregrinations around the realm largely unempowered to operate a local court. Nevertheless, as a judicial figure he remained relatively accessible. During the fourteenth century, the court of the Justiciar was becoming increasingly overloaded with litigation, so much so in fact that it was frequently unable to deal in one octave session with the volume of cases moved before it.[56] By contrast, the Tavernicus, owing to the decline of the *conditionarii* network and his increasing involvement with financial and administrative matters proved more readily available to hear disputes. Because of this availability, the Tavernicus might on occasions earlier on in the century be deputed to take charge of county *congregationes* although this task legally best befitted other royal justices.[57] Similarly, for reasons of expediency, the Chancellery steadily directed to his court such pleas involving the townsfolk as would otherwise be brought before the overburdened Justiciar. Thereby, the progress of individual cases might be hastened and, moreover, adjudicated by a figure well apprised of town conditions.

An increasing involvement with the realm's towns did not, however, automatically render the Tavernicus favourably disposed or even mildly sympathetic to town interests. The activities of one Tavernicus during the 1370's, Johann Dunajeci, and his unwarranted opposition to the town of Kassa—an opposition which King Louis was later obliged to redress—may be taken to illustrate this point clearly.[58] Yet the events following hard upon this incident suggest that additional and hitherto unapparent forces were at work within the development of Tavernical jurisdiction. Hitherto, we have regarded the administration of such pleas as involved the less well defined areas of municipal jurisdiction firstly in terms of their absorption within the developing structure of *praesentia regia* procedure and, secondly, by reference to innovations embarked upon by the central Chancellery "clearing house." Nevertheless, it is evident that the towns themselves might exert a powerful influence within the arrangement of such matters as touched upon themselves.

The dismissal of Johann Dunajeci and temporary suspension of the office of Tavernicus left the way open for the Justiciar, Jacob of Szepes, to assume the unprecedented title of Judge of All the Towns. Therewith he took over to his court those pleas arising from the towns which had hitherto been divided between the Justiciar and the Tavernicus.[59] The reasons behind this extraordinary development remain unclear. Quite possibly, the institution of Judge of All the Towns represents an early attempt to introduce a unified structure for the resolution of disputes passing before the "royal presence." Alternatively, since King Louis was at this time much concerned with the growth of magnate power, the new authority put in the hands of the loyal Jacob of Szepes may suggest a measure aimed at investing one of the monarch's most trusted officials with a much extended competence.[60] In this respect, it may be significant that during the 1370's Jacob of Szepes held also the office of Judge of All Jews in the Realm.[61]

Whatever the motives behind this new appointment, the towns reacted sharply. In 1378, Sopron complained to the King that any citation before Jacob was contrary to its liberties.[62] Opposition from other towns of the realm to the new powers of the Justiciar obliged Louis to transfer Kolozsvár in Transylvania to the jurisdiction of the region's Voevod, while Zagreb compelled him to reiterate its right only to be summoned by warrants of the King or Tavernicus.[63] Anxious not to alienate himself from the towns whose continued cash support was necessary for his military adventures, Louis bowed under pressure. The Tavernical court was re-established and, as its new incumbent, Thomas (Temlin) of St. George was appointed.[64]

Certainly, the opposition raised by the townsfolk may have been prompted by the same considerations as had earlier influenced the Chancellery. If the Justiciar's court had previous to Jacob's appointment been overloaded with business, then in view of its greatly extended competence, the speedy passage of litigation was now rendered all but impossible. The towns, thus, reacted merely to overcome administrative difficulties inherent in the new system. Nonetheless, the study of an action which involved the town of Pozsony and

was in 1377 brought before Jacob as Judge of All Towns suggests an additional interpretation.[65]

This case concerning the robbery of a servant in the town had first been
brought by the victim's noble master, whose money had been stolen, before
the Pozsony Council. The latter refused to take any appropriate action and the
case proceeded along the usual channels to Jacob of Szepes' court. The town,
however, demanded that the case be tried according to its own customary law.
Jacob refused. He was only empowered to adjudicate within the bounds of
consuetudo regni. Helpfully, the servant's master proclaimed that providing
his money was returned he had no objection to either legal system being
employed. Nevertheless, despite the nobleman's declaration, as far as the
townsfolk were concerned some respect for the principles of town law was
important. Already, well before this time, as the Kunclin case amply demonstrates, local custom could act as a complicating factor in the resolution of
disputes involving the towns. Crucially though, by the 1370's, town law had
assumed an unprecedented significance for the central court justices.

As the 1377 Pozsony case suggests, the distinction between an action
involving the town as a corporate entity represented by its Council and an
appeal against an actual verdict delivered by the same remained in the context
of this period only minor. During the second half of the fourteenth century,
appeal procedures were gradually developed in the towns and even accorded
sanction in some royal privileges.[66] Although, in this respect, the individual
Town Councils most probably operated in the function of *loca credibilia,*
cases once appealed entered the established system of *praesentia regia* jurisdiction. Obviously though, a case which had been first adjudicated by a town
magistracy according to the precepts of municipal custom could hardly be
moved before a forum which judged exclusively by reference to differing
consuetudo regni. Yet, in this respect, the Justiciar's court proved quite inflex-
ible. As a forum dealing primarily with the affairs of the nobility, it was bound
to adhere to the principles of "custom of the realm" even when these clearly
conflicted with local *consuetudo.*[67] By contrast, the Tavernicus's court was less
constrained.

During the 1380's reference occurs to a judgment being delivered at the
Tavernicus's court in accordance with the precepts of municipal law—
"consuetudine civium requirente necnon libertate civitatis . . . exigente."[68]
Seemingly though, well before this date, the Tavernicus might set aside *consuetudo regni* in the interests of local law. Hence, as early as 1344, in a
judgment delivered in conjunction with the Palatine and involving the town of
Zagreb, the Tavernicus adjudicated according to Croat customs.[69] Evidently,
moreover, as a result of his travels around the kingdom, the Tavernicus was

well aware of local conditions and rights which might obstruct proceedings narrowly following the path of *consuetudo regni.* As the Kunclin case suggests, "on the spot" discussions could reveal peculiar municipal procedures impeding the fulfilment of requests drawn up at a distance. With the development of the appeal and the new need to adjudicate exclusively by reference to local law, the inadequacies of the Justiciar's court could but stand starkly revealed. Nor did the grant to the Justiciar of the title Judge of All the Towns make the yoke of his overburdened jurisdiction any more tolerable. Rather, it only excited opposition from the towns and the formal expression of their preference for the legally less-constrained court of the Tavernicus. Accordingly, under pressure from the towns, the Justiciar's new title of Judge of All the Towns was revoked and the Tavernical office reestablished. But with the reappearance of this office came no renewal of the jurisdictional parallelism in municipal pleas which so characterises the relative positions of Justiciar and Tavernicus in the period before Jacob of Szepes. For, within little more than a year of his appointment, the new Tavernicus, Thomas of St. George, had himself adopted the Judge of All the Towns title, thereby assuming directly the preeminence of Jacob's former role.[70]

Should one wish to fix any one point at which the Tavernicus's authority in municipal pleas passing before the "royal presence" came to achieve a position greater than that of any other official, then one may with justification single out the elevation of Thomas of St. George. Actions arising from the towns now passed almost exclusively before his court while a large number of royal mandates attest to his special judicial status in regard to the townsfolk of the realm.[71] The continuing history of the dispute between Esztergom town and chapter reveals for this period the Tavernicus as the sole official charged with the duty of passing judgment in the various legal actions.[72] Such is a significant contrast to the 1347 process in which, as we have seen, a number of dignitaries participated issuing judgments in their own name. Now from the Tavernicus were stripped many of his wider financial functions which were henceforward performed by a separate *thesaurarius regius.*[73] In place of these, the Tavernicus assumed special responsibilities within the towns—acting as, for instance, the protector of the enfeebled town of Zsolna, or, as in the case of Buda, operating together with the Castellan of the palace as an overseer in municipal elections and a guarantor for the toll collections and weighing scales belonging to a local convent.[74] Unlike any other royal official, the Tavernicus's agents were, moreover, permitted to perform *statutiones* within towns, but, respecting urban rights, only when accompanied by Council members.[75]

But it is within the actual framework and operation of the Tavernical court that the most striking developments were to occur. Availability and accessibility had first prompted the Chancellery to address to the Tavernicus certain cases proceeding before the "royal presence." In this development, the Tavernicus's knowledge of local conditions and customs had also influenced the Chancellery's decision while later his readiness to examine and adjudicate by reference to municipal law made the townsfolk reluctant to have actions involving themselves pressed before any one else but him. It is hardly, then, surprising that these factors were to receive due prominence in the revived Tavernical court of the 1380's and 90's. The court now ceased to operate solely in a central capacity, functioning only within the royal *curia*. Rather it increasingly tended towards a peripatetic function with the Tavernicus on occasions sallying forth either on his own initiative or under royal direction to hear urgent disputes and apply the necessary judgment. Henceforth, he carried with him his special seals of office which allowed him to issue and confirm documents relating to cases heard outside the royal *curia*. Buda, Esztergom, Zsolna, Besztercebánya, Zagreb, Kassa and Nagyszombat all witnessed the immediate presence of the Tavernicus and the exercise of his renewed judicial authority amongst them.[76]

Changes, however, took place not only in the location but also in the internal organisation of the Tavernical court. The necessity for determining and defining more exactly local rights and customs had already led to certain inquisitions being conducted in conjunction with individual town magistracies.[77] So that local town custom might all the more be appreciated, similar procedures were now employed within the Tavernical court. In 1389, mention is made of the Tavernicus Michael "discerning the just path of law" and "judging all municipal cases proceeding before us," in association with the Judge and sworn men of Kassa.[78] Indeed, some years earlier, in both 1382 and 1383, representatives of a number of towns had even appeared as assessors within the main Tavernical court at Visegrád, there passing judgment together with the Tavernicus and other dignitaries of the realm.[79]

By the turn of the century, Tavernical jurisdiction had moved considerably away from its earlier role as an adjunct of *praesentia regia* procedure. Against the currents of a century which saw the principal organs of justice merging into and developing within the central *curia* apparatus, the Tavernical court assumed an itinerant character. Unlike other bodies, non-noble assessors were allowed to participate in its deliberations, and judgments were framed in accordance with local law. Some recognition of these extraordinary developments was afforded in the *Decretum Minus* of 1405.[80] The Tavernical court was admitted to be no longer incorporated within *praesentia regia* jurisdiction. Henceforward, it should operate as a forum largely independent of the *curia* organisation. Moreover, the court's valuable ability to adjudicate according to town custom was indirectly conceded. Hence, its role as a forum for municipal appeals was sanctioned and over the succeeding period the resolution of disputes at the second instance became its primary and preoccupying concern.

Nevertheless, despite the Tavernical court's obvious peculiarities, the 1405 decree was at pains to stress that there was little intrinsically remarkable about its organisation. Thus, the appeal system outlined, proceeding from the town courts to the Tavernicus and, thereafter, as it turned out, to the King himself, was likened to structures already evident within other branches of the realm's administration. It was pointed out that appeals from the seigneurial courts might also be addressed through a second and third instance—namely, to the county courts and, thereafter, to the monarch. Thus, while Tavernical jurisdiction was admitted to have departed from its earlier *praesentia regia* function, through an adept comparison, it was theoretically reabsorbed within the wider judicial organisation of the realm. Thus, already by 1405, trends which were to mark the development of the Tavernical court during the succeeding century came in part to be anticipated. Pressures urging a unique and almost independent form of jurisdictional organisation, relevant to the needs of the towns, were met and held in check by forces compelling the semblance of administrative integration.

Tavernicus and Mother-Town Court

During the fourteenth century, in the more momentous events surrounding the development of Tavernical jurisdiction, Buda appears to have played a role of little significance. Nor, with the valuable exception of the action *Hospitallers versus Kunclin,* does much material survive illustrating the town's relations with the Tavernical court. Such omissions are not to be found in the fifteenth century. From this period substantial material remains both in charter form and in the pages of the town *Stadtrecht.* Moreover, from these it is well evident that in the organisation of Tavernical jurisdiction Buda was increasingly able to exert a decisive influence. Also suggested is the continued pressure the towns were collectively able to apply on the institution thereby fundamentally determining its essential shape and jurisdictional framework. Thus, the initiative seized by the towns during the 1370's came to be maintained for much of the succeeding period and, as new forces were applied, the

Tavernical court so impelled to assume an institutional character not unfamiliar outside Hungary's own boundaries.

The traditional European *Schöffenstuhl* developed out of the system whereby one town came to be endowed with the same privileges as had formerly been given to an earlier foundation. Not surprisingly, when judicial difficulties and discords arose in the new town, recourse might be had or advice sought from the more experienced court of the mother-town.[81] This system appears as early as the twelfth century. Frederick Barbarossa's privilege for the merchants of Flanders allowed for one of their number who was denied justice "in a lesser place" to appeal "to the greater place from which the lesser has received its laws of justice."[82]

Although Lübeck and Magdeburg emerged as the most important of these mother-towns, many other cities also possessed forums for the solution of disputes arising in such foundations as had received their law. These higher courts, the *Schöffenstühle,* were staffed almost entirely by persons well versed in matters of town law, either members of the current *Rat* or learned jurists. Primarily judicial institutions with their own independent legal framework, the *Schöffenstühle* engaged in a wide variety of judicial actions. Indeed, the breadth of business undertaken by one of these courts is evident from a brief study of the Iglau (Jihlava) *Schöffenstuhl* which, as far as the towns of Bohemia and Moravia were concerned, dealt out "the highest law in this kingly regiment."[83]

Under the heading of *sentencia diffinitiva* a number of different types of litigation were resolved by the Iglau *schöffen.* Should a citizen object to a judgment given out by the Council of a town, be it in regard to either a civil or criminal action, an appeal might be lodged with the *schöffen* and the case reviewed. Likewise, if a Council was itself unable to arrive at a decision or when "judgment was hurled against judgment," the matter could be transmitted to the Iglau court with the request "that you advise us rightly with your knowledge of the law." Should the *schöffen* of Iglau find themselves unable to perform this task, they were obliged to swear an oath affirming that they could not reach judgment. By extension, the Iglau *schöffen* acted also as intermediaries between individual towns or local officials and townsfolk functioning mainly in such negotiations *"ad modum informationis. "*[84]

During the fifteenth century, the Tavernical court in Hungary performed a task almost parallel to that of the Iglau mother-town court and other European *Schöffenstühle.* In Hungary, however, the contrasting origins of this court, springing as it did out of the *curia* and the system of *praesentia regia* adjudication, produced certain jurisdictional distortions. Previous analyses of the Tavernical court and office have tended to view the institution from above, looking down with the Tavernicus on to the scattered communities of the realm.[85] This can only produce an uneven picture. Remedy must be sought with the townsfolk themselves. Only thus become fully apparent the changing nature of Tavernical jurisdiction and the complex stages through which the institution subtly developed—that is, from a branch of the *curia* into a Hungarian form of *Schöffenstuhl* and one wherein the town of Buda came to play an increasingly significant role.

Following the pattern laid down in the 1380's, representatives of a number of communities might be present at sessions of the often itinerant Tavernical court. Certainly this need not always be the case. In 1404 only the Óbuda magistracy was mentioned by name in the records of a meeting of the court held in that town.[86] But the Buda *Stadtrecht* makes it clear that, when the Tavernicus on a visit to Buda wished to pronounce in any matter, he was obliged to summon not only the Town Council but also the Judges and sworn men of other communities visiting the town.[87] Almost certainly, it is this seeming informality in the arrangement of the Tavernical court which explains the variety and changing number of towns whose representatives were recorded at its sessions. This situation was to continue unresolved despite the use, from the 1420's, of summonses of attendance.[88] Hence, when the Tavernical court met in 1416 at Kassa, Council members from Székesfehérvár, Esztergom, Pest and Selmecbánya were also in attendance.[89] In the same year, at Buda, magistrates from eleven towns appeared although fourteen years later only three towns were here so represented.[90] Although, as the examples from 1416 suggest, Council members from quite distant towns might participate, usually sessions of the Tavernical court witnessed the presence of representatives from only nearby communities. In 1426, at a session held in Körmöcbánya, the Judges and sworn men from just five northern towns appeared.[91] A Judge and sworn man of Nagyszombat and two *iurati* from Pozsony account for the sum total of municipal representatives specifically named as participants at the Tavernical court held the year before at Sopron.[92]

Generally, town councillors were unwilling to attend sessions of the Tavernical court held a great way off and, later, penalties even had to be threatened for such towns as failed to send the requisite number of representatives.[93] Equally reluctant to participate in this wider area of municipal jurisdiction was the town of Buda which seems to have played little part in Tavernical court sessions held outside the town. Although in 1426 members of the Buda council appeared at Sopron together with the headmen of Pozsony, Nagyszombat, Bártfa, Lőcse and "the Judges and sworn men of other free towns," it was to participate not in a Tavernical court but rather in a special royal court convened there to prosecute some rebellious local citizens.[94]

The reluctance of the towns to participate in inconvenient sessions of the court was accompanied by the gradual exclusion of non-burghers from its deliberations. When in 1382–3 the townsfolk had first appeared at sessions of the Tavernical court, they had taken their place beside the high dignitaries and nobles of the realm.[95] While, subsequently, greater officials were to play little part at these sessions, the nobility until the middle years of the fifteenth century continued to exercise a presence there. Indeed, they were, according to a judgment of Sigismund, fully entitled to a share in the deliberations of this court as in those other courts of the realm presided over by major dignitaries.[96] Thus, in 1409, in a matter brought before the Tavernicus and concerning the unlawful seizure of properties in Buda, judgment was passed in the presence "of the nobles of the realm and of the Judge and sworn men of the city."[97] Again, in 1430, the Tavernicus passed judgment in conjunction with nobles of the realm as well as members of the Buda, Pest and Esztergom Town Councils.[98]

Nevertheless, the burghers came consistently to oppose the continued presence of the nobility. Certainly, the Buda *Stadtrecht* is silent on the question of their participation. But later articles and statutes treating on the operation of the court prove less evasive; the nobility were specifically excluded from judicial sessions, delegates alone from the principal towns of the realm being permitted.[99] Already as early as 1407 at Kassa no nobles appear to have been in attendance and by the reign of Matthias their absence had been rendered permanent.[100] Yet the banishment of the nobility cannot be seen just against a background of burgher antagonism to the feudal classes.[101]

Representatives of the towns performed an important function in defining the nature of municipal customs and local conditions. Indeed, the necessity for obtaining this sort of information had first occasioned their participation at the Tavernical court. Documents issued by the Tavernicus relating to actions in which citizens of Buda were involved note this dignitary as passing judgment *"quesito et assumpto consilio"* of the municipal and other representatives.[102] More illustrative are the events of 1434 when the Tavernicus, Johann Rozgo-nyi, confronted by a complicated municipal action, was obliged to summon urgently the delegates of one town to Buda since, in his own words, "on account of the ambiguity and difficult nature of the case we are unwilling to proceed and pass judgment without your circumspect selves being in attendance."[103] Unable to comment usefully on either town affairs or customs, representatives of the nobility were of little value in what was essentially a municipal court. Thus their place was taken by burghers whose position gave them a fuller insight into the workings of the towns. Indeed, a parallel to this development is evident at the close of the fifteenth century within the highest court of the land, the court of the royal "personal presence." For in 1499 Vlászló II was to declare that pleas brought by townsfolk before this tribunal should be judged not by protonotaries of the court accustomed as they were to the "law of the nobles" but rather by persons versed in the law of the towns.[104]

Changes, however, occurred within not only the composition of the Tavernical court, but, importantly also, the types of action proceeding before it. Originally, during the fourteenth century, the court had adjudicated as a judicial tribunal of the first instance. It had heard pleas conjointly involving citizens and outsiders as well as actions concerning towns drawn into litigation as corporate units. By extension, the Tavernical court came later in the century to be involved in appeal cases arising from the towns. Clearly though, by the early fifteenth century, this wide competence had suffered a marked redress and been altogether reduced to embrace only one category of action: the appeal. Thus, the 1405 *Decretum Minus* makes no mention of the Tavernical court's hitherto established capacity to adjudicate cases brought before it in the first instance.[105] Likewise, the Buda *Stadtrecht* refers to a competence extending but to the *Berufung* or appeal. Later collections and protocols of procedural law are equally emphatic.[106] Beyond this, a study of individual cases affirms that almost without exception only cases brought by appeal from the towns could be heard by the Tavernical court.[107]

Certainly, as far as cases initiated by outsiders against individual citizens were concerned, the development of appeal procedures largely obviated the immediate need for a legally removed and impartial court of the first instance. An outsider who received unjust treatment at the hands of a Town Council or, alternatively, found the proper prosecution of his plaint impeded by local customs might address an appeal before the Tavernicus and seek due remedy from his court. In this respect, it can be no coincidence that the provisions treating on appeal procedures in the 1405 *Decretum Minus* were accompanied by a categorical reaffirmation of the old *actor sequitur forum rei* principle.[108] The Buda *Stadtrecht* similarly pronounced that no citizen might be directly impleaded in the first instance before any ordinary of the realm and that included the Tavernicus. All prosecutions of citizens were to be directed before the Judge and Council for primary adjudication.[109] Nevertheless, it remained of course impossible for a municipal Council to pass judgment in actions wherein its own town as a corporate entity was involved in litigation. Yet, in this crucial respect and despite a mass of historical precedents, the Tavernical court was in the fifteenth century generally held to exercise no jurisdictional competence. In view of the organisational changes of the late fourteenth and early fifteenth centuries, however, the imposition of this restriction may be considered a not entirely unpredictable development. As we have seen, the basis for the Tavernicus's former involvement in the adjudication of towns as corporate entities derived from his early role in *praesentia regia* jurisdiction. But now, with the separation of his court from the royal *curia* and the established *praesentia regia* system of adjudication, cases affecting the towns which proceeded before the "royal presence" for primary adjudication ceased to be viewed as the Tavernicus's concern. Although some confusion evidently persisted, these types of actions were henceforward directed to those courts which, unlike the Tavernicus's, still adjudicated in a *praesentia regia* capacity. At times this might, as of old, be the Justiciar's court although, with the abolition of the Chancellery court of the "special presence," the court of the royal "personal presence" was mainly involved.[110] Stripped then of that authority which had been acquired by his former assumption of the role of royal *alter ego,* the basis of the Tavernicus's jurisdictional competence shifted. It became increasingly dependent upon earlier charters and decrees which had, in fact, invested him with a more limited judicial authority.

The majority of municipal charters had allowed for a process wherein a superior authority might be invoked in a legal action proceeding before a Town Council. This superior authority was usually the King, although some earlier thirteenth century charters omitted reference to him in favour of a more accessible figure: a local castellan, perhaps, or the Transylvanian Voevod.[111] Although certain of the early charters had allowed for royal or outside involvement in cases proving too difficult for a Town Council to handle alone (the *arduae causae*),[112] this early form of transmission came to be largely eclipsed. In its place were enunciated provisions allowing for the impeachment of town magistrates.[113]

It is within this last category that the Buda charter of 1244 fell. Should the *villicus* fail to dispense justice to any person, then it became possible to have the judge of the town summoned before the King—*"vel cui duxerimus committendum."* The earlier Nagyszombat charter of 1238 suggests that such an indictment could result in the forfeiture of office.[114] Charters issued during the course of the fourteenth century tended, however, to substitute a more substantial definition for the vague formula "or to whom we entrust the matter"—a formula by no means unique to the Buda charter.[115] With the increased participation of the Tavernicus in town affairs, this figure came to be accorded a greater role within the texts of municipal liberties. Thus, impeachments of a judge or magistracy might be directed *"ad nostram (regiam) vel magistri tavernicorum nostrorum (regalium) praesentiam."* [116]

The original impeachment provisions as laid down in the 1244 charter were duly incorporated in the Buda *Stadtrecht.* Significantly though, the loose entrustment formula was modified in the light of the fourteenth century charters bestowed on other towns: only before the King or Tavernicus might a mischievous Judge be indicted.[117] Generally, however, the impeachment process came itself to be omitted in charters of the late fourteenth century in favour of provisions allowing for a specific case to be sent up to a higher tribunal for review. This procedure was, furthermore, adopted in the *Decretum Minus* of 1405.[118]

Already by the second half of the fourteenth century, it had been recognised that the various town charters differed considerably from one another in many respects and that these discrepancies could be exploited by landowners and magnates to the disadvantage of the burghers.[119] In those of its clauses which touched on municipal jurisdiction, the 1405 *Decretum Minus* was intended to bring contrasting town customs into line with one another through an overall review of the often anachronistic procedures framed in earlier charters. Thus, procedure for the appeal of a case, already replacing in more recent charters the older impeachment clause, now came to be extended by the decree to other towns of an older foundation. The role and significance of the Tavernicus in determining actions of appeal was accordingly recognised.

These clauses treating on the role of a superior authority in municipal appeal actions seem clearly intended to provide the statutory basis upon which the towns might substitute for the outworn and seldom employed impeachment process the appeal proper. Thus a town like Buda was brought into line with procedural developments operating elsewhere—not just within the more recently chartered foundations but within the kingdom as a whole where the notion of the *novum* or retrial at the first instance and individual case transmission, often proceeding under the fiction of the *prorogatio*, had already made progress.[120]

Seemingly then, changes surrounding the general conception of Tavernical authority in the fifteenth century were occasioned by two interrelated developments. As the Tavernicus lost that authority deriving from his erstwhile *praesentia regia* rights of adjudication, so the basis for his continued competence in the affairs of the townsfolk came increasingly to rely on statutory instruments—namely, the towns' charters and, by extension, the updating of these undertaken in the 1405 decree. Strikingly though, as the Buda *Stadtrecht* makes clear, the townsfolk felt themselves in no way rigidly bound to follow every provision of these statutory instruments. Thus, for instance, the possibility of directing an appeal from the Tavernical court to the King himself, a principle laid down in 1405, found no mention in the *Stadtrecht*. More importantly, grievances involving certain types of litigation were categorically refused admission to the Tavernical court.

The *Stadtrecht* declared that a citizen of Buda "might appeal to the court of the Tavernicus nothing that relates to other than inherited lands and possessions and large debts." In any action which centred around "a shameful think, namely the spilling of blood" the Tavernical court might exercise no jurisdiction whatsoever.[121] Almost certainly, the *Stadtrecht* represents the first formal attempt to limit in this way the competence of the Tavernical court. For this institution had quite evidently possessed an earlier jurisdiction over "shameful" matters.[122] Thus, Selmecbánya's *Gemayne Stattrecht,* which probably predates by some years the *Stadtrecht* of Buda, imposed no qualification on the types of appeal action which might be brought before the court.[123] Exactly by what point the Buda *Stadtrecht's* limitations on Tavernical jurisdiction came to be more widely adopted remains unclear. The *Laws and Customs of the Seven Towns,* probably circulated in the mid-fifteenth century at a session of the Tavernical court, made no procedural distinction between the "shameful" and "unshameful" action.[124] On the other hand, since the actual purpose to which these articles were put remains somewhat uncertain, it would be unwise to draw too great a conclusion on the basis of this source alone.

Certainly though, by the 1450's, the provisions of the *Stadtrecht* appear to have been more widely observed. Thus, the Buda Articles of 1456, drawn up at Buda by the free towns of the realm, noted that the competence of the Tavernical court extended only to "inherited property *(Eribtayll)* or debt which is above the sum of sixty gold florins and in other matters, as murder, wounding or robbery, nothing." The later Pozsony Articles stated also that "the Tavernicus and his deputy may not involve themselves or venture into (matters concerning) blows, wounds, incapacitating injuries and murder." Only actions involving debt and inherited possessions might be appealed before him and his court.[125]

Much of the explanation for the limitation on appeals referable to the Tavernical court may be deemed to lie in the general distrust exhibited by the townsfolk for the institution as a whole. Indeed, these sentiments were not altogether misplaced. Certainly, the townsfolk were throughout the first half of the fifteenth century gaining greater and eventually exclusive representation at the court. But until such a time as the office became entirely subordinate to the court, the institution posed a not inconsiderable threat to the burghers. The Tavernici were throughout the medieval period drawn without exception from the ranks of the powerful landed class and, as such, tended to represent interests opposed to those of the burghers.[126] Although, for much of the latter part of Sigismund's reign, the Tavernicus was a certain Peter Berzeviczy, himself related to leading citizens of Buda,[127] and although the town seems to have come into little conflict generally with the Tavernici, it is evident that this relationship was not always to be repeated elsewhere.

Examples of conflict between Tavernicus and townsfolk are not infrequent occurring indeed within the fourteenth century in regard to the already mentioned Johann Dunajeci.[128] But even more troublesome to the townsfolk than Dunajeci was one Johann Bubek, Tavernicus between 1410 and 1419. Shortly after assuming office, Bubek so insulted the burghers of one community by refusing to sit at table with them and shamefully plucking their beards that he was subsequently to be shut out of the town.[129] In 1417, Sigismund condemned him roundly for having held court "not with the Judges and sworn men of our free towns . . . but with whomsoever you wished." Additionally and for good measure, the King noted that "busying and dishonouring yourself with many ill, base, deceitful and condemnable words, you, moreover, beat some of the citizens, boxing their ears. You and your deputy . . have performed damning injuries and exquisite calumnies."[130] A few years later, a former incumbent of the Tavernical office was reported to have molested the town of Sopron. There, Stephen of Kanizsa had apparently seized lands and cattle belonging to the townsfolk, persecuted citizens working in their vineyards and interfered in the judicial business of the town thereby earning for himself "most surely the not immoderate displeasure of Our Majesty."[131]

Less certain although no less interesting is the conceptual view entertained by the towns in regard to appeal procedures. Whether the possibility of appeal from one court to another imposes a direct limitation on any rights of jurisdictional independence claimed by the former is a complicated theoretical question made even more problematic in this case by the nature and composition of the higher tribunal. Nevertheless, it is suggestive that King Matthias's attempts to extent his own authority in the realm at the expense of baronial privilege was partly pursued, as we have seen, by an amplification of his own prerogatives in the matter of appeal jurisdiction.[132] Significantly also, the *Stadtrecht,* while prepared to countenance appeals from the Council as essentially necessary, sensed these yet to be in some way a slight on the authority of the same. Hence, it pronounced that, should a Council verdict be upheld by the Tavernical court, the party which brought the appeal was obliged to pay a substantial fine.[133]

But even accepting burgher anxiety as the principal reason for the restrictions imposed by both the *Stadtrecht* and later articles on the categories of appeal referable to the Tavernicus, such cannot be taken to explain why it should be that only certain types of civil action were allowed access there. Nor, indeed, are any historical precedents evident in this regard. In fact, the

opposite seems to be the case. For certain of the earlier charters bestowed on
towns of the realm had allowed external judges to intervene in municipal
affairs only when the so-called "shameful" matters were involved—*"furti,
videlicet, homicidii et sanguinis."*[134] Similar provisions existed also on some
baronial estates.[135] Yet it was precisely in respect to these actions that the
Tavernicus was deemed to exercise no jurisdiction whatsoever.

In order to understand the reason for the burghers' refusal to countenance
appeals other than those arising out of inherited property and debt cases, it is
necessary first to apprehend the townsfolk's essentially practical disposition. It
was not their aim to endow the Tavernical court with a legal framework that
comfortably locked into the procedural system operating outside the towns.
Rather, town representatives called to attend sessions of the court found these
to be tedious and best avoided. Moreover, the institution as a whole and the
Tavernicus in particular constituted a possible threat to the townsfolk and
their notion of immune status. Accordingly, from those types of action which
might be satisfactorily resolved at a local level the opportunity of appeal was
removed. By the same token, only litigants involved in the more complex sorts
of action were granted this right.

In criminal cases or disputes around recently bought properties where no
question of inheritance law came in to complicate the issue, a fairly reliable
verdict might be reckoned on first time. The proceedings were quite straightforward and the evidence usually too clear cut to make appeal seem anything
more than a delaying tactic. Indeed, it was for this very reason that, in the
sixteenth century, a variety of debt action—the *debitum liquidum* or
bankruptcy—was put outside the jurisdiction of the Tavernical court. For
"notorious and manifest debt" was deemed too obvious a status to merit the
need for appeal.[136]

In complete contrast, actions involving inherited property and debt proved
invariably to be of a long and complicated nature. Examples from Buda
indicate that in these cases litigants might produce a welter of ancient family
claims and conflicting documents all of which were in need of corroboration
and analysis. Thus, in one early appeal proceeding from Buda, the thorough
investigation of all claims put forward by the plaintiffs was necessary before it
proved possible to deny to one townsman the property seized by him. For
although this had been obvious from the start, only then was the Tavernical
court able unequivocally to confirm that, in contrast to the plaintiffs, the
defendant "could produce no pertinent document of reasonable credibility."[137]
Total ignorance might, furthermore, make for additional complications. One
attorney presenting a case before the Buda Council "according to the rite and
custom of the town did not know how to make the relevant responses" and as

a result lost his client's case.[138] Another defendant had clearly no idea by what terms he held a house in the town.[139] Equally illustrative is a case in 1429 involving some citizens of Lőcse but which ultimately came to be resolved by the Town Council of Buda. The dispute, arising out of debt and the wrongful seizure of property had proved so complex that it had been *"diucius actitata et ventilata"* through a number of courts as well as the Tavernical. Claims of confession under duress, false imprisonment and forgery had to be investigated in conjunction with the main features of the case. Indeed, the whole action was to drag on for five years with Sigismund himself finally intervening to resolve the matter—*"propter sui arduitatem."* [140]

Under these circumstances it might well be that a Town Council felt itself unable to give out a judgment binding for all time.[141] In the absence of procedures allowing for transmission on the grounds of *ardua causa,* the possibility of appeal was thus not denied in those matters wherein a Council felt itself less capable of delivering a satisfactory verdict. Some indication of this may be preserved in the later Pozsony Articles. Here, special reference is made to the appeal of property actions when a "dispute around the facts" had arisen.[142] It is, however, equally likely that because litigants found the judgments of Town Councils unconvincing, they simply prosecuted their claims elsewhere. Indeed, only the threat of execution from the Buda Council could stay one such plaintiff's frantic attempts to remedy his grievances.[143] Accordingly, for actions concerning inherited property and debt, it was desirable to have available a court of appeal for the final settlement of problematic cases. Such a function the Tavernical court performed most effectively, since no other institution possessed the capacity for determining so expertly those appeals arising out of the knottier points of law.

The court consisted of persons drawn up from the membership of the Town Councils, persons therefore well able to cope with such problems of municipal precedure and custom as might emerge in their own and other communities. Later, in the second half of the fifteenth century, town jurists appear to have taken their place also at the court to resolve the peculiar legal difficulties which might occur there.[144] Nor was the Tavernicus a redundant figure at these deliberations. For although a separate treasury office had developed during the fourteenth century, the Tavernicus still maintained many contacts with the financial life of the towns. Indeed, even in the fifteenth century, one town appears to have sent its account books to him for auditing.[145] Again, the Tavernicus seems for a time to have acted as an ordinary for merchants, both native and foreign, although this function was later assumed by his court.[146] Documents, likewise, might be brought before the Tavernicus for confirmation. In 1409, for instance, the long-serving Judge of Buda, Johann Siebenlinder, requested the Tavernicus to confirm a payment of compensation even though this had already been ratified by Master Jacob, a Chancellery official, and two *iurati* of the town.[147]

Like the Iglau *Schöffenstuhl* and similar institutions elsewhere in Europe, membership of the Tavernical court consisted of persons well versed in matters of town law before whom cases might be transferred from the individual Town Councils. As we have seen, the Iglau *schöffen* occupied themselves mainly in appeals and matters referred up as *arduae causae*. Certainly, the Tavernical court's membership corresponds closely with such *Schöffenstühle*. But contrastingly, in Hungary, a distortion seems to have occurred in the types of action which might be moved before the court. Notions of *ardua causa* and appeal became interjoined. For only such appeals as arose out of *arduae causae,* as involved problematic cases of law, were allowed access. Thus, the competence of the institution became confined but to property and debt actions. For, as far as the townsfolk were concerned, the Tavernical court represented, at one and the same time, a tedious task, a possible threat and yet a convenient forum for problematic cases. In the reconciliation of these various aspects, peculiarities of jurisdiction were to develop—peculiarities, indeed, first evident within the text of the Buda *Stadtrecht.*

The traditional European *Schöffenstuhl* largely developed out of the mother-town system, the arrangement whereby one town might be endowed with the liberties of an older foundation and to which place certain types of action might also be directed for settlement. Contrastingly, in Hungary, the Tavernical court, which resembles closely these *Schöffenstühle,* developed out of the *curia* and contemporary notions of *praesentia regia* jurisdiction. Yet one must not presume that in Hungary no mother-town system existed.

Charters bestowed during the thirteenth century often alluded to Székesfehérvár alleging that they adhered to the form of liberty bestowed on that town. Liberties were, thus, defined *"ad instar civium Albensium"* or *"more civium Albensium."*[148] During the course of the thirteenth and fourteenth centuries, references to Székesfehérvár decline as other towns appear more regularly in the texts of the municipal privileges. Occasionally, a number of communities are so mentioned. The privilege of Dézsakna in 1291 endowed the community with the same rights as "are enjoyed by the citizens of Buda, Esztergom, the *hospites* of Szatmár and of our other free towns."[149] The Kassa charter of 1342 mentions only the example "of our principal towns."[150] During the course of the fourteenth century, however, there emerged three towns whose liberties largely provided the basis for such privileges as might be granted out to other towns: Selmecbánya, Korpona and, particularly, Buda.[151] Reference to the reception of Buda's liberties by another town of the realm first occurs in 1253.[152] Thereafter, such bestowals become commonplace. Certain towns appear to have been endowed with the entirety of Buda's privilege, written out word for word; others with only its market rights.[153] However, it is evident that towns, even though not endowed with Buda's privilege, might still refer to it and construct therefrom their own procedures. The citizens of Bars, much to the chagrin of some local nobles, declared that property transactions within the town followed the "rite and custom of Buda city" even though Bars's charter had itself been drawn up in 1240 prior to the foundation of Buda.[154]

Out of the system of charter bestowal, there emerged the possibility of referring an action for adjudication at the mother-town. This idea soon fused with the developing notion of the appeal proper. In 1370, Korpona declared to one of its daughter-towns that if any inhabitant of the latter were unsatisfied with a verdict given out by their magistracy they might proceed directly to Korpona.[155] A few years later, it was allowed the town of Privigye that, in the event of legal difficulties, a case might be referred to Korpona "for counsel and information."[156] The town of Debrecen was, likewise, granted the right to appeal an action "to the judgment, examination and discussion" of the town of Buda whose privilege it enjoyed. Similar rights were awarded the town of Rév in Bihar county.[157] The royal decree of 1405 noted also the development of mother-town jurisdiction. Thus, it was declared possible to appeal an action from a Town Council to either the Tavernicus or, alternatively, the judiciary of that town "by whose liberty such a city or free town operates."[158] Hence, two seemingly parallel institutions were enunciated: the Tavernicus and his court on the one hand; on the other the various mother-town courts.

Yet the clear cut distinction between the two systems of municipal government rapidly became blurred. Nor did the growing confusion of competences confine itself to the conflicting jurisdictions of the Tavernical court and the mother-towns. Also involved were the developing geographical regions of municipal jurisdiction, notably the Szepesség town conglomerate and the emerging confederation of the northern towns. Amongst the various structures of municipal jurisdiction, cases were moved from one system to another without apparent protest or procedural difficulty. Thus, the dispute between Eperjes and Bártfa concerning rights to bleach cloth was heard in 1446 by a court of the northern towns specially convened for that purpose. But, following a decision unfavourable to Eperjes, an appeal was lodged with the Tavernicus and the matter despatched to his court for review.[159] Even more illustrative are the activities of Conrad Imbert, a citizen of Lőcse. For having contested the judgment of his own town magistracy, Conrad brought his case before a session of the Tavernical court. Unsatisfied with the verdict given there, he took the matter before the regional court of the Szepesség towns, presided over by the Judge of Késmárk. Thereafter, with Conrad still having been denied satisfaction, the case was in 1429 brought before a session of the Buda mother-town court for final adjudication.[160] Likewise, for mediatised Debrecen, Iványi has indicated the existence during the fifteenth century of eight specific and largely contradictory pronouncements on the town's appeal procedures. The Buda mother-town court, the Tavernicus, local count, lord and county court were all postulated in various sequences as Debrecen's relevant appeal tribunals.[161]

Nevertheless, this seeming confusion amongst the various systems of municipal jurisdiction had partly resolved itself by the second half of the fifteenth century. Specific regional courts were established for both the mining towns of Upper and Lower Hungary and for the Transylvanian communities.[162] Lőcse, Esztergom and Székesfehévár were subordinated directly to the court of the royal "personal presence" in a development apparent from perhaps as early as the 1440's.[163] Likewise, Tavernical jurisdiction which had originally embraced all the free towns of the realm was now formally confined to a single group: Buda, Kassa, Pozsony, Sopron, Nagyszombat, Eperjes and Bártfa.[164]

An oblique reference to this last group of seven towns first occurs in 1441, in a letter sent to the Queen by the burghers of Pozsony.[165] A few years later, the text of a royal decree makes it clear that these seven towns alone possessed the right to participate at sessions of the Tavernical court.[166] Although there were evidently a few exceptions, the Buda and Pozsony Articles convey also the strong impression that only appeals arising from out of the seven towns might be heard.[167] Thus, in contrast to its earlier role, the Tavernical court had become no more than "the common court of the seven towns."[168]

These seven towns represented the foremost commercial centres of the realm being, moreover, all occupied to varying degrees by a powerful German-speaking class. All seven had successfully fought off attempts at mediatisation, thereby avoiding the fate which overhangs the history of so many towns during the last decades of Sigismund's reign. Another equally significant bond is also evident. For of those communities which joined together with Buda to form the seven Tavernical towns, all but one had received either wholly or in part the liberties of Buda.[169] The exception was Nagyszombat, not surprisingly since its charter predates the actual foundation of Buda during the 1240's.[170]

The new significance acquired by Buda within the revised Tavernical court of the mid-fifteenth century is made manifest in this court's administration and location. Already by this time the Vice-Tavernicus had assumed particular responsibilities within the court's organisation, maintaining close links with the Chancellery and often presiding over judicial sessions in the absence of his master.[171] It is, however, quite impossible to accept Szekfű's view that the Vice-Tavernici were no more than *familiares* introduced from out of the Tavernicus's own household.[172] For only one such deputy appears to have enjoyed this background. Contrastingly, at least four Vice-Tavernici from the fifteenth century—Sigismund of Gemerew, Francis Bernhard, Ladislas of Erd and George the Deacon—are known to have been citizens of Buda.[173]

Certainly, this connection between appointments to the office of Vice-Tavernicus and the town of Buda may be considered just another manifestation of the prominent role assumed generally by the citizenry in the day to day affairs of royal government. But undoubtedly, it reflects also the changing geographical location of the Tavernical court. For, by the middle of the fifteenth century, this court had become firmly fixed in Buda and the possibility of its operating sessions outside the town was accordingly revoked.[174] The Buda Articles of 1456 suggest the practicality of this arrangement. Buda occupied a central position within the realm. Thus, a summons to the town might prove "quite reasonable" *(gern pillich)*. Also, by this time, Buda ranked as the "capital wherein the law of the nobility is pronounced and determined." The Pozsony Articles, likewise, attest to the court's permanent location in Buda, since this town "is considered most eminent and all matters concerning inhabitants of the kingdom are decided here."[175]

Despite this comparison with the realm's wider judicial organisation, the Tavernical court did not take up residence in Buda as but another adjunct of royal government. It may well be that earlier on in the century the Tavernicus while visiting Buda had dispensed justice from the palace compound. But, by the 1450's, the position of his court had evidently moved entirely out of the traditional centre of the kingdom's judicial organisation. Thus, the Tavernicus, so it was declared, might preside only over judicial sessions held within the actual town of Buda "and not in the palace of Buda or any other town." In Buda either the Tavernicus or his deputy were required to be permanently available for consultation and they were ordered to keep in the town certain lodgings.[176] Indeed, as early as 1436 proceedings are recorded as having taken place *"in domo . . . Tavernicali Budensi."*[177]

Seemingly though, the dominant position now assumed by Buda within the Tavernical court and amongst the organisation of the seven towns extended on to a far deeper level. Already in the fourteenth century, certain daughter-towns had not only been bestowed with their mother foundation's liberties but placed under its *"iure et consuetudine"* as well.[178] A similar development now

appears to have occurred amongst the seven towns which fell under Tavernical jurisdiction.

About the middle years of the fifteenth century there was drawn up a code
of customary procedure known as the *Laws and Customs of the Seven Towns*
or, more correctly, the *Iura Civilia et Consuetudines Antiquae septem libera-
rum civitatum.* The ostensible purpose of this work is obscure and some
historians have proposed that it served none at all. Certainly, despite its
publication early last century under the title of *Codex Authenticus Iuris
Tavernicalis,*[179] this work could hardly have been intended for use at sessions
of the Tavernical court. For it contains provisions treating on criminal actions
and constitutional matters which quite clearly fell outside the competence of
this institution. Nonetheless, as is amply suggested by its title, the *Laws and
Customs of the Seven Towns* was inherently bound up with the general conception of Tavernical jurisdiction in so far as this had become synonymous
with the organisation of the seven towns.

As was indicated long ago by the great Gusztáv Wenzel, the *Laws
and Customs of the Seven Towns* might well alternatively be entitled the
"Laws and Customs of Fifteenth Century Buda." For the provisions of the
former conform strikingly to what we know from its *Stadtrecht* and charters
to be Buda's own legal principles and procedures. This close resemblance
embraces all aspects of law—property, criminal, marriage, and contract—as
well as minor details concerning, for instance, the proper siting of buildings.[180]
Nor can this remarkable coincidence be explained away by simple reference
to a commonality of social and legal pressures making for the formulation of
identical customs and procedures. For an electoral college of a hundred persons, an institution born in Buda out of seemingly unique circumstances, is
enunciated also in the *Laws and Customs of the Seven Towns.*[181]

Particularly relevant to any enquiry into this work and its provenance is a
most magnificent version of the *Laws and Customs* drawn up in the early
sixteenth century for the town of Újlak (Illok) in southern Hungary.[182] In the
mid-fifteenth century this town had been awarded "the laws, statutes, customs
and ordinances, in their entirety, which our city of Buda and its citizens use
and enjoy."[183] A brief compendium of Buda's principal legal precepts together
with substantial sections from its early charters was accordingly written out
and approved by the town's local lord.[184] When these were redrafted in 1525,
the *Laws and Customs of the Seven Towns* was appended and submitted for
royal confirmation with the claim that these represented the "ancient and
accepted rights, laws and customs of the aforesaid town of Újlak."[185] Since
Újlak was never considered subject to the Tavernical court of the seven towns,
the *Laws and Customs* must accordingly have been included in the 1525

compendium as a consequence of Újlak's special relationship to Buda and its earlier assumption of that town's customary laws and procedures. The example of Újlak only further reinforces the claims advanced by Wenzel. Almost certainly, the *Laws and Customs of the Seven Towns* was nothing less than an official compilation of Buda's town law as it was understood during the second half of the fifteenth century. The title of the work, moreover, forces the assumption that the compilation was specifically intended for use and adoption by the seven Tavernical towns. In this respect, it is indeed suggestive that in 1563 the town of Kassa, which had earlier produced its own customary law compilation, caused the *Laws and Customs* to be fully written out in a German translation. This was bound together with statutes and decrees treating on the more general aspects of Tavernical jurisdiction.[186]

Already a close correlation has been indicated between the Tavernical court and town *Schöffenstühle* in other parts of Europe. In their internal composition and the types of action proceeding before them clear similarities are evident. Contrastingly through, the traditional European *Schöffenstuhl* grew up and developed out of the mother-town arrangement of charter bestowal. In Hungary, however, Tavernical jurisdiction derived originally from notions of *praesentia regia* procedure with the various mother-towns developing as separate institutions. Yet if Buda's freshly acquired dominance among the seven Tavernical towns extended to the actual bestowal of its customary law to them, a new and interesting twist is given to the chequered history of the Tavernical court. For as such the institution would seem now totally to have assumed the historical antecedents of *Schöffenstuhl* development grafting on to itself a system of mother-town adjudication centred upon the town and legal precepts of Buda.

Whatever our interpretation of the *Laws and Customs of the Seven Towns,* it can hardly be denied that by the mid-fifteenth century the Tavernical court had progressed and developed far away from its earlier place as but an adjunct of *praesentia regia* procedure. By a series of complicated shifts and changes it had assumed the character of a specifically municipal court and, as a study of its organisation, jurisdiction and legal framework suggests, come in form to differ little from the *Schöffenstuhl* mother-town court common elsewhere in Europe. Yet the final culminative stage of this development—that is, the severing of all bonds with the royal administrative apparatus out of which the court originated—never came to be fully achieved. Thus, despite various attempts to restrict his authority, the Tavernicus who was, after all, a royally appointed official was never dispensed with entirely. His presence remained altogether necessary for the proper and legal functioning of his court. Indeed, in seeming compensation for his reduced official powers, the Tavernicus over the course of the fifteenth century came increasingly to assume the symbolic role of guardian of urban freedoms. It was he who preserved the *civitas* "in its liberties and privileges, given, awarded and confirmed by godly Kings"; he who should plead before the monarch should a town be "seemingly deprived of its rights." For his good services, the towns were held liable to pay a yearly tribute.[187]

Nor did it prove possible to sever the procedural link binding the court of the Tavernicus to the monarch. The 1405 *Decretum Minus* had allowed for a process whereby a dissatisfied party might appeal an action from the Tavernical court to the royal "personal presence."[188] The existence of this higher stage of adjudicature continued throughout the fifteenth century and appeals to the monarch, therefore, became a quite regular phenomenon. Thus, in 1424, a dispute around, in fact, that same piece of land as Kunclin and the Hospitallers had earlier quarrelled over, was moved by appeal from the Buda Town Council to the Tavernical court. The noble Galgóczi family which had become drawn into the dispute was, however, unsatisfied with the judgment delivered at the Tavernical court and appealed the action to the monarch.[189]

Despite the seeming fusion of Tavernical jurisdiction with the Buda mother-town court, appeals involving Buda continued to be addressed from the Tavernical court of the seven towns to the court of the royal "personal presence." In the 1450's a long running and *"diucius ventilata"* dispute about some houses and vineyards in the town was moved by appeal before the Tavernicus. But the measured judgment of his court was rejected and the matter accordingly despatched to the monarch for a final and, as it turned out, unsatisfactory verdict.[190] Still, in the sixteenth century, an action involving Buda proceeded by appeal first to the Tavernical court and, thereafter, for eventual judgment to the royal court of the "personal presence."[191]

There is, moreover, much to suggest that parties in an action who were dissatisfied with a verdict delivered by a Town Council often sought to bypass the Tavernical court in favour of a direct appeal to the monarch. Thus, in 1453, Ladislas V noted that persons intent upon circumventing the Tavernical court were illicitly taking appeals against the judgment of one council "directly to the royal court of the 'personal presence'."[192] Most probably, the motives behind this development may be sought in the plaintiffs' own common sense. To pursue any action was a time-consuming and costly business and one, moreover, which could be dragged out for perhaps as long as six or seven years by further appeal.[193] Hence, it proved expedient for a party to proceed directly to the highest court in the land firm in the knowledge that the judgment of this forum was considered by all both binding and final. During the reign of Matthias, the institutional and judicial centralisation process undertaken by the new monarch further facilitated the direction of appeals from the Tavernical court to the "personal presence." Under Matthias's direction, a written clarification of procedures was embarked upon which greatly elaborated the administrative principles involved in case transmission to the "personal presence." This was duly published by the Tavernicus, Johann Thuz de Lak, widely disseminated and, thereafter, incorporated to form the later Pozsony Articles.[194] During the reign of Vlászló II, so as to obviate legal difficulties brought about by local town custom, cases involving the town which proceeded by appeal before the royal "personal presence" were heard and adjudicated by assessors well versed in municipal law.[195]

The development and definition of jurisdictional mechanisms linking the towns to the monarch through the agency of the Tavernical court could, however, yet be reinforced in such a way as to bypass the Tavernical court altogether. Thus, as Werbőczy pronounced and as indeed occurred in a case proceeding from Buda in 1514, should the monarch after hearing a doubly appealed action recommend a Town Council through *novum* procedure to rehear a case, any further appeal from the Council's revised decision could only be addressed before the court of the royal "personal presence."[196]

Thus, while fast assuming the characteristics of the institutionally quite independent and jurisdictionally self-sufficient central European *Schöffenstuhl,* the Tavernical court remained both legally and administratively closely associated with the royal judicial apparatus from out of which it had first emerged. On the lower level, an almost independent appeal system of municipal jurisdiction was carved out by the towns and yet, higher up, this structure met and merged into the realm's central judicial machinery. Nor was the resolution of these two conflicting features of the court's character ever achieved. With the Turkish conquest and the imposition of Habsburg rule, the Tavernical court was frozen in the form it had acquired by the opening years of the sixteenth century. Thus, it endured until its eventual abolition in 1849 as but a distorted almost hybrid institution.

Chapter 8

CONCLUSION

The long history of the Tavernical court may perhaps suggest on a wider plane certain problems encountered also in the governmental and jurisdictional life of medieval Buda. In the development of the Tavernical court two conflicting trends are apparent. The towns from the 1370's onwards collectively strove, and with much success, to exercise a determining influence on the institutional character of the court and assert their own jurisdictional exclusiveness. Once the Tavernical court had been lifted out of its former role in *praesentia regia* jurisdiction, it became increasingly subject to pressures applied by the towns and was, thus, forced to assume characteristics not dissimilar to those evident in the jurisdictional organisation of the politically less constrained towns of the west. Nevertheless, as the early history of *praesentia regia* jurisdiction and, moreover, the continued links maintained between the Tavernical court and the realm's central judicial apparatus both suggest, the towns were from the first drawn towards and even at the end unable entirely to free themselves from the organs of kingly majesty and the royal administration.

A corresponding pattern is apparent also in medieval Buda. The town was founded and, like other towns of the realm, entrusted with extensive judicial and governmental rights. These effectively gave the town its own special legal identity and an institutional organisation quite separate and removed from both the realm as a whole and the agencies of the royal administration. But early in the town's history, Buda's basic right to appoint its own chief magistrate was overridden, by almost a whim of royal policy, and Rectors were imposed on the new community. Nevertheless, under the guidance of its long serving patrician families and imbued with the associative idea transferred from the west, Buda was well able to recover from this early assault on its liberties. Over the succeeding period, the town's governmental and jurisdictional organisation was successfully made to accord with the principles laid

161

down in its charter and an independent institutional life was fashioned out within the town. Buda was indeed able to advance and reinforce its immune status in the realm through the territorial extension of its own jurisdictional rights.

Yet, despite these marked successes, elements suggestive of fragility begin to re-emerge in the fifteenth century. These first make their appearance in social organisation. The established alliance of wealth with power evident earlier in Buda's history and the development of Hungarian and European towns as a whole was severed. The lure of the royal palace set close beside the town drew off a whole class of wealthy burghers and left political power in the hands of a poorer social elite. In the wake of this development came the 1439 revolt which, in its turn, occasioned changes in the governmental organisation of the town. At the same time, the expansion of royal authority threatened the principles laid down in Buda's foundation charter which very much provided the legal basis for the town's governmental and judicial autonomy. While the basic institutional organisation of the town survived intact, the new measure of royal power yet provoked a reversal of jurisdictional trends evident earlier in the preceding century. Furthermore, the ideology of government, already set in disarray as a consequence of the 1439 revolt, strikingly altered to recognise the new authority possessed by the monarch.

The history of the Tavernical court may with some justification be taken to illustrate how the towns' desire for an independent jurisdictional organisation never quite came to be reconciled with diverging tendencies urging some form of integration with the royal administration. Although here the personal influence of the monarch is more keenly perceived, the history of Buda can be seen in very much the same light. On the one side, there is the by no means unsuccessful attempt to preserve and develop the spirit and letter of the town's earliest charter and the principle of municipal independence which this afforded; on the other, the problems imposed by the sheer weight of monarchical authority in its turn periodically subverting the fulfilment of burgher aspirations. It is, however, precisely this correlation between the governmental and jurisdictional history of Buda and the development of the Tavernical court, the collective jurisdictional organisation of the realm's towns, that makes impossible any too narrow an interpretation of events occurring within this one community. Rather, the problems faced by Buda, because they may be shown to have their parallels elsewhere, suggest the existence of perhaps far more deep-rooted difficulties inherent in the history of Hungary's towns.

For the greater part of their history, Hungary's towns radiate what may excusably be called an impression of "German-ness." Their leading citizen families were largely of German origin; their most important records often ornately written in the German language and in a flowing Gothic hand. For the laws and institutions of the towns, both individually and collectively established, direct parallels may be found in the lands to the west. Nor is this impression to any degree misplaced or in historical terms falsely conceived. For Béla IV himself, in order to populate the realm's nascent urban centres, had encouraged to his country immigrants from, in the main, Germany awarding these of necessity the rights and privileges to which they were accustomed in their homeland. Thus, the initial and determining conception of town life assumed in Hungary was one derived from abroad and, however much the realm may have matured to accommodate this, one essentially that had been already defined by circumstances quite outside the realm and its own historical experience. Certainly, a town such as Buda proved well capable of furthering and, in its institutional development, reinforcing the principles expounded in its first charter. Yet this partial success, for at least the reason that it proved incomplete, should not be allowed to obscure the fundamental nature of the Hungarian state in which Buda and the other towns of the realm were set. For even the most casual acquaintance with Hungarian history, such as one hopes may additionally be gained from this work, reveals the kingdom to be quite different from the neighbouring Empire out of whose political conditions and dissensions the seminal notions of municipal autonomy had been transferred.

Throughout the medieval period, the Hungarian monarchs exercised full rights over that most crucial of political barometers, the kingdom's coinage. The Crown was possessed of a substantial income deriving from regalian revenues. These might at times be supplemented by the personal ownership of extensive properties within the realm. An effective Chancellery apparatus functioned during even the darkest days while, through the *loca credibilia* and county courts, decisions and judgments fashioned in the *curia* could be immediately relayed and effected at a local level. Thus, on no occasion was there room for self-appointed peasant or knightly agencies of justice to emerge in compensation for any absence of central authority. Certainly, at times, baronial leagues cast their grim shadow over the kingdom. But normally the appearance of these was only rendered possibly by long absences on the part of the monarch or the weaknesses imposed by regencies and minority rule. In any event, it must be conceded that Sigismund's alliance with the barons of the Hungarian *Order of the Dragon* proved far more fruitful than his overtures to the Swabian League. More regularly though, the magnates sought no upstart rival power to monarch, but instead an immediate influence over his person and policy through their assumption of high administrative and judicial offices. Thus, almost unwittingly, they brought their might down on the side of the Crown and central government. Extending their power in the name of the King, they thereby expanded the perimeters of monarchical authority.

As has been recently pointed out by Karl Leuschner,[1] the extent of local autonomy attainable by a town depends not so much upon charters or any advanced legal conceptions as rather upon the degree of weakness inherent within the organisation of the state and the relative impotence of central authority. Thus, the independent powers gradually acquired by Nuremberg over the medieval period were won step by step as a consequence of a corresponding decline of political influence by the monarch and his imperial officials. Certainly, towards the close of the medieval period and during the course of the sixteenth century, we may observe the general imposition of practical restraints on the exercise of municipal authority by the towns of the Empire. Yet this development only further endorses Leuschner's argument. As newly felt centripetal influences were applied within the individual princedoms of the Empire, an independent life was quite simply squeezed out of the great *Reichstädte*. In Hungary, a peculiar variant to these sequences is clearly demonstrable.

German towns were established in the realm, endowed with German rights and for the greater part of their history developed very much as German cities. Yet precisely because Hungary was a relatively well ordered state with an immediately apparent and persuasive central authority, the unhindered pursuit and attainment of autonomy by the towns of the realm could never be entirely achieved and maintained. Through the character of the monarchy and the royal administration, realm impinged into town periodically upsetting and impeding the full untrammelled realisation of those principles and ambitions first expounded in the foundation charters. Such is clearly apparent in not only the collective organisation of the realm's towns, but, moreover, in the history of one of Hungary's greatest and most successful communities: Buda. The practicalities and fundamental notions which underlay this town's governmental and jurisdictional life could, once transferred from their birthplace in Germany, but in Hungary enjoy a mixed and at times uneasy history.

APPENDIX I

The Pest-Buda Charter of 1244

In nomine Sancte Trinitatis et Individue Unitatis amen. Bela Dei gratia Hungarie, Dalmatie, Croatie, Rame, Servie, Gallitie, Lodomerie Comanieque rex in perpetuum. Omnibus Christi fidelibus presentem paginam inspecturis salutem in omnium Salvatore. Cum in multitudine populorum regum ac principum gloria sumpmopere attendatur, non inmerito regalis decrevit sublimitas suos subditos provisionibus amplioribus ordinare, ut populus sibi serviens et fidelitate et numero augeatur. Ad universorum igitur notitiam presentium ac posterum harum tenore volumus pervenire, quod cum tempore persecutionis Tartarorum, quorum impetus et sevitia Domino permittente grave dispendium intulit regno nostro, hospites nostri de Pesth privilegium super ipsorum libertate confectum et concessum ammisissent, nos seriem libertatis memorate, cum esset notoria, duximus renovandum et presentibus annotandam, que talis est, videlicet quod in expeditionem, in quam personaliter ibimus, debent nobiscum mittere decem milites decenter armatos. Item infra limites regni nostri ab omni tributo, salva tricesima et salvo iure ecclesie Budensis, quantum ad tributa de salibus exigenda, sint exempti. Item de vineis eorundem cibriones nullatenus exigantur. Item nullus principum nostrorum violentum descensum facere possit super eos, nec aliquid contra eorum recipere voluntatem, sed descendens justo pretio sibi necessaria debeat comparare. Item nullus hospes ex ipsis possessiones suas vel domos vendere valeat alicui extraneo, nisi in eadem villa volenti a modo habitare. Item quicunque ex ipsis sine herede decesserit, possessiones suas dimmittendi facultatem habeat, cui volet. Item quicunque ex eis possessiones emerit, si per annum et diem nullus ipsum super hoc impetierit, de cetero eas sine contradictione aliqua possideat pacifice et quiete. Item habeant liberam electionem plebani, cum eorum ecclesia vacaverit, nec plebanus vicarios constituat eis

165

invitis. Item ipsi maiorem ville eligant, quem volent et nobis electum present-
ent, qui omnes causas eorum mundanas debeat judicare. Sed si per ipsum
debita justitia alicui non fuerit exhibita, ipse villicus et non villa debeat con-
veniri coram nobis, vel illo, cui duxerimus committendum. Item vicepalatinus
violenter descendere non possit super eos, nec eosdem judicare. Item omnia,
qui eis post recessum Tartarorum . . . *(lacuna)* . . . possint sine contradictione
qualibet possidere. Item quicunque cum eis habitare voluerint habentes
ibidem possessiones, cum eis teneantur servitia debita exercere. Item duellum
inter eos non judicetur, sed secundum quantitatem et qualitatem commissi,
super quo quis impetitur, purgationem exhibeat congruentem. Item cum im-
petiti fuerint per quempiam, ab aliquo extraneo non possint produci testes
contra eos, nisi ex ipsis vel aliis habentibus consimilem libertatem. Item tam
terram Kuer, quam eis de novo contulimus, quam alias, quas prius habuerunt,
dividant in communi, habita contemplatione facultatis cuiuslibet, quantam
possit facere araturam, ne terre supradicte inculte remaneant et inanes. Item
naves at carine descendentes et ascendentes cum mercibus et curribus apud
eos descendant et forum sicut prius habeant cottidianum. Item Minor Pesth
ultra Danubium sita quantum ad naves ascendentes et descendentes et cibriones non solvendos consimili gaudeat libertate. Item homo magistri
thawarnicorum nostrorum non debeat stare cum monetariis inter ipsos, sed
unus ex ipsa villa fidedignus illis associetur, qui super receptionem monete
regalis curam adhibeat pervigilem et undique diligentem. Ut autem huius
prenotate libertatis series salva semper et inconcussa perseveret in posterum,
nec aliquo successu temporum possit aliquatenus retractari, presentem eisdem
paginam duximus concedendam caractere bulle nostre auree perhenniter
roboratam. Verum quia exhibitio privilegii ipsorum existens sub aurea bulla
propter viarum discrimina esse periculosa videbatur, transcriptum eiusdem de
verbo ad verbum sub munimine dupplicis sigilli nostri concessimus, tantam
presentibus fidem volentes adhiberi, ut ad exhibitionem illius nullatenus
conpellantur. Datum per manus venerabilis patris Benedicti Colocensis
archiepiscopo, aule nostre cancellarii, venerabili patre Stephano archiepiscopo
Strigoniensi, Bartholomeo Quinqueecclesiensi, Cleto Agriensi, Stephano
Zagrabiensi, Blasio Chanadiensi, Artolpho Ultrasilvano episcopis, ecclesias
Dei salubriter gubernantibus, Vincenio in episcopum ecclesie Waradiensis
electo et confirmato, Jauriensi et Wesprimiensi sedibus vacantibus, Ladislao
palatino et comite Simigiensi, Dionisio bano et duce totius Sclavonie, Matheo
magistro thawarnicorum et comite Posoniensi, Demetrio iudice curie et
comite Musuniensi, Laurentio waiawada Ultrasilvano, Rolando magistro
Dapiferorum et comite Suppruniensi, Mauritio magistro pincernarum et
comite Jauriensi, Stephano magistro agazonorum et comite de Orbaz,

Arnoldo comite Nitriensi, Herrico Ferrei Castri ac ceteris magistratus et comitatus regni nostri tenentibus, anno ab incarnatione Domini millesimo ducentisimo quadragesimo quarto, regni autem nostri anno nono et octavo Kalendas Decembris.

(Dezső Csánki & Albert Gárdonyi, *Monumenta diplomatica civitatis Budapest, 1148–1301*, Budapest, 1936, pp. 41–3.)

APPENDIX II

The Judges and Councillors of Medieval Buda

1259-1264:   Peter *villicus*.[1]

The Period of the Rectors

c.1265–1267:   Rector Preussel[2]
                 Rector Mykud[3]
1268–1276:   Rector Walter[4]
1276:   Rector Charles[5]
before 1279–88: Rector Hench[6]
1288-96:   Rector Werner[7]
                 1289: George and Rudolf, *iurati* [8]
                 1292: Gusman, Jacob, Rudolf, Helelus, Kunc, Vasuath, Kunc
                 examinator, Fridul, Nicolas, Volfard, Weidner, Nicolas,
                 iurati [9]
1296–c.1304:   Rector Ladislas[10]
c.1304–1307:   Rector Petermann[11]
1307–before 1319: Rector Ladislas (second term of office)[12]
1317/9–36:   Rector Johann[13]
                 1317: Kunclin son of Hertlieb, Bartholomew, Albert son of
                 Ruprecht, Nicolas son of Weidner, Kunclin Megerdorf-
                 er, Ulving, Nicolas Lohrer, Ulmann, Permann, Tilmann,
                 Johann, Demeter, *iurati*[14]
                 1318: Benus, Kunclin son of Hertlieb, Bartholomew, Albrus,
                 Kunclin Megerdorfer, Ulving, Ulmann, Nicolas Lohrer,
                 Permann, Tilmann, Nicolas de Eger, Nicolas son of
                 Mykó, *iurati*[15]
                 1322: Tilmann, Albert, Kunclin Megerdorfer, Ulving, Mat-
                 thias, Hench, Lanthmann, Nicolas son of Mykó, Rued-

lin, Petermann, Nicolas son of Hailman, Johann de
Eger, *iurati* [16]

1329: Tilmann *vice-iudex,* Kunclin Megerdorfer, Ulving,
Jacob de Eger, Nicolas de Győr, Ruedlin, Nicolas
brother of Tilmann, Kunclin son of Johann, Michael
son of Ulmann, Sedulin Pernhauser, Peter son of Mykó,
Johann son of Bocuk, *iurati*[17]

1332: Tilmann *vice-iudex,* Kunclin Megerdorfer, Ulving,
Jacob de Eger, Nicolas brother of Tilmann, Ruedlin,
Sedulin Pernhauser, Nicolas de Győr, Michael son of
Ulmann, Peter son of Mykó, Johann son of Bocuk,
iurati [18]

1337-1346/7:   Rector Nicolas[19]

1337: Tilmann, Kunclin Megerdorfer, Ulving, Jacob de Eger,
Ruedlin, Nicolas brother of Tilmann, Michael son of
Ulmann, Sedulin Pernhauser, Nicolas son of Gudrann,
Lorand, Peter son of Mykó, Johann son of Matuch,
iurati [20]

1341: Kunclin *vice-iudex,* Ulving, Jacob de Eger, Ruedlin,
Michael son of Ulmann, Sedulin Pernhauser, Lorand,
Nicolas Rabensteiner, Jenslin Megerdorfer, Peter son of
Nicolas de Győr, Peter son of Mykó, Johann son of
Bocuk, *iurati* [21]

1342: Nicolas son of Gudrann *vice-iudex,* Jacob de Eger,
Nicolas son-in-law of Ulving, Ruedlin, Michael son of
Ulmann, Sedulin Pernhauser, Kunclin son of Johann,
Lorand, Nicolas Rabensteiner, Peter de Győr, Jenslin
Megerdorfer, Peter son of Mykó, Johann son of Bocuk,
iurati [22]

1343: Kunclin son of Johann, *iuratus* [23]
1344: Kunclin son of Johann, Lorand, *iurati* [24]
1345: Jacob de Eger, *iuratus* [25]

The Period 1346-1529

1346/7:   Lorand *iudex,* Kunclin son of Johann, Nicolas Ulving, Johann de
Eger, Nicolas Rabensteiner, Peter de Győr, Nicolas de Losnych
(Labinth), Michael son of Kunclin, Nicolas *examinator,* Peter *de
foro Danubii,* Nicolas son of Peter, Peter brother of the Crusader,
iurati. [26]

1347:   Lorand *iudex,* Kunclin son of Johann, Nicolas Ulving, Johann de
Eger, Nicolas Rabensteiner, Peter de Győr, Nicolas de Labinth
(Losnych), Michael son of Kunclin, Nicolas *examinator,* Johann

Crispus, Nicolas son of Leopold, Nicolas son of Peter, Peter brother of the Crusader, *iurati* [27]

1348/9:   Tilmann *iudex* [28]

1350:   Michael son of Kunclin *iudex* [29]

1351:   Michael son of Kunclin *iudex* [30]

1353:   Lorand *iudex* [31]

1354:   Lorand *iudex,* Michael son of Kunclin, Nicolas Ulving, Peter de Győr, Johann de Eger, Nicolas de Losnych (Labinth), Ludlinus Styczunpah, Jenslin Hailmann, Nicolas son of Leopold, Stephen Lorand, Nicolas son of Seydlin Megerdorfer, Paul son of Lambert, Johann Tuzan, *iurati* [32]

1362:   Lorand *iudex* [33]

1364:   Stephen Lorand *iudex* [34]

1365:   Lorand *iudex,* Hans Pernhauser, Stephen Lorand, Andrew Litteratus, *iurati* [35]

1366:   Michael son of Kunclin, *iudex* [36]

1367:   Michael son of Kunclin, *iudex* [37]

1370:   Michael son of Kunclin *iudex,* Hans Pernhauser, Johann Weyguel *institor,* Lawrence son of Chamar, Jacob Longus *pellifex,* Peter Schreiber, Henry Rechperger, Nicolas Longus, Ulrich *collector hospitum,* Nicolas Tilmann, Andrew *Litteratus,* Paul de Pilis, *iurati* [38]

?1371–4:   Ulving *iudex* (mentioned in 1375 as "former judge") [39]

1374:   Johann the Cock, son of Tilmann, *iudex* [40]

1375:   Ulving son of Nicolas *iudex* [41] (= Ulving II)

1376:   Ulving son of Nicolas *iudex* [42]

1377:   Nicolas Gleczel *iudex,* Jacob Longus, *pellifex et iuratus* [43]

1378:   Ulving son of Nicolas *iudex,* Frederick Chratzer, Lawrence son of Chamar, Johann Greczinger, Jacob *pellifex,* Peter *scriptor* (Schreiber), Johann Pernhauser, Nicolas Stoyan, Ladislas im Gezzel, Nicolas Lorand, Hans *tricesimator,* Johann Tuzan, Ladislas Magnus, *iurati* [44]

1380:   Johannes Hunrer *iudex* [45]

1381:   Lawrence son of Chamar *iudex,* Jacob *Kuerschner (pellifex) iuratus* [46]

1383:   Ulving son of Nicolas *iudex* [47]

1384:   Ulving son of Nicolas *iudex,* Peter *scriptor,* Johann Gleczel, Nicolas Stoyan, Ladislas *de vico,* Michael Roessler, Ulrich Rabensteiner, Michael Nadler, Stephen Ruebsam, Johann Hatus, Ladislas Vasarus, Briccius son of Nicolas, Johann son of Thomas, *iurati* [48]

1385:   Ulving son of Nicolas *iudex,* Peter *scriptor,* Johann Gleczel, Nicolas Stoyan, Michael Nadler, Michael Roessler, Ladislas *de vico,* Ulrich Rabensteiner, Stephen Ruebsam, Johann *Litteratus,* Henslin son of Vitus, Briccius son of Nicolas, Johann son of Thomas, *iurati* [49]

1388:	Johann Gleczel *iudex* [50]
1389:	Ulrich Rabensteiner *iudex* [51]
1390:	Johann Pernhauser *iudex* [52]
1392:	Johann Gleczel *iudex,* Johann Pernhauser, Mark Stoyan, Lawrence Nynderthaym, Johann Omicheim, Hertlin, Berchtold Kraft, George Kasse, Johann *Litteratus,* Nicolas de Senche, Johann son of Vitus, Michael Nadler, *iurati* [53]
1393:	Ulrich Rabensteiner *iudex* [54]
1395:	Mark Stoyan *iudex,* Johann Pernhauser, Johann Gleczel, Michael Nadler, Lawrence Nynderthaym, Hertlin, Nicolas de Eger, Ladislas Lorand, Jacob Hailman, Johann son of Thomas, Matthias de Tobayd, Johann son of Vitus, Michael Potroch, *iurati* [55]
1396:	Johann Pernhauser *iudex* [56]
1397:	Hertlin *iudex* [57]
1398:	Hertlin *iudex* (possibly Mark Stoyan served also in this capacity for part of the year), Johann *Litteratus,* (Hans) Groland, *iurati* [58]
1401:	Hertlin *iudex,* Johann *Litteratus,* Nicolas de Eger, Ladislas son of Stephen Lorand, *iurati* [59]
1402:	Andrew son of Frederick *iudex* [60]
1403:	Peter Rauczan *iudex,* Rigo Rechperger, Lawrence Nynderthaym, Andrew, *iurati* [61]
1404:	Peter Rauczan *iudex* [62]
1406:	Johann Siebenlinder *iudex* [63]
1409:	(?) Johann Siebenlinder *iudex,* Johann son of Thomas, Jacob *sartor,* Stephen of Szepes, Gaspar, Peter Borgyas *aurifisor, iurati* [64]
1410:	Rigo Rechperger *iudex* [65]
1411:	Johann Siebenlinder *iudex* [66]
1412:	Rigo Rechperger *iudex* [67]
1414:	Johann Siebenlinder *iudex* [68]
1415:	Johann Stadler *iudex* [69]
1416:	Johann Budwisser *iudex,* Matthias Visi, Benedict Bator, *iurati* [70]
?1417:	Johann *rasor iudex,* Michael, Peter, Ponawrar, Jacob Longus *pellifex,* Ludwig Sachs, Peter Paldauff, Gaspar Bernhart, Michael de Erd, *iurati* [71]
1418:	Michael Nadler *iudex* [72]
1419:	Michael Nadler *iudex* [73]
1420:	Ludwig Sachs *iuratus* [74]
1421:	Gaspar Bernhart *iudex* [75]
(before) 1422:	Conrad (probably Gündelwein) *iudex* [76]
1422:	Peter Paldauff *iudex* (*iudex* title also claimed for this year by Johann Rotenburg, but probably only out of bravado) [77]
1423:	Peter Paldauff *iudex* [78]

1424:	Peter Paldauff *iudex*—followed by Conrad Gündelwein *iudex*[79]
1425:	Michael Nadler *iudex*[80]
1426:	Michael Nadler *iudex*, Peter de Kesző, Blaise *pellifex, iurati*[81]
1427:	Michael Nadler *iudex*, Conrad Mehlmeister, Paul Haz, *iurati*[82]
1428:	Peter Paldauff *iudex*, Ladislas de Erd *iuratus*[83]
1429:	Nicolas (Wolfgang) Farkas-Hyko *iudex*, Andrew Stubihen, Martin Hohnauer, Erhard Kremer, Jacob von dem Pach, Günther, Paul Haz, Matthias *aurifisor*, Johann *carnifex*, Ladislas de Erd, Matthias *Litteratus*, George *Litteratus*, Johann *pellifex, iurati*[84]
1432:	Martin Hohnauer *iudex*[85]
1433:	Michael Nadler *iudex*[86]
1434:	Michael Nadler *iudex*, Ulrich Lemmel *iuratus*[87]
1435:	Peter Onwein (Bornemisza) *iudex*[88]
1437:	Ladislas Farkas *iudex*, Paul Haz, Michael Weiss *mercator, iurati*[89]
1439:	Ladislas Farkas *iudex*[90]
1440:	Dionysius de Kopách *iudex*, Michael Fodor *iuratus*[91]
1441:	Peter Onwein (Bornemisza) *iudex*[92]
1445:	Peter Onwein (Bornemisza) *iudex*[93]
1446:	Stephen *Litteratus* de Mykola *iudex*, Stephen the Apothecary *iuratus*[94]
1447:	Johann Münzer *iudex*[95]
1448:	Peter Vitus, Nicolas, Maeyer, *iurati*[96]
1451:	Martin Weissenstein *iudex*[97]
1452:	Stephen Cristini *iudex*[98]
1453:	Johann Münzer *iudex*[99]
1454:	Stephen de Mykola *iudex*[100]
1456:	Dionysius *Litteratus* de Albaregali (Székesfehérvár) *iudex*, Thomas *vitripar*, Johann Hertauf *iurati.*[101]
1457:	Johann Münzer *iudex*, Anthony Zekel, Cristianus Bebel, Stephen *Litteratus* de Buda (Ermen) *iurati*[102]
1459:	Johann Münzer *iudex*[103]
1460:	Stephen *Litteratus* de Buda (Ermen) *iudex*[104]
1461:	Johann Münzer *iudex*[105]
1462:	Stephen *Litteratus* de Buda (Ermen) *iudex*, Cristianus Bebel, Korlath Polgar, Johann Pronus *(apothecarius)*, Gregory *pellifex*, Koncz Polgar (= Conrad Wan), Dionysius *Litteratus*, Stephen Pirger, Ladislas Polgar, Johann Alch, Matthias *vitripar*, George Makrai *iurati*[106]
1463:	Johann Münzer *iudex*[107]
1464:	George Makrai *iudex*, Egidius Sthoz *iudex pecuniarium*, Stephen Purger, Pongracz, Johann Kalmar, Benedict *pellifex*, Matthias *vitripar*, Anthony Zunchu, Nicolas Thegez, Ladislas *Litteratus*, Johann Alch, Nicolas Porkelab *alias* Zekel, Johann Hertauf *iurati*[108]

1465:   Johann Münzer *iudex,* Johann Alcs, Pongracz Swer, Michael
              Fodor *iurati* [109]
1466:   Stephen *Litteratus* de Buda (Ermen) *iudex* [110]
1467:   Johann Münzer *iudex* [111]
1468:   Stephen de Mykola (Angyal) *iudex* [112]
1469:   Lucas Agsch *iudex* [113]
1470:   Stephen Kovach *iudex* [114]
1471:   Leopold Dax *iudex,* Matthias *vitripar et iuratus* [115]
1472:   Stephen Kovach *iudex* [116]
1473:   Leopold Dax *iudex,* Johann *carpentarius,* Matthias *vitripar*
              iurati [117]
1474:   Lawrence de Bayon *iudex* [118]
1475:   Johann Münzer *iudex* (dies and is succeeded by George Forster),
              Stephen de Mykola (Angyal) *iudex pecuniarum,* Conrad Wan,
              Nicolas Thegez, Herman Kranacher, Dionysius *Litteratus,* George
              Forster, Gregory *pellifex,* Johann *carpentarius,* Johann *Litteratus,*
              Thomas Sigel, Peter Tharnak, Nicolas Ebendorffer *iurati* [119]
1476:   Stephen Kovach *iudex,* Gregory *pellifex,* Nicolas Ebendorffer
              iurati [120]
1478:   Matthias Vitripar *iudex,* Thomas Meixner, Demetrius Keneres
              iurati [121]
1479:   George Forster *iudex* [122]
1480:   Lawrence *Litteratus* de Bayon *iudex,* Leopold Dax *iudex pecuni-*
              arum, Gregory *pellifex,* Conrad Wan *iurati* [123]
1481:   Leopold Dax *iudex,* Nicolas Thegez *iudex pecuniarum,* Conrad
              Wan, Valentine Themeskezy, Thomas Meixner, Benedict Proby
              (Pechy), Nicolas Ebendorffer, Clement Berki, Sebald Nessinger,
              Gregory Adam, Johann Pramperger, Peter Tharnak, Thomas
              Engl *iurati* [124]
1482:   Gregory Adam *iudex* [125]
1483:   George Foster *iudex,* Lawrence *Litteratus* de Bayon *iudex pecu-*
              niarum, Nicholas Ebendorffer, Thomas Maingos *iurati* [126]
1486:   Kerezthus *iudex,* Clement Berki *iurati* [127]
1487:   Goerge Forster *iudex,* Clement Berki *iuratus* [128]
1488:   Gregory Adam *iudex,* Nicolas Thegez, Johann *Litteratus*
              iurati [129]
1489:   Thomas Maingos *iudex* (possibly for a short period in January
              1490, Laurence *Litteratus* de Bayon), Nicolas Ebendorffer, Nico-
              las Thegez, Johann *Litteratus,* Martin *aurifaber iurati* [130]
1490:   Gregory Adam *iudex,* Ruprecht Haller, Johann Arnolth *iurati* [131]
1491:   Johann Pemfflinger *iudex* [132]
1492:   Gregory Adam *iudex,* Demetrius Kalmar, Nicolas Thegez, Martin
              aurifaber iurati [133]
1493:   Johann Pemfflinger *iudex* [134]

1494:   Gregory Adam *iudex,* Barnabus Yo, Demetrius Kalmar *iurati*
                (possibly also Matthias Ewthwes Harber) [135]
1495:   Johann Pemfflinger *iudex* [136]
1496:   Gregory Adam *iudex* [137]
1497:   Johann Pemfflinger *iudex* [138]
1498:   Johann Kanczlyr *iudex,* Johann Arnolth *iudex pecuniarum,*
                George Sweg, Paul Polyak, Barnabus Yo, Nicolas Ebendorffer,
                Demetrius Kalmar, Thomas Schaur, Johann Pechy, Johann
                Harber, Peter Tetemy, Sigismund Kronsfelder, Barnabus *Littera-*
                tus (Nicolas Malosas) *iurati* [139]
1499:   Johann Pemfflinger *iudex,* Gregory Kuntstock *doctor et iuratus* [140]
1500:   Gregory Adam *iudex,* Johann Pechy, Johann Arnolth, Nicolas
                Malosas *iurati* [141]
1501:   Johann Pemfflinger *iudex,* Thomas Schaur, Caspar *pistor, iurati* [142]
1502:   Peter Tetemy *iudex,* George Sweg, Johann Arnolth, Nicolas
                Malosas *iurati* [143]
1503:   Matthias Harber *iudex,* Erhard Mulner *iuratus* [144]
1504:   Peter Tetemy *iudex,* Thomas Schaur, Johann Arnolth *iurati* [145]
1505:   Johann Pemfflinger *iudex* [146]
1506:   Peter Tetemy *iudex* [147]
1507:   Johann Harber *iudex* [148]
1509:   Johann Pemfflinger *iudex* [149]
1511:   Wolfgang Hamburger (possibly Hainburger) *iudex,* George *pistor*
                semellarum (Kreus, Kömlődy), George Sweg, Johann Arnolth
                iurati [150]
1512:   Wolfgang Hamburger *iudex minor,* George *pistor semellarum et*
                iuratus [151]
1513:   Ruprecht Haller *iudex* [152]
1514:   Stephen Zekel *iudex,* Johann Kalmar *iuratus* [153]
1515:   Johann Harber *iudex,* Thomas Schawer, Blaise Bodrogyi, George
                pistor iurati [154]
1516:   Michael *aromatarius iudex,* Michael Gazon (Gailsam), Wolfgang
                Litteratus iurati [155]
1517:   Wolfgang Hamburger *iudex* [156]
1518:   Michael *aromatarius iudex,* Johann Kalmar, Michael Stancze,
                Nicolas Kreen *iurati* [157]
1519:   Stephen Tetemy *iudex* [158]
1520:   Thomas Pechy *iudex* [159]
1521:   Johann Harber *iudex* [160]
1523:   Johann Harber *iudex,* Thomas Zaboztho, Stephen Zekel, Nicolas
                Thorma, Michael Gazon, Johann Sarhajo, Wolfgang, Blaise
                Weres, Johann Zabo, Johann Bodo, Paul Malosas, Leonard, Gre-
                gory Nyirew *iurati* [161]
1524:   Johann de Attád *iudex* [162]

1525: Wolfgang Freiberger *iudex* [163]

before 1526: Barnabus Kesztyűgyártó *iuratus* [164]

1527: Johann Zabo *iudex*, Peter Palczan *iuratus* [165]

1528: Johann de Attád *iudex* [166]

1529: Wolfgang Freiberger *pannicida et iudex* (killed by the Turks and succeeded by Albert Ettyeki) [167]

ABBREVIATIONS USED FOR COMMONLY CITED
SOURCES AND ARCHIVES

AK, 1973:

András Kubinyi, "A budai német patriciátus társadalmi helyzete családi összeköttetéseinek tükrében a XIII. századtól a XV. század második feléig," *Levéltári közlemények,* 42, 1973, pp. 203-264.

AMB:

Archív mesta Bratislavy, (ed) D. Lehotská, D. Handzová, I, Praha, 1956.

Annales USB:

Annales Universitatis Scientiarum Budapestiensis de Rolando Eötvös nominatae, Sectio historica, I etc, 1957 etc.

AO:

Anjou-kori okmánytár (Codex diplomaticus Hungaricus Andegavensis), (ed) Imre Nagy, Gyula Nagy, I-VII, Budapest, 1878-1920.

ÁÚO:

Árpád-kori új okmánytár (Codex diplomaticus Arpadianus continuatus), (ed) Gusztáv Wenzel, I-VIII, Pest-Budapest, 1860-78.

Bártfai Szabó, *Pest:*

(ed) László Bártfai Szabó, *Pest megye történetének okleveles emlékei 1002-1588,* Budapest, 1938.

BStAN:

Bayerische Staatsarchiv, Nuremberg.

177

Bud.Tört.:	*Budapest története,* (ed) László Gerevich, I-II, Budapest, 1973.
CD:	*Codex diplomaticus regni Hungariae ecclesiasticus et civilis,* (ed) György Fejér, 42 parts in Volumes I-XII, Buda, 1829-44.
CJH:	*Corpus Juris Hungarici (Magyar törvenytár), 1000-1526,* (ed) Dezső Márkus, Budapest, 1899.
Csánki, *Földrajza*:	Dezső Csánki, *Magyarország történeti földrajza a Hunyadiak korában,* I-III, V, Budapest, 1890-1913.
Csánki, *Mon.Bud.*:	(ed) Dezső Csánki, Albert Gárdonyi, *Monumenta diplomatica civitatis Budapest (Budapest történetének okleveles emlékei), 1148-1301,* Budapest, 1936.
Df:	Budapest, Országos Levéltár, *Fényképgyűjtemény,* (this collection is at present undergoing reclassification. Former serial numbers are, where relevant, given in parentheses in the notes).
Dl:	Budapest, Országos Levéltár, *Mohács előtti gyűjtemény.*
DRH:	*Decreta Regni Hungariae (Gesetze und Verordnungen Ungarns), 1301-1457,* (ed) Ferenc Döry, György Bónis, Vera Bácskai, Budapest, 1976.
Endlicher:	(ed) Stephanus Ladislaus Endlicher, *Rerum Hungaricarum Monumenta Arpadiana,* Sangalli, 1849.
Gombos, *Catalogus*:	(ed) Albinus Franciscus Gombos, *Catalogus fontium historiae Hungaricae,* I-III, Budapestini, 1937-8.
Házi, *Sopron*:	(ed) Jenő Házi, *Sopron szabad királyi város története,* I-II (13 parts), Sopron, 1921-43.

HO:	*Hazai okmánytár (Codex diplomaticus patrius),* (ed) Imre Nagy, Imre Paur, K. Ráth, D. Véghely, I-VIII, Győr-Budapest, 1865-91.
Hóman-Szekfű:	Bálint Hóman, Gyula Szekfű, *Magyar történet,* I-II, Budapest, 1935-6.
Horváth & Huszár:	T. A. Horváth, Lajos Huszár, "Kamaragrófok a középkorban," *Numizmatikai közlöny,* 54-5, 1955-6, pp. 21-33.
Iványi, *Bártfa*:	Béla Iványi, *Bártfa szabad királyi város levéltára, 1319-1526,* Budapest, 1910.
Iványi, *Eperjes*:	Béla Iványi, *Eperjes szabad királyi város levéltára, 1245-1519,* I-II, Szeged, 1931-2.
LK:	*Levéltári közlemények,* I etc, 1923-46, 1954 etc.
Mon.Strig.:	*Monumenta ecclesiae Strigoniensis,* (ed) F. Knauz, L. C. Dedek, I-III, Strigonii, 1874-1924.
Mon.Vesp.:	*Monumenta Romana episcopatus Vesprimiensis (A veszprémi püspökség római oklevéltár),* (ed) A római magyar történeti intézet, I-III, Budapest, 1896-1902.
MTT:	*Magyar történelmi tár,* (ed) A magyar tudományos akadémia, I-XXV, Pest-Budapest, 1855-78.
MZsO:	*Magyar zsidó oklevéltár,* (ed) Sándor Scheiber, Fülöp Grünwald, Armin Friss, I-XV, Budapest, 1903-72.
Quellen Wien:	*Quellen zur Geschichte der Stadt Wien,* (ed) Anton Mayer, I-III, Wien, 1895-1911.
Regesta Regum:	*Regesta Regum stirpis Arpadianae critico-diplomatica (Az Árpádházi királyok okleveleinek*

kritikai jegyzéke, (ed) Imre Szentpétery, Iván Borsa, I-II, Budapest, 1923-61.

Smičiklas:

(ed) T. Smičiklas, *Codex diplomaticus Regni Croatiae, Dalmatiae et Slavoniae,* II-XIV, Zagrabiae, 1904-16.

Stadtrecht:

Das Ofner Stadtrecht, (ed) Karl Mollay, Budapest, 1959.

SRH:

Scriptores rerum Hungaricarum, (ed) Emericus Szentpétery, I-II, Budapestini, 1937-8.

TBM:

Tanulmányok Budapest múltjából, I *etc,* Budapest, 1932 *etc.*

Tkalčić:

(ed) Tkalčić, *Monumenta liberae regiae civitatis Zagrabiensis,* I-XII, Zagreb, 1889-1905.

TT:

Történelmi tár, (ed) A magyar tudományos akadémia, Budapest, 1879-1911.

Werbőczy, *Tripartitum:*

István Werbőczy (Stephanus de Werbewcz), *Tripartitum opus iuris consuetudinarii regni Hungariae,* Millenniumi emlékkiadás, (ed) Sándor Kolozsvári & Kelemen Óvári, Budapest, 1897.

Zichy:

Codex diplomaticus domus senioris comitum Zichy de Zich et Vasonkéő, (ed) Imre Nagy, Iván Nagy, D. Véghely, E. Kammerer, P. Lukcsics, I-XII, Budapest, 1871-1931.

Zimmermann-Werner:

(ed) Franz Zimmermann, Carl Werner, *Urkundenbuch zur Geschichte der Deutschen in Siebenburgen,* I-III, Hermannstadt, 1892-1902.

ZO:

Zsigmondkori oklevéltár, (ed) Elemér Mályusz, I-II, Budapest, 1951-8.

NOTES

Chapter 1

1. On Roman and Dark Age Aquincum, *Bud. Tört.,* I.
2. *Anonymi Gesta Hungarorum,* ch 46 (*SRH,* I, p. 94).
3. György Györffy, "Lés débuts de l'évolution urbaine en Hongrie," *Cahiers de civilisation médiévale,* 12, 1969, p. 255.
4. András Kubinyi, *Die Anfänge Ofens,* Berlin, 1972, p. 12.
5. *Anonymi Gesta Hungarorum,* ch 46 (*SRH,* I, p. 94); discussed by Györffy in *Bud. Tört.,* I, p. 273.
6. Gombos, *Catalogus,* I, pp. 292, 305.
7. *Rogerii Carmen Miserabile,* ch 15 (*SRH,* II, p. 561); Csánki, *Mon.Bud.,* p. 243.
8. *Bud. Tört.,* I, p. 274.
9. E. Fügedi, "Topográfia és városi fejlődes a középkori Óbudán," *TBM,* 13, 1959, pp. 31-6.
10. Dezső Pais, "Budapest kialakulásának kezdetei," *Magyar Nyelv,* 50, 1954; *Bud. Tört.,* I, pp. 251, 259.
11. *Anonymi Gesta Hungarorum,* ch 57 (*SRH,* I, pp. 114-5).
12. Györffy, "Les débuts. (see above, n. 3)," pp. 256-8.
13. Csánki, *Mon.Bud.,* p. 16.
14. Dezső Pais in *SRH,* I, p. 115 n. 1; H. Helbig, L. Weinrich, *Urkunden und erzählende Quellen zur deutschen Ostsiedlung im Mittelalter,* II, Darmstadt, p. 511, n. 1.
15. Csánki, *Mon.Bud.,* p. 200; *HO,* III, p. 79.
16. Csánki, *Mon.Bud.,* p. 21; *ÁÚO,* II, pp. 113-125.
17. György Granasztói, *A középkori magyar város,* Budapest, 1980, p. 70.
18. Csánki, *Mon.Bud.,* pp. 37-8.
19. *Rogerii Carmen Miserabile,* ch 16 (*SRH,* II, p. 562).
20. András Kubinyi, "Buda város pecséthasználatának kialakulása," *TBM,* 14, 1961, p. 114.
21. Csánki, *Mon.Bud.,* pp. 37-8; E. Fügedi, "Das mittelalterliche Königreich Un-

182   NOTES

garn als Gastland," in (ed) Walter Schlesinger, *Die deutsche Ostsiedlung des Mittelalters als Problem der europäischen Geschichte (Reichenau Vorträge, 1970-2), Vorträge
und Forschungen,* XVIII, Konstanz, 1975, p. 507.

22. *Rogerii Carmen Miserabile,* ch 28 (*SRH,* II, p. 571).

23. The text of the 1244 charter is reproduced above as Appendix I.

24. Henrik Marczali, *Magyarország története az Árpádok korában* (Volume II of
the series edited by Sándor Szilágyi, *A magyar nemzet története*), Budapest, 1896,
p. 506; *CD,* IV/2, p. 222.

25. Csánki, *Mon.Bud.,* p. 55.

26. András Kubinyi, *Die Anfänge Ofens,* Berlin, 1972, pp. 56-8; László Gerevich,
"A pesti és budai vár," *Budapest régiségei,* 24, 1976; M. Jankovich, "Buda környék
plébániáinak középkori kialakulása és a királyi kápolnák intézménye," *Budapest régiségei,* 19, 1959, pp. 82-3.

27. András Kubinyi, "Topographic Growth of Buda up to 1541," *Nouvelles
Études Historiques,* I, Budapest, 1965, p. 137; E. Fügedi, "Középkori magyar városprivilégiumok," *TBM,* 14, 1961, pp. 78-81; by the same author, "Burgstadt, Vorburgstadt und Stadtburg: Zur Morphologie des mittelalterlichen Buda," *Acta Archaeologica,* 33, 1981, p. 175.

28. See above, pp. 40-41.

29. András Kubinyi, "Topographic Growth . . . (see above, n. 27)," p. 138.

30. *Ibid.,* pp. 138-41.

31. (Ed) A római magyar történeti intézet, *Monumenta Romana Episcopatus Vesprimiensis,* I, Budapest, 1896, pp. 291, 297.

32. András Kubinyi, "Buda város pecséthasználatának kialakulása," *TBM,* 14,
1961, p. 114; by the same author, *Die Anfänge Ofens,* Berlin, 1972, p. 79.

33. Both names may be employed even within a single text, Österreichische
Nationalbibliothek, Handschriftensammlung, *Cod. Lat.* 4470, *fol* 243r, 350v.

34. H. Fischer, *Die Siedlungsverlegung im Zeitalter der Stadtbildung,* Wien, 1952,
pp. 49-59.

35. Elemér Mályusz, "A mezővárosi fejlődés," in (ed) György Székely, *Tanulmányok a parasztság történetéhez Magyarországon a 14. században,* Budapest, 1953,
p. 142.

36. Csánki, *Mon.Bud.,* pp. 71-4, 177, 243, 247-9, 263, 282-3, 291, 298, 321;
Mon.Vesp., I, pp. 291, 294, 297, 315, 331.

37. Csánki, *Mon.Bud.,* p. 283.

38. *Ibid.,* pp. 157-8.

39. The first reference to "duodecim iurati" occurs in 1268, Csánki, *Mon.Bud.,*
p. 100.

40. *Mon.Bud.,* pp. 71-3.

41. (Ed) Karl Mollay, *Das Ofner Stadtrecht,* Budapest, 1959; an earlier edition
was published in Pressburg (Pozsony-Bratislava), 1849, edited by Andreas Michnay
and Karl Lichner.

42. György Székely, "A pannóniai települések kontinuitásának kérdése és a hazai
városfejlődes kezdetei," *TBM,* 12, 1957; "Le sort des agglomerations pannoniennes au

NOTES 183

début du moyen age et les origines de l'urbanisme en Hongrie," *Annales USB,* 3, 1961;
see also, Aladár Radnóti, "Pannóniai városok élete a korai feudalizmusban," *Magyar
tudományos akadémia II. osztályának közleményei,* 5, 1954.

43. Ambrus Pleidell, "A magyar várostörténet első fejezete," *Századok,* 68, 1934,
pp. 180-1; *Bud.Tört.,* I, p. 222; E. Fügedi, "Der Stadtplan von Stuhlweissenburg und
die Anfänge des Bürgertums in Ungarn," *Acta Historica,* 15, Budapest, 1969, p. 105;
paper delivered by László Gerevich at the Anglo-Hungarian Conference of Archaeolo-
gists held at the British Museum, August, 1978.

44. *Gesta Friderici I imperatoris,* I, xxxii; (trans) C. C. Mierow, *The Deeds of
Frederick Barbarossa,* 1966, New York, p. 66.

45. Gombos, *Catalogus,* III, p. 1720.

46. E. Fügedi, "Középkori magyar városprivilégiumok," *TBM,* 14, 1961, pp. 20,
83, citing Tadeusz Lewicki, *Polska i kraje sasednie w świetle "Ksiega Rogera" geo-
grafa arabskiego z XII w. Al-Idrisiego (Prace Komisji Orientalistycznej, 34),* Krakow,
1945, pp. 128-30, 219.

47. Ivan Hrbek, "Ein arabischer Bericht über Ungarn," *Acta Orientalia,* 5, 1955,
p. 213. For the sometimes confusing terminology applied by Arab writers to the
Hungarians, see Tadeusz Lewicki, "Les noms de Hongrois et de la Hongrie chez les
médiévaux geographes arabes et persans," *Folia Orientalia,* 19, 1978.

48. Ambrus Pleidell, "A magyar városok első fejezete," *Századok,* 68, 1934,
pp. 308-9.

49. Lajos Huszár, "Der Umlauf ungarischer Münzen des 11. Jahrhunderts im
Nordeuropa," *Acta Archaeologica,* 19, 1967.

50. Csánki, *Mon.Bud.,* pp. 234-5, 247-8; György Granasztói, *A középkori magyar
város,* Budapest, 1980, pp. 47-8, 59; Oskar von Mitis, *Urkundenbuch zur Geschichte
der Babenberger in Österreich,* II, Wien, 1955, p. 64.

51. *CJH,* p. 60 (I Lad: I: 31).

52. Gombos, *Catalogus,* I, p. 37.

53. Ambrus Pleidell, "A magyar városok első fejezete," *Századok,* 68, 1934,
p. 280.

54. Gombos, *Catalogus,* III, p. 2258.

55. György Székely, "Wallons et Italiens en Europe centrale aux XIe-XVIe
siècles," *AnnalesUSB,* 6, 1964, pp. 10-11.

56. E. Fügedi, "Középkori magyar városprivilégiumok," *TBM,* 14, 1961, p. 21.

57. *Ibid.,* p. 22.

58. (Ed) János Luczenbacher, *Tudománytár,* 15, 1844, pp. 155-6.

59. Gy. Pauler, *A magyar nemzet története az árpádházi királyok alatt,* I,
Budapest, 1899, p. 254; Henrik Marczali, *Magyarország története (A műveltség
könyvtára),* Budapest, 1911, p. 108.

60. *Gesta Friderici I imperatoris,* I, xxxii; (trans) C. C. Mierow (see above n. 44),
p. 67.

61. *CJH,* p. 86 (I Lad: III; 25); Emil Jakubovich, "I Endre király tőrvénybeidéző
ércbilloga," *Turul,* 47, 1933; Péter Váczy, "A királyi kúria bírósága és I Endre tőrvénybeidéző ércbilloga," *Századok,* 68, 1934.

184

NOTES

62. *CJH,* p. 106 (Col: I; 37); discussed in László Erdélyi, *Magyarország társadalma a XI. századi tőrvenyeiben,* Budapest, 1907, p. 109.

63. Péter Váczy, *Die erste Epoche des ungarischen Königtums,* Pécs, 1935, pp. 30, 36, 40-1; György Györffy, *István király és műve,* Budapest, 1977, pp. 204-5; the relationship of the *bilochi* to the county lieutenants is discussed briefly in the 1222 Golden Bull, the best edition of which is provided by Géza Érszegi in *Fejér megyei történeti évkönyv,* 6, 1972, pp. 1-15.

64. *CJH,* pp. 76-8 (I Lad III: 3); for the Golden Bull, see above n. 63.

65. Péter Váczy, "Immunitas és jurisdictio," *A bécsi-magyar intézet évkönyve,* I, 1931.

66. Josef Deér, *Heidnisches und Christliches in der altungarischen Monarchie (Acta Litterarum ac Scientiarum Regiae Universitatis Hungaricae Francisco-Josephinae, Sectio Geographica-Historica, Tom.* I, *Fasc.* 2*),* Szeged, 1934, p. 79.

67. Gyula Szekfű, *Serviensek és familiarisok (Értekezések a történelmi tudományok köréből),* Budapest, 1912, p. 13; Péter Váczy, *Die erste Epoche des ungarischen Königtums,* Pécs, 1935, pp. 35-49; Ándor Csizmadia, Kálmán Kovács, László Asztalos, *Magyar állam- és jogtörténet,* Budapest, 1978, p. 49.

68. Elemér Mályusz, "A patrimoniális királyság," *Társadalomtudomány,* 13, 1933, pp. 38-9.

69. György Györffy, "Honfoglalás, megtelepedés és kalandozások," in (ed) Antal Bartha, Károly Czeglédy, András Róna-Tas, *Magyar őstörténeti tanulmányok,* Budapest, 1977, p. 136.

70. Hóman-Szekfű, I, pp. 208-9.

71. László Erdélyi, *Magyarország társadalma a XI. századi tőrvenyeiben,* Budapest, 1907, pp. 24-5.

72. Péter Váczy, *Die erste Epoche des ungarischen Königtums,* Pécs, 1935, pp. 36-7.

73. Gyula Szekfű, *Serviensek és familiarisok* (see above, n. 67), pp. 21-4; Lajos Elekes, Emma Lederer, György Székely, *Magyarország története,* I, Budapest, 1961, pp. 106, 112-3.

74. Kamill Szoika, *A földesúri biráskodás az árpádkori Magyarországon,* Budapest, 1944, pp. 17-8.

75. Hóman-Szekfű, I, pp. 404, 477-80.

76. *Ibid.,* pp. 405-6.

77. Endre Varga, György Bónis, Alajos Degré, *A magyar birósági szervezet és perjog,* Budapest, 1961, p. 12; Iván Bertényi, "Vármegyei tisztviselők a középkorban," *História,* II, 1980, p. 26.

78. Péter Váczy, "Immunitas és jurisdictio," *A bécsi-magyar intézet évkönyve,* I, 1931, pp. 33-40.

79. Endre Varga, György Bónis, Alajos Degré, *op.cit.* (see above, n. 77), p. 8.

80. Kamill Szoika, *A földesúri biráskodás az árpádkori Magyarországon,* Budapest, 1944, pp. 36-9, 62-3; Ignatius de Battyán, *Leges Ecclesiasticae Regni Hungariae,* II, Claudiopolis, 1827, p. 401.

81. Imre Hajnik, *A magyar birósági szervezet és perjog,* Budapest, 1899, p. 290;

Tivadar Botka, *Trensini Csák Máté és kortársai (Értekezések a történelmi tudományok köréből)*, Budapest, 1873, p. 62.

82. Gyula Kristó, *Csák Máté tartományúri hatalma*, Budapest, 1973, pp. 157, 162-4.

83. Jenő Szűcs, "Theoretical Elements in Master Simon of Kéza's *Gesta Hungarorum* (1282-85)," *Études Historiques Hongroises,* 1975, pp. 243-7; for an alternative examination of the process of "westernisation" in Hungary, see Z. J. Kosztolnyik, *Five Eleventh Century Hungarian Kings: Their Policies and Their Relations with Rome,* East European Monographs 79, New York, 1981, and my criticisms of the same in *The Slavonic and East European Review,* 61, 1983, pp. 445-6.

84. E. Fügedi, "La formation des villes et les ordres mendiants en Hongrie," *Annales Économies, Sociétiés, Civilisations,* 25, 1970, p. 977.

85. E. Fügedi, "Das mittelalterliche Königreich Ungarn als Gastland," in (ed) Walter Schlesinger, *Die deutsche Ostsiedlung des Mittelalters als Problem der europäischen Geschichte (Reichenau Vorträge,* 1970-2), *Vorträge und Forschungen,* XVIII, Konstanz, 1975, pp. 502-4; by the same author, ' "Németjogú" falvak települése a szlovák és német nyelvterületen,' in (ed) György Székely, *Tanulmányok a parasztság történetéhez Magyarországon a 14. században,* Budapest, 1953.

86. *Rogerii Carmen Miserabile (SRH,* II, pp. 551-88).

87. György Györffy, "Einwohnerzahl und Bevölkerungsdichte in Ungarn bis zum XIV. Jahrhundert," (ed) Commission Nationale des Historiens Hongrois, *Études Historiques,* I, Budapest, 1960, pp. 184-5.

88. Endlicher, pp. 444-7; *ÁÚO,* VII, p. 103.

89. *Csánki, Mon.Bud.,* p. 41; *CD,* IV/1, pp. 329, 332.

90. Endlicher, pp. 451, 498, 471, 482.

91. Endlicher, pp. 489, 503, 505, 517, 526, 545, 551, 623; Iványi, *Eperjes,* no. 8.

92. E. Fügedi, "La formation des villes et les ordres mendiants en Hongrie," *Annales Économies, Sociétiés, Civilisations,* 25, 1970, p. 977; by the same author, "Der Stadtplan von Stuhlweissenburg und die Anfänge des Bürgertums in Ungarn," *Acta Historica,* 15, 1969, p. 124.

93. Bálint Hóman, *A magyar városok az Árpádok korában,* Budapest, 1908, pp. 20, 24-5.

94. Endlicher, pp. 528, 548.

95. András Kubinyi, "Zur Frage der deutschen Ostsiedlung im mittleren Teil des Königreichs Ungarn, 1200-1541," *Vorträge und Forschungen,* XVIII (see above, n. 85), p. 544.

96. József Szalay, "Városaink nemzetiségi viszonyai a XIII. században," *Századok,* 14, 1880, pp. 541-2; István Orosz, "Jobbágyköltözés és köznemesség kelet-Európában a XV-XVI. században," *Egyetemes történeti tanulmányok,* 11, 1977 (Debrecen), pp. 3-4.

97. *DRH,* pp. 155, 195-6 (1397:1; 1405:6).

98. E. Fügedi, "Das mittelalterliche Königreich Ungarn als Gastland," *Vorträge und Forschungen,* XVIII (see above, n. 85), p. 488.

186 NOTES

99. György Györffy, *Az árpádkori Magyarország történeti földrazja,* Budapest, 1963, pp. 103-5.

100. György Györffy, *Az árpádkori Magyarország történeti földrajza,* Budapest, 1963, pp. 103-5, 558; András Kubinyi, "Zur Frage der deutsche Ostsiedlung im mittleren Teil des Königreich Ungarn," *Vorträge und Forschungen,* XVIII, Konstanz, 1975 (see above, n. 85), pp. 549-50; György Granasztói, *A középkori magyar város,* Budapest, 1980, pp. 93-7.

101. Bálint Hóman, *A magyar városok az Árpádok korában,* Budapest, 1908, pp. 39-40.

102. "Hospitibus iuxta castrum Valkow commorantibus, videlicet Teutonicis, Saxonibus, Hungaris et Slavis," Endlicher, p. 434.

103. *Dl.* 24536; *Dl.* 14451-2; *Dl.* 76696; *Dl.* 83256; György Komoróczy, "Debrecen város képviseleti rendszere," in (ed) György Bónis, Alajos Degré. *Tanulmányok a magyar helyi önkormányzat múltjából,* Budapest, 1971, p. 90.

104. László Fejérpataky, *A pannonhalmi apátság alapitó oklevele,* Budapest, 1878, pp. 20, 25-6, 151.

105. *CD,* II, p. 102.

106. Hóman-Szekfű, I, p. 537; Imre Hajnik, *A magyar birósági szervezet és perjog,* Budapest, 1899, pp. 104-7.

107. Endlicher, p. 623, see also pp. 446, 499.

108. *Ibid.,* p. 499.

109. *Ibid.,* p. 489.

110. F. Keutgen, *Urkunden zur städtischen Verfassungsgeschichte,* Berlin, 1899, pp. 103, 159, 204, 252-3.

111. Endlicher, p. 445.

112. *HO,* VI, p. 42.

113. Endlicher, pp. 471, 518; *Dl.* 76696.

114. András Kubinyi, "Zur Frage der deutschen Ostsiedlung im mittleren Teil des Königreichs Ungarn," *Vorträge und Forschungen,* XVIII (see above, n. 85), p. 543.

115. Edith Ennen, *The Medieval Town,* Amsterdam-New York-Oxford (North Holland Publishing Co.), 1979, p. 111.

116. Endlicher, p. 625; see also, *ibid.,* pp. 404, 443, 446-7, 469, 490, 625.

117. Vaclav Chaloupecký, *Kniha Žilinska,* Bratislava, 1934, pp. 197-202.

118. F. Keutgen, *Urkunden zur städtischen Verfassungsgeschichte,* Berlin, 1899, p. 467; see above, Chapter III (ii), and especially p. 60.

119. Csánki, *Mon.Bud.,* pp. 157-8; F. Keutgen, *op. cit.* (see above, n. 118), p. 204; Oskar von Mitis, *Urkundenbuch zur Geschichte der Babenberger in Österreich,* II, pp. 39-47.

120. Endlicher, pp. 435, 445, 497; *HO,* V, p. 61; Keutgen, *op. cit.* (see above, n. 118), pp. 52, 104, 142, 178, 188, 194; Imre Hajnik, *A perdöntő eskü és az előzetes tanúbizonyitás a középkori magyar perjogban (Értekezések a társadalmi tudományok köréből),* Budapest, 1881, p. 3; by the same author, *A magyar birósági szervezet és perjog,* Budapest, 1899, pp. 259-61.

Chapter 2

1. Gyula Kristó, *Az aranybullák évszázada,* Budapest, 1976, p. 127; György Granasztói, *A középkori magyar város,* Budapest, 1980, p. 89.

2. Csánki, *Mon.Bud.,* pp. 71-3.

3. *Ibid.,* pp. 247-9.

4. Endlicher, p. 623.

5. *Mon.Vesp.,* I, p. 302.

6. *AO,* I, p. 595 (in the case brought by the Count of Cherne against the inhabitants of Mány in Fehér county).

7. SRH, I, p. 482 (*Chronicon Pictum,* ch. 190).

8. (Ed) Oskar von Mitis, *Urkundenbuch zur Geschichte der Babenberger in Österreich,* II, Wien, 1955, pp. 184, 186, 237, 317, 319, 320; *Mon.Strig.,* II, pp. 54-5; Csánki, *Mon.Bud.,* p. 73.

9. Zimmermann-Werner, I, pp. 137-8.

10. *AK,* 1973, p. 218.

11. *Ibid.;* Ferenc Eckhart, "Néhány kiadatlan árpádkori oklevél," *Fejérpataky emlékkönyv,* Budapest, 1917, p. 77.

12. Zimmermann-Werner, I, pp. 137-8.

13. Csánki, *Mon.Bud.,* pp. 71-2; discussed by András Kubinyi, *Die Anfänge Ofens,* Berlin, 1972, p. 71, n. 361.

14. Csánki, *Mon.Bud.,* p. 100.

15. *Ibid.,* pp. 157-8.

16. (Ed) Dezső Csánki, Albert Gárdonyi, *Monumenta diplomatica civitatis Budapest (Budapest történetének okleveles emlékei), 1148-1301,* Budapest, 1936; (ed) Gusztáv Wenzel, "Budai regeszták," *MTT,* I, IV, 1855-7.

17. See below, n. 46.

18. Horváth & Huszár, pp. 21-33.

19. (Ed) Henrik Marczali, *A magyar történet kútfőinek kézikönyve (Enchiridion fontium historiae Hungarorum),* Budapest, 1901, p. 141.

20. *Ibid.,* pp. 129-30.

21. *DRH,* p. 77.

22. *Ibid.,* pp. 99, 113, 117; Hóman-Szekfű, II, p. 120.

23. For the Hungarian coinage of this period and related topics, see particularly, Bálint Hóman, *Magyar pénztörténet,* 1000-1325, Budapest, 1916, and by the same author, *A magyar királyság pénzügyei és gazdaságpolitikája Károly Róbert korában,* Budapest, 1921, of which pp. 10-46 are devoted almost entirely to the Árpád period.

24. *Fejér megyei történeti évkonyv,* 6, 1972, pp. 13-4.

25. Hóman, *Pénztörténet* (see above, n. 23), p. 459; for the Friesach denar and its role as an "export coinage," D. M. Metcalf, *The Coinage of Southern Germany in the Thirteenth Century,* London, 1961, pp. 50-5.

26. Hóman, *Pénztörténet* (see above, n. 23), p. 289.

27. F. Király, "Éremlelet Örkénypusztán a XIII. századból," *Numizmatikai közlöny,* 52-3, 1953-4; the remainder of the hoard consists of Friesach denars.

28. Hóman, *Pénztörténet* (see above, n. 23), pp. 457-9; the Csanád mint, first mentioned in a letter of 1221, seems to have ceased functioning as a result of the Mongol devastation of the town only later being revived by the Angevins — Hóman, *Pénztörténet,* p. 458 and, by the same author, *A magyar királyság pénzügyei és gazdaságpolitikája Károly Róbert korában,* Budapest, 1921, p. 198.

29. Georgius Pray, *Specimen Hierarchiae Hungaricae,* II, Posonii et Cassoviae, 1779, p. 62.

30. (1256) "idem episcopus (zagrebiensis) una cum bano Stephano vice nostra procuraverat Cameram de ultra Dravam"—C. Truhelka, "Die slavonische Banaldenare," *Wissenschaftliche Mittheilungen aus Bosnien und der Hercegovina,* Sarajevo, 6, 1899, p. 333; Smičiklas, IV, pp. 42-3.

31. D. M. Metcalf, *Coinage in the Balkans, 820-1355 (Institute for Balkan Studies, no. 80)* Thessaloniki, 1965, p. 147.

32. Csánki, *Mon.Bud.,* p. 57.

33. *Mon.Strig.,* I, p. 456.

34. Truhelka, *op. cit.* (see above, n. 30), p. 335.

35. Truhelka's assertion that Stephen did not at this time possess the Sirmium mint is confirmed by Hóman, *Pénztörténet* (see above, n. 23), p. 334, n. 1. In Stephen's ratification of this grant, the careful avoidance of any reference to his father's donation suggests that Stephen felt himself to possess the primary legal claim to the mint, Truhelka, *op. cit.* (see above, n. 30), p. 458.

36. *Mon.Strig.,* I, p. 379.

37. *Ibid.,* pp. 520-21.

38. *DRH,* pp. 88, 101, 207; *Stadtrecht,* ch. 278.

39. Endlicher, pp. 451-4.

40. Smičiklas, V, p. 410.

41. *Ibid.*

42. Klaus-Detlev Grothusen, *Entstehung und Geschichte Zagrebs bis zum Ausgang des 14 Jahrhunderts,* Wiesbaden, 1967, pp. 279-81.

43. László Zolnay, "Az esztergomi latinusokról," *Esztergom évlapjai (Annales Strigonienses),* I, 1960, p. 161.

44. Horváth & Huszár, p. 22.

45. Smičiklas, VII, p. 103.

46. Csánki, *Mon.Bud.,* p. 130; for further examples, Horváth & Huszár, p. 22.

47. Csánki, *Mon.Bud.,* p. 100.

48. *DRH,* p. 118; *AO,* IV, pp. 234, 349.

49. Lajos Huszár, *A budai pénzverés története a középkorban,* Budapest, 1958, p. 25.

50. For Perchin, see Horváth & Huszár, p. 22, and Lajos Huszár, *op. cit.* (see above, n. 49), p. 25; the last has Perchin as principal administrator of the mint.

51. See above, n. 5; *AK,* 1973, p. 217.

52. Csánki, *Mon.Bud.,* p. 177; Zimmermann-Werner, I, pp. 99-100; *Dl.* 73625.

53. László Zolnay, "'Opus Castri Budensis,' A XIII. századi budai vár kialakulása," *TBM,* 15, 1963, p. 67; Horvath & Huszar, p. 25.

NOTES   189

54. *Mon.Strig.*, II, p. 156.
55. Csánki, *Mon.Bud.*, pp. 283, 353.
56. *Mon.Strig.*, III, p. 558; Horvath & Huszar, p. 25.
57. *Mon.Strig.*, I, p. 456.
58. András Kubinyi, *Die Anfänge Ofens*, Berlin, 1972, p. 74.
59. Friedrich Keutgen, *Urkunden zw städtischen Verfassungsgeschichte*, Berlin, 1901, pp. 118, 186, 8, 126-7.
60. *Ibid.*, p. 260.
61. Csánki, *Mon.Bud.*, pp. 234, 247.
62. A. Dopsch, "Zur Geschichte der Finanzverwaltung Österreichs im 13. Jahrhundert," in, by the same author, *Verfassungs- und Wirtschaftsgeschichte des Mittelalters*, Wien, 1928, pp. 445-50.
63. (Ed) Die Historische Kommission der kaiserlichen Akademie der Wissenschaften in Wien, *Fontes Rerum Austriacarum*, II/3, Wien, 1851, pp. 343, 462-3.
64. *Ibid.*, I, Wien, 1849, p. 107; Dopsch, *op. cit.* (see above, n. 62), pp. 459-60.
65. Dopsch, *op. cit.* (see above, n. 62), pp. 459-60.
66. Horváth & Huszár, p. 24.
67. *Bud.Tört.*, I, p. 331.
68. *MTT*, IV, p. 162.
69. *AO*, I, p. 645; *Mon.Strig.*, II, p. 520.
70. *Dl.* 2568; for uses of the term *capitaneus*, A. Bartal, *Glossarium media et infimae latinitatis regni Hungariae*, Budapest, 1901, p. 103.
71. *MTT*, I, p. 112 (Dubravius, *Historia Bohemiae*, VIII).
72. András Kubinyi, "Topographic Growth of Buda up to 1541," in (ed) Commission Nationale des Historiens Hongrois, *Nouvelles Études Historiques*, I, Budapest, 1965, p. 152; György Györffy, "Les débuts de l'évolution urbaine en Hongrie," *Cahiers de Civilisation Médiévale*, 12, 1969, p. 264.
73. *Df.* 249009 (Arch. Primat. Strig. *Arch. Eccl. Vetus*, no. 46); Lajos Kemény, "A kassai pénzverőház," *Magyar gazdaságtörténelmi szemle*, 9, 1902, p. 248; *DRH*, pp. 87, 97, 112, 121-2, 152.
74. "Darnach fuorten si in/Inder kamerhof hin/In der selben kluse/Wont der kunic mit huse."—Gombos, *Catalogus*, III, p. 1905; *Dl.* 11384.
75. István Sugár, *A budai vár és ostromai*, Budapest, 1979, p. 14; *Stadtrecht*, ch. 10, item 241.
76. László Zolnay, '"Opus Castri Budensis," A XIII. századi budai vár kialakulása,' *TBM*, 15, 1963, p. 45; by the same author, *Ünnep és hétköznap a középkori Budán*, Budapest (2nd Revised Edition), 1975, pp. 20-21.
77. *MTT*, IV, p. 166.
78. *CD*, X/4, p. 239.
79. Josef Deér, "Die dalmatinische Munizipalverfassung unter der ungarischen Herrschaft bis zur Mitte des 12. Jahrhunderts," *Ungarische Jahrbücher*, 1931, p. 379; Smičiklas, II, pp. 15, 18; *Monumenta spectantia Historiam Slavorum Meridionalium*, XXVI, Zagreb, 1894, pp. 60-62 (*Chronicle of Thomas of Spalato*, ch. 18).
80. Csánki, *Mon.Bud.*, pp. 22-33.

81. *Ibid.,* p. 199; György Györffy, "Les débuts de l'évolution urbaine en Hongrie," *Cahiers de Civilisation Médiévale,* 12, 1969, p. 264; *AK,* 1973, pp. 219-221.

82. Csánki, *Mon.Bud.,* pp. 73-4.

83. *MTT,* I, p. 113.

84. Csánki, *Mon.Bud.,* pp. 157-8.

85. *Ibid.,* pp. 71-3; see above, n. 5.

86. *AO,* I, p. 512.

87. *AO,* III, pp. 251-2.

88. Namely, the families of Kunclin, Megerdorfer and Petromann Karaz, (ed) K. Géresi, *Codex diplomaticus comitum Károlyi de Nagy-Károlyi,* I, Budapest, 1882, p. 53.

89. *AK,* 1973, p. 225-8.

90. Tilmann and his brother Nicolas, Ulving, Jacob de Eger and Ruedlin Redner.

91. *AO,* II, pp. 247-8, 274; *ZO,* II/2, no. 7043.

92. *MTT,* IV, p. 133.

93. *Ibid.,* p. 127.

94. *Dl.* 2570.

95. Csánki, *Mon.Bud.,* p. 299.

96. For this and much of what follows, György Székely, "Le développement de la magistrature de la ville de Buda au XIVe siècle," *Folia Diplomatica,* I, 1971, pp. 280-4.

97. *Chronicon Pictum,* ch. 190 (*SRH,* I, pp. 481-2).

98. Bártfai Szabó, *Pest,* no. 169.

99. *Chronicon Pictum,* ch. 193 (*SRH,* I, p. 485).

100. *MTT,* IV, p. 112; *AO,* V, p. 613.

101. *MTT,* IV, p. 123.

102. *Ibid.,* IV, p. 128; see above, Chapter VII(ii), and especially pp. 152-3.

103. *MTT,* IV, p. 139.

104. Csánki, *Mon.Bud.,* p. 230.

105. *Ibid.,* pp. 199-200.

106. *MTT,* IV, p. 130.

107. *Ibid.,* p. 130; *Dl.* 2568.

108. *Mon.Strig.,* III, p. 222.

109. *Dl.* 3554.

110. *Mon.Strig.,* III, p. 619. Lorand is first recorded as *iudex* in February 1347; the last reference to Nicolas as Rector is in the September of the previous year (*Dl.* 3858).

Chapter 3

1. *Mon.Strig.,* II, p. 717.

2. For this and much of what follows, see, András Kubinyi, "Topographic Growth of Buda up to 1541," in (ed) Commission National des Historiens Hongrois, *Nouvelles Études Historiques,* I, Budapest, 1965, pp. 138-40; by the same author, *Die Anfänge Ofens,* Berlin, 1972, pp. 34-41.

NOTES   191

3. Xystus Schier, *Buda sacra sub priscis regibus,* Viennae, 1774, p. 171; R.D.P.
Hieronymus Pez, *Scriptores rerum Austriacarum,* II, Lipsiae, 1725, col. 628.
    4. Schier, *op. cit.* (see above, n. 3), *ibid.; Mon.Vesp.,* II, pp. 383-4; Csánki,
Mon.Bud., pp. 343-4.
    5. Kubinyi, "Topographic Growth (see above n. 2)," pp. 139-41.
    6. *Bud.Tört.,* II, pp. 17-8.
    7. Kubinyi, "Topographic Growth (see above, n. 2)," pp. 142-3.
    8. F. Palacky, *Urkundenliche Beiträge zur Geschichte des Hussitenkrieges,* II,
Prag, 1873, pp. 473-5.
    9. László Borsos, "Régi budai házösszeirások," *TBM,* XIX, 1972, pp. 57-9.
    10. *ZO,* II/1, nos. 2199, 3101; *Dl.* 9821; *Dl.* 12461; *Dl.* 17323.
    11. *AO,* VI, p. 192; *Mon.Strig.,* II, p. 523; *Dl.* 24536; *Dl.* 17500; *Dl.* 9821, and
particularly, *MTT,* XXIII, p. 109.
    12. Jenő Szűcs, *Városok és kézművesség a XV. századi Magyarországon,* Budapest,
1955, pp. 42-3.
    13. *ZO,* II/1, no. 2199; *Dl.* 9937; Vidor Pataki, "A budai vár középkori helyrajza,"
Budapest régiségei, 1950, 15, p. 285, n. 17.
    14. Kubinyi, "Topographic Growth (see above, n. 2)," p. 149; Károly Pereházy,
Régi házak Pest-Budán, Budapest, 1976, p. 57.
    15. András *Kubinyi, "A mezőgazdaság* történetéhez a Mohács előtti Budán (Gal-
linczer Lénárt számadáskönyve 1525-ből')," *Agrártörténelmi szemle,* 6, 1964, p. 398.
    16. Imre Palugyay, *Buda-Pest szabad királyi városok leirása (Magyarország
leirása,* I), Pest, 1852, pp. 161, 172.
    17. Kubinyi, "Topographic Growth (see above, n. 2)," pp. 155-57.
    18. *Városok és kézművesség* (see above, n. 12), pp. 42-3.
    19. Csánki, *Mon.Bud.,* p. 54; András Kubinyi, *Die Anfänge Ofens,* Berlin, 1972,
p. 46.
    20. *Stadtrecht,* ch. 154.
    21. *Stadtrecht,* ch. 130, 154, 227; *Mon.Vesp.,* II, p. 203.
    22. *Stadtrecht,* ch. 227, 154.
    23. *ZO,* I, no. 434.
    24. *Stadtrecht,* ch. 427.
    25. *Ibid.;* Karl Otto Müller, *Welthandelsbraüche 1480-1540 (Deutsche Handel-
sakten des Mittelalters und der Neuzeit, V),* Stuttgart & Berlin, 1934, p. 199; *Dl.*
44478.
    26. *Stadtrecht,* ch. 211.
    27. Csánki, *Mon.Bud.,* pp. 229-30 (discussed by E. Fügedi, "Középkori magyar
városprivilégiumok," *TBM,* 14, 1961, pp. 89-91); *Dl.* 24678.
    28. Karl Otto Müller, *op. cit.* (see above, n. 25), p. 199.
    29. *Stadtrecht,* ch. 183, 189, 238-43, 353, 399.
    30. Edited with an introduction by Karl Mollay, *Das Ofner Stadtrecht,* Budapest,
1959; an earlier edition was published by Andreas Michnay and Paul Lichner, *Buda
városának törvénykönyve,* Pressburg, 1845.
    31. For the texts involved, see the introduction to the Mollay edition (see above, n.

192 NOTES

30), pp. 6-31; Néda Relković, "A budai jogkönyv harmadik kézirata a Fővárosi Könyvtárban," *A Fővárosi Könyvtár évkönyve*, 11, 1941, pp. 121-41.

32. *DRH*, p. 193 (1405:2).

33. Discussed further above, pp. 141-52.

34. Fővárosi Levéltár, no. 9.

35. Discussed further above, p. 109.

36. E. T. Gaupp, *Das alte Magdeburgische und Hallische Recht*, Breslau, 1826, p. 270.

37. *Ibid.*, p. 305.

38. George Bartal de Beleháza, *Commentariorum ad historiam status jurisque publici Hungariae Aevi mediae*, III, Posonii, 1847, p. 86; Iványi, *Eperjes*, no. 169 (discussed by Béla Iványi, "Jogtörténeti vonatkozások Eperjes város középkori számadáskönyveiben," *Fejérpataky Emkékkönyv*, Budapest, 1917, pp. 243-4).

39. J. G. Heineccius, *Historia Iuris Romani et Germanici*, Magdeburg-Halle, 1733, *Lib.* II, p. 428.

40. *Ungrisches Magazin oder Beitraege zur ungrischen Geschichte*, I, Pressburg, 1781, pp. 169-170, citing Frankenstein's *Brev. Originum nationum et praecipue Saxonicae in Transylvania*, Claudiopolis, 1697, p. 37.

41. George Bartal de Beleháza, *op. cit.* (see above, n. 38), *ibid.*

42. Andreas Michnay, Paul Lichner, *Buda városának tőrvénykönyve*, Pressburg, 1845, p. 36; E. T. Gaupp, *Das schlesische Landrecht*, Leipzig, 1828, pp. 56-7; Cecil Headlam, *The Story of Nuremberg*, London, 1899, p. 157.

43. *Stadtrecht*, ch. 374: *cf* F.L.A. von Lassberg *Der Schwabenspiegel*, Tübingen, 1840, p. 115; *Stadtrecht*, ch. 375: *cf* Heinrich Maria Schuster, *Das Wiener Stadtrechts-oder Weichbildbuch*, Wien, 1873, p. 71; *Stadtrecht*, ch. 376: *cf* Theodor Ortvay, *Geschichte der Stadt Pressburg*, II/4, p. 282.

44. Emma Lederer, *A középkori pénzüzletek története Magyarországon, 1000-1458*, Budapest, 1932, p. 85, n. 14.

45. For *Stadtrecht*, ch. 159 & 162, see back, n. 36-7; *Stadtrecht*, ch. 161 & 164: *cf* E. T. Gaupp, *Das alte Magdeburgische und Hallische Recht*, Breslau, 1826, pp. 294-299; *Stadtrecht*, ch. 163: *cf* Karl August Eckhardt, *Sachsenspiegel Landrecht*, Berlin-Frankfurt, 1955, p. 99.

46. Néda Relković, *Buda város jogkönyve*, Budapest, 1905, especially Chapter III, "A budai jogkönyv forrásbeli kapcsolatai."

47. *Stadtrecht*, ch. 302, 304; Wilhelm Ebel, "Über die rechtschöpferische Leistung des mittelalterlichen deutschen Bürgertums," *Vorträge und Forschungen*, XI, Konstanz-Stuttgart, 1966, p. 245.

48. (Ed) Wilhelm Altmann, *Eberhart Windeckes Denkwürdigkeiten zur Geschichte des Zeitalters Kaiser Sigismunds*, Berlin, 1893, p. 479; *Dl.* 64201.

49. Hence, for rape: *Stadtrecht*, ch. 284-6; Jacob Grimm, *Deutsche Rechtsalterthümer*, Göttingen, 1828, pp. 633-4; János Király, *Pozsony város joga a középkorban*, Budapest, 1894, pp. 285-6. For dicing: *Stadtrecht*, ch. 190; Selmecbánya's *Gemayne Stattrecht*, ch. 28 (*ÁÚO*, III, p. 215); Király, *op. cit.*, pp. 257-8.

50. Borrowing of this sort seems a quite common practice—Gerald Strauss,

Nuremberg in the Sixteenth Century, Bloomington & London (Indiana University Press, Second Edition), 1976, p. 57.

51. *Stadtrecht,* ch. 358.

52. *Ibid., Prologus,* i-ii.

53. *Stadtrecht,* ch. 29, 30, 167, 172.

54. *Ibid.,* ch. 153, 233, 235.

55. *Ibid.,* ch. 202, 352, 356.

56. Georg von Below, *Das altere deutsche Städtewesen und Bürgertum,* Bielefeld & Leipzig, 1898, p. 72.

57. "Nos N. Judex castri novi montis Pestiensis, Jurati et universi cives de eodem memorie commendamus, quod *etc.*"

58. János Király, *Pozsony város joga a középkorban,* Budapest, 1894, p. 69.

59. *Mon.Strig.,* III, p. 527; *Stadtrecht,* ch. 37; see also, Imre Palugyay, *Buda-Pest szabad királyi városok leirása,* Pest, 1852, p. 45.

60. *Stadtrecht,* ch. 24, 27, 32.

61. M. G. Kovachich, *Formulae Solennes Styli,* Pesthini, 1799, pp. 27, 32.

62. *Stadtrecht,* ch. 168, 235, 352, 356.

63. *Stadtrecht,* ch. 204-5, 404-440.

64. *TT,* 1889, pp. 372-384.

65. *Stadtrecht,* ch. 399.

66. *Ibid.,* ch. 33, 45.

67. *Stadtrecht,* ch. 49, 51, 68, 130, 144-5, 152-3, 218, 341, 394.

68. Lajos Kemény, "Kassai kereskedelmi társaság 1518-ban," *Magyar gazdaságtörténelmi szemle,* IV, 1897, p. 482.

69. *Stadtrecht,* ch. 307; Imre Hajnik, *A magyar birósági szervezet és perjog,* Budapest: *TT,* 1889, p. 374.

70. *Stadtrecht,* ch. 335.

71. *Stadtrecht,* ch. 31, 215; *Bud. Tört.,* II, p. 84.

72. *Dl.* 100032; see also, *Dl.* 17675; *MTT,* XII, p. 69.

73. *Zichy,* III, p. 289.

74. *Mon.Strig.,* III, p. 527.

75. *ZO,* II/1, nos. 3092, 3101; *Dl.* 11924; *Dl.* 11944; *Dl.* 13608; *Dl.* 15153; *Dl.* 15196; *Dl.* 93040; *Dl.* 46663.

76. *Dl.* 12461; *Dl.* 16355; *Df.* 270205 (Arch. civ. Cassovien., *Coll. Schwartzenbachiana,* no. 165.)—published in Gusztáv Wenzel, *Nevezetes per lőcsei polgárok között, 1421-9 (Értekezések a történeti tudományok köréből),* Budapest, 1873, pp. 16-34.

77. Loránd Szilágyi, "A magyar királyi kancellária szerepe az államkormányzatban, 1458-1526," *Turul,* 44, 1930, p. 55; Imre Szentpétery, *Magyar oklevéltan,* Budapest, 1930, pp. 173-4.

78. *Dl.* 45484.

79. *Stadtrecht,* ch. 29, 30.

80. *Ibid.,* ch. 167, 170-72.

81. M. G. Kovachich, *Codex Authenticus Iuris Tavernicalis,* Budae, 1803, p. 92;

194   NOTES

from 1464, the designation *iudex pecuniarum* may be found in the magistracy
lists—see above, Appendix II.

82. George von Below, *Das altere deutsche Städtewesen und Bürgertum,* Leipzig &
Bielefeld, 1898, p. 72.

83. Győző Ember, *Az újkori magyar közigazgatás története Mohácstól a török
kiűzéséig,* Budapest, 1946, p. 557; József Tirnitz, "Sopron szabad királyi város külső
tanácsa, 1526-1711," in (ed) György Bónis, Alajos Degré, *Tanulmányok a magyar helyi
önkormányzat múltjából,* Budapest, 1971, p. 54; and, in the same volume, Vera Bácskai,
"A mezővárosi önkormányzat a XV. században és a XVI. század elején," p. 12.

84. Discussed above, pp. 156-7.

85. Discussed above, pp. 105-6.

86. *CD,* X/4, pp. 237-41.

87. Jenő Szűcs, *Városok és kézművesség a XV. száazadi Magyarországon,* Budapest, 1955, pp. 303, 316.

88. *Stadtrecht,* ch. 12-15, 236/a-b.

89. *Ibid.,* ch. 61.

90. *Mon.Strig.,* II, p. 717.

91. *Stadtrecht,* ch. 55-6.

92. Kovachich, *Codex Authenticus* (see above, n. 81), p. 94.

93. Iványi, *Bártfa,* nos. 541, 1110, 1128, 1760.

94. *MTT,* XII, p. 66.

95. *Stadtrecht,* ch. 55.

96. *Ibid.,* ch. 54.

97. M. G. Kovachich, *Formulae Solennes Styli,* Pesthini, 1799, p. 23.

98. *Stadtrecht,* ch. 54.

99. *Ibid.,* ch. 56, 331.

100. Franz Kováts, "Pressburger Grundbuchführung und Liegenschaftsrecht im
Spätmittelalter," *Zeitschrift der Savigny Stiftung für Rechtsgeschichte (Germanische
Abteilung),* 39, 1918, p. 45; László Fejérpataky, *Magyarországi városok régi számadáskönyvei,* Budapest, 1885, pp. 76-101; "Liber civitatis Szomolnok," Országos Széchenyi könyvtár, *Cod.Lat. Medii Aevi,* no. 385; Oswald Redlich, *Die Privaturkunden
des Mittelalters,* München & Berlin, 1911, pp. 189-90.

101. Redlich, *op. cit.* (see above, n. 100), *ibid.*

102. *Stadtrecht,* ch. 274.

103. *Ibid.,* ch. 52, 54.

104. *MTT,* XII, p. 69; *HO,* 1, pp. 351-2, 388.

105. *Dl.* 38821.

106. Franz Eckhart, "Die glaubwürdigen Orte Ungarns im Mittelalter," *Mitteilungen des Instituts für Österreichische Geschichtsforschung, Ergänzungsband* IX, 1915,
pp. 473-81.

107. Imre Hajnik, *A királyi könyvek a vegyes házakbeli királyok korszakában
(Értekezések a történelmi tudományok köréből),* Budapest, 1879, pp. 14-15; Imre
Szentpétery, *Magyar oklevéltan,* Budapest, 1930, pp. 181-3; possibly this practice goes
back to the late Árpád period—*Dl.* 10295/9.

108. M. G. Kovachich, *Formulae Solennes Styli,* Pesthini, 1799, p. 123.

109. József Holub, *Zala megye története a középkorban,* I, Zala megye közönsége, 1929, pp.

312-327; Gyula Gábor, *A megyei intézmény alakulása és működése Nagy Lajos alatt,* Budapest, 1908, pp. 109-11, 214; Antal Főglein, "A vármegyei jegyzőkönyv," *LK,* 1938, pp. 142-3; by the same author, "A vármegyei notárius," *LK,* XIV, 1936; Géza Istványi, "A XIV. századbeli megyei oklevéladáshoz," *Turul,* 50, 1936, pp. 81-3; L. Bernát Kumorovitz, "Az authentikus pecsét," *Turul,* 50, 1936, pp. 62-3.

110. János Király, *Pozsony város joga a középkorban,* Budapest, 1894, pp. 338-340; *MTT,* XII, p. 69; *Dl.* 46636.

111. László Fejérpataky, *Magyarországi városok régi számadáskönyvei,* Budapest, 1885, pp. 78, 81, 84, 86, 88, 90, 93-5.

112. *Stadtrecht,* ch. 52.

113. *CD,* X/2, p. 408.

114. *Stadtrecht,* ch. 54.

115. Franz Eckhart, "Die glaubwürdigen Orte Ungarns (see above, n. 106)," pp. 521-2.

116. See generally in this context, R. Aubenas, "La famille dans l'ancienne Provence," *Annales d'Histoire Économique et Sociale,* 8, 1936, p. 529.

117. József Illés, *A magyar szerződési jog az Árpádok korában,* Budapest, 1901, pp. 65-6.

118. *ZO,* I, no. 4196.

119. M. G. Kovachich, *Codex Authenticus Iuris Tavernicalis,* Budae, 1803, p. 124.

120. *Stadtrecht,* ch. 200, 313, 370, 379, 397; see generally in this context, Ákos Timon, *Magyar alkotmány- és jogtörténet,* Budapest, 1919, pp. 397-8.

121. *Stadtrecht,* ch. 282, 392-3.

122. *Ibid.,* ch. 379.

123. Eckhart, "Die glaubwürdigen Orte Ungarns (see above, n. 106)," pp. 524-5; Imre Hajnik, *A magyar bírósági szervezet és perjog,* Budapest, 1899, pp. 171-4; József Illés, *A magyar szerződési jog az Árpádok korában,* Budapest, 1901, pp. 100-102.

124. (Ed) Die Historische Kommission der kaiserlichen Akademie der Wissenschaften in Wien, *Fontes Rerum Austriacarum,* II/1, Wien, pp. 181, 289; BStAN, *Stadt und Landalmosenampt, Urkunden,* nr. 116.

125. György Bónis, *Középkori jogunk elemei,* Budapest, 1972, p. 99.

126. *Df.* 229964 (Veszprémi kápt. hiteleshelyi levéltára, *Instr. Regni, Capsa P,* 237); *Df.* 263191 (Szepesi kápt. levéltára, *Misc. div. cott., Scr. 9, f. 13, nr 25*).

127. "Auch wan ainer ainem ain erb verkaufft, es sein hewser oder weingertn, so sol der verkauffer des kauffers vorstandt sein Jar und tag, fur al Zuspruch und hinderung"— János Király, *Pozsony város joga a középkorban,* Budapest, 1894, p. 398.

128. *Stadtrecht,* ch. 360; M. G. Kovachich, *Formulae Solennes Styli,* Pesthini, 1799, p. 269; Vilmos Fraknói, *Oklevéltár a magyar királyi kegyúri jog történetéhez,* Budapest, 1899, pp. 2-3; the *praescriptio* period for citizens was according to Werbőczy twelve years—Werbőczy, *Tripartitum,* I: 78; 2.

129. Imre Hajnik, *A magyar bírósági szervezet és perjog,* Budapest, 1899, p. 172; József Illés, *A magyar szerződési jog az Árpádok korában,* Budapest, 1901, p. 102.

130. *ZO*, II/1, no. 2199.

131. *Stadtrecht*, ch. 377-8.

132. Eckhart, "Die glaubwürdigen Orte Ungarns (see above, n. 106), " p. 465.

133. Gerhart Burger, *Die südwestdeutschen Stadtschreiber im Mittelalter*, Boblingen, 1960, pp. 2, 44-5.

134. Elemér Mályusz, "A magyarság és a városi élet a középkorban," *Századok*, 78, 1944, p. 12.

135. *Mon.Strig.*, II, p. 717; *ZO*, II/1, no. 3597; Házi, *Sopron*, I/2, p. 221; Iványi, *Bártfa*, no. 1760.

136. *Df.* 270205 (Arch. civ. Cassovien., *Coll. Schwartzenbachiana*, nr 165).

137. György Bónis, "Magyi János formuláskönyve és a gyakorlati jogtanitás," in (ed) Ándor Csizmadia, *A pécsi egyetem történetéből, Jubileumi tanulmányok*, I, Pécs, 1967 pp. 235, 239-40.

138. M. G. Kovachich, *Formulae Solennes Styli*, Pesthini, 1799, pp. 21-33, 206-9, 433-55.

139. *Ibid.*, p. 33

140. The standard work on the *loca credibilia* remains Franz Eckhart, "Die glaubwürdigen Orte Ungarns im Mittelalter," *Mitteilungen des Instituts für Österreichische Geschichtsforschung*, Ergänzungsband IX, 1915.

141. *AO*, VI, p. 270; *ZO*, II/1, no. 3732; *Dl.* 21967.

142. Eckhart, *op. cit.* (see above, n. 140), pp. 497-503.

143. András Kubinyi, "Buda város pecséthasználatának kialakulása," *TBM*, XIV, 1961, pp. 109-112, 120.

144. Házi, *Sopron*, I/2, p. 310; *Df.* 240434 (Arch. civ. Poson., *Chart. nr.*, 1803); Béla Iványi, "Eperjes szabad királyi város czimerei és pecsétjei," *Turul*, 29, 1911, p. 20; Géza Érszegi, "Körmend középkori pecsétjei és cimere," *Vasi szemle*, 33, 1979, p. 355; from the 1440's, a third and much smaller impressed seal was in the employ of the town: the *sigillum minus*. This had a limited credibility, though, and could not be used to confirm land transactions: *Dl.* 44478; *Dl.* 44704

145. *Mon.Strig.*, III, pp. 619-20; *Dl.* 3926; *Dl.* 3953; *AO*, VI, pp. 269-70; *Dl.* 5865; *Dl.* 6273; *Dl.* 7089.

146. Patents: *Zo*, I, nos. 539, 710, 1379, 1186, 1435, 1814, 1921, 2619, 2719, 3072, 3118, 3566, 4193, 4196, 4367, 4461, 5218, 5489, 5596, 5599, 5601; *ibid.*, II/1, nos. 2043, 2199, 3101, 3732, 5025; *Zichy*, IV, pp. 360-61; *MTT*, IV, pp. 158-9; *MTT*, IX, pp. 43-4. Privileges: *ZO*, I, nos. 2727, 4266; (ed) Imre Nagy, *Zala vármegye történetének oklevéltára*, II, Budapest, 1890, pp. 257-8.

147. *Dl.* 6273; *ZO*, I, nos. 2727, 4266.

148. *Dl.* 5866.

149. András Kubinyi, "Buda város pecséthasználatának kialakulása," *TBM*, XIV, 1961, p. 128.

150. (Ed) Levente Závodszky, *A hédervári család oklevéltára*, I, Budapest, 1909, p. 99; *CD*, X/2, p. 408.

151. *Stadtrecht*, ch. 53, 73, 404.

152. *Dl.* 50564; A Tiszántúli Református Egyházkerület Nagykönyvtára, Református Kollégium, Debrecen, R 1110/134; Fővárosi levéltár, no. 4.

153. See back, n. 146; during the late fourteenth and fifteenth centuries, the notion became increasingly current that town privileges only held an authentic status when applied to transactions involving properties actually within the area of municipal jurisdiction. For transactions falling outside this category, recourse to the more established *loca credibilia* was necessary. Hence, in Buda the circumstances under which a burgher or inhabitant might proceed before the Council for a privilege of confirmation came yet further to be reduced. It is for this reason that only one privilege issued by the Buda Council to confirm a land transaction survives from the fifteenth century: *Df.* 252008 (*Zágrábi érseki ltár, priv.* 40, dated 1475).

154. *Stadtrecht,* ch. 55.

155. Eckhart, *op. cit.* (see above, n. 140), p. 533.

156. *ZO,* I, nos. 4666, 4705.

157. *Stadtrecht,* ch. 203.

158. László Papp, "A birtokba-iktatás *(statutio)* lefolyása," *Szentpétery emlékkönyv,* Budapest, 1938.

159. *Ibid.,* p. 377.

160. *Dl.* 16355; *Dl.* 17675; *Dl.* 100190; *Dl.* 22637.

161. *Dl.* 100032.

162. *Bud.Tört.,* II, p. 83.

Chapter 4

1. For what follows, see Werbőczy, *Tripartitum,* III:8.

2. Such may be well illustrated by the words of one eleventh century Spanish writer, "I wish to found a city within my town," Pierre Michaud-Quantin, *Universitas; Expressions du Mouvement Communautaire dans le Moyen-Age Latin,* Paris, 1970, p. 113 *et seq.*

3. Iványi, *Bártfa,* no. 211; *CD,* VI/1, p. 225; István Petrovics, "Oklevelek Szeged középkori történetéhez," *Acta Universitatis Szegediensis: Acta Historica,* 56, 1979, p. 62.

4. Béla Iványi, *A városi polgárjog keletkezése és fejlődese figyelemmel Buda és Pest városokra,* Budapest, undated, p. 6.

5. Wilhelm Ebel, "Über die rechtschöpferische Leistung des mittelalterlichen deutschen Bürgertums," *Vorträge und Forschungen,* XI, 1966, pp. 242-3.

6. *Df.* 243327 (Arch. civ. Poson., *Chart.* nr 5283).

7. *Stadtrecht,* ch. 1; Ebel, *op. cit.* (see above, n. 5), *ibid.*

8. Otto von Gierke, *Die Genossenschaftstheorie und die deutsche Rechtssprechung,* 1887, pp. 22-3:—cited by John D. Lewis, *The Genossenschaft-Theory of Otto von Gierke (University of Wisconsin Studies in the Social Sciences and History,* no. 25), Madison, 1935, p. 56.

9. Sándor Kolozsvári, Kelemen Óvári, *Corpus Statutorum Hungariae Municipalium (Monumenta Hungariae Juridico-Historiae)*, V/2, Budapest, 1904, pp. 5-6.

10. Országos Széchenyi Könyvtár, *Cod. Lat. Medii Aevi*, no. 124, *fol* 2r, 3v, 4v, 7r, 9v, 11r.

11. Béla Iványi, *op. cit.* (see above, n. 4), pp. 30-33.

12. *Stadtrecht*, ch. 66.

13. Hans Planitz, "Die deutsche Stadtgemeinde," *Zeitschrift der Savigny Stiftung für Rechtsgeschichte (Germanische Abteilung)*, 64, 1944, pp. 34-5.

14. *Stadtrecht*, ch. 40-46.

15. Walter Ullmann, *Medieval Political Thought*, London *(Penguin-Peregrine)*, 1975, pp. 159-61.

16. *Stadtrecht, Prologus* iv.

17. *Stadtrecht*, ch. 59, 334; Néda Relković, *Buda város jogkönyve*, Budapest, 1905, p. 164; Jacob Grimm, *Deutsche Rechtsalterthümer*, Göttingen, 1828, pp. 135, 761.

18. Csánki, *Mon.Bud.*, pp. 157-8.

19. Adalbert Erler, *Bürgerrecht und Steuerpflicht im mittelalterlichen Städtewesen mit besonderer Untersuchung des Steuereides (Frankfurter wissenschaftliche Beiträge, Rechts-und Wirtschaftswissenschaftliche Reihe, Bd* 2), Frankfurt a M., 1939.

20. *DRH*, p. 155, 195-6 (1397:1; 1405:6), *Stadtrecht*, ch. 311.

21. Eötvös Loránd Tudományi Egyetem, Könyvtár, *Collectio Hevenesiana*, LXV, p. 254; *DRH*, p. 197 (1405:7); Ákos Timon *Magyar alkotmány- és jogtörténet*, Budapest, 1919, p. 755; Werbőczy, *Tripartitum*, III:13 & 20; *Bud.Tört.*, II, p. 170.

22. György, Bónis, "Die Entwicklung der geistlichen Gerichtsbarkeit in Ungarn vor 1526," *Zeitschrift der Savigny Stiftung für Rechtsgeschiche (Kanonische Abteilung)*, 80, 1963, p. 229-231.

23. *Stadtrecht*, ch. 207.

24. *Ibid.*, ch. 309.

25. *Ibid.*, ch. 295, 297.

26. Bónis, *op. cit.* (see above, n. 22), pp. 230-1.

27. *ZO*, I, no. 4518; Ottó B. Kelényi, "Iparosok és kereskedők Budán és Pesten a középkorban," *Budapest régiségei*, 13, 1943, p. 329.

28. M. G. Kovachich, *Formulae Solennes Styli*, Pesthini, 1799, pp. 212-3; for the execution by the Buda Council of a priest in 1535, (ed) Gusztáv Wenzel, György Szerémi, *Emlékirat Magyarország romlásáról*, Pest, 1857, p. 280.

29. See back, p. 25.

30. *DRH*, pp. 88, 92, 99, 122.

31. Lajos Huszár, *A budai pénzverés története a középkorban*, Budapest, 1958, p. 29.

32. Gyula Szekfű, "Oklevelek I Károly pénzverési reformjához," *TT*, XII, 1911, p. 36.

33. *CD*, X/4, pp. 799-800.

34. *Stadtrecht*, ch. 98, 175.

35. *Ibid.*, ch. 97.

36. Lajos Huszár, *A budai pénzverés története a középkorban*, Budapest, 1958, p. 70.

37. See back, pp. 30, 91.

38. Hans Planitz, *Die deutsche Stadt im Mittelalter*, Graz-Köln, 1954, pp. 287-9.

39. *DRH*, pp. 88, 101, 207 (1405:18); *Stadtrecht*, ch. 278.

40. Emma Lederer, "A legrégibb magyar iparososztály kialakulása," *Századok*, 62, 1928, p. 642, citing W. Gallion, *Der Ursprung der Zünfte in Paris*, Berlin & Leipzig, 1910.

41. (Ed) David Herlihy, *Medieval Culture and Society*, London & Melbourne *(Macmillans)*, 1968, pp. 184-5.

42. *ÁÚO*, VIII, pp. 262-3; *CD*, IV/3, pp. 479-80; *CD*, V/3, p. 299.

43. *MTT*, XII, p. 32; *ÁÚO*, VIII, pp. 262-3; *AO*, III, p. 314.

44. For this and much of what follows, see Emma Lederer, *A feudalizmus kialakulása Magyarországon*, Budapest, 1959, pp. 107-115, 144-7; György Györffy, *István király és műve*, Budapest, 1977, pp. 233-48; (ed) K. Géresi, *Codex diplomaticus comitum Károlyi de Nagy-Károlyi*, I, Budapest, 1882, p. 161; *TT*, 1893, pp. 8, 13; A. Bartal, *Glossarium mediae et infimae Latinitatis Regni Hungariae*, Budapest, 1901, p. 134.

45. *SRH*, I, p. 193 (*Gesta Hungarorum Simonis de Keza*, ch. 96).

46. *CD*, IX/2, p. 372.

47. *AO*, III, pp. 312-4.

48. "Tributum fori Geyzae et tributum portus Pest et kerepes navium"—*CD*, II, p. 129. For "kerepes," see *TT*, 1893, p. 13.

49. Lederer, *op. cit.* (see above, n. 44), pp. 147-9.

50. Gusztáv Heckenast, *Fejedelmi (királyi) szologálónépek a korai Árpádkorban (Értekezések a történeti tudományok köréből, Új sorozat*, 53), Budapest, 1970, pp. 82-86.

51. Nicolas Isthvánfi, *De rebus Hungaricis*, Coloniae Agrippinae, 1622, p. 273; Antal Mocsáry, *Nemes Nógrád vármegyének esmertetése*, I, Pest, 1826, p. 306; Csánki, *Földrajza*, I, p. 93; *Ibid.*, II, pp. 580, 656; András Kubinyi, "A budai vár udvarbírói hivatala, 1458-1541," *LK*, 35, 1964, p. 79.

52. *ÁÚO*, VII, pp. 262-3: dated by Szentpétery (*Regesta Regum*, I/3, no. 1542). Jenő was still in the possession of the Margitsziget nuns in 1462—Országos Levéltár, *Kúriai levéltár*, no. 4-2810 (transcription available in the Budapesti történeti múzeum, Register Collection, notes of Elemér Mályusz, no. 33).

53. L. Bernát Kumorovitz, *Veszprémi regeszták, 1301–1387*, Budapest, 1953, no. 624.

54. *AO*, IV, p. 297.

55. *CD*, IX/2, pp. 370-75.

56. E. Fügedi, "Topográfia és városi fejlődes a középkori Óbudán," *TBM*, 13, 1959, p. 11.

57. *MTT*, XII, pp. 24, 31, 118-23.

58. M. G. Kovachich, *Formulae Solennes Styli*, Pesthini, 1799, p. 388.

59. *MTT*, XII, p. 29.

60. *CD,* IV/3, pp. 479-80; *ibid.,* V/3, pp. 299-303.

61. *CD,* V/3, p. 349.

62. *CD,* VI/1, p. 359.

63. *CD,* VI/1, p. 225.

64. *CD,* VI/1, p. 224.

65. *CD,* VI/2, pp. 319-20.

66. *SRH,* I, pp. 481-2 (*Chronicon Pictum,* ch. 190).

67. *AO,* III, pp. 312-4.

68. *MTT,* XII, p. 115.

69. *MTT,* XII, p. 114; *CD,* X/7, pp. 862-4; *MTT,* XII, pp. 119-23.

70. *AO,* III, pp. 312-4.

71. More correctly, *infertor* or *dapifer*—György Györffy, *István király és műve,* Budapest, 1977, p. 242.

72. Béla Bevilaqua Borsody, *A budai és pesti mészáros céhek ládainak okiratai, 1270-1872,* I, Budapest, 1931, pp. 29-31.

73. Bártfai Szabó, *Pest,* no. 249.

74. *ZO,* II/1, no. 3859.

75. Fővárosi levéltár, no. 9.

76. *Stadtrecht,* ch. 110-111.

77. For Jewish dress: *MZsO,* I, p. 52; *Stadtrecht,* ch. 193; Sándor Büchler, *A zsidók története Budapesten a legrégibb időktől 1867-ig;* Budapest, 1901, pp. 31-2; for pogroms: MZsO, IV, pp. 87-8, 92; A. Neubauer, 'Le Memorbuch de Mayence," *Revue des Études Juives,* IV, 1882, pp. 24, 28. For a possible thirteenth century pogrom in Buda, Büchler, *op. cit.,* p. 43.

78. *Stadtrecht,* ch. 191.

79. *MZsO,* I, pp. 27-30.

80. (Ed) Andreas von Meiler, "Österreichische Stadtrechte und Satzungen aus der Zeit der Babenberger," *Archiv für Kunde österreichischer Geschichts-Quellen,* X, 1853, pp. 146-48. This same privilege was adopted also in Bohemia in 1254 and in Poland in 1264.

81. *MZsO,* I, pp. 107-9, 124-5, 165, 169-72, 174-6, 190-92, 198-200, 202-4; *MZsO,* IV, p. 82.

82. Sámuel Kohn, *A zsidók története Magyarországon,* Budapest, 1884, pp. 146-7.

83. The Jews were temporarily expelled from the realm in 1367 and their possessions seized; see also, Kohn, *op. cit.* (see above, n. 82), p. 422.

84. *MZsO,* V/1, p. 87, 112-3, 129-30; *MZsO,* IV, p. 59.

85. 1251:29.

86. For the implications elsewhere of the term "cameral servitude," Guido Kisch, *The Jews in Medieval Germany,* Chicago (University of Chicago Press), 1949, pp. 129-35, 421-2.

87. Alexander (Sándor) Scheiber, "A Medieval Form of Jewish Oath," *Journal of Jewish Studies,* 25, 1974, pp. 181-2.

88. László Zolnay, *Buda középkori zsidósága,* Budapest *(TIT budapesti szervezete),* 1968, pp. 21-2; Kohn, *op. cit.* (see above, n. 82), pp. 148-50.

89. *MZsO,* I, pp. 170, 172; *ibid.,* IV, p. 85; *ibid.,* VIII, p. 37; *ibid.,* IX, p. 34. Later on this figure was elected by the local Jewish community, *MZsO,* I, p. 318.

90. *MZsO,* I, pp. 2, 10-13; *ibid.,* IV, p. 99; *ibid.,* XI, p. 34; Kohn, *op. cit.* (see above, n. 82), p. 476.

91. *MZsO,* I, p. 206.

92. *AO,* V, p. 410.

93. *MZsO,* IX, pp. 36-7.

94. Kohn, *op. cit.* (see above, n. 82), p. 111.

95. János Király, *Pozsony város joga a középkorban,* Budapest, 1894, p. 372.

96. *Stadtrecht,* ch. 50, 52; Kohn, *op. cit.* (see above, n. 82), p. 34.

97. *MZsO,* I, pp. 120-21, 122-23; *ibid.,* IV, p. 83; *ibid.,* IX, pp. 35-36. See also, *MZsO,* I, pp. 96, 132-33, 150, 154-7, 172; *ibid.,* V/1, p. 34; *ibid.,* VIII, p. 69.

98. *MZsO,* I, pp. 89-90; *ibid.,* IX, pp. 35-6; Kohn, *op. cit.* (see above, n. 82), pp. 162-3. The deputy of the Judge of All Jews was the Castellan of Buda, *MZsO,* I, p. 150; *ibid.,* V/1, pp. 34, 41.

99. *MZsO,* X, pp. 45-6.

100. *MZsO,* X, p. 249; *ibid.,* V/1, pp. 52-4; *ibid.,* X, pp. 72-3.

101. Many loans were recorded in private documents not issued by the *loca credibilia* and, thus, held no value in law: *MZsO,* I, pp. 125, 144; *ibid.,* V/1, p. 81; *ibid.,* VIII, pp. 69-70.

102. *MZsO,* VIII, p. 112.

103. The usual formula, "with relatives having been consulted," is frequently omitted from documents treating on these matters.

104. On the history of equity in Hungarian law: Imre Szabó, "Le traitement de l'Equité dans le système juridique hongrois," in (ed) Zoltán Péteri, *Droit hongrois-Droit comparé, Hungarian Law—Comparative Law,* Budapest, 1970; József Holub, "Ordinaria potentia, absoluta potentia," *Revue Historique de droit francais et étranger,* Series 4, 27 (1950).

105. György Bónis, *Középkori jogunk elemei,* Budapest, 1972, pp. 68-73; for the relationship between equity and *plenitudo potestatis,* Kohn, *op. cit.* (see above, n. 82), p. 422.

106. *CD,* VI/1, p. 360; Házi, *Sopron,* I/2, p. 296.

107. *MZsO,* V/1, pp. 52-4; *ibid.,* VIII, p. 78.

Chapter 5

1. (ed) G. Veesenmeyer, *Fratris Felicis Fabri Tractatus de civitate Ulmensi, de eius origine, ordine, regimine de civibus eius et statu,* Tübingen *(Bibliothek des litterari-schen Vereins in Stuttgart, 186),* 1889, pp. 59, 63; for recent research on German town patriciates, see particularly: Erich Maschke, *Die Familien in der deutschen Stadt des späten Mittelalters,* Heidelberg, 1980; F.R.H. Du Boulay, *Germany in the Later Middle Ages,* London *(Athlone),* 1983, pp. 141-59.

2. "Chronica der Staat Augspurg bis auf 1569," British Library, Additional MS 22475, *fol* 290r-291v.

3. Hanns Hubert Hofmann, "Nobiles Norimbergenses, Beobachtungen zur Struktur der reichstädtischen Oberschicht," *Vorträge und Forschungen,* XI, p. 72.

4. Isolde Brunner-Schubert, "Wilhelm und Matthäus Runtinger: zwei Regensburger Kaufleute," *Verhandlungen des Historischen Vereins fur Oberpfalz und Regensburg,* 110, 1970, p. 53.

5. Hanns Hubert Hofmann, *op. cit.* (see above, n. 3), pp. 72-3.

6. Jenő Szűcs, *Városok és kézművesség a XV. századi Magyarországon,* Budapest, 1955, pp. 268-9.

7. *ZO,* II/1, nos. 1882, 5025; *ibid.,* II/2, no. 6740; *Mon.Vesp.,* III, p. 85.

8. *Stadtrecht,* ch. 35, 36, 354.

9. *ZO,* I, nos. 8, 877, 924, 2710, 3072, 3118, 3566, 4234, 5218, 5489; *ibid.,* II/2, nos 5438, 6943, 7379; (ed) Imre Nagy, Dezső Véghely, Gyula Nagy, *Zala vármegye történetének oklevéltára,* II, Budapest, 1890, p. 257; *Dl.* 87002; *Df.* 239418 (Arch. civit. Poson., *ch. nr* 790).

10. "Ulman Stromers Peuchel von meim geslecht und von abenteur," in (ed) Die historische Commission bei der königlichen Academie der Wissenschaften, *Die Chroniken der deutschen Städte,* I, Leipzig, 1862.

11. (Ed) Ernő Krammerer, *A Pécz nemzetség Apponyi ágának oklevelei,* I, Budapest, 1906, pp. 7, 14-5, 20.

12. Bálint Surányi, "Pozsonyi biródinasztiák a XIII-XIV. században," *LK,* 35, 1964.

13. Dezső Csánki, "Kuncz ispán majora Budán," *Századok,* 40, 1906, p. 687; a list of Buda's judges and councillors for the period covered in this chapter is included as an appendix, pp. 169-76.

14. *AK,* 1973, pp. 228-234.

15. *Dl.* 91295; *AK,* 1973, p. 227; *AO,* III, p. 505; *ibid.,* IV, p. 432.

16. Dezső Csánki, "Szent-Erzsébetfalva—Pest mellett," *Századok,* 27, 1893, p. 20.

17. As was the case with the de Eger family, *AK,* 1973, p. 234.

18. Zimmermann-Werner, I, pp. 506-8; discussed by László Makkai, *Társadalom és nemzetiség a középkori Kolozsváron,* Kolozsvár, 1943, p. 19.

19. *Mon.Vesp.,* II, pp. 85, 105; *AO,* III, p. 505.

20. Ulving: *AO,* III, p. 182; *CD,* VIII/3, p. 509; *Dl.* 6260; *Dl.* 6273; *Zichy,* III, p. 275; Lorand: *MTT,* IV, pp. 136, 146-7; Bártfai Szabó, *Pest,* no 458; *Dl.* 3554; Gyula Alapi, *Komárom megye levéltárának középkori oklevelei,* Komárom, 1917, pp. 12, 14, 42-3; *ZO,* II/1, no. 3181; de Eger: *AO,* II, p. 193; *Zichy,* II, pp. 381-4.

21. Otto Brunner, *Neue Wege der Sozialgeschichte,* Göttingen, 1956, p. 143.

22. *DRH,* p. 119; *Zichy,* II, p. 124.

23. Ladislas Ulving was the son of Nicolas Ulving, the heir and son-in-law of Ulving I—*Dl.* 74836; *MTT,* IV, p. 141. On Frederick Chratzer and his relation to the Ulving family—*ZO,* I, no. 4196, 4734; Horváth & Huszár, p. 26.

24. *Dl.* 100032; *Mon.Vesp.,* II, p. 133.

25. *Monumenta Vaticana Historiam Regni Hungariae Illustrantia,* I/1, "Rationes Collectorum Pontificorum in Hungaria," Budapest, 1887, pp. 25, 402-3, 419.
26. *MTT,* IV, p. 137.
27. Surányi, *op.cit.* (see above, n. 12), p. 177; Emma Lederer, *A középkori pénzüzletek története Magyarországon (1000-1458),* Budapest, 1932, pp. 129-30, 134, 163.
28. Lederer, *op.cit.* (see above, n. 27), pp. 34-5; Theodor Ortvay, *Geschichte der Stadt Pressburg,* II/4, Pressburg, p. 65.
29. *Stadtrecht,* ch. 50, 173, 225, 249.
30. Alapi, *op.cit.* (see above, n. 20), pp. 12, 14, 42-3.
31. *AO,* III, p. 182; (ed) Elemér Varjú, *Oklevéltár a Tomaj nemzetségbeli Losonczi Bánffy család történetéhez,* I, Budapest, 1908, pp. 436-7.
32. *ZO,* II/2, no. 7043; *Dl.* 91295; *AO,* IV, p. 432.
33. *AO,* VII, pp. 5-6, 24-6; *MTT,* IV, pp. 136, 146-7.
34. Lederer, *op.cit* (see above, n. 27), Chapter I ("A birtokzálogüzlet kialakulása"), and especially pp. 40-46; *ZO,* I, no. 877, 2710, 3072, 3118, 3566.
35. A collateral line of both the Ulving and Tilmann, the Nadler, later take over the Szenterzsébet and Régenszenttamás estates—Csánki, "Szent-Erzsébetfalva . . (see above, n. 16)," p. 20; Csánki, *Földrajza,* III, p. 381. An offshoot of the de Győr, the Stoyan, one of whose members later became Town Judge, take over the de Győr estates in the 1390's—*AK,* p. 1973, p. 238.
36. *CD,* IX/2, p. 254; *ZO,* II/2, no. 7043; *MTT,* IV, pp. 136, 141, 146-7; *CD,* VIII/4, p. 369.
37. Gerhard Pfeiffer, *Das Breslauer Patriziat im Mittelalter,* Breslau, 1929, pp. 206-22.
38. Richard C. Hoffmann, "Wroclaw Citizens as Rural Landholders," in (ed) Harry A. Miskimin, David Herlihy and A. L. Udovitch, *The Medieval City,* New Haven & London *(Yale University Press),* 1977.
39. (Ed) Ernő Krammerer, *A Pécz . . . oklevelei* (see above, n. 11), I, pp. 7, 9-16, 80-82, 108-9.
40. *AO,* IV, p. 510.
41. *CD,* X/4, pp. 595-6.
42. *CD,* IX/7, pp. 288-9; *ibid.,* IX/4, pp. 435-7.
43. *CD,* VIII/3, p. 511; Bártfai Szabó, *Pest,* no. 282; Leopold Sailer, "Die Wiener Ratsbürger des 14. Jahrhunderts," *Studien aus dem Archiv der Stadt Wien,* 3-4, Wien, 1931, p. 239.
44. (Ed) Ernő Krammerer, *A Pécz nemzetség . . . oklevelei* (see above, n. 11), p. 80; *ZO,* II/1, no. 1219.
45. *ZO,* II/1, no. 3181; *ibid,* II/2, no. 7794; *AO,* I, pp. 366-67.
46. *AK,* 1973, p. 236.
47. *AO,* III, p. 182; Surányi, *op.cit.* (see above, n. 12), p. 176.
48. Árpád Bossányi, *Regesta Supplicationum: A papai kérvénykönyvek magyar vonatkozású okmányai, Avignoni korszak,* I, Budapest, 1916, p. 245; *Mon.Vesp.,* II, p. 133.

49. László Zolnay, "A középkori Budavári Szent-László és Szent-Mihály kápolna," *Budapest régiségei,* 21, 1964, pp. 380-82; Alapi, *op.cit.* (see above, n. 20), p. 39; Bártfai-Szabó, *Pest,* no. 628.

50. (Ed) Elemér Varjú, *Oklevéltár a Tomaj nemzetségbeli Losonczi Bánffy család történetéhez,* I, Budapest, 1908, pp. 436-37; *ZO,* I, no. 2105.

51. *Dl.* 6273.

52. (Ed) László Fejérpataky, *Magyarországi városok régi számadáskönyvei,* Budapest, 1885, pp. 80, 83.

53. Szűcs, *op.cit.* (see above, n. 6), p. 266.

54. Makkai, *op.cit.* (see above, n. 18), p. 23; Peter Csendes, "Die Donaustädte von Passau bis Pressburg im 15. Jahrhundert," in (ed) Wilhelm Rausch, *Die Stadt am Ausgang des Mittelalters,* Linz-Donau, 1974, p. 100.

55. István Szabó, *A magyar mezőgazdaság története a XIV. századtól az 1530-as évekig (Agrártörténeti tanulmányok, 2),* Budapest, 1975, p. 9.

56. *Bud.Tört.,* II, p. 35; Csánki, *Földrajza,* I, 17, 20-21, 44, 46.

57. András Kubinyi, "A mezőgazdaság történetéhez a Mohács előtti Budán (Gallinczer Lénárt számadáskönyve 1525-ből)," *Agrártörténelmi szemle,* 6, 1964, pp. 385-7.

58. Kubinyi, *op.cit.* (see above, n. 57), p. 399; István Szamota, *Régi utazások Magyarországon és a Balkán Félszigeten, 1054-1717,* Budapest, 1891, p. 93; *Stadtrecht,* ch. 208, 210, 211; *CD,* IX/6, p. 168.

59. Stadtarchiv, Nuremberg, *FA Schürstab,* nr 1a, membranes E and M.

60. (Ed) Gusztáv Wenzel, *Magyar diplomácziai emlékek az Anjou-korból (Monumenta Hungariae Historica: Acta Extera),* I, Budapest, 1874, pp. 343-6; *ibid.,* II, 1875, p. 47; discussed: Ambrus Pleidell, *A nyugatra irányuló magyar külkereskedelem a középkorban,* Budapest, 1925, pp. 33-8; Theodor Mayer, *Der auswärtige Handel des Herzogtums Österreich im Mittelalter,* Innsbruck, 1909, pp. 28-31; Bálint Homan, *A magyar királyság pénzügyei és gazdaságpolitikája Károly Róbert korában,* Budapest, 1921, pp. 64-9.

61. Gerhard Hirschmann, "Nürnbergs Handelsprivilegien, Zollfreiheiten und Zollverträge bis 1399," in (ed) Stadtarchiv Nürnberg, *Beiträge zur Wirtschaftsgeschichte Nürnbergs,* I, Nürnberg, 1967, nos. 74, 99-100, 111, 127-9; Johannes Müllner, *Die Annalen der Reichstadt Nürnberg von 1623 (Quellen zur Geschichte und Kultur der Stadt Nürnberg),* Nürnberg, 1972, pp. 398-9.

62. *Magyar gazdaságtörténelmi szemle,* 5, 1898, p. 237 (citing J. H. Wylie, *History of England under Henry IV).*

63. (Ed) George Warner, *The Libelle of Englyshe Polycye,* Oxford, 1926, p. 17.

64. *Quellen Wien,* I/3, no. 3209; II/5, nos. 37, 39; discussed: *AK,* 1973, pp. 239-40; *Quellen Wien,* III/1, no. 1021; Stadt- und Landesarchiv, Vienna, *Testament-und Geschäftsbücher, Hs 9/1, fol* a 2r.

65. Christoph Petzch, "Die Nürnberger Familie von Lochaim: Eine Kaufmannsgeschlecht des 14-16. Jahrhunderts," *Zeitschrift für bayerische Landesgeschichte,* 29, 1966, p. 218; Dénes Radocsay, "Les principaux monuments funéraires médiévaux conservés à Budapest," in (ed) Adhémar, le Comte de Panat; le chevalier Xavier de

Ghellinck Vaerewyck; Pierre Brière; *Mélanges offerts à Szabolcs de Vajay*, Braga, 1971, p. 472, no. 30.

66. In 1398, reference is made simply to "Grolonth." Two Groland brothers, Hans and Jacob, are known to have represented the Stromer in Buda, but during the judicial year 1398-99 Jacob is clearly resident in Nuremberg—Wolfgang von Stomer, *Oberdeutsche Hochfinanz (Vierteljahrschrift für Sozial- und Wirtschaftsgeschichte, Beihefte 55-57)*, Wiesbaden, 1970, p. 133; *Archive der Freiherren Haller von Hallerstein in Schloss Gründlach (Bayerische Archivinventare, 26)*, I, Munich, 1965, *Archiv Henfenfeld U*171. For Greczinger, British Library, Department of Manuscripts, *Additional Charter* 71495.

67. Bayerische Staatsarchiv, Nuremberg, *Stadt- und Landalmosenampt, Urkunden*, nos. 113, 114, 116.

68. *Stadtrecht*, ch. 72-78, 84, 87, 408, 423-7; *DRH*, pp. 204-5; *ZO*, II/1, no. 1949.

69. See back, p. 50.

70. Házi, *Sopron*, 1/2, pp. 215-6.

71. *Dl*. 9791; see above, n. 66.

72. (Ed) Wilhelm Altmann, *Eberhart Windeckes Denkwürdigkeiten zur Geschichte des Zeitalters Kaiser Sigismunds*, Berlin, 1893, p. 9.

73. Szűcs, *op.cit.* (see above, n. 16), pp. 295-322.

74. *CD*, X/4, p. 318; Szűcs, op.cit. (see above, n. 6), pp. 278-9; András Kubinyi, "Népmozgalmak Budapesten a feudalizmus korában," *TBM*, 14, 1961, pp. 8-9.

75. *ZO*, I, no. 5218; *ibid.*, II/1, no. 2199; *Dl*. 7114; *Dl*. 93303; Vidor Pataki, "A budai vár középkori helyrajza," *Budapest régiségei*, 15, 1950, pp. 284-5, 291, 294.

76. "Carnifices in suburbio huius civitatis . . . Budensis residentes," Fővárosi levéltár, no 9; Budapesti történeti múzeum, Register Collection, typescript no. 91 (citing *Arch. Conv. S. Montis Pann.*, Tihany, *fasc.* 18, *nr* 2)

77. Fővárosi levéltár, no. 9; Béla Bevilaqua Borsody, *A budai és pesti mészáros céhek ládainak okiratai*, I, Budapest, 1931, pp. 123, 147, 150.

78. Fővárosi Levéltár, nos. 3-5; Szűcs, *op.cit.* (see above, n. 6), pp. 142-50.

79. (Ed) Gusztáv Wenzel, *Magyar diplomácziai emlékek* (see above, n. 60), II, p. 54; *CD*, IX/4, pp. 136, 168.

80. *ZO*, I, no. 5604; *CD*, IX/3, p. 47; *ibid.*, IX/5, p. 628; *ibid.*, IX/7, p. 298; *ZO*, II/1, no. 3329.

81. Bártfai Szabó, *Pest*, no. 538; *Zichy*, V, p. 586; *ZO*, II/1, nos. 1221, 1882; *Dl*. 71362; Péter Váczy, *A városi polgárok vérdíja Werbőczynél és a budai jog*, Miskolc, 1929, p. 9.

82. *CD*, IX/5, pp. 249-50, 384, 490; *ibid.*, X/1, pp. 431-3; *ibid.*, X/4, pp. 128-9; *Quellen Wien*, 2/1, nos. 663, 1161.

83. *CD*, X/4, pp. 108-16; *DRH*, pp. 199-200 (1405:11).

84. Emma Lederer, *A középkori pénzüzletek története Magyarországon (1000-1458)*, Budapest, 1932, p. 171; *AK*, 1973, pp. 253-5.

85. Stadt- und Landesarchiv, Vienna, *Testament- und Geschäftsbücher*, Hs 9/3, *fol* 157v; Házi, *Sopron*, 1/2, pp. 215-6.

206 NOTES

86. Házi, *Sopron,* 1/2, pp. 226, 243-4; (ed) Bruno Kuske, *Quellen zur Geschichte des Kölner Handels und Verkehrs im Mittelalter,* I, Bonn, 1923, no. 295.

87. László Gerevich, *The Art of Buda and Pest in the Middle Ages,* Budapest, 1971, pp. 83-86. A study of issue places appended to charters given out by the Justiciar suggests the move from Visegrád to Buda occurred gradually from 1404 to 1406—*ZO,* II/1, nos. 2901, 3219, 3274, 3285, 3444, 3483, 3485, 3835, 3961, 4049, 4131, 4138, 4246, 4268, 4289, 4301, 4307, 4311, 4471, 4487, 4505, 4520, 4672, 4673-7, 4694-5, 4738, 4757, 4766, 4853, 4956, 4962-3, 5063, 5107, 5133; *ibid.,* II/2, nos. 5281, 5306, 5331, 5340, 5542, 5546, 5555, 5647, 5689, 5707, 5760, 5784, 5810, 5814.

88. *CD,* X/5, p. 302.

89. András Kubinyi, "Budai kereskedők udvari szállitásai a Jagellókorban," *Budapest régiségei,* 19, 1959.

90. Dénes Huszti, *Olasz-Magyar kereskedelmi kapcsolatok a középkorban,* Budapest, 1941, p. 72, citing A. Wesselofsky, *Il Paradiso degli Alberti,* III, Bologna, 1867, pp. 100-112.

91. Lederer, *op.cit.* (see above, n. 84), p. 85 n. 14; *Zichy,* V, p. 586; *ZO,* II/2, no. 7094.

92. András Kubinyi, "Budai és pesti polgárok családi összeköttetései a Jagellókorban," *LK,* 37, 1966, p. 242; *Quellen Wien,* II/2, nos. 2593, 2617, 3675.

93. *CD,* X/4, pp. 595-6.

94. *AK,* 1973, p. 251.

95. *CD,* X/8, p. 662; (ed) W. Altmann, *Regesta Imperii,* XI, Innsbruck, 1896-7, no. 11315.

96. Horváth & Huszár, pp. 27-8; *TT,* 1907, p. 321; *CD,* XI, pp. 107-8.

97. (Ed & trans) Károly Mollay, *A korona elrablása: Kottanner Jánosné emlékirata,* Budapest, 1978, p. 31.

98. *CD,* X/6, pp. 780-4; Házi, *Sopron,* 1/2, p. 271; *AMB,* no. 1026.

99. Horváth & Huszár, p. 28; (ed) Das Institut für oesterreichische Geschichtsforschung, *Die Matrikel der Universität Wien,* I, Graz-Köln, 1956, p. 212.

100. *Dl.* 10359; *Dl.* 11562; *Dl.* 13972; *Dl.* 14486; Házi, *Sopron,* 1/3, p. 131; *Regesta Imperii* (see above, n. 95), XI, nos. 11305a-b; *Matrikel Wien* (see above, n. 99), p. 212.

101. *Quellen Wien,* II/2, nos 2739, 2741; Ernst Birk, "Beiträge zur Geschichte der Königin Elisabeth von Ungarn und ihres Sohnes König Ladislas," *Quellen und Forschungen,* 1849, Wien, pp. 242-3.

102. *DRH,* p. 327; Lajos Elekes, *Hunyadi,* Budapest, 1952, p. 273, n. 47.

103. See above, n. 101; An excellent biography of Farkas is provided by Elemér Mályusz, "Budai Farkas László," *TBM,* 15, 1963.

104. See below, n. 131.

105. Ernst Birk, *op.cit.* (see above, n. 101), p. 233.

106. Through his son-in-law, Henry Munich; András Kubinyi, "Die Nürnberger Haller in Ofen: Ein Beitrag zur Geschichte des Südosthandels im Spätmittelalter," *Mitteilungen des Vereins für Geschichte der Stadt Nürnberg,* 52, 1963-4, pp. 8-9; Ferencz Kováts, *Nyugatmagyarország árúforgalma a XV. században a pozsonyi har-*

minczadkönyv alapján, Budapest, 1902, pp. 152, 200; von Stromer, *Oberdeutsche Hochfinanz* (see above, n. 66), p. 136.

107. Von Stromer, *Oberdeutsche Hochfinanz* (see above, n. 66), pp. 100-106.

108. Käthe Dettling, "Der Metallhandel Nürnbergs im 16. Jahrhundert," *Mitteilungen des Vereins für Geschichte der Stadt Nürnberg,* 27, 1928; R. A. Peltzer, "Geschichte der Messingindustrie," *Zeitschrift des Aachener Geschichtsvereins,* 30, 1908.

109. Ondrej R. Halaga, "Kaufleute und Handelsgüter der Hanse im Karpatengebiet," *Hansische Geschichtsblätter,* 85, 1967, p. 66.

110. M. C. Rady, "The Hungarian Copper Trade and Industry in the Later Middle Ages," in (ed) C.M.A. McCauley and J. Screen, *Occasional Papers of the School of Slavonic and East European Studies,* forthcoming.

111. Gusztáv Wenzel, *Magyarország bányászatának kritikai története,* Budapest, 1880, p. 46; "Liber civitatis Szomolnok," Országos Széchenyi könyvtár, Kézirattár, *Cod. Lat. Medii Aevi,* no. 385, *fol* 38r.

112. Edward Browne, *A Brief Account of some Travels in divers Parts of Europe viz Hungary . . . With some Observations on the Gold, Copper, Quick-Silver Mines,* London (Second Edition), 1685, p. 64; thus, also, from a Körmöcbánya mining book, "Im Monat Januarii (1511), An einem Dienstag ist Peter Holy Im perg verfallen, und gestorben, und die Perckwerch und Schacht ettlich tag geprenndt und zu Poden gangenn . . . gleichzfals ist die wasserkhunst aufgelassen," Pál Krizskó, *A körmöczi régi kamara és grófjai,* Budapest, 1880, p. 42.

113. Oszkár Paulinyi, "A középkori magyar réztermelés gazdasági jelentősége," *Károlyi Árpád emlékkönyv,* Budapest, 1933, pp. 420-33.

114. Richard Klier, "Nürnberg und Kuttenberg," *Mitteilungen des Vereins für Geschichte der Stadt Nürnberg,* 48, 1958, p. 65.

115. Rady, *op.cit.* (see above, n. 110).

116. *Ibid.*

117. *ZO,* I, no. 272; more generally on this subject, Bálint Hóman, *A magyar királyság* (see above, n. 60), pp. 151-4, 201-10, 213.

118. Günther von Probszt, "Deutsches Kapital in den Niederungarischen Bergstädten im Zeitalter des Frühkapitalismus," *Zeitschrift für Ostforschung,* 10, 1961, p. 7; *verleger* arrangements might still continue illegally after 1405—*CD,* X/6, pp. 682-4.

119. *DRH,* p. 203 (1405:15); Wolfgang von Stromer, "Nürnberger Unternehmer im Karpatenraum: Ein oberdeutsches Buntmetall-Oligopol, 1396-1412," *Kwartalnik Historii Kultury Materialnej,* 16, 1968, Warsaw, p. 649.

120. *Monumenta Medii Aevi Historica res gestas Poloniae illustrantia,* IV/2, Cracow, 1878, *Acta Consularia,* pp. 167-9; von Stromer, *Oberdeutsche Hochfinanz* (see above, n. 66), pp. 114-6.

121. *Monumenta..Poloniae* (see above, n. 120), *ibid.; ZO,* I, no. 3398.

122. Horváth & Huszár, p. 27; Csánki, *Földrajza,* I, p. 45; László Fejérpataky, *Magyarországi városok régi számadáskönyvei,* Budapest, 1885, p. 625; BStAN, *Losungsampt,* Bände, no. 69, *fol* 37r; (ed) Bruno Kuske, *Quellen zur Geschichte des Kölner Handels und Verkehrs im Mittelalter,* I, Bonn, 1923, no. 836. For Lutz Stein-

208   NOTES

linger's liquation plant in Nuremberg—Wolfgang von Stromer, "Fränkische und schwäbische Unternehmer in den Donau- und Karpatenländern im Zeitalter der Luxemburger, 1347-1437," *Jahrbuch für fränkische Landesforschung*, 31, 1971, p. 363.

123. von Stromer, *Oberdeutsche Hochfinanz* (see above, n. 66), p. 269.

124. Horváth & Huszár, pp. 27-8; von Stromer, *Oberdeutsche Hochfinanz* (see above, n. 66), pp. 126-136; von Stromer, "Fränkische und schwäbische Unternehmer" (see above, n. 22), pp. 361-4; *CD*, X/6, pp. 897-8; Herbert E. Lemmel, *Herkunft und Schicksal der Bamberger Lemmel des 15. Jahrhunderts (Historischer Verein Bamberg, 101 Bericht)*, Bamberg, 1965, Chapter V; *TT*, 1907, p. 321.

125. Pál Krizskó, *A körmöczi régi kamara és grófjai*, Budapest, 1880, pp. 18-20.

126. Ferencz Kováts, *Nyugatmagyarország árúforgalma a XV. században a pozsonyi harminczadkönyv alapján*, Budapest, 1902, p. 197; András Kubinyi, "Die Städte Ofen und Pest und der Fernhandel am Ende des 15. und am Anfang des 16. Jahrhunderts," in (ed) Ingomar Bog, *Der Aussenhandel Ostmitteleuropas, 1450-1650*, Köln-Wien, 1971, p. 371.

127. *AK*, 1973, pp. 247-50.

128. Csánki, *Földrajza*, I, pp. 45, 273; (ed) Bruno Kuske, *Quellen zur Geschichte des Kölner Handels* (see above, n. 122), no. 836; BStAN, *Briefbücher des innern Rates*, no. 29, *fol.* 53r; *Dl.* 13608.

129. *TT*, 1907, pp. 321-2; *CD*, XI, p. 108; Emma Lederer, *A középkori pénzüzletek története Magyarországon, 1000-1458*, Budapest, 1932, p. 167.

130. (Ed) Das Institut für oesterreichische Geschichtsforschung, *Die Matrikel der Universität Wien*, I, Graz-Köln, 1956, p. 113; (ed) Julius Weizsäcker, *Deutsche Reichstagsakten*, IV, Gotha, 1882, nr 357:11—discussed by von Stromer, *Oberdeutsche Hochfinanz* (see above, n. 66), pp. 205-18.

131. BStAN, *Briefbücher des innern Rates*, no. 14, *fol* 121r; ibid., no. 29, *fol* 53v-54r; BStAN, *Nürnberger Stadtrechnungen*, no. 179, *fol* 242v; *Dl.* 14256.

132. *CD*, XI, p. 108.

133. von Stromer, *Oberdeutsche Hochfinanz* (see above, n. 66), p. 136.

134. *Quellen Wien*, 2/2, nos 2739-41; *ibid*, 1/10, no 18657.

135. *AMB*, no. 1872.

136. BStAN, *Urkunden des sieben farbigen Alphabets*, nos. 3476, 3498, 4001; *ibid., Briefbücher des innern Rates*, no. 34B, *fol* 30v-31r; *ibid., Stadtrechnungsbelege, Urkunden und Briefe*, no. 35.

137. András Kubinyi, "Budai és pesti polgárok családi összeköttetései a Jagellókorban," *LK*, 37, 1966, pp. 272, 286.

138. Rhiman A. Rotz, "Investigating Urban Uprisings with Examples from Hanseatic Towns" in (ed) W. Jordan *et al., Order and Innovation in the Middle Ages: Essays in Honour of Joseph R. Strayer*, Princeton University Press, 1976.

139. See back, p. 41.

140. *Stadtrecht*, ch. 27-29.

141. *AK*, 1973, pp. 234-5; *Stadtrecht*, ch. 24, 32, 66; *CD*, X/4, p. 239.

142. *Dl.* 11924; Ferenc Salamon, *Budapest története*, III, Budapest, 1885, p. 356.

143. See generally in this context, András Kubinyi, "Polgári értelmiség és hivatalnokrétege Budán és Pesten a Hunyadi- es Jagellókorban," *LK,* 39, 1968.
144. *ZO,* II/2, nos. 7094, 5405, 7562; *CD,* X/3, p. 196; *Zichy,* IV, p. 497.
145. (Ed) Johannes Janssen, *Frankfurts Reichscorrespondenz,* I, Freiburg im Breisgau, 1863, pp. 435, 471.
146. *DRH,* p. 288 (1439: 5-6); Janssen, *op.cit.* (see above, n. 145), p. 484.
147. *Bud.Tört.,* II, p. 71.
148. Ernst Birk, "Beiträge zur Geschichte der Königin Elisabeth" (see back, n. 101), p. 230.
149. A number of accounts survive of which the most detailed is given by Thuróczy (I. G. Schwandtner, *Scriptores rerum Hungaricarum,* I, Vindobonae, 1746, pp. 237-8). Other, largely supportative, versions include: Thomas Ebendorffer's *Chronicon Austriacum Libris V. Comprehensum* in R.D.P. Hieronymus Pez, *Scriptores Rerum Austriacarum,* II, Lipsiae, 1725, col. 853; Ebendorffer's *Chronica Regum Romanorum,* in A. F. Pribram, *Mitteilungen des Instituts für österreichische Geschichtsforschung, Erg.Band 3,* Innsbruck 1890-94, p. 129; accounts by Aeneas Silvius preserved in *CD,* XI, pp. 135-6, 392; Albert to Master of the Teutonic Order, *Rozprawy Akademii Umietjetnosci wydziat Historyczno-Filozoficzny, Serya* II, *Tom* XII, Krakow, 1899, pp. 315-6; Chiphenwerger's interestingly abusive poem in (ed) R. V. Liliencron, *Die historische Volkslieder der Deutschen von 13. bis 16. Jahrhundert,* I, Leipzig, 1865, pp. 367-371; Károly Mollay, *A korona elrablása: Kottanner Jánosné emlékirata,* Budapest, 1978, p. 6; Gaspar Heltai's *Chronica Az Magyaroknac Dolgairol,* Colosvarot, 1575, *fol* 77r.
150. *Df.* 249009 (Esztergom primási levéltára, *Arch. Eccl. Vetus,* no. 46).
151. István Szamota, *Régi utazások Magyarországon és a Balkán Félszigeten, 1054-1717,* Budapest, 1891, p. 93.
152. *Bud.Tört.,* II, p. 71.
153. Ernst Birk, "Beiträge zur Geschichte der Königin Elisabeth" (see above, n. 101), p. 258; György Székely, "A Huszitizmus és a magyar nép," *Századok,* 90, 1956, pp. 579-80.
154. (Ed) Elek Jakab, *Kolozsvár történetének oklevéltára,* I, Buda, 1870, pp. 281-2.

Chapter 6

1. This work is alternatively known as the *Liber* or *Cronica Cronicarum* and was first published in Nuremberg in 1493. The relevant illustration is double-paged, *fol* CXXXVIIIv-CXXXIXr. The features discussed are even more pronounced in the later Nuremberg 1497 edition, *fol* CLVIv.
2. Theodor Mayer, *Der auswärtige Handel des Herzogtums Österreich im Mittelalter (Forschungen zur inneren Geschichte Österreichs, 6),* Innsbruck, 1909, p. 123-4; more particularly, András Kubinyi, "Die Städte Ofen und Pest und der

Fernhandel am Ende des 15. und am Anfang des 16. Jahrhunderts," in (ed) Ingomar Bog, *Der Aussenhandel Ostmitteleuropas, 1450-1650,* Köln-Wien, 1971, p. 360.

3. István Szamota, *Régi utazáok Magyarországon és a Balkán Félszigeten,* 1054-1717, Budapest, 1891, p. 94; Pál Szende, *Magyar városok a középkor végén,* Budapest, 1913, p. 29; *Bud.Tört.,* II, pp. 99-101, 144.

4. On Buda's later fifteenth century patriciate: András Kubinyi, "Budai és pesti polgárok családi összeköttetései a Jagellókorban," *LK,* 37, 1966; and by the same author, "Die Nürnberger Haller in Ofen: Ein Beitrag zur Geschichte des Südosthandels im Spätmittelalter," *Mitteilungen des Vereins für die Geschichte der Stadt Nürnberg,* 52, 1963-4; Helmut Freiherr Haller von Hallerstein, "Deutsche Kaufleute in Ofen zur Zeit der Jagellonen," *Mitteilungen des Vereins für die Geschichte der Stadt Nürnberg,* 51, 1962.

5. For the dispersal and massacre of Buda's Germans in the period after Mohács, we are forced to rely on the highly coloured accounts of only a few contemporaries: György Szerémi, *Emlékirat Magyarország romlásáról, 1484-1543* (ed. Gusztáv Wenzel, Pest, 1857, pp. 264-5) and Miklós Istvánffy, *A magyarok történetéből (Monumenta Hungarica,* VI, Budapest, 1962, pp. 123-4). After 1529, only one German, Thomas Drailinger, may be found on the Council lists all other places being occupied by Hungarians: *Verancsics Antal összes munkái* (ed. László Szalay, *Monumenta Hungariae Historica: Scriptores,* III, Pest, 1857, p. 51); Albert Gárdonyi, "A budai városi tanács árulása 1541-ben," *TBM,* 7, 1939, p. 10; Imre Palugyay, *Buda-Pest szabad királyi városok leirása,* Pest, 1852, pp. 33-46.

6. András Kubinyi, "Budai és pesti polgárok" (see above, n. 4), pp. 259-63.

7. *Bud.Tört.,* II, p. 145.

8. *Ibid.,* p. 167.

9. András Kubinyi, "A budai vár udvarbirói hivatala, 1458-1541," *LK,* 35, 1964, p. 93; Katalin Kisfaludy, *Matthias Rex,* Budapest, 1983, p. 74.

10. For much of what follows, Lajos Elekes, *Mátyás es kora,* Budapest, 1956; by the same author, *Essai de centralisation de l'état hongrois dans la seconde moitié du XVe siècle (Studia Historica, 22),* Budapest, 1960; János Bak, *Königtum und Stände in Ungarn im 14-16. Jahrhundert,* Wiesbaden, 1973, pp. 54-61.

11. Lajos Elekes, *Mátyás és kora,* Budapest, 1956, pp. 129-30.

12. *Ibid.,* p. 132.

13. *Ibid.,* p. 132.

14. Imre Hajnik, *A magyar birósági szervezet és perjog,* Budapest, 1899, p. 424, n. 21.

15. *Ibid.,* pp. 54-57.

16. *CJH,* p. 422 (1486:21).

17. Elemér Mályusz, "A magyar társadalom a Hunyadiak korában," in (ed) Imre Lukinich, *Mátyás király emlékkönyv,* Budapest, undated, I, pp. 372-3.

18. Lajos Elekes, *Mátyás és kora,* Budapest, 1956, p. 121.

19. *Ibid.,* pp. 109-111.

20. *Ibid.,* p. 91; *MTT,* XXII, 1877, pp. 113, 151, 179, 181, 213-4, 235-6.

21. (Ed) A magyar tudományos akadémia: Lajos Thallóczy & Antal Áldásy,

Monumenta Hungariae Historica, Diplomataria, 33, Budapest, 1907, p. 378; Hajdú-Bihar megyei levéltár (Debrecen), *Ftsz,* IV A, 1021/a, *MuO* 13 (formerly, no. 58).
22. *MZsO,* I, pp. 218, 249-50; *ibid.,* IV, p. 92; *ibid.,* V/1, p. 146; *ibid.,* VIII, p. 113; Sámuel Kohn, *A zsidók története Magyarországon,* Budapest, 1884, pp. 432, 473.
23. *MZsO,* I, pp. 214, 274-7, 282, 319-20; *ibid.,* V/1, pp. 87, 112-3; *ibid.,* VIII, p. 113; Sámuel Kohn, *A zsidók története Magyarországon,* Budapest, 1884, pp. 470-71.
24. M. G. Kovachich, *Codex Authenticus Iuris Tavernicalis,* Budapest, 1803, p. 50.
25. *MZsO,* I, pp. 122-23; *ibid.,* IX, p. 35.
26. László Zolnay, *Buda középkori zsidósága,* Budapest, *(TIT Budapesti szervezete),* 1968, pp. 23-24; Kohn, *op.cit.* (see above, n. 23), pp. 214-6.
27. Ernő Birk, "Adalék Magyarország pénztörténetéhez V László idejében," *Új Magyar Múzeum,* III/1, 1853, p. 509; M. G. Kovachich, *Scriptores rerum Hungaricarum minores,* II, Buda, 1798, p. 31; Johann von Engel, *Geschichte des Ungrischen Reichs und seiner Nebenländer,* Halle, 1797, pp. 17-18; L. von Schedius, "Etwas über den Zustand des ungrischen Finanzen im Anfänge des XVI Jahrhunderts," *Zeitschrift von und für Ungarn,* III, Pesth, 1803, p. 101; *TT,* 1880, p. 168; Kohn, *op.cit.* (see above, n. 23), pp. 230-8.
28. *MZsO,* IV, pp. 95-7, 100-102; Kohn, *op.cit.* (see above, n. 23), pp. 458-9, 462-3, 470.
29. *MZsO,* I, pp. 65, 168; Kohn, *op.cit.* (see above, n. 23), pp. 424, 446.
30. László Zolnay, *Buda középkori zsidósága,* Budapest *(TIT Budapesti szervezete),* 1968, pp. 22-3.
31. György Bónis, "Ständisches Finanzwesen in Ungarn im frühen 16. Jahrhundert," in (ed) Commission Nationale des Historiens Hongrois, *Nouvelles Études Historiques,* I, Budapest, 1965, pp. 94, 100; *Bud.Tört.,* II, p. 172.
32. Elemér Mályusz, "Geschichte des Bürgertums in Ungarn," *Vierteljahrschrift für Sozial- und Wirtschaftsgeschichte,* XX, 1927, pp. 371-5.
33. Béla Sebestyén, *A magyar királyok tartózkodási helyei,* Budapest, undated, pp. 62-79.
34. Dezső Csánki, "Mátyás király mint városépítő," *Századok,* 38, 1904, pp. 408-410.
35. Iványi, *Bártfa,* no. 1760.
36. Elemér Mályusz, *op.cit.* (see above, n. 32), p. 374.
37. *TT,* 1889, p. 376.
38. *Stadtrecht,* ch. 23; András Kubinyi, "Polgári értelmiség és hivatalnokrétege Budán és Pesten a Hunyadi és a Jagellókorban," *LK,* 39, 1968, pp. 217-9.
39. BStAN, *Losungsampt, Bände,* no. 69, *fol* 113v.
40. András Kubinyi, *op.cit.* (see above, n. 38), p. 217.
41. Endre Kovács, *A krakkói egyetem és a magyar művelödés,* Budapest, 1964, pp. 55-8.
42. Iványi, *Bártfa,* no. 1760.
43. Werbőczy, *Tripartitum,* Prologus 2:9.

44. Fővárosi levéltár, no. 9.

45. Transcripts of both letters are preserved in Fővárosi levéltár, no. 9.

46. András Kubinyi, "A budai vár udvarbirói hivatala, 1458-1541," *LK,* 35, 1964, pp. 78-80.

47. József Fógel, *II Vlászló udvartartása,* Budapest, 1913, p. 138.

48. M. G. Kovachich, *Formulae Solennes Styli,* Pesthini, 1799, pp. 388-9.

49. Kubinyi, *op.cit.* (see above, n. 46), p. 79.

50. *Stadtrecht,* ch. 66.

51. S: CONFRATERNITATIS CORPORIS TEUTUNORUM BUDE, BStAN, *Urkunden des siebenfarbigen Alphabets,* no. 3890.

52. Fővárosi levéltár, no. 3; *Dl.* 50564; A tiszántúli református egyházkerület nagykönyvtára, Református kollégium, Debrecen, *R* 1110/134; *ibid., R* 764/2; Béla Bevilaqua Borsody, *A budai és pesti mészáros céhek ládainak okiratai, 1270-1872,* I, Budapest, 1931, pp. 146-7, 162-3, 168-9, 171-2.

53. *Stadtrecht,* ch. 34, 37.

54. *Ibid.,* ch. 404.

55. *Ibid.,* ch. 46; see back also, n. 52.

56. John M. Najemy, "Guild Republicanism in Trecento Florence, The Successes and Ultimate Failure of Corporate Politics," *American Historical Review,* 84, 1979, pp. 55-7.

57. M. G. Kovachich, *Codex Authenticus Iuris Tavernicalis,* Budae, 1803, p. 88.

58. (Ed) Elek Jakab, *Kolozsvár történetének oklevéltára,* Buda, 1870, p. 282.

59. *Ibid.,* pp. 281-2.

60. *Ibid.,* p. 281.

61. Kovachich, *op.cit.* (see above, n. 57), p. 88.

62. *Dl.* 44704; *Dl.* 15153; *Dl.* 15196 *etc.*

63. For the text of the *Summa Legum,* (ed) Alexander Gál, *Die Summa Legum brevis, levis et utilis des sogenannten Doctor Raymundus von Wiener Neustadt,* I-II, Weimar, 1926; for the Pozsony text, *ibid.,* I, p. 14; for other texts; György Bónis, "Der Zusammenhang der *Summa Legum* mit dem *Tripartitum,"* *Studia Slavica,* XI, 1965; by the same author, *Középkori jogunk elemei,* Budapest, 1977, p. 283, n. 11; Iványi, *Eperjes,* no. 585; Iványi, *Bártfa,* no. 3471.

64. Országos Széchenyi könyvtár, Kézirattár, *Cod. Lat. Medii Aevi,* no. 365, *fol* 29*r-v,* 58*v*-61*r.*

65. Gál, *op.cit.* (see above, n. 63), I, pp. 132, 227; Aegidius Colonna, *De regimine principum,* III: 2; iii (using the unpaginated Augsburg 1473 edition); Colonna's work was also available in Buda: *Matthias Corvinus und die Renaissance in Ungarn* (1982 Schallaburg Exhibition Catalogue), p. 549.

66. M. G. Kovachich, *Codex Authenticus Iuris Tavernicalis,* Budae, 1803, p. 217; Nationalbibliothek, Vienna, *Handschriftensammlung, Ser. Nov.,* 4644, *fol.* 26*v.*

Chapter 7

1. For documents relevant to the case, Hospitallers *versus* Kunclin, see, *Mon. Strig,* III, pp. 500-501, 525-9, 539, 552; *CD,* IX/1, pp. 147-53; *Dl.* 87002.

2. For *recaptivatio* procedure, Imre Hajnik, *A magyar bírósági szervezet és perjog,* Budapest, 1899, p. 194.

3. *Dl.* 42161; *Dl.* 89412; *Dl.* 42388.

4. *Dl.* 3661.

5. For further information on the *praescriptio,* see back, pp. 60, 65.

6. György Bónis, *Középkori jogunk elemei,* Budapest, 1972, p. 106.

7. *ZO,* I, no. 3499; *Zichy,* VII, p. 619; on the Jews, see back, Chapter IV(ii).

8. Endlicher, pp. 443-4, 445, 453, 482, 489, 496-7, 499, 503, 505, 526, 545, 552, 623; *ÁÚO,* VIII, p. 10; *CD,* V/2, pp. 345-6; Elek Jakab, *Kolozsvár történetének oklevéltára,* I, Buda, 1870, p. 32; *CD,* VIII/3, pp. 280-1, 296, 532; *HO,* VI, p. 42; *CD,* IV/1, pp. 330, 332; *CD,* VIII/2, pp. 514-5; *ibid.,* VIII/4, pp. 376-8, 652; *ibid.,* VIII/3, pp. 416-7; *ibid.,* IV/3, p. 9.

9. *ÁÚO,* VII, pp. 79-80, 386; Imre Hajnik, *A perdöntő eskü és az előzetes tanúbizonyítás a középkori magyar perjogban (Értekezések a társadalmi tudományok köréből),* Budapest, 1881, pp. 5-8.

10. See back, p. 20.

11. *MTT,* II, 1855, pp. 192-8.

12. *Dl.* 71362.

13. Országos Levéltár, *Filmtár,* Microfilm Box 8016, 23 cim; I would like to thank Dr. András Kubinyi for making available to me a photographic reproduction of this document.

14. Iványi, *Eperjes,* no. 97.

15. *Mon.Strig.,* III, p. 340.

16. István Katona, *Historia critica regum Hungariae,* II/4, Pest, pp. 702-4.

17. Elemér Mályusz, "Geschichte des Bürgertums in Ungarn," *Vierteljahrschrift für Sozial- und Wirtschaftsgeschichte,* 20, 1927, pp. 373-4.

18. *Zichy,* III, pp. 289-90; *AO,* IV, pp. 325-6; Franz Eckhart, "Die glaubwürdigen Orte Ungarns im Mittelalter," *Mittheilungen des Instituts für österreichische Geschichtsforschung, Ergänzungband,* IX, 1915, p. 534.

19. The fine prescribed for non-attendance at a county court was derisory, József Holub, *Zala megye története a középkorban,* I, Pécs, 1929, pp. 236-7; *Stadtrecht,* ch. 203.

20. Endre Varga, György Bónis, Alajos Degré, *A magyar bírósági szervezet és perjog,* Budapest, 1961, p. 41.

21. *Stadtrecht,* ch. 362; "friendly judgment" would appear to be a rendering of the legal term 'amicabilis ordinacio'—*Dl.* 39212.

22. Imre Szentpétery (the younger), "A tárnoki ítélőszék kialakulása," *Századok,* 68 *(Pótfüzet),* 1934, p. 535.

23. *Zichy,* III, pp. 291, 408-9; *Mon.Strig.,* III, p. 226; (ed) Elemér Varjú, *Oklevéltár a Tomaj nemzetségbeli Losonczi Bánffy család történetéhez,* I, Budapest, 1908,

214   NOTES

pp. 63-4, 234; Imre Hajnik, *A magyar birósági szervezet és perjog,* Budapest, 1899,
p. 190; CD, X/3, pp. 129-30; Házi, *Sopron,* 1/1, p. 176; *Zichy,* V, pp. 423-4.
    24. *CD,* X/4, pp. 318-9; Jenő Szűcs, *Városok és kézművesség a XV. századi
Magyarországon,* Budapest, 1955, pp. 279-80.
    25. Iván Bertényi, "Zur Gerichtstätigkeit des Palatins und des Landesrichters
(Judex Curiae Regis) in Ungarn im XIV. Jahrhundert," *AnnalesUSB,* 7, 1965, p. 29;
Imre Hajnik, *A magyar birósági szervezet és perjog,* Budapest, 1899, p. 33.
    26. *Dl.* 71423.
    27. *Mon.Strig.,* III, pp. 58-61.
    28. *Zichy,* III, pp. 152-3; *Dl.* 83256; *Dl.* 94422; *Dl.* 2800; *Dl.* 30651.
    29. Discussed further, pp. 137-39.
    30. *Dl.* 3661; *Dl.* 41495.
    31. Erik Fügedi, "Középkori magyar városprivilégiumok," *TBM,* 14, 1961, p. 64.
    32. *DRH,* pp. 197-8, 200 (1405: 8, 12).
    33. András Kubinyi, "Der ungarische König und seine Städte im 14. und am
Beginn des 15. Jahrhunderts," in (ed) Wilhelm Rausch, *Stadt und Stadtherr im 14.
Jahrhundert,* Linz-Donau, 1972, pp. 201-2.
    34. Iván Bertényi, "Die städtischen Bürger und das Gericht der königlichen
Anwesenheit im 14. Jahrhundert," *AnnalesUSB,* 11, 1970, pp. 10-14.
    35. *Mon.Strig.,* III, p. 526; *cf. ibid.,* pp. 228-30, 319; (ed) Elemér Varjú,
Oklevéltár a Tomaj nemzetségbeli Losonczi Bánffy család történetéhez, I, Budapest,
1908, p. 84; Tkalčić, I, p. 445; *CD,* VIII/2, p. 404.
    36. *CD,* IX/1, p. 152; *cf. ibid.,* p. 148; *Mon.Strig.,* III, p. 526.
    37. *Dl.* 3661; *Dl.* 41495; *Dl.* 89412; *Dl.* 91789.
    38. Smičiklas, XII, p. 417.
    39. Imre Szentpétery, *Magyar Oklevéltan,* Budapest, 1930, pp. 154-164, 213-5.
    40. Iván Bertényi, "Zur Gerichtstätigkeit des Palatins und des Landesrichters
(Judex Curiae Regiae) in Ungarn im XIV. Jahrhundert," *AnnalesUSB,* 7, 1965,
pp. 31-3; by the same author, "Die städtischen Bürger und das Gericht der königlichen
Anwesenheit im 14. Jahrhundert," *AnnalesUSB,* 11, 1970, p. 5; (ed) Gyula Nagy, *A
nagymihályi és sztárai gróf Sztáray család oklevéltára,* I, Budapest, 1887, p. 440.
    41. Imre Hajnik, *A magyar birósági szervezet és perjog,* Budapest, 1889, pp. 33-8;
György Bónis, *A jogtudó értelmiség a Mohács előtti Magyarországon,* Budapest, 1971,
pp. 120-48; Erik Fügedi, "Középkori magyar városprivilégiumok," *TBM,* 14, 1961,
pp. 66-71.
    42. Imre Hajnik, *op.cit.* (see above, n. 41), p. 33; Hóman-Szekfű, II, p. 140;
Vilmos Fraknói, *A nádori és az országbirói hivatal eredete és hatáskörének történeti
kifejlődése,* Pest, 1863, pp. 140-141.
    43. Iván Bertényi, *Az országbirói intézmény története XIV. századi Magyaror-
szágon,* Budapest, 1976, pp. 49-50; József Gerics, "Beiträge zur Geschichte der
Gerichtstätigkeit im ungarischen Hof und der Zentralverwaltung im 14. Jahrhundert,"
AnnalesUSB, 7, 1965, pp. 8-10; Hajnik, *op.cit.* (see above, n. 41), pp. 33-38.
    44. *Mon.Strig.,* III, pp. 627-30; Antal Pór, "Háborúság Esztergom város és az
Esztergomi káptalan közt a vám miatt," *Magyar gazdaságtörténelmi szemle,* 9, 1904;
cf. AO, III, pp. 2, 132.

45. László Fejérpataky, *Magyarországi városok régi számadáskönyvei,* Budapest, 1885, p. 89; for background to the *scansor,* Günther von Probszt, *Die neiderungarische Bergstädte,* München, 1966, p. 45.

46. *Dl.* 50823; Házi, *Sopron,* 1/1, p. 160; *Hospitallers v. Kunclin* is, of course, a further instance.

47. Iván Bertényi, "Die städtischen Bürger und das Gericht der Königlichen Anwesenheit im 14. Jahrhundert," *AnnalesUSB,* 11, 1970, p. 11; by the same author, "Városi polgárok az országbiró itélőszéke előtt a 14. században," in (ed) Ándor Csizmadia, *Jogtörténeti tanulmányok,* III, Budapest, 1974, p. 125.

48. L. Bernát Kumorovitz, "Audientia, praesentia," in (ed) Pál Angyal, Jusztin Baranyay, Mihály Móra, *Notter Antal emlékkönyv,* Budapest, 1941, p. 711; by the same author, "A királyi kápolnaispán oklevéladó műdödése," *Regnum,* 5, 1942, p. 462; Albert Gárdonyi, "A királyi titkos kanczellária eredete és kialakulása Magyarországon," *Századok,* 48, 1914, pp. 176-81; Franz Eckhart, "Die glaubwürdigen Orte Ungarns im Mittelalter" (see above, n. 18), pp. 546-8; *Dl.* 84688; *Dl.* 89412; *Dl.* 42388.

49. Elemér Boreczky, *A királyi tárnokmester hivatala 1405-ig,* Budapest, 1904, pp. 6-16.

50. *Mon.Strig.,* I, p. 282; *CD,* II, p. 120; *DRH,* pp. 86-9, 91-3.

51. Bálint Hóman, *A magyar királyság pénzügyei és gazdaságpolitikája Károly Róbert korában,* Budapest, 1921, p. 35; Boreczky, *op.cit.* (see above, n. 49), p. 18.

52. Similar rights were awarded to Vasvár in 1279—*HO,* V, p. 62.

53. László Fejérpataky, *Magyarországi városok régi számadáskönyvei,* Budapest, 1885, pp. 4, 7, 83.

54. *MTT,* XII, pp. 114, 119-23; *CD,* X/7, pp. 862-4; *Dl.* 76696; *Dl.* 50823.

55. *Dl.* 93906; *Dl.* 75160; *Dl.* 93907-8; *Dl.* 75517; *AO,* I, p. 223; *Dl.* 50736; *Dl.* 50823; *Dl.* 40530; *Dl.* 40609; *D1.* 76696; *Dl.* 87159.

56. Iván Bertényi, *Az országbirói intézmény története a XIV. században,* Budapest, 1976, p. 121; by the same author, "Die städtische Bürger und das Gericht der königlichen Anwesenheit im 14. Jahrhundert," *AnnalesUSB,* 11, 1970, p. 8.

57. *Dl.* 40581; *Dl.* 40584.

58. Iván Bertényi, *Az országbirói intézmény* (see above, n. 56), pp. 162-3.

59. *Ibid.,* pp. 159-60.

60. *Ibid.,* pp. 39, 161-2; Iván Bertényi, "Városi polgárok az országbiró itélőszéke előtt a 14. században," in (ed) Ándor Csizmadia, *Jogtörténeti tanulmányok,* III, Budapest, 1974, pp. 127-8; József Gerics, "Beiträge zur Geschichte der Gerichtsbarkeit im ungarischen königlichen Hof und der Zentralverwaltung im 14. Jahrhundert," *AnnalesUSB,* 7, 1965, pp. 18-20.

61. *MZsO,* I, p. 89.

62. Házi, *Sopron,* 1/1, p. 176.

63. Zimmermann-Werner, II, p. 464; Tkalčić, I, pp. 249-50.

64. László Fejérpataky, *Magyarországi városok régi számadáskönyvei,* Budapest, 1885, p. 20.

65. *Dl.* 42042; see also, *Df* 238948 (*Pozsony v. lt.,* no. 328).

66. Tkalčić, V, pp. 42-3, 156; *CD*, X/1, pp. 61-2; *CD*, XI, p. 531; *ZO*, I, no. 4424.
67. Iván Bertényi, *Az országbírói intézmény története a XIV. században*, Budapest, 1976, p. 116; András Kubinyi, "Der ungarische König und seine Städte im 14. und am Beginn des 15. Jahrhunderts," in (ed) Wilhelm Rausch, *Stadt und Stadtherr im 14. Jahrhundert*, Linz-Donau, 1972, p. 200.
68. *Dl.* 6998.
69. *Dl.* 32879.
70. Tkalčić, I, p. 287.
71. *Dl.* 42161; *Dl.* 42279; *Dl.* 42287; *Dl.* 42388; *ZO*, I, nos. 1759, 2203, 2988, 3039, 3370, 4424, 5027; see however, *Dl.* 71423.
72. *ZO*, I, no. 5629; *CD*, X/1, p. 558.
73. András Kubinyi, "A királyi kincstartók oklevéladó működése Mátyástól Mohácsig," *LK*, 28, 1958, p. 35; Hóman-Szekfű, II, p. 124.
74. *CD*, XI, pp. 527-8; *CD*, X/4, p. 239; *ZO*, I, nos. 3939-40.
75. *ZO*, II/2, no. 6423; *MZsO*, V/1, p. 53; *Bud.Tört.*, II, p. 83.
76. *Dl.* 42287; *ZO*, I, nos. 291, 5689, 5629; Fejérpataky, *op.cit.* (see above, n. 64), pp. 83, 88; Tkalčić, I, p. 287; *ibid.*, V, p. 102; *ZO*, I, no. 1017; *ibid.*, II/1, no. 731.
77. (Ed) Imre Nagy, *Sopron vármegye történetének oklevéltára*, I, Sopron, 1889, p. 171.
78. *ZO*, I, no. 1017.
79. *Dl.* 71362; *Dl.* 6998.
80. *DRH*, pp. 197, 200 (1405: 7, 11).
81. Wilhelm Ebel, *Deutsches Recht im Osten (Göttinger Arbeitskreis Schriftenreih, 21)*, 1952, pp. 11-14.
82. F. Keutgen, *Urkunden zur städtischen Verfassungsgeschichte*, Berlin, 1899, p. 52.
83. J. A. Tomaschek, *Der Oberhof Iglau in Mähren und Schöffensprüche aus dem XIII-XVI. Jahrhundert*, Innsbruck, 1868, p. 19; for the text of the *aeltere Schöffensprüche*, pp. 56-261.
84. Tomaschek, *op.cit.* (see above, n. 83), pp. 18-19, 77-8, 183-4, 209, 236-7.
85. Such an approach is largely favoured in what still remains the best work on this subject—Imre Szentpétery (the younger), "A tárnoki itélőszék kialakulása," *Századok*, 68 *(Pótfüzet)*, 1934.
86. *ZO*, II/1, no. 3270.
87. *Stadtrecht*, ch. 16.
88. Házi, *Sopron*, 1/2, pp. 191-2; *AMB*, nos. 1031, 1347, 1397.
89. *Df.* 27051 *(Arch. Civ. Cassoviensis, Coll. Schwartzenbachiana*, nr 109*)*.
90. Imre Hajnik, *A magyar bírósági szervezet és perjog*, Budapest, 1899, p. 93, n. 13, n. 15.
91. Házi, *Sopron*, 1/2, p. 289.
92. *Ibid.*, p. 293.
93. Hajnik, *op.cit.* (see above, n. 90), p. 95.
94. Házi, *Sopron*, 1/2, p. 296.
95. *Dl.* 71362; *Dl.* 6998.

96. *DRH,* p. 261; Hajnik, *op.cit.* (see above, n. 90), p. 52. Still on very rare occasions, nobles might be represented at the Tavernical court as late as the last quarter of the fifteenth century, M. G. Kovachich, *Formulae Solennes Styli,* Pesthini, 1799, p. 300.

97. *ZO,* II/2, no. 6740.

98. See above, n. 90.

99. *Buda Articles of 1456:* 5 (*Századok,* 68/*Pótfüzet*/1934, pp. 587-9); *Pozsony Articles:* 16 (János Király, *Pozsony város joga a középkorban,* Budapest, 1894, pp. 420-4.)

100. *ZO,* II/2, no. 5385.

101. As suggested in Ándor Csizmadia, Kálmán Kovács, László Asztalos, *Magyar állam- és jogtörténet,* Budapest, 1978, p. 136.

102. *ZO,* II/2, nos. 6423, 6740.

103. *AMB,* no. 1347; see also, Imre Szentpétery (the younger), "A tárnoki itélőszék kialakulása," *Századok,* 68 (*Pótfüzet*), 1934, p. 565.

104. M. G. Kovachich, *Codex Authenticus Iuris Tavernicalis,* Budae, 1803, p. 49.

105. *DRH,* pp. 197, 200 (1405: 8, 12).

106. *Stadtrecht,* ch. 16, 202, 310, 312; *Buda Articles of 1456:* 1; *Pozsony Articles:* 3, 11, 23, 24 (see above, n. 99); Werbőczy, *Tripartitum,* III:10.

107. An exception may be provided in *ZO,* II/2, no. 6923.

108. *DRH,* pp. 196-7 (1407:7).

109. *Stadtrecht,* ch. 165, 206.

110. *Dl.* 31604-5; *Dl.* 26418; *Df.* 237216 (Arch. Cap. Strig.; *Priv., Lad.* 41, *fasc.* 1, nr 20); Szentpétery (the younger), *op.cit.* (see above, n. 103), p. 556.

111. Endlicher, pp. 434, 447, 552; *CD,* IV/1, p. 330; *ÁÚO,* VIII, p. 7; Alexander Húščava, *Jan Literát a Liptovské Falzá,* Bratislava, 1936, p. 162.

112. *CD,* IV/1, pp. 330, 333; *ibid.,* VIII/3, p. 532; Endlicher, p. 499.

113. *CD,* VIII/3, p. 296; *ibid.,* IX/5, p. 99; Endlicher, pp. 445, 454, 505, 526, 625; Gyula Osváth, *Adalékok Kassa város közjogi helyzetéhez és közigazgatási szervezetéhez I Lipót koráig,* Kassa, 1918, p. 81.

114. Endlicher, p. 455.

115. Osváth, *op.cit.* (see above, n. 113), p. 84; *CD,* IV/2, p. 296.

116. Osváth, *op.cit.* (see above, n. 113), p. 82; *CD,* VIII/3, p. 532; *ibid.,* IX/5, p. 99; Endlicher, p. 621.

117. *Stadtrecht,* ch. 206.

118. *CD,* X/1, p. 62; *CD,* XI, pp. 528-33; *DRH,* pp. 197, 200 (1405: 8, 12).

119. M. G. Kovachich, *Formulae Solennes Styli,* Pesthini, 1799, p. 21.

120. Imre Hajnik, *A magyar birósági szervezet és perjog,* Budapest, 1899, pp. 432-3; (ed) K. Géresi, *Codex diplomaticus comitum Károlyi de Nagy-Károlyi,* I, Budapest, 1882, pp. 555, 559-60; *CD,* VIII/4, p. 425; Zichy, IV, p. 6; *Dl.* 64321.

121. *Stadtrecht,* ch. 16, 310.

122. Tkalčić, V, pp. 42-3; *Dl.* 71362.

123. *ÁÚO,* III, pp. 212-3.

124. M. G. Kovachich, *Codex Authenticus iuris Tavernicalis,* Budae, 1803, pp. 87-255.

125. *Buda Articles of 1456:* 1; *Pozsony Articles:* 1-3 (see back, n. 99).

126. A list of Tavernici is provided in Imre Szentpétery (the younger), "A tárnoki itélőszék kialakulása," *Századok,* 68 *(Pótfüzet),* 1934, pp. 524-5.

127. *Bud.Tört.,* II, p. 86.

128. See back, to the first part of this chapter, pp. 136-37.

129. Elemér Mályusz, "Geschichte des Bürgertums in Ungarn," *Vierteljahrschrift für Sozial- und Wirtschaftsgeschichte,* 20, 1927, p. 387.

130. Gusztáv Wenzel, *A XV. századi tárnoki jog,* Budapest, 1878, pp. 37-8, 40-1.

131. Házi, *Sopron,* 1/2, pp. 180-83.

132. See back, Chapter VI(i), and especially p. 114.

133. *Stadtrecht,* ch. 202.

134. *CD,* IV/1, pp. 330, 333; *ibid.,* V/1, p. 177; *ÁÚO,* VII, p. 103, Endlicher, pp. 434, 471, 518.

135. *ZO,* II/1, no 4748; *ibid.,* II/2, no. 5208.

136. Imre Szentpétery (The younger), *op.cit.* (see above, n. 126), p. 578; 1486: 29: 1; 1492: 92 *(CJH,* pp. 431, 542).

137. *ZO,* II/1, no. 2168, 6740.

138. *MZsO,* V/1, p. 128.

140. M. G. Kovachich, *Formulae Solennes Styli,* Pesthini, 1798, p. 300; *cf, ZO,* II/2, no. 5385.

140. *Df.* 270205 (Arch. civ. Cassoviensis, *Collectio Schwartzenbachiana,* nr 165); the text of this charter is reproduced in Gusztáv Wenzel, *Nevezetes per lőcsei polgárok között (Értekezések a történelmi tudományok köréből),* Budapest, 1873, pp. 16-34.

141. The terminology of one case may possibly reflect this. The Council of Sopron are in 1429 declared to have given a *deliberacio* and not, as one might expect, a *iudicium* in a case subsequently proceeding before the Tavernical court—Házi, *Sopron,* 1/2, pp. 379-80.

142. "Ob die sachen kriegisch entsteen werden"—*Pozsony Articles:* 2 (see above, n. 99); M. G. Kovachich, *Codex Authenticus Iuris Tavernicalis,* Budae, 1803, p. 256 ("si causae litigiosae exortae fuerint").

143. *Df.* 270205 (Arch. civ. Cassoviensis, *Collectio Schwartzenbachiana,* nr. 165).

144. István Kaprinai, *Hungarica diplomatica,* II, Vindobonae, 1771, p. 187; Házi, *Sopron,* 1/6, p. 94; *Df.* 240464 (Arch. civ. Posoniensis, *Chart.,* nr. 1834); *Df.* 270412 (Arch. civ. Cassoviensis, *Collectio Schwartzenbachiana,* nr. 374).

145. *CD,* X/4, pp. 152-4; Iványi, *Bártfa,* no. 295; Házi, *Sopron,* 1/2, pp. 211-2, 285.

146. *ZO,* II/2, no. 7326; Iványi, *Bártfa,* no. 735.

147. *ZO,* II/2, no. 7094; see also, *Dl.* 92491; *Dl.* 93580.

148. Erik Fügedi, "Középkori magyar városprivilégiumok," *TBM,* 14, 1961, p. 65.

149. *ÁÚO,* V, p. 21.

150. Gyula Osváth, *Adalékok Kassa város közjogi helyzetéhez és közigazgatási szervezetéhez I Lipót koráig,* Kassa, 1918, p. 81.

151. Erik Fügedi, *op.cit.* (see above, n. 148), p. 66.

152. *ÁÚO,* III, p. 38.

153. Osváth, *op.cit.* (see above, n. 150), pp. 83-4; *CD,* IX/6, p. 178; Zimmermann-Werner, II, pp. 98, 212-3, 219.

154. *AO,* VII, pp. 402-6.

155. *CD,* XI, p. 523.

156. *CD,* X/1, pp. 61-2.

157. *ZO,* II/1, nos. 3767, 3921.

158. *DRH,* pp. 193, 200 (1405: 4, 12).

159. Iványi, *Bártfa,* no. 466; Iványi, *Eperjes,* nos. 309, 315, 318.

160. *Df.* 270205 (Arch. civ. Cassoviensis, *Collectio Schwartzenbachiana,* nr. 165).

161. Béla Iványi, *Debrecen és a budai jog,* Debrecen, 1924, pp. 10-11; such confusion persisted until well into the sixteenth century—István Gazdag, *Debrecen város magistratusának jegyzőkönyvei 1547,* Debrecen, 1979, no. 450.

162. Ákos Timon, *Magyar alkotmány-és jogtörténet,* Budapest, 1919, pp. 751-2; *LK,* 12, 1934, p. 70.

163. Házi, *Sopron,* 1/3, p. 293.

164. See generally in this context, Werbőczy, *Tripartitum,* III: 8; 2 by which time Pest had been admitted as an eighth member.

165. Imre Hajnik, *A magyar birósági szervezet és perjog,* Budapest, 1899, p. 91, n. 37.

166. J. Teleki, *Hunyadiak kora Magyarországon,* X, Pest, 1853, pp. 370-1.

167. J. Teleki, *Hunyadiak kora Magyarországon,* XII, Pest, 1857, pp. 72-3; *Buda Articles of 1456:* 5 & 10; *Pozsony Articles:* 2 & 6 (see above, n. 99).

168. *Pozsony Articles:* 19 (see above, n. 99).

169. Béla Iványi, *Debrecen és a budai jog,* Debrecen, 1924, p. 13; *CD,* VIII/2, pp. 74-5; *ibid.,* IX/1, p. 204; *ibid.,* IX/6, p. 178; Gyula Osváth, *Adalékok Kassa város közjogi helyzetéhez és közigazgatási szervezetéhez I Lipót koráig,* Kassa, 1918, pp. 83-4.

170. Endlicher, pp. 444-47.

171. *Df.* 239418 (Arch. civ. Posoniensis, *Chart.,* nr. 790); Iványi, *Bártfa,* no. 1578; *CD,* X/4, pp. 400-2; Házi, *Sopron,* 1/2, p. 289; *ZO,* II/2, no. 5213.

172. Gyula Szekfű, *Serviensek és familiarisok (Értekezések a történelmi tudományok köréből),* Budapest, 1912, p. 107.

173. Házi, *Sopron,* 1/2, pp. 123, 212, 380; *ibid.,* 1/3, p. 76.

174. M. G. Kovachich, *Codex Authenticus Iuris Tavernicalis,* Budae, 1803, pp. 259-60, 268. Already by 1436 it was recognised that the Tavernical court was normally held at Buda—Országos Széchenyi Könyvtár, Kézirattár, *Cod. Lat. Medii Aevi,* no. 124, *fol 6v.*

175. *Buda Articles of 1456:* 12, 17; *Pozsony Articles:* 4 (see above, n. 99).

176. *Pozsony Articles:* 4 (see above, n. 99); M. G. Kovachich, *Codex Authenticus Iuris Tavernicalis,* Budae, 1803, p. 264.

177. *CD,* X/8, p. 661; noted by András Kubinyi, *LK,* 28, 1958, p. 35.

178. Erik Fügedi, "Középkori magyar városprivilégiumok," *TBM,* 14, 1961, p. 70.

179. Edited by M. G. Kovachich and published in Buda, 1803. The relevant section is contained in pp. 87-255.

180. Gusztáv Wenzel, *A XV. századi tárnoki jog,* Budapest, 1878, pp. 11-12, 14-15, 19-33.

181. M. G. Kovachich, *op.cit.* (see above, n. 176), p. 88-9.

182. "Livra civitatis Wylak," Nationalbibliothek, Vienna, Handschriftensammlung, *Cod. no.* 8624; published, Rudolf Schmidt, *Statuta Grada Iloka z Godine 1525 (Monumenta Historica—Juridica Slav. Merid., Volumen* XII*),* Zagreb, 1938.

183. Gusztáv Wenzel, *op.cit.* (see above, n. 180), p. 7.

184. "Livra civitatis Wylak" (see above, n. 182), *fol* 5r-10r.

185. *Ibid., fol* 5r, 11r-36r.

186. "Liber Civitatis Cassoviensis," Nationalbibliothek, Vienna, Handschriftensammlung, *Ser. Nov.,* 4644.

187. György Bónis, "Die ungarischen Städte am Ausgang des Mittelalters," in (ed) Wilhelm Rausch, *Die Stadt am Ausgang des Mittelalters,* Linz-Donau, 1974, p. 85; *Stadtrecht,* ch. 17.

188. *DRH,* pp. 197, 200 (1405: 8, 12).

189. *Dl.* 87002; Dezső Csánki, "Kuncz ispán majora Budán," *Századok,* 40, 1906, pp. 694-6.

190. *Dl.* 15766.

191. *MTT,* XII, 1863, pp. 79-80.

192. J. Teleki, *Hunyadiak kora Magyarországon,* X, Pest, 1853, p. 371.

193. Kovachich, *op.cit.* (see above, n. 176), p. 260.

194. M. G. Kovachich, *Codex Authenticus Iuris Tavernicalis,* Budae, 1803, pp. 256-70; Országos Széchényi Könyvtár, Kézirattár, *Cod. Lat. Medii Aevi,* no. 365, *fol* 59v-61r; *ibid.,* no. 323, *fol* 5r-v; Nationalbibliothek, Vienna, *Handschriftensammlung, Ser. Nov.,* 4644, fol 42v; for *Pozsony Articles,* see above, n. 99.

195. Kovachich, *op.cit.* (see above, n. 194), p. 49.

196. Werbőczy, *Tripartitum,* III:11; *MZsO,* V/1, pp. 128-9.

Chapter 8

1. Joachim Leuschner, *Deutschland im späten Mittelalter,* Göttingen, 1975, p. 190-2.

Appendix II

1. Csánki, *Mon.Bud.,* pp. 71, 73.

2. Zimmermann-Werner, I, pp. 137-8.

3. Ferenc Eckhart, "Néhány kiadatlan árpádkori oklevél," *Fejérpataky Emlékkönyv,* Budapest, 1917, p. 77.

4. Csánki, *Mon.Bud.,* p. 100; *MTT,* I, p. 113.

5. *Mon.Vesp.*, I, p. 302.
6. Csánki, *Mon.Bud.*, p. 177.
7. *Ibid.*, pp. 246, 301.
8. *Ibid.*, pp. 247-8.
9. *Ibid.*, p. 283.
10. *SRH*, I, pp. 481-2.
11. *Ibid.*
12. *AO*, I, p. 512.
13. *Df.* 229964 (Veszp. kápt. hh. levéltár, *Inst. Regni, Capsa* P, no. 237).
14. *Ibid.*
15. *Df.* 236191 (Szepesi kápt. o. levéltár, *Misc. div. cott., fasc.* 13, no. 25).
16. *MTT*, IV, p. 126.
17. *Ibid.*, p. 130; *Dl.* 2568.
18. *Mon.Strig.*, III, p. 222.
19. *MTT*, IV, p. 136; *Mon.Strig.*, III, p. 619; see above, p. 190, note 110.
20. *MTT*, IV, p. 136.
21. *Dl.* 24678; *Df.* 229965 (Veszp. kápt. hh. levéltár, *Inst. Regni, Capsa* P, no. 238).
22. *Dl.* 3554; *Dl.* 76690.
23. *Mon.Strig.*, III, p. 515.
24. *Ibid.*, III, p. 539; Horváth & Huszár, p. 25.
25. *AO*, IV, p. 510.
26. *Mon.Strig.*, III, p. 619.
27. *Dl.* 3926; *Dl.* 3953.
28. *CD*, IX/2, p. 254.
29. *AO*, V, p. 407; *Dl.* 87265.
30. *AO*, V, p. 563; *Dl.* 4265.
31. *AO*, VI, p. 81.
32. *Ibid.*, p. 269.
33. *AMB*, no. 194.
34. *CD*, IX/3, pp. 458-9.
35. *Zichy*, III, pp. 289, 296.
36. *Dl.* 5545.
37. *Dl.* 5566.
38. *Dl.* 5865-6.
39. *Dl.* 6260.
40. *Df.* 238149 (Eszt. kápt. mag. levéltár, *Lad.* 64, *fasc.* 1, *nr.* 2).
41. *Dl.* 6334.
42. *Dl.* 6354.
43. *Dl.* 74836.
44. *Dl.* 6273.
45. *Dl.* 6767.
46. *Dl.* 6894; *Quellen Wien*, II/1, no. 1023.
47. *MTT*, IV, p. 155; *Dl.* 7094.

48. *Dl.* 7089.
49. Levente Závodszky, *A Hédervári család oklevéltár,* I, Budapest, 1909, p. 98.
50. *ZO,* I, nos. 539, 710.
51. *Ibid.,* I, nos. 1186, 1379.
52. *Ibid.,* I, nos. 1814, 1921.
53. *Ibid.,* I, no. 2727; Imre Nagy, Dezső Véghelyi, Gyula Nagy, *Zala vármegye történetének oklevéltára,* II, Budapest, 1890, p. 257.
54. *ZO,* I, no. 3072.
55. *Ibid.,* no. 4266.
56. *CD,* X/2, p. 408.
57. *ZO,* I, no. 5218.
58. *Ibid.,* I, nos. 5489, 5596.
59. *Ibid.,* II/1, nos. 1177, 1219.
60. *Ibid.,* II/1, nos. 2043, 4199.
61. *Ibid.,* II/1, nos. 3092, 3101, 3104; Házi, *Sopron,* I/1, p. 279.
62. *ZO,* II/1, no. 3732.
63. *Ibid.,* II/1, no. 5025; *CD,* X/4, p. 595.
64. *ZO,* II/2, nos. 6846, 6943, 7094.
65. *Dl.* 9766.
66. *Dl.* 5866, *Dl.* 9821.
67. *Dl.* 9937.
68. *Dl.* 10119.
69. *Dl.* 10359.
70. *Dl.* 10547; *Bud.Tört.,* II, p. 69.
71. *AK,* 1973, p. 264; *Bud.Tört,* II, p. 69.
72. *Dl.* 95811.
73. *Dl.* 64201.
74. *Dl.* 43472.
75. Házi, *Sopron,* I/2, p. 216; *Stadtrecht,* ch. 404.
76. *AK,* 1973, p. 264.
77. *Dl.* 11239; Emil Jakubovich, Dezső Pais, *Ó-magyar olvasókönyv,* Pécs, 1929, p. 282.
78. Fővárosi levéltár, no. 9.
79. *Dl.* 11562; *Dl.* 11625; *Dl.* 11629.
80. Házi, *Sopron,* I/2, p. 291.
81. *AK,* 1973, p. 264; *Bud.Tört.,* II, p. 70.
82. *Dl.* 11924; *Dl.* 11944.
83. *Df.* 270205 (Arch. civ. Cassovien., *Coll. Schwartzenbachiana,* no. 165).
84. *Quellen Wien,* II/3A, no. 31; *Dl.* 12126.
85. *Dl.* 12461.
86. *Dl.* 12550.
87. *AK,* 1973, p. 264; *Quellen Wien,* II/2, no. 2489.
88. *CD,* X/7, p. 740; Ferenc Salamon, *Budapest története,* III, Budapest, 1885, p. 356.

89. *Quellen Wien*, II/2, nos. 2625, 2633; *CD*, X/8, p. 663.
90. Házi, *Sopron*, I/3, p. 186.
91. *Dl.* 13608.
92. *Df.* 249009 (Eszt. primási levéltár, *Arch. Eccl. Vetus*, no. 46).
93. *Dl.* 13972.
94. *Dl.* 93040.
95. *Dl.* 44478.
96. *Dl.* 14205.
97. *Dl.* 44622.
98. *Df.* 237582 (Eszt. Kápt. magánltára, *Lad.* 45, *fasc.* 12, *nr.* 10).
99. *Dl.* 44704.
100. *LK,* 42, 1973, p. 264, citing Jászói levéltár, *sub.* PP25.
101. *Dl.* 15133.
102. *Dl.* 15196; *Df.* 238096 (Eszt. kápt. magánltára, *Lad.* 53, *fasc.* 3, *nr.* 12).
103. *Dl.* 30842.
104. *Dl.* 93303.
105. *Dl.* 15670.
106. *Dl.* 15785; *Dl.* 15766.
107. *Dl.* 15867.
108. *Dl.* 16188.
109. Fővárosi levéltár, no. 2; *Dl.* 16188-9.
110. *Dl.* 16355.
111. *Dl.* 93370.
112. Bártfai Szabó, *Pest,* p. 252.
113. *Quellen Wien,* II/3, no. 4321.
114. *Dl.* 16626.
115. *Dl.* 45484.
116. *Dl.* 17323.
117. *Dl.* 17500; *Df.* 252007 (Zágrábi érseki ltár, *priv.* 39).
118. *Df.* 238272 (Eszt. kápt. magánltára, *Lad.* 67, *fasc.* 7, *nr.* 3).
119. *Dl.* 17675; *Dl.* 50311; *Századok,* 52, 1918, p. 58; Register in Budapesti történeti múzeum, unnumbered typescript.
120. Károly Fabritius, *Pemfflinger Márk élete,* Budapest, 1875, p. 101.
121. *Dl.* 88620; Egri kápt. magánlevéltára, *no.* 29, *fasc.* 4-5 (Országos levéltár, *Filmtár,* Microfilm box 1349, 218 *cim*).
122. *Dl.* 18208.
123. *Dl.* 45908; *Dl.* 18468; *Dl.* 18366; *Df.* 238098 (Eszt. kápt. magánltár, *Lad.* 53, *fasc.* 3, *nr.* 14).
124. *Dl.* 18570; *Dl.* 93548; *Dl.* 93580; Fővárosi levéltár, no. 4.
125. *Df.* 238161 (Eszt. kápt. magánltár, *Lad.* 64, *fasc.* 1, *nr.* 16).
126. *LK,* 37, 1966, p. 285; *Dl.* 45955.
127. *Dl.* 19250; *Df.* 238162 (Eszt. kápt. magánltára, *Lad.* 64, *fasc.* 1, *nr.* 17).
128. *Df.* 238102 (Eszt. kápt. magánltára, *Lad.* 53, *fasc.* 3, *nr.* 18).
129. *Dl.* 19491.

130. Bártfai Szabó, *Pest,* nos. 1141, 1144; *Dl.* 82070; *Dl.* 19567; Eötvös Loránd tudományi egyetem, Könyvtár, *Diplomatarium autographum,* no. 40; *Df.* 208830 (Eszt. kápt. országos levéltár, *Capsa* 18, *fasc.* 7, *nr.* 5).

131. *Df.* 208831 (Eszt. kápt. országos levéltár, *Capsa* 18, *fasc.* 7, *nr.* 2).

132. *Dl.* 19768.

133. Tiszántúli református egyházkerület, Református kollégium nagykönyvtára, Debrecen, R1110/134; *Dl.* 82070.

134. *Dl.* 20051.

135. *Dl.* 39212; *Dl.* 39213; Bártfai Szabó, *Pest,* no. 1182.

136. *Df.* 238300 (Eszt. kápt. magánltár, *Lad.* 71, *fasc.* 1, *nr.* 14).

137. *Df.* 283138 (Veszpr. püsp. ltár, *Epp. Dec. Bud.* 25).

138. *Df.* 238314 (Eszt. kápt. magánltár, *Lad.* 71, *fasc.* 2, *nr.* 12).

139. Országos levéltár, *Filmtár,* Microfilm box 8016, 23 *cim;* copy in, Eötvös Loránd tudományi egyetem, Könyvtár, *Collectio Hevenesiana,* 71, pp. 205-209; *Df.* 236393 (Eszt. kápt. magánltár, *Lad.* 25, *fasc.* 3, *nr.* 21).

140. *Df.* 238104 (Eszt. kápt. magánltár, *Lad.* 53, *fasc.* 3, *nr.* 20).

141. *Df.* 238305 (Eszt. kápt. magánltár, *Lad.* 71, *fasc.* 1, *nr.* 19) *Df.* 238169 (*ibid.,* 64, 1, 24).

142. *Dl.* 46582.

143. *Dl.* 21148.

144. *Dl.* 46636.

145. *Dl.* 46663.

146. *Df.* 216776 (Bártfa városi levéltára, *Okl* 3887).

147. Df. 206404 (Garamszentbenedeki konvent levéltára, *fasc.* 141, *nr* 29).

148. *MTT,* XII, p. 67.

149. *Df.* 216984 (Bártfa városi levéltára, *Okl* 4089).

150. *MTT,* XII, pp. 66-7, 93; *Dl.* 106083/72, *Dl.* 22279.

151. *Df.* 238124 (Eszt. kápt. magánltár, *Lad.* 53, *fasc.* 3, *nr.* 33).

152. András Kubinyi, "Die Nürnberger Haller in Ofen," *Mitteilungen des Vereins für Geschichte der Stadt Nürnberg,* 52, 1963-64, p. 96.

153. *Dl.* 22637.

154. *Dl.* 106748; *cf* Bártfai Szabó, *Pest,* no. 1376.

155. *Dl.* 22770; *Df.* 236377 (Eszt. kápt. magánltár, *Lad.* 25, *fasc.* 3, *nr.* 2).

156. *Dl.* 106075.

157. *Dl.* 23032.

158. *LK,* 37, 1966, p. 263.

159. *LK,* 37, 1966, p. 285.

160. György Szerémi, *Emlékirat Magyarország romlásáról,* (ed. Gusztáv Wenzel), Pest, 1857, p. 97.

161. *Dl.* 90430.

162. *Dl.* 87628.

163. *LK,* 37, 1966, p. 286.

164. *Dl.* 32685/8.

165. Szerémi, *op.cit.,* p. 175; Haus- Hof- und Staatsarchiv, Vienna, *Ungarische Urkunden,* February 11-18, 1528.

166. *LK,* 37, 1966, p. 286.

167. Szerémi, *op.cit.,* pp. 264, 267.

BIBLIOGRAPHY

Manuscript Collections Consulted

Hungary

Budapest: Országos levéltár (National Archive).

Országos Széchenyi könyvtár, Kézirattár (National Széchenyi Library, Manuscript Collection).

Fővárosi levéltár (Municipal Archive).

Eötvös Loránd tudományi egyetem, Könyvtár (Loránd Eötvös University of Budapest, Library).

Register Collection in the Budapesti történeti múzeum (Budapest Historical Museum).

Debrecen: Hajdú-Bihar megyei levéltár (Hajdú-Bihar County Archive).

A tiszántúli református egyházkerület nagykönyvtára, Református kollégium (The Great Library of the Reformed Church Diocese beyond-the-Tisza, College of the Reformed Church).

Austria

Vienna: Nationalbibliothek, Handschriftensammlung.

Stadt- und Landesarchiv.

228   BIBLIOGRAPHY

Germany

Nuremberg: Bayerische Staatsarchiv.

Stadtarchiv.

England

London: British Library, Department of Manuscripts.

Primary Sources

Adalékok Kassa város közjogi helyzetéhez és közigazgatása szervezetéhez I Lipót koráig, (ed) Gyula Osváth, Kassa, 1918.

Analecta Scepusii sacri et profani, I-IV, (ed) Carolus Wagner, Viennae, 1774-8.

Anjou-kori okmánytár (Codex diplomaticus Hungaricus Andegavensis), I-VII, (ed) Imre Nagy, Gyula Nagy, Budapest, 1878-1920.

Die Annalen der Reichstadt Nürnberg von 1623, Johannes Müllner *(Quellen zur Geschichte und Kultur der Stadt Nürnberg),* Nürnberg, 1972.

"Az Aranybulla," (ed) Géza Érszegi, *Fejér megyei történeti évkönyv,* 6, 1972, pp. 1-15.

Archív mesta Bratislavy, I, (ed) D. Lehotská, D. Handzová, Praha, 1956.

Archive der Freiherren Haller von Hallerstein in Schloss Gründlach (Bayerische Archivinventare, 26), I, Munchen, 1965.

Árpád-kori új okmánytár (Codex diplomaticus Arpadianus continuatus), I-VIII, (ed) Gusztáv Wenzel, Pest-Budapest, 1860-78.

Bártfa szabad királyi város levéltára, Béla Iványi, Budapest, 1910.

Buda városnak törvénykönyve, (ed) Andreas Michnay, Karl Lichner, Pressburg (Pozsony), 1845.

Budai török számadáskönyvei, 1510-1580, (ed) Gyula Káldy-Nagy, Lajos Fekete, Budapest, 1962.

Catalogus fontium historiae Hungaricae, I-III, (ed) Albinus Franciscus Gombos, Budapest, 1937-8.

Chronica Az Magyaroknac Dolgairol, Gaspar Heltai, Colosvarot, 1575.

Die Chroniken der deutschen Städte, (ed) Die Historische Commission bei der Königliche Akademie der Wissenschaften, I. Leipzig, 1862.

Codex Authenticus Iuris Tavernicalis, M. G. Kovachich, Budae, 1803.

Codex Diplomaticus comitum Károlyi de Nagy-Károlyi, I, (ed) K. Géresi, Budapest, 1882.

Codex Diplomaticus domus senioris comitum Zichy de Zich et Vasonkéő, I-XII, (ed) Imre Nagy, Iván Nagy, D. Véghely, E. Kammerer, P. Lukcsics, Budapest, 1871-1931.

Codex Diplomaticus Regni Croatiae, Dalmatiae et Slavoniae, II-XIV, (ed) T. Smičiklas, Zagrabiae, 1904-1916.

BIBLIOGRAPHY 229

Codex Diplomaticus Regni Hungariae ecclesiasticus et civilis, I-XI, (ed) György/ Georgius/Fejér, Budae, 1829-44.

Corpus Juris Hungarici (Magyar törvénytár), 1000-1526, (ed) Dezső Márkus, Budapest, 1899.

Corpus Statutorum Hungariae Municipalium (Monumenta Hungariae Juridico-Historiae), V/2, (ed) Sándor Kolozsvári, Kelemen Óvári, Budapest, 1904.

De rebus Hungaricis, Nicolas Istvánfi, Coloniae Agrippinae, 1622.

Debrecen szabad királyi város levéltára diplomagyűjteményének regesztai, (ed) Gábor Herpay, Debrecen, 1916.

Debrecen város magistratusának jegyzőkönyvei, 1547, (ed) István Gazdag, Debrecen, 1979.

Decreta Regni Hungariae (Gesetze und Verordnungen Ungarns), 1301-1457, (ed) Ferenc Döry, György Bónis, Vera Bácskai, Budapest, 1976.

Deutsche Reichstagakten, IV, (ed) Julius Weizsäcker, Gotha, 1882.

Eberhart Windeckes Denkwürdigkeiten zur Geschichte des Zeitalters Kaiser Sigismunds, (ed) Wilhelm Altmann, Berlin, 1893.

Emlékirat Magyarország romlásáról, György Szerémi, (ed) Gusztáv Wenzel, Pest, 1857.

Eperjes szabad királyi város levéltára, 1245-1519, I-II, Béla Iványi, Szeged, 1931-2.

Formulae Solennes Styli, M. G. Kovachich, Pesthini, 1799.

Frankfurts Reichscorrespondenz, I, (ed) Johannes Janssen, Freiburg-im-Breisgau, 1863.

Fratris Felicis Fabri Tractatus de Civitate Ulmensi, de eius origine, ordine, regimine, de civibus eius et statu, (ed) G. Veesenmayer *(Bibliothek des litterarischen Vereins in Stuttgart, 186)*, Tübingen, 1889.

Gesta Friderici Imperatoris Ottonis Frisingensis episcopi, (ed & trans) C. C. Mierow, *The Deeds of Frederick Barbarossa*, New York, 1966.

Hazai okmánytár (Codex diplomaticus patrius), I-VIII, (ed) Imre Nagy, Imre Paur, K. Ráth, D. Véghely, Győr-Budapest, 1865-1891.

A Hédervári család oklevéltára, I, (ed) Levente Závodszky, Budapest, 1909.

Hungaria Diplomatica temporibus Mathiae de Hunyad Regis Hungariae, I-II, (ed) István Kaprinai, Vindobonae, 1767-77.

Hunyadiak kora Magyarországon, oklevéltár, X-XII, (ed) József Teleki, Pest, 1853-57.

Kolozsvár történetének oklevéltára, I, (ed) Elek Jakab, Buda, 1870.

Komárom megye levéltárának középkori oklevelei, (ed) Gyula Alapi, Komárom, 1917.

(A korona elrablása:) Kottanner Jánosné emlékirata, (ed) Károly Mollay, Budapest, 1978.

Leges Ecclesiasticae Regni Hungariae, II, (ed) Ignatius de Battyán, Claudiopolis, 1827.

The Libelle of Englyshe Polycyce, (ed) George Warner, Oxford, 1926.

Das alte Magdeburgische und Hallische Recht, (ed) E. T. Gaupp, Breslau, 1826.

Magyar diplomácziai emlékek az Anjou-korból (Monumenta Hungariae Historica, Acta Extera), I-III, (ed) Gusztáv Wenzel, Budapest, 1874-76.

Magyar történelmi tár, I-XXV, (ed) A magyar tudományos akadémia, Pest-Budapest, 1855-78.

Magyar-zsidó oklevéltár, I-XV, (ed) Sándor Scheiber, Fülöp Grünwald, Armin Friss, Budapest, 1903-72.

Magyarországi városok régi számadáskönyvei, (ed) László Fejérpataky, Budapest, 1885.

A márkusfalvi Máriássy család levéltára, 1243-1803, (ed) Béla Iványi, Lőcse, 1917.

Die Matrikel der Universität Wien, I, (ed) Das Institut für Österreichische Geschichtsforschung, Graz-Köln, 1956.

Monumenta Diplomatica civitatis Budapest (Budapest történetének okleveles emlékei), 1148-1301, (ed) Dezső Csánki, Albert Gárdonyi, Budapest, 1936.

Monumenta Ecclesiae Strigoniensis, I-III, (ed) F. Knauz, L. C. Dedek, Strigonii, 1874-1924.

Monumenta ecclesiastica tempora innovatae in Hungaria Religionis Illustrantia, I-III, (ed) V. Bunyityay, R. Rapaics, I. Karácsonyi, Budapestini, 1902-06.

Monumenta liberae regiae civitatis Zagrabiensis, I-XII, (ed) Tkalčić, Zagreb, 1889-1905.

Monumenta Medii Aevi Historica res gestas Poloniae illustrantia, IV/2, *Acta Consularia,* Cracow, 1878.

Monumenta Romana episcopatus Vesprimiensis (A veszprémi püspökség római oklevéltár), I-III, (ed) A római magyar történeti intézet, Budapest, 1896-1902.

Monumenta Vaticana Historiam Regni Hungariae Illustrantia, I/1, *Rationes Collectorum Pontificorum in Hungaria,* Budapest, 1887.

A nagymihályi és sztárai gróf Sztáray család oklevéltára, I, (ed) Gyula Nagy, Budapest, 1887.

Österreichische Stadtrechte und Satzungen aus der Zeit der Babenberger," (ed) Andreas von Meiler, *Archiv für Kunde österreichischer Geschichts-Quellen,* 10, 1853, pp. 87-173.

Das Ofner Stadrecht, (ed) Karl Mollay, Budapest, 1959.

Oklevéltár a magyar királyi kegyúri jog történetéhez, (ed) Vilmos Fraknói, Budapest, 1899.

Oklevéltár a Tomaj nemzetségbeli Losonczi Bánffy család történetéhez, I, (ed) Elemer Varjú, Budapest, 1908.

A Pécz nemzetség Apponyi ágának oklevelei, I, (ed) Ernő Krammerer, Budapest, 1906.

Pest-Budai hivatali utasitások a XVIII században, (ed) György Bónis, Budapest, 1974.

Pest megye történetének okleveles emlékei, 1002-1588, (ed) László Bártfai Szabó, Budapest, 1938.

Quellen zur Geschichte des Kölner Handels und Verkehrs im Mittelalter, (ed) Bruno Kuske, Bonn, 1923.

Quellen zur Geschichte der Stadt Wien, I-III, (ed) Anton Mayer, Wien, 1895-1911.

Regesta Imperii, XI, (ed) W. Altmann, Innsbruck, 1896-7.

Regesta Regum stirpis Arpadianae critico-diplomatica (Az árpádházi királyok okleveleinek kritikai jegyzéke), I-II, (ed) Imre Szentpétery, Iván Borsa, Budapest, 1923-61.

Regesta Supplicationum: A papai kérvénykönyvek magyar vonatkozású okmányai, Avignoni korszak, I, (ed) Árpád Bossányi, Budapest, 1916.

Régi utazások Magyarországon és a Balkán Félszigeten, 1054-1717, (ed) István Szamota, Budapest, 1891.

Rerum Hungaricarum Monumenta Arpadiana, (ed) Stephanus Ladislaus Endlicher, Sangalli, 1849.

Sachsenspiegel Landrecht, (ed) Karl August Eckhardt, Berlin & Frankfurt, 1955.

Das schlesische Landrecht, (ed) S. Gaupp, Leipzig, 1823.

Das Schwabenspiegel, (ed) F.L.A. von Lassberg, Tubingen, 1840.

Scriptores rerum Austriacarum, II, (ed) R.D.P. Hieronymus Pez, Lipsiae, 1725.

Scriptores rerum Hungaricarum, I-III, (ed) I. G. Schwandtner, Vindobonae, 1746-48.

Scriptores rerum Hungaricarum, I-II, (ed) Imre Szentpétery, Budapestini, 1937-8.

Scriptores rerum Hungaricarum minores, I-II, (ed) M. G. Kovachich, Budae, 1798.

Sopron szabad királyi város története, I-II, (ed) Jenő Házi, Sopron, 1921-43.

Sopron vármegye történetének oklevéltára, I, (ed) Imre Nagy, Sopron, 1889.

Specimen Hierarchiae Hungaricae, Georgius Pray, Posonii et Cassoviae, 1779.

Statuta Grada Iloka z Godine 1525 (Monumenta Historica Juridica Slavorum Meridionalium, XII), (ed) Rudolf Schmidt, Zagreb, 1938.

Die Summa Legum brevis, levis et utilis des sogenannten Doctor Raymundus von Wiener Neustadt, I-II, (ed) Alexander Gál, Weimar, 1926.

Supplementum analectorum terrae Scepusiensis, I-III, (ed) János Bárdosy, M. Schmauk, J. Hradszky, Samu Weber, Leutschoviae-Szepesváralja-Lőcse, 1802-1908.

Történelmi tár, (ed) A magyar tudományos akadémia, Budapest, 1878-1911.

Tripartitum opus iuris consuetudinarii regni Hungariae a Stephano de Werbewcz (Werbőczy) scriptum, (ed) Kelemen Óvári, Sándor Kolozsvári, Millenniumi emlékkiadás, Budapest, 1897.

Urkundenbuch zur Geschichte der Babenberger in Österr--ch, II, (ed) Oskar von Mitis, Wien, 1955.

Urkundenbuch zur Geschichte der Deutschen in Siebenburgen, I-III, (ed) Franz Zimmermann, Carl Werner, Hermannstadt, 1892-1902.

Urkunden zur städtischen Verfassungsgeschichte, (ed) F. Keutgen, Berlin, 1899.

Urkundliche Beiträge zur Geschichte des Hussitenkrieges, II, (ed) F. Palacky, Prag. 1873.

Veszprémi reveszták, 1301-1387, (ed) L. Bernát Kumorovitz, Budapest, 1953.

Das Wiener Stadtrechts- oder Weichbildbuch, (ed) Heinrich Maria Schuster, Wien, 1873.

Welthandelsbräuche, 1480-1540, (ed) Karl Otto Müller *(Deutsche Handelsakten des Mittelalters und der Neuzeit,* V), Stuttgart & Berlin, 1934.

Zala vármegye történetének oklevéltára, I-II, (ed) Imre Nagy, Dezső Véghely, Gyula Nagy, Budapest, 1886-90.

Zsigmondkori oklevéltár, I-II, (ed) Elemér Mályusz, Budapest, 1951-8.

Secondary Sources

Bácska, Vera; "A mezővárosi önkormányzat," in (ed) György Bónis, Alajos Degré, *Tanulmányok a magyar helyi önkormányzat múltjából*, Budapest, 1971, pp. 9-34.

Bak, János; *Königtum und Stände in Ungarn im 14-16. Jahrhundert*, Wiesbaden, 1973.

Balog, Szidónia; *A magyarországi zsidók kamaraszolgasága és igazságszolgáltatása a középkorban*, Budapest, 1907.

Bartal, A.; *Glossarium mediae et infimae Latinitatis Regni Hungariae*, Budapest, 1901.

Bartal de Beleháza, George; *Commentariorum ad historiam status jurisque publici Hungariae Aevi mediae*, III, Posonii, 1847.

Barth, Reinhard; *Argumentation und Selbstverständnis der Bürgeropposition in städtischen Auseinandersetzungen des Spätmittelalters*, Böhlau-Köln, 1974.

von Below, Georg; *Das altere deutsche Städtewesen und Bürgertum*, Bielefeld & Leipzig, 1898.

Bertényi, Iván; "Zur Gerichtstätigkeit des Palatins und des Landesrichters (Judex Curiae Regiae) in Ungarn im XIV. Jahrhundert," *Annales Universitatis Scientiarum Budapestiensis (Sectio Historica)*, 7, 1965, pp. 29-42.

Bertényi, Iván; "Die städtischen Bürger und das Gericht der königlichen Anwesenheit im 14. Jahrhundert," *Annales Universitatis Scientiarum Budapestiensis (Sectio Historica)*, 11, 1970, pp. 3-31.

Bertényi, Iván; "Városi polgárok az országbiró itélőszéke előtt a 14. században," in (ed) Ándor Csizmadia, *Jogtörténeti tanulmányok*, III, Budapest, 1974, pp. 123-137.

Bertényi, Iván; *Az országbirói intézmény története a XIV. századi Magyarországon*, Budapest, 1976.

Birk, Ernő; "Adalék Magyarország pénztörténetéhez V László idejében," *Új Magyar Múzeum*, III/1, 1853, pp. 509-515.

Birk, Ernst (Ernő); "Beiträge zur Geschichte der Königin Elisabeth von Ungarn und ihres Sohnes König Ladislas," *Quellen und Forschungen*, Wien, 1859, pp. 209-258.

Bónis, György; *Hűbériség és rendiség a középkori magyar jogban*, Kolozvár, undated (1943?).

Bónis, György; 'A kúriai irodák munkája a XIV. és XV. században', *Levéltári Közlemenyek*, 34, 1963, pp. 197-246.

Bónis, György; "Die Entwicklung der geistlichen Gerichtsbarkeit in Ungarn vor 1526," *Zeitschrift der Savigny Stiftung für Rechtsgeschichte (Kanonische Abteilung)*, 80, 1963, pp. 174-235.

Bónis, György; "Ständisches Finanzwesen in Ungarn im frühen 16. Jahrhundert," *Nouvelles Études Historiques*, I, Budapest, 1965, pp. 83-103.

Bónis, György; "Der Zusammenhang der Summa Legum mit dem Tripartitum," *Studia Slavica*, 11, 1965, pp. 373-409.

Bónis György; "Magyi János formuláskönyve és a gyakorlati jogtanitás," in (ed) Ándor Csizmadia, *A pécsi egyetem történetéből, Jubileumi tanulmányok*, I, Pécs, 1967, pp. 225-260.

Bónis, György; *A jogtudó értelmiség a Mohács előtti Magyarországon*, Budapest, 1971.

Bónis, György; "L'état corporatif hongrois au début du XVIe siècle," *Anciens Pays et Assemblées d'États (Standen en Landen),* 70, 1971, pp. 313-25.

Bónis, György; *Középkori jogunk elemei,* Budapest, 1972.

Bónis, György; "Die ungarischen Städte am Ausgang des Mittelalters," in (ed) Wilhelm Rausch, *Die Stadt am Ausgang des Mittelalters,* Linz-Donau, 1974, pp. 79-92.

Bónis, György; "Men Learned in the Law in Medieval Hungary," *East Central Europe,* 4, 1977, pp. 181-191.

Boreczky, Elemér; *A királyi tárnokmester hivatala 1405-ig,* Budapest, 1904.

Borsody, Béla Bevilaqua; *A budai és pesti mészáros céhek ládainak okiratai, 1270-1872,* I, Budapest, 1931.

Borsos, László; "Régi budai házösszeirások," *Tanulmányok Budapest múltjából,* 19, 1972, pp. 57-78.

Botka, Tivadar; *Trensini Csák Máté és kortársai (Értekezések a történelmi tudományok köréből),* Budapest, 1873.

Browne, Edward; *A Brief Account of Some Travels in Divers Parts of Europe viz Hungary . . . With some Observations on the Gold, Copper, Quick-Silver Mines,* London (Second Edition), 1685.

Brunner, Otto; *Neue Wege der Sozialgeschichte,* Göttingen, 1956.

Brunner-Schubert, Isolde; "Wilhelm und Matthäus Runtinger: Zwei Regensburger Kaufleute," *Verhandlungen des Historischen Vereins für Oberpfalz und Regensburg,* 110, 1970, pp. 35-59.

Burger, Gerhart; *Die südwestdeutschen Stadtschreiber im Mittelalter,* Boblingen, 1960.

Büchler, Sándor; *A zsidók története Budapesten a legrégibb időktől 1867-ig,* Budapest, 1901.

Chaloupecký, Vaclav; *Kniha Žilinska,* Bratislava, 1934.

Csánki, Dezső; "Szent-Erzesébetfalva—Pest mellett," *Századok,* 27, 1893, pp. 16-26.

Csánki, Dezső; "Mátyás király mint városépitő," *Századok,* 38, 1904, pp. 297-321, 395-412.

Csánki, Dezső; "Kuncz ispán majora Budán," *Századok,* 40, 1906, pp. 685-725.

Csánki, Dezső; *Magyarország történeti földrajza a Hunyadiak korában,* I-III, V, Budapest, 1890-1913.

Csendes, Peter; "Die Donaustädte von Passau bis Pressburg im 15. Jahrhundert," in (ed) Wilhelm Rausch, *Die Stadt am Ausgang des Mittelalters,* Linz-Donau, 1974, pp. 95-106.

Csizmadia, Ándor; *Győr városjoga az Árpádok alatt,* Győr, 1940.

Csizmadia, Ándor; Kovács, Kálmán; Asztalos, László; *Magyar állam- és jogtörtenet,* Budapest, 1978.

Czok, Karl; "Zur Volksbewegungen in den deutschen Städten des 14. Jahrhunderts: Bürgerkämpfe und antikuriale Opposition," in (ed) Die deutsche Historikergesellschaft, *Städtische Volksbewegungen im 14. Jahrhundert,* Berlin, 1960, pp. 156-69.

Deér, Josef; "Die dalmatinische Munizipalverfassung unter der ungarischen Herrschaft bis zum Mitte des 12. Jahrhunderts," *Ungarische Jahrbücher,* XI, 1931, pp. 377-87.

Deér, Josef; *Heidnisches und Christliches in der altungarischen Monarchie* (Acta

234 BIBLIOGRAPHY

Litterarum ac Scientiarum Regiae Universitatis Hungaricae Francisco-Josephinae Sectio Geographica-Historica, Tom I, fasc 2), Szeged, 1934.

Demkó, Kálmán; *A felső-magyarországi bányavárosok életéről a XVI-XVII. században,* Budapest, 1890.

Demkó, Kálmán; *Lőcse története, Lőcse,* 1897.

Dettling, Käthe; "Der Metallhandel Nürnbergs im 16. Jahrhundert," *Mitteilungen des Vereins für Geschichte der Stadt Nürnberg,* 27, 1928, pp. 97-241.

Domanovszky, Sándor; *A szepesi városok árúmegallitó joga,* Budapest, 1922.

Dopsch, A.; *Verfassungs- und Wirtschaftsgeschichte des Mittelalters,* Wien, 1928.

Du Boulay, F.R.H.; *Germany in the Later Middle Ages,* London *(The Athlone Press),* 1983.

Ebel, Wilhelm; *Deutsches Recht im Osten (Göttinger Arbeitskreis, Schriftenreihe 21),* 1952.

Ebel, Wilhelm; "Über die rechtschöpferische Leistung des mittelalterlichen deutschen Bürgertums," *Vorträge und Forschungen,* XI, 1966, pp. 241-258.

Eckhart, Ferenc (Franz); "Die glaubwürdigen Orte Ungarns im Mittelalter," *Mitteilungen des Instituts für österreichische Geschichtsforschung, Ergänzungsband IX,* 1915, pp. 395-558.

Eckhart, Ferenc; "Néhány kiadatlan Árpádkori oklevél," *Fejérpataky emlékkönyv,* Budapest, 1917, pp. 75-81.

Eckhart, Ferenc; *A szentkorona-eszme története,* Budapest, 1941.

Eckhart, Ferenc; *Magyar alkotmány- és jogtörténet,* Budapest, 1946.

Elekes, Lajos; *Hunyadi,* Budapest, 1952.

Elekes, Lajos; *Mátyás és kora,* Budapest, 1956.

Elekes, Lajos; *Essai de centralisation de l'État hongrois dans la seconde moitié du XVe siècle (Studia Historica, 22),* Budapest, 1960.

Elekes, Lajos; Lederer, Emma; Székely, Gyorgy; *Magyarország története,* I, Budapest, 1961.

Ember, Győző, *Az újkori magyar közigazgatás története Mohácstól a török kiűzéséig,* Budapest, 1946.

Ember, Győző, *Zur Geschichte des Aussenhandels Ungarns im XVI. Jahrhundert (Studia Historica, 44),* Budapest, 1960.

von Engel, Johann; *Geschichte des Ungrischen Reichs und seiner Nebenländer,* Halle, 1797.

Ennen, Edith; *The Medieval Town,* Amsterdam-New York-Oxford *(North Holland Publishing Co.),* 1979.

Erdélyi, László; *Magyarország társadalma a XI. századi törvényeiben,* Budapest, 1907.

Erler, Adalbert; *Bürgerrecht und Steuerpflicht im mittelalterlichen Städtewesen mit besonderer Untersuchung des Steureides (Frankfurter wissenschaftliche Beiträge, Rechts- und Wirtschaftswissenschaftliche Reihe, 2),* Frankfurt am Main, 1939.

Érszegi, Géza; "Körmend középkori pecsétjei és cimere," *Vasi szemle,* 33, 1979.

d'Eszláry, Charles; *Histoire des Institutions publiques hongroises,* I-II, Paris, 1959-63.

Fabritius, Károly; *Pemfflinger Mark szász gróf élete (Értekezések a történelmi tudományok köréből),* Budapest, 1875.

Fejérpataky, László; *A pannonhalmi apátság alapitó oklevele,* Budapest, 1878.

Fischer, Hans; *Die Siedlungsverlegung im Zeitalter der Stadtbildung,* Wien, 1952.

Fógel, József; *II Vlászló udvartartása,* Budapest, 1913.

Főglein, Antal; "A vármegyei notárius," *Levéltári közlemények,* 14, 1936, pp. 149-171.

Főglein, Antal; "A vármegyei jegyzőkönyv," *Levéltári közlemények,* 16, 1938, pp. 142-167.

Fraknói, Vilmos; *A nádori és az országbirói hivatal eredete és hatáskörének történeti kifejlődése,* Pest, 1863.

Fritze, Konrad; *Bürger und Bauern zur Hansezeit: Studien zu den Stadt-Land Beziehungen an der südwestlichen Ostseeküste von 13. bis zum 16. Jahrhundert,* Weimer, 1976.

Fügedi, Erik; " 'Németjogú' falvak települése a szlovák és német nyelvterületen," in (ed) György Székely, *Tanulmányok a parasztság történetéhez Magyarországon a 14. században,* Budapest, 1953, pp. 225-239.

Fügedi, Erik; "Topográfia és városi fejlődés a középkori Óbudán," *Tanulmányok Budapest múltjából,* 13, 1959, pp. 7-56.

Fügedi, Erik; "Középkori magyar városprivilégiumok," *Tanulmányok Budapest múltjából,* 14, 1961, pp. 17-107.

Fügedi, Erik; "Der Stadtplan von Stuhlweissenburg und die Anfänge des Bürgertums in Ungarn," *Acta Historica,* 15, 1969, pp. 103-136.

Fügedi, Erik; "La formation des villes et les ordres mendiants en Hongrie," *Annales Économies, Sociétiés, Civilisations,* 25, 1970, pp. 966-987.

Fügedi, Erik; "Das mittelalterliche Königreich Ungarn als Gastland," *Vorträge und Forschungen,* XVIII, 1975, pp. 471-507.

Gábor, Gyula; *A megyei intézmény alakulása és működése Nagy Lajos alatt,* Budapest, 1908.

Gárdonyi, Albert; "Buda legrégibb pecsétje," *Turul,* 29, 1911, pp. 115-23.

Gárdonyi, Albert; "A királyi titkos kanczellária eredete és kialakulása Magyarországon," *Századok,* 48, 1914, pp. 174-196.

Gárdonyi, Albert; "Buda középkori levéltáráról," *Levéltári közlemények,* 12, 1934, p. 159-165.

Gárdonyi, Albert; "Buda középkori helyrajza," *Tanulmányok Budapest múltjából,* 4, 1936, pp. 59-86.

Gárdonyi, Albert; "A budai városi tanács árulása 1541-ben," *Tanulmányok Budapest múltjából,* 7, 1939, pp. 1-10.

Gárdonyi, Albert; "Középkori települések Pest határában," *Tanulmányok Budapest múltjából,* 8, 1940, pp. 14-27.

Gárdonyi, Albert; "A középkori Buda határai," *Budapest régiségei,* 14, 1945, pp. 379-395.

Gerevich, László; *The Art of Buda and Pest in the Middle Ages,* Budapest, 1971.

Gerevich, László (ed); *Budapest története,* I-II, Budapest, 1973.

Gerevich, László; "A pesti és budai vár," *Budapest régiségei,* 24, 1976, pp. 43-58.

Gerics, József; "Beiträge zur Geschichte der Gerichtstätigkeit im ungarischen Hof und der Zentralverwaltung im 14. Jahrhundert," *Annales Universitatis Scientiarum Budapestiensis (Sectio Historica),* 7, 1965, pp. 3-28.

Granasztói, György; *A középkori magyar város,* Budapest, 1980.

Grimm, Jacob; *Deutsche Rechtsalterthümer,* Göttingen, 1828.

Grothusen, Klaus-Detlev; *Entstehung und Geschichte Zagrebs bis zum Ausgang des 14. Jahrhunderts,* Wiesbaden, 1967.

Guldescu, S.; *History of Medieval Croatia,* The Hague, 1964.

Györffy, György; "Einwohnerzahl und Bevölkerungsdichte in Ungarn bis zum XIV. Jahrhundert," in (ed) Commission Nationale des Historiens Hongrois, *Études Historiques,* I, Budapest, 1960, pp. 163-193.

Györffy, György; *Az árpádkori Magyarország történeti földrajza,* Budapest, 1963.

Györffy, György; "Les débuts de l'évolution urbaine en Hongrie," *Cahiers de Civilisation Médiévale,* 12, 1969, pp. 127-146, 253-64.

Györffy, György; "Honfoglalás, megtelepedés és kalandozások," in (ed) Antal Bartha, Károly Czeglédy, András Róna-Tas, *Magyar őstörténeti tanulmányok,* Budapest, 1977, pp. 123-156.

Györffy, György; *István király és műve,* Budapest, 1977.

Hajnik, Imre; *A királyi könyvek a vegyes házakbeli királyok korszakában (Értekezések a történelmi tudományok köréből),* Budapest, 1879.

Hajnik, Imre; *A perdöntő eskü és az előzetes tanúbizonyítás a középkori magyar perjogban (Értekezések a társadalmi tudományok köréből),* Budapest, 1881.

Hajnik, Imre; *A magyar bírósági szervezet és perjog,* Budapest, 1899.

Halaga, Ondrej R.; "Kaufleute und Handelsgüter der Hanse im Karpatengebiet," *Hansische Geschichtsblätter,* 85, 1967, pp. 58-84.

Haller von Hallerstein, Helmut; "Deutsche Kaufleute in Ofen zur Zeit der Jagellonen," *Mitteilungen des Vereins für die Geschichte des Stadt Nürnberg,* 51, 1962, pp. 467-480.

Heckenast, Gusztáv; *Fejedelmi (királyi) szolgálónépek a korai Árpádkorban (Értekezések a történeti tudományok köréből, Új sorozat, 53),* Budapest, 1970.

Heineccius, J. G.; *Historia iuris Romani et Germani,* Magdeburg-Halle, 1733.

Hirschmann, Gerhard; "Nürnbergs Handelsprivilegien, Zollfreiheiten und Zollverträge bis 1399," in (ed) Stadtarchiv Nürnberg, *Beiträge zur Wirtschaftsgeschichte Nürnbergs,* I, Nürnberg, 1967, pp. 1-48.

Hoffman, Richard C.; "Wroclaw Citizens as Rural Landholders," in (ed) Harry A. Miskimin, David Herlihy, A. L. Udovitch, *The Medieval City,* New Haven & New York (Yale University Press), 1977, pp. 293-311.

Hofmann, Hanns Hubert; "*Nobiles Norimbergenses,* Beobachtungen zur Struktur der reichstädtischen Oberschicht," *Vorträge und Forschungen,* XI, 1966, pp. 53-92.

Holub, József; *Zala megye története a középkorban,* I, Zala megye közönsége, 1929.

Holub, József; "Ordinaria potentia, absoluta potentia," *Revue Historique de droit francais et étranger,* Series 4, 27, 1950, pp. 92-99.

Hóman, Bálint; *A magyar városok az Árpádok korában,* Budapest, 1908.

Hóman, Bálint; *A magyar királyság pénzügyei és gazdaságpolitikája Károly Róbert korában,* Budapest, 1921.

Hóman, Bálint; *Magyar pénztörténet, 1000-1325,* Budapest, 1921.

Hóman, Bálint; Szekfű, Gyula; *Magyar történet,* I-II, Budapest, 1935-6.

Horváth, Henrik; *Buda a középkorban,* Budapest, 1932.

Horváth, J.; "Meister P. und sein Werk," *Acta Antiqua,* 18, 1970, pp. 371-412.

Horváth, T. A.; Huszár, Lajos; "Kamaragrófok a középkorban," *Numizmatikai közlöny,* LIV-LV, 1955-56, pp. 21-33.

Hrbek, Ivan; "Ein arabischer Bericht über Ungarn," *Acta Orientalia,* 5, 1955, pp. 205-230.

Húščava, Alexander; *Ján Literát a Liptovské Falzá,* Bratislava, 1936.

Huszár, Lajos; *A budai pénzverés története a középkorban,* Budapest, 1958.

Huszár, Lajos; "Der Umlauf ungarischer Münzen des 11. Jahrhunderts im Nordeuropa," *Acta Archaeologica,* 19, 1967, pp. 175-200.

Huszti, Dénes; *Olasz-Magyar kereskedelmi kapcsolatak a középkorban,* Budapest, 1941.

Illés, József; *A magyar szerződési jog az Árpádok korában,* Budapest, 1901.

Istványi, Géza; "A XIV. századbeli megyei oklevéladáshoz," *Turul,* 50, 1936, pp. 81-83.

Iványi, Béla; "Eperjes szabad királyi város czimerei és pecsétjei," *Turul,* 29, 1911, pp. 16-32.

Iványi, Béla; "Jogtörténeti vonatkozások Eperjes város középkori számadáskönyveiben," *Fejérpataky emlékkönyv,* Budapest, 1917, pp. 243-62.

Iványi, Béla; *Debrecen és a budai jog,* Debrecen, 1924.

Jakubovich, Emil; "I Endre király tőrvénybeidéző ércbilloga," *Turul,* 47, 1933, pp. 56-74.

Jankovich, M.; "Buda környék plébániáinak középkori kialakulása és a királyi kápolnák intézménye," *Budapest régiségei,* 19, 1959, pp. 57-98.

Jecht, Horst; "Studien zur gesellschaftliche Struktur der mittelalterlichen Städte," *Vierteljahrschrift für Sozial- und Wirtschaftsgeschichte,* 19, 1926, pp. 48-85.

Jireček, Constantin; *Die Handelsstrassen und Bergwerke Serbien und Bosnien während des Mittelalters,* Prag, 1879.

Jurčić, H.; "Die sogenannten "Pacta Conventa" in kroatischer Sicht," *Ungarn-Jahrbuch,* I, 1969, pp. 11-22.

Karsai, G.; "Ki volt Anonymus?," in (ed) J. Horváth; Gy. Székely; *Középkori kútfőinek kritikus kérdései,* Budapest, 1974, pp. 39-59.

Katona, István (Stephanus); *Historia critica,* I-XLII, Pest, 1779-1817.

Kelényi, Ottó, B.; "Iparosok és kereskedők Budán és Pesten a középkorban," *Budapest régiségei,* 13, 1943, pp. 319-334.

Kemény, Lajos; "Kassa kereskedelmi társaság 1518-ban," *Magyar gazdaságtörténelmi szemle,* 4, 1897, p. 482.

Kemény, Lajos; "A kassai pénzverőház," *Magyar gazdaságtörténelmi szemle,* 9, 1902, pp. 248-253.

Király, F.; "Éremlelet Örkénypusztán a XIII. századból," *Numizmatikai közlöny,* 52-53, 1953-4, pp. 9-12.

Király, János; *A pozsonyi nagy-dunai vám- és révjog története,* Pozsony, 1890.

Király, János; *Pozsony város joga a középkorban*, Budapest, 1894.

Kisfaludy, Katalin; *Matthias Rex*, Budapest, 1983.

Klier, Richard; "Nürnberg und Kuttenberg," *Mitteilungen des Vereins für Geschichte der Stadt Nürnberg*, 48, 1958, pp. 51-78.

Komoróczy, György; "Debrecen város képviseleti rendszere," in (ed) György Bónis, Alajos Degré, *Tanulmányok a magyar helyi önkormányzat múltjából*, Budapest, 1971, pp. 81-115.

Kohn, Sámuel; *A zsidók története Magyarországon*, Budapest, 1884.

Kovács, Endre; *A krakkói egyetem és a magyar művelődés*, Budapest, 1964.

Kováts, Ferencz; *Nyugatmagyarország árúforgalma a XV. században a pozsonyi harmincadkönyv alapján*, Budapest, 1902.

Kováts, Ferencz (Franz); "Pressburger Grundbuchführung und Liegenschaftrecht im Spätmittelalter," *Zeitschrift der Savigny Stiftung für Rechtsgeschichte (Germanische Abteilung)*, 39, 1918, pp. 45-87.

Kováts, Ferencz; "A magyar arany világtörténeti jelentősége és kereskedelmi összeköttetéseink a nyugattal a középkorban," *Történeti szemle*, 11, 1922, pp. 104-143.

Kristó, Gyula; *Csák Máté tartományúri hatalma*, Budapest, 1973.

Kristó, Gyula; *Az aranybullák évszázada*, Budapest, 1976.

Kristó, Gyula; "Ki volt és mikor élt Anonymus?," *História*, 2, 1979, pp. 14-15.

Krizskó, Pál; *A körmöczi régi kamara és grófjai*, Budapest, 1880.

Kubinyi, András; "A kincstári személyzet a XIV. század második felében," *Tanulmányok Budapest múltjából*, 12, 1957, pp. 25-49.

Kubinyi, András; "A királyi kincstartók oklevéladó működése Mátyástól Mohácsig," *Levéltári közlemények*, 28, 1958, pp. 35-60.

Kubinyi, András; "A király és a királyné kúriai a XIII. századi Budán," *Archaeológiai értesítő*, 89, 1962, pp. 160-169.

Kubinyi, András; "Budai kereskedők udvari szállitásai a Jagellókorban," *Budapest régiségei*, 19, 1959, pp. 99-119.

Kubinyi, András; "Népmozgalmak Budapesten a feudalizmus korában," *Tanulmányok Budapest múltjából*, 14, 1961, pp. 7-15.

Kubinyi, András; "Buda város pecséthasználatának kialakulása," *Tanulmányok Budapest múltjából*, 14, 1961, pp. 109-146.

Kubinyi, András; "A városi rend kialakulásának gazdasági feltételei és a főváros kereskedelme a XV. sząad végén," *Tanulmányok Budapest múltjából*, 15, 1963, pp. 189-226.

Kubinyi András (Andreas); "Die Nürnberg Haller in Ofen: Ein Beitrag zur Geschichte des Südosthandels im Spätmittelalter," *Mitteilungen des Vereins für die Geschichte der Stadt Nürnberg*, 52, 1963-4, pp. 80-129.

Kubinyi, András; "A budai vár udvarbirói hivatala, 1458-1541," *Levéltári közlemények*, 35, 1964, pp. 67-98.

Kubinyi, András; "A mezőgazdaság történetéhez a Mohács előtti Budán (Gallinczer Lénárt számadáskönyve 1525-ből)," *Agrártörténelmi szemle*, 6, 1964, pp. 371-404.

Kubinyi, András; "Topographic Growth of Buda up to 1541," *Nouvelles Études Historiques*, I, Budapest, 1965, pp. 133-157.

Kubinyi, András; "Budai és pesti polgárok családi összeköttelései a Jagellókorban," *Levéltári közlemények,* 37, 1966, pp. 227-291.

Kubinyi, András; "Polgári értelmiség és hivatalrétege Budán és Pesten a Hunyadi- és Jagellókorban," *Levéltári közlemények,* 39, 1968, pp. 205-231.

Kubinyi, András; "Die Städte Ofen und Pest und der Fernhandel am Ende des 15. und am Anfang des 16. Jahrhunderts," in (ed) Ingomar Bog, *Der Aussenhandel Ostmitteleuropas 1450-1650,* Köln-Wien, 1971, pp. 342-433.

Kubinyi, András; "A magyarországi városhálózat XIV-XV. századi fejlődésének néhány kérdése," *Tanulmányok Budapest múltjából,* 19, 1972, pp. 39-56.

Kubinyi, András; *Die Anfänge Ofens (Giessener Abhandlungen zur Agrar- und Wirtschaftsforschung, 60),* Berlin, 1972.

Kubinyi, András; "Der ungarische König und seine Städte im 14. und am Beginn des 15. Jahrhundert," in (ed) Wilhelm Rausch, *Stadt und Stadtherr im 14. Jahrhundert,* Linz-Donau, 1972, pp. 193-220.

Kubinyi, András; "A budai német patriciátus társadalmi helyzete családi összeköttetései tükrében a XIII. századtól a XV. század második feléig," *Levéltári közlemények,* 42, 1973, pp. 203-264.

Kubinyi, András; "Budapest im Mittelalter," *Cashiers Bruxelloises,* 20, 1975, pp. 39-54.

Kubinyi, András; "Zur Frage der deutschen Ostsiedlung im mittleren Teil des Königreichs Ungarn, 1200-1541," *Vorträge und Forschungen,* XVIII, 1975, pp. 527-66.

Kubinyi, András; "Die Pemfflinger in Wien und Buda," *Jahrbuch des Vereins für Geschichte der Stadt Wien,* 34, 1978, pp. 67-88.

Kubinyi, András, "A magyarországi városok országrendiségének kérdésének," *Tanulmányok Budapest múltjából,* 21, 1979.

Kubinyi, András; "Burgstadt, Vorburgstadt und Stadtburg: Zur Morphologie des mittelalterlichen Buda," *Acta Archaeologia,* 33, 1981, pp. 161-178.

Kubinyi, András; Nagy, L.; Vörös, K.; "Zur Erforschung der Geschichte von Budapest," *Acta Historica,* 3, 1967, pp. 171-198.

Kumorovitz, L. Bernát; "Az authentikus pecsét," *Turul,* 50, 1936, pp. 45-68.

Kumorovitz, L. Bernát; "A magyar királyi egyszerű- és titkospecsét használatának alakulása a középkorban," *A Gróf Klebelsberg Kunó Magyar történetkutató intézet évkönyve,* 7, 1937, pp. 69-112.

Kumorovitz, L. Bernát; "Audientia, praesentia," *Notter Antal emlékkönyv,* Budapest, 1941, pp. 684-711.

Kumorovitz, L. Bernát; "A királyi kápolnaispán oklevéladó működése," *Regnum,* 5, 1942.

Lang, Grete; *Die Nationalitatenkämpfe in Klausenburg im ausgehenden Mittelalter (Veröffentlichungen des Südostinstituts München, 23),* München, 1941.

Lederer, Emma; "A legrégibb magyar iparososztály kialakulása," *Századok,* 62, 1928, pp. 492-528, 633-645.

Lemmel, Herbert E.; *Herkunft und Schicksal der Bamberger Lemmel des 15. Jahrhunderts (Historischer Verein Bamberg,* 101 Bericht*),* Bamberg, 1965.

Lewicki, Tadeusz; "Les noms de Hongrois et de la Hongrie chez les médiévaux geographes arabes et persans," *Folia Orientalia,* 19, 1978, pp. 35-55.

Lewis, John D.; *The Genossenschaft-Theory of Otto von Gierke (University of Wisconsin Studies in the Social Sciences and History,* 25*),* Madison, 1935.

Liliencron, R. V.; *Die historische Volkslieder der Deutschen von 13. bis 16. Jahrhundert,* I, Leipzig, 1865.

Lócsy, Erzsébet; "Középkori telekviszonyok a budai várnegyedben," *Budapest régiségei,* 21, 1964, pp. 191-208.

Lütge, Friedrich; "Der Handel Nürnbergs nach dem Osten im 15-16. Jahrhundert," in (ed) Stadtarchiv Nürnberg, *Beiträge zur Wirtschaftsgeschichte Nürnbergs,* I, Nürnberg, 1967, pp. 318-76.

Macartney, C. A.; *The Origin of the Hun Chronicle (Studies on the Earliest Hungarian Historical Sources,* VI-VII*),* Oxford, 1951.

Macartney, C. A.; *The Medieval Hungarian Historians,* Cambridge, 1953.

Makkai, László; *Társadalom és nemzetiség a középkori Kolozsváron,* Kolozsvár, 1943.

Mályusz, Elemér; "A magyar társadalom a Hunyadiak korában," in (ed) Imre Lukinich, *Mátyás király emlékkönyv,* I, Budapest, undated, pp. 309-433.

Mályusz, Elemér; "Geschichte des Bürgertums in Ungarn," *Vierteljahrschrift für Sozial- und Wirtschaftsgeschichte,* 20, 1927, pp. 356-407.

Mályusz, Elemér; "Polgárságunk részvétele a középkori országgyűléseken', *Protestáns szemle,* 36, 1927, pp. 142-146.

Mályusz, Elemér; "A patrimoniális királyság," *Társadalomtudomány,* 13, 1933, pp. 37-49.

Mályusz, Elemér; "A magyarság és a városi élet a középkorban," *Századok,* 78, 1944, pp. 36-62.

Mályusz, Elemér; "A mezővárosi fejlődés," in (ed) György Székely, *Tanulmányok a parasztság történetéhez Magyarországon a 14. században,* Budapest, 1953, pp. 128-191.

Mályusz, Elemér; "Zsigmond király központosító törekvései Magyarországon," *Történelmi szemle,* 2-3, 1960 (Különnyomat).

Mályusz, Elemér; "Budai Farkas László," *Tanulmányok Budapest múltjából,* 15, 1963, pp. 153-187.

Marczali, Henrik; *Magyarország története az Árpádok korában* (ed. Sándor Szilágyi, *A magyar nemzet története,* II*),* Budapest, 1896.

Marczali, Henrik; *Magyarország története (A műveltség könyvtára),* Budapest, 1911.

Maschke, Erich; "Verfassung und sociale Kräfte in der deutschen Stadt des späten Mittelalters vornehmlich in Oberdeutschland," *Vierteljahrschrift für Sozial-und Wirtschaftsgeschichte,* 46, 1959, p. 289-349, 433-76.

Maschke, Erich, *Die Familien in der deutschen Stadt des späten Mittelalters,* Heidelberg, 1980.

Matthias Corvinus und die Renaissance in Ungarn (1982 Schallaburg Exhibition Catalogue).

Mayer, Theodor; *der auswärtige Handel des Herzogtums Österreich im Mittelalter,* Innsbruck, 1909.

Metcalf, D. M.; *The Coinage of Southern Germany in the Thirteenth Century*, London, 1961.

Metcalf, D. M.; *Coinage in the Balkans, 820-1355 (Institute for Balkan Studies, 80)*, Thessaloniki, 1965.

Michaud-Quantin, Pierre; *Universitas; Expressions du Mouvement Communautaire dans le Moyen-Age latin*, Paris, 1970.

Mierow, C. C.; *The Deeds of Frederick Barbarossa*, New York, 1966.

Mitgau, Hermann; "Geschlossene Heiratskreise sozialer Inzucht," in (ed) Helmuth Rössler, *Deutsches Patriziat, 1430-1740* (Budinger Vorträge, 1965), Limburg-Lahn, 1968, pp. 1-25.

Mocsáry, Antal; *Nemes Nógrád vármegyének . . . esmertetése*, I, Pest, 1826.

Molnár, Erik; *A magyar társadalom története az Árpádkorból Mohácsig*, Budapest, 1949.

Molnár, Erik; Pamlényi, Ervin; Székely, György, *Magyarország története*, I, Budapest, 1964.

Nagy, Lajos; "Pest város eredete," *Tanulmányok Budapest múltjából*, 3, 1934, pp. 7-24.

Najemy, John M.; "Guild Republicanism in Trecento Florence, The Successes and Ultimate Failure of Corporate Politics," *American Historical Review*, 84, 1979, pp. 53-71.

Neubauer, A.; "Le Memorbuch de Mayence," *Revue des Études Juives*, IV, 1882, pp. 1-30.

Nuber, C. F.; "Beitrag zur Chronologie slavonischer Münzen," *Wissenschaftliche Mittheilungen aus Bosnien und der Hercegovina*, 6, Sarajevo, 1899, pp. 467-477.

Orosz, István; "Jobbágyköltözés és köznemesség kelet-Europában a XV-XVI századiban," *Egyetemes történeti tanulmányok*, 11, 1977.

Ortvay, Theodor; *Geschichte der Stadt Pressburg*, I-IV, Pressburg, 1892-1912.

Pais, Dezső; "Budapest kialakulásának kezdetei," *Magyar nyelv*, 50, 1954, pp. 506-513.

Palugyay, Imre; *Pest-Buda szabad királyi városok leirása (Magyarszag leirása, I)*, Pest, 1852.

Papp, László; "A birtokba-iktatás *(statutio)* lefolyása," *Szentpétery emlékkönyv*, Budapest, 1938.

Pataki, Vidor; "A budai vár középkori helyrajza," *Budapest régiségei*, 15, 1950, pp. 239-299.

Pauler, Gyula; *A magyar nemzet története az árpádházi királyok alatt*, I-II, Budapest, 1899 (Second Edition).

Paulinyi, Oszkár; "A középkori magyar réztermelés gazdasági jelentősége," *Károlyi Árpád emlékkönyv*, Budapest, 1933, pp. 402-439.

Paulinyi, Oszkár; "Nemesfémgazdaságunk és országos gazdaságunk alakulása a bontakozó és kifejlett feudalizmus korszakában, 1000-1526. Gazdag föld— szegény ország," *Századok*, 106, 1972, pp. 561-608.

Peltzer, R. A.; "Geschichte der Messingindustrie," *Zeitschrift des Aachener Geschichtsverein*, 30, 1908, pp. 235-463.

Pereházy, Károly; *Régi házak Pest-Budán*, Budapest, 1976.

242

BIBLIOGRAPHY

Petrovics, István; "Oklevelek Szeged középkori történetéhez," *Acta Universitatis Szegediensis: Acta Historica,* 56, 1979, pp. 61-65.

Petzsch, Christoph; "Die Nürnberger Familie von Lochaim: Eine Kaufmanngeschlecht des 14-16. Jahrhundert," *Zeitschrift für bayerische Landesgeschichte,* 29, 1966, pp. 212-238.

Pfeiffer, Gerhard; *Das Breslauer Patriziat im Mittelalter,* Breslau, 1929.

Planitz, Hans; "Die deutsche Stadtgemeinde," *Zeitschrift der Savigny Stiftung für Rechtsgeschichte (Germanische Abteilung),* 64, 1944, pp. 1-85.

Planitz, Hans; "Zur Geschichte des städtischen Meliorats," *Zeitschrift der Savigny Stiftung für Rechtsgeschichte (Germanische Abteilung),* 67, 1950, pp. 141-75.

Planitz, Hans; *Die deutsche Stadt im Mittelalter,* Graz-Köln, 1954.

Pleidell, Ambrus; *A nyugatra irányuló magyar külkereskedelem a középkorban,* Budapest, 1925.

Pleidell, Ambrus; "A magyar várostörténet első fejezete," *Századok,* 68, 1934, pp. 1-44, 158-200, 276-313.

Pór, Antal; "A királyi tárnokmesterek a XIV században," *Századok,* 25, 1891, pp. 227-232.

Pór, Antal; "Háborúság Esztergom és az esztergomi káptalan közt a vám miatt," *Magyar gazdaságtörténelmi szemle,* 11, 1904, pp. 161-205.

von Probszt, Günther; "Deutsches Kapital in den Niederungarischen Bergstädte im Zeitalter des Frühkapitalismus," *Zeitschrift für Ostforschung,* 10, 1961, pp. 1-25.

von Probszt, Günther; *Die niederungarischen Bergstädte,* München, 1966.

Radnóti, Aladár; "Pannóniai városok élete a korai feudalizmusban," *MTA (Magyar tudományos akadémia) II osztályának közleményei,* 5, 1954, pp. 489-508.

Radocsay, Dénes; "Les principaux monuments funéraires médiévaux conservés a Budapest," *Mélanges offerts à Szabolcs de Vajay,* Braga, 1971, pp. 461-486.

Rady, M. C.; "The Hungarian Copper Trade and Industry in the Later Middle Ages," (ed) C.M.A. McCauley and J. Screen, *Occasional Papers of the School of Slavonic and East European Studies* (University of London), forthcoming.

Redlich, Oswald; *Die Privaturkunden des Mittelalters,* München & Berlin, 1911.

Relković, Néda; *Buda város jogkönyve,* Budapest, 1905.

Relković, Néda; *A budai jogkönyv harmadik kézirata a Fővárosi könyvtárban (A Fővárosi könyvtár évkönyve, 4)* Budapest, 1941.

Révhelyi, E.; 'Kelenföld (Tabán) helye és neve', *Tanulmányok Budapest múltjából,* 4, 1936, pp. 34-58.

Rotz, Rhiman A.; "Investigating urban uprisings, with examples from Hanseatic towns, 1374-1416," in (ed) William C. Jordan, *Order and Innovation in the Middle Ages—Essays in Honour of Joseph R. Strayer,* Princeton University Press, 1976, pp. 215-33.

Rupp, Jakab; *Buda-Pest és környékének helyrajzi története,* Pest, 1868.

Ságvári, Ágnes (ed); *Budapest: The History of a Capital,* 1973.

Sailer, Leopold; "Die Wiener Ratsbürger des 14. Jahrhunderts," *Studien aus dem Archiv der Stadt Wien,* 3-4, 1931.

Salamon, Ferenc; *Budapest története,* I-III, Budapest, 1878-85.

Sander, Paul; *Die Reichstädtische Haushaltung Nürnbergs von 1431 bis 1440*, Leipzig, 1902.

von Schedius, L.; "Etwas über den Zustand des ungrischen Finanzen im Anfänge des XVI Jahrhunderts," *Zeitschrift von und für Ungarn*, III, Pesth, 1803, pp. 99-106.

Scheiber, Sándor (Alexander); "A medieval form of Jewish Oath," *Journal of Jewish Studies*, 25, 1974, pp. 181-2.

Schier, Xystus; *Buda sacra sub priscis regibus*, Viennae, 1774.

Schröder, R; Künssberg, Eberhard; *Lehrbuch der deutschen Rechtsgeschichte*, Berlin & Leipzig, 1919-22.

Sebestyén, Béla; *A magyar királyok tartózkodási helyei*, Budapest, undated.

Sipos, Gábor; "A kolozsmonostori konvent hiteleshelyi működése," in (ed) Elek Csetri, Zsigmond Jakó, Sándor Tonk, *Művelödéstörténeti tanulmányok*, Bukarest, 1979, pp. 33-50.

Strauss, Gerald; *Nuremberg in the Sixteenth Century*, Bloomington & London (Indiana University Press: Second Revised Edition), 1976.

von Stromer, Wolfgang; "Nürnberger Unternehmer im Karpatenraum: Ein oberdeutsches Buntmetall-Oligopol, 1396-1412," *Kwartalnik Historii Kultury Materialnej*, 16, 1968, pp. 641-662.

von Stromer, Wolfgang; "Nuremberg in the International Economics of the Middle Ages," *Business History Review*, 44, 1970, pp. 210-225.

von Stromer, Wolfgang; *Oberdeutsche Hochfinanz (Vierteljahschrift für Sozial- und Wirtschaftsgeschichte, Beihefte 55-7)*, Wiesbaden, 1970.

von Stromer, Wolfgang; "Fränkische und schwäbische Unternehmer in den Donau- und Karpatenländern im Zeitalter der Luxemburger, 1347-1437," *Jahrbuch für fränkische Landesforschung*, 31, 1971, pp. 355-365.

Surányi, Bálint; "Pozsonyi biródinasztiák a XIII-XIV században," *Levéltári közlemények*, 35, 1964, pp. 173-186.

Szadeczky, Lajos; *A czéhek történetéről Magyarországon*, Budapest, 1889.

Szabó, Imre; "Le traitement de l'Equité dans le système juridique hongrois," in (ed) Zoltán Péteri, *Droit hongrois—Droit comparé, Hungarian Law—Comparative Law*, Budapest, 1970, pp. 23-50.

Szabó, István; *A magyar mezőgazdaság története a XIV. századtól az 1530-as évekig (Agrártörténeti tanulmányok, 2)*, Budapest, 1975.

Szabó, István; *Jobbágyok-parasztok*, Budapest, 1976.

Szabó, László Bártfai; *Óbuda egyházi intézményei a középkorban*, Budapest, 1935.

Szalay, József; 'Városaink nemzetiségi viszonyai a XIII. században', *Századok*, 14, 1880, pp. 533-557.

Székely, György; "A Huszitizmus és a magyar nép," *Századok*, 90, 1956, pp. 331-367, 556-590.

Székely, György; "A pannóniai települések kontinuitásának kérdése és a hazai városfejlődés kezdetei," *Tanulmányok Budapest múltjából*, 12, 1957, pp. 7-23.

Székely, György; "Le sort des agglomerations pannoniennes au début du moyen âge et les origines de la'urbanisme en Hongrie," *Annales Universitatis Scientiarum Budapestiensis (Sectio historica)*, 3, 1961, pp. 59-96.

244

BIBLIOGRAPHY

Székely, György; "Wallons et Italiens en Europe centrale aux XIe-XVIe siècles," *Annales Universitatis Scientiarum Budapestiensis (Sectio Historica),* 6, 1964, pp. 3-71.

Székely, György; "Le developpement de la magistrature de la ville de Buda au XIVe siècle," *Folia Diplomatica,* I, Brno, 1971.

Szekfű, Gyula; "Oklevelek I Károly pénzverési reformjához," *Történelmi tár,* 12, 1911, pp. 1-36.

Szekfű, Gyula; *Serviensek és familiarisok (Értekezések a történelmi tudományok köréből),* Budapest, 1912.

Szende, Pál; *Magyar városok a középkor végén,* Budapest, 1913.

Szentpétery, Imre; *Magyar oklevéltan,* Budapest, 1930.

Szentpétery, Imre; "A kancelláriai jegyzetek az Anjoukori okleveles gyakorlatban," *Károlyi Árpád emlékkönyv,* Budapest, 1933, pp. 471-490.

Szentpétery, Imre (the younger); *A tárnoki itelőszék kialakulása Századok,* 68, *(Pótfüzet),* Budapest, 1934.

Szentpétery, Imre (the younger); "A vörös viaszpecsét bizonyitó ereje a középkorban," *Szentpétery emlékkönyv,* Budapest, 1938.

Szilágyi, Loránd; "A magyar királyi kancellária szerepe az államkormányzatban, 1458-1526," *Turul,* 44, 1930, pp. 45-83.

Szoika, Kamill; *A földesúri biráskodás az árpádkori Magyarországon,* Budapest, 1944.

Szűcs, Jenő; *Városok és kézművesség a XV. századi Magyarországon,* Budapest, 1955.

Szűcs, Jenő; "Das Städtewesen in Ungarn im 15-17. Jahrhundert" *(Studia Historica, 53),* Budapest, 1963.

Szűcs, Jenő; "Theoretical Elements in Master Simon of Kéza's *Gesta Hungarorum,* 1282-1285," *Études Historiques Hongroises,* 1975, pp. 239-281.

Thallóczy, Lajos; *A kamara haszna (lucrum camerae) története,* Budapest, 1879.

Timon, Ákos; *Magyar alkotmány- és jogtörténet,* Budapest, 1919.

Tirnitz, József; "Sopron szabad királyi város külső tanácsa, 1526-1711," in (ed) György Bónis, Alajos Degré; *Tanulmányok a magyar helyi önkormányzat múltjából,* Budapest, 1971, pp. 53-79.

Tomaschek, J. A.; *Der Oberhof Iglau in Mähren und seine Schöffensprüche aus dem XIII-XVI. Jahrhundert,* Innsbruck, 1868.

Truhelka, C.; "Die slavonischen Banaldenare," *Wissenschaftliche Mittheilungen aus Bosnien und der Hercegovina,* Sarajevo, 6, 1899, pp. 328-466.

Ullmann, Walter; *Medieval Political Thought,* London (Peregrine-Penguin), 1975.

Váczy, Péter; *A városi polgárok vérdija Werbőczynél és a budai jog,* Miskolc, 1929.

Váczy, Péter; "Immunitas és jurisdictio," *A bécsi-magyar történeti intézet évkönyve (A Gróf Klebelsberg Kunó magyar történetkutató intézet évkönyve),* I, 1931, pp. 13-40.

Váczy, Péter; "A királyi kúria birósága és I Endre tőrvénybeidéző ércbilloga," *Századok,* 68, 1934, pp. 484-489.

Váczy, Péter; *Die erste Epoche des ungarischen Königtums,* Pécs, 1935.

Varga, Endre; Bónis, György; Degré, Alajos; *A magyar birósági szervezet és perjog,* Budapest, 1961.

Wendt, Heinrich; *Schlesien und der Orient (Darstellungen und Quellen zur schlesischen Geschichte, 21)*, Breslau, 1916.

Wenzel, Gusztáv; *Nevezetes per lőcsei polgárok között, 1421-29 (Értekezések a történelmi tudományok köréből)*, Budapest, 1873.

Wenzel, Gusztáv; *A XV. századi tárnoki jog (Értekezések a történelmi tudományok köréből)*, Budapest, 1878.

Wenzel, Gusztáv; *Magyarország bányászatának kritikai története*, Budapest, 1880.

Zolnay, László; "Az esztergomi latinusokról," *Esztergomi évlapjai (Annales Strigonienses)*, I, 1960.

Zolnay, László; *"Opus Castri Budensis;* A XIII. századi budai vár kialakulása," *Tanulmányok Budapest múltjából*, 15, 1963, pp. 43-107.

Zolnay, László; "A középkori Budavári Szent-László és Szent-Mihály kápolna," *Budapest régiségei*, 21, 1964, pp. 375-388.

Zolnay, László; *Buda középkori zsidósága*, Budapest *(TIT Budapesti szervezet)*, 1968.

Zolnay, László; *Ünnep és hétköznap a középkori Budán*, Budapest (Second Revised Edition), 1975.

INDEX

Aachen, 101
Abaújvár county, 131
Abdullah Jakut, 9
absoluta potentia, 85
Abu Hamid, 8
actor sequitur forum rei, 83, 129, 145
Aigen, 42
Ainweg, Leonard, 88
Albert I (1437–39), 100, 107, 122
Aldoth family, 97
Aloch, Stephen, 118
Altsohl, *see* Zólyom
Ammann-Kammerer-Seiler-Grau, merchant
  firm, 103
Amsterdam, 8
Andrew II (1205–35), 3, 25, 26
Anger, 42
Angevin dynasty, 19, 26, 36, 80, 134; *see also*
  Charles Robert, Louis I
Anonymus Chronicle, 2
Antwerp, 101
apothecaries, 108
Apothecaries' Row, 42
appeal, 114, 138, 141-2, 145, 147-54, 158,
  159
Aquincum, 1
Arbitration, 51, 131
Archynus of Venice, chamberlain and judge,
  27-30
ardua causa, 52, 142, 146, 151, 152
Árpád dynasty, 2, 11-13, 57, 77, 115; Árpád,
  prince, 11; *see also,* Stephen I, Ladislas I,
  Koloman, Béla II, Géza II, Stephen III,
  Béla III, Andrew II, Béla IV, Stephen V,
  Ladislas IV
Ars Notarialis, 50, 56, 62

Attád, Johann de, 113, 175-76
Attila, 1, 2
Augsburg, 87
Austria, 5, 15, 20, 32, 34, 60, 82, 84, 112

Bábaszék, 15
Bács, 7
Baghdad, 8
Bailiff of Buda, 113, 116, 119
Banská Bystrica, *see* Besztercebánya
Banská Štiavnica, *see* Selmecbánya
Barancs, 8
Bars, town, 15, 130, 153; county, 24
Bártfa (Bardejov, Bartfeld), 72, 123, 143, 153,
  154
Basle, Council of, 41, 107
de Bathe family, 106
Batu Khan, 14-15
Bauman, Christian, 61
Bavaria, 36
Bayon, Lawrence de, 113, 174
Béla II (1131-41), 26
Béla III (1173-96), 2, 12
Béla IV (1235-1270), 2-4, 15, 16, 24, 26, 27,
  30, 31, 33, 35-8, 43, 82, 83, 163
Belgrade, 8
Below, Georg von, 49
Berki, Clement, 113, 174
Berne, 31
Bernhard, Francis, 89, 155
Bernhart, Gaspar, 96, 172
Berruer, Martin, 41
Bertényi, Iván, 135
Berzeviczy, Peter, 148

247

Besztercebánya (Banská Bystrica, Neusohl), 15, 19, 58, 72, 102, 140
Beth-Din, 82-3
Bihar county, 153
bilochi, 9-11, 184
boatmen, *see* sailors
Bodrog county, 129
Bohemia, 24, 32, 33, 36, 95, 142
Bonfini, Antonio, 99
Borgyas, Peter, 106
Bornemisza, *see* Onwein
Brassó (Brasov, Kronstadt), 17, 94
Bratislava, *see* Pozsony
brigandage, 98, 130
Browne, Edward, 102
Bruges, 20
Brunner, Otto, 91
Brunner-Schubert, Isolde, 87
Bubek, Emerich, 132; Johann, 149
Buda (main references only), origins of name, 2; early history of region, 1-2; foundation, 3-5; topography, 4, 40-42, 108; population, 4-5, 40-42, 105-6; charters, 4-6, 23, 34-35, 37, 53-4, 73, 130-1, Appendix I; early government, 4-6, 23-25; Rectors, 23-39; Judge and Council, 6, 24, 37-39, 43, 49-51, 99-100, 121-2, 182, Appendix II; elections, 6, 50, 72-3, 106-109, 121, 139; churches and priests, 40, 74-5, 108, 111, 118; markets and fairs, 4, 42, 45; taxes, 53-4, 117; municipal custom and law, 6, 20, 23, 46-68, 70-71 *(see also, Stadtrecht);* municipal records and record-keeping, 55-66, 122; patriciate, 34-37, 89-109, 112-3; revolts, 50, 53-4, 96-97, 105-9, 132; relations with Tavernicus, 127-8, 141-59.
Buda Chapter, 2, 62, 78-80, 93, 127
Budafelhéviz (Felhéviz), 78, 79, 92, 127
burgher oath, 70-72
butchers, 45, 64, 81, 97
Byzantium, 2, 8, 99

capitaneus, 32
Castellan of Buda, 33, 81, 116, 139, 201
Castellan of Óbuda, 78, 79, 81, 100
census iudeorum, 82, 116

chamberlains, minting organisation, 6, 25-33, 75-77, 81-85, 100-103
Chacellery, Chancellor, 12, 57, 62, 114, 116, 118, 119, 134-37, 140, 152, 155, 163
Charles Robert (1308–42), 19, 26, 35-37, 80, 81
Charles of Óbuda, Rector, 24, 32, 35, 169
chirograph, 57, 62
Chratzer, family, 95; Frederick, 91, 171
civis, 17
clergy, 36, 74-5, 80, 198
cliciarii (clicium), 77, 78
cloth, 8, 95, 97-100, 153
Cluj, *see* Kolozsvár
coins, coinage, 2, 8, 12, 16, 19, 25, 26, 28, 30, 77, 163, 187
Cologne, 95, 98, 104
Colonna, Aegidius, 123
comes, 93
comites curiales, 78
commerce, *see* trade
commission *(commissio),* notarial mark, 51-2
Committee of One Hundred, 109, 121, 122, 156
conditionarii, 77, 79, 119, 136
coniuratio, 70-72, 91
consent formula, 58-9, 84, 201
Contra-Aquincum, 1
copper, *see* metals
corporation, 71, 120
Corpus Christi Brotherhood, 104, 107, 120
corroboratio, 63
Council House of Buda, *see* Town Hall
county administration, 10-13, 16, 57, 78, 114, 129, 131, 132, 136, 154
Croatia, 15, 27, 138
Crusades, 14
Csák, Matthew, 13; Gabriel, 84
Csanád, 8, 27
Csepel Island, 1, 36
Csongrád county, 93
Cumans, 18
curia, 13, 33, 108, 114, 131-36, 140-43, 152, 163
"custom of the realm," 6, 13, 23, 127, 129, 138-9

Dalmatia, 34
Danube, 1-4, 77, 80, 81, 98, 111
Dax family, 112, 174
Debrecen, 115, 153
debt, 44, 83, 148, 150, 152
Decretum minus (1405), 44, 133, 140-41, 145, 147, 158
Dézsakna, 152
Diet *(országgyűlés),* 100, 107, 114-17, 122-23
Dionysius of Buda, 113, 173
Dionysius, son of Apod, 12
Dobronya, 15
Drailinger, Thomas, 210
duel, 20, 130
Dunajeci, Johann, 136, 149

Ebel, Wilhelm, 70
Ebendorffer, Nicolas, 123, 174-75
Ebner family, 103
de Eger family, 90-93, 169-72; Jacob, 92-93, 170; Johann, 91, 170
Eidgenossenschaft, see coniuratio
Eisvogel family, 101; Ulrich, 101
elections, 44, 49-50, 53, 73, 88, 89, 106, 109, 118, 120-23, 139
Electoral College, *see* Committee of One Hundred
Ellenpek, Johann, 88
England, 60, 95
Eperjes (Preschau, Prešov), 15, 46, 70, 72, 123, 131, 153, 154
equity, 84-85
Erler, Adalbert, 73
Ermen, Stephen, *Litteratus de Buda,* 113, 174
Esztergom (Gran), town, 7, 8, 27, 29, 30, 32, 36, 135, 139, 140, 143, 144, 152, 154; archbishop and primatial chapter, 13, 24, 36, 79, 80, 133, 135, 139; consistory court, 75
Etzelburg, 1
evictio (expeditio), 59-62
evidence, 130

Fabri, Felix, of Ulm, 87
Falconers, 78
Farkas, Ladislas, 100, 101, 104, 107, 173

Fejér county, 35, 92, 93, 100, 113
Felhéviz, *see* Budafelhéviz
fishermen, 45, 75, 81, 83, 85, 119
Fisher Street *(Halász utca),* 81
fishmongers, 45
Flanders, 20, 95, 142
Flextorfer-Kegler-Zenner, merchant firm, 103
Forster family, 112, 174
forum Geyzae, 78
Frankenstein, Count, antiquary, 47
Frankfurt, 107
Frankochorion, 8
Frederick Barbarossa, 2, 8, 142
Frederick II (Hohenstaufen), 31
Frederick of Babenberg, 82, 83
Freiburg, 31
Fuggers, 112
furs, furriers, 8, 97
Fügedi, Erik, 14
Fünfkirchen, *see* Pecs

Gabriel, Chancellor, 118, 123
Gailsam family, 98, 101, 112, 175
Galgóczi family, 158
Gara, Nicolas of, 61
Gellért Hill, 3
Gemayne Stattrecht of Selmecbánya, 148
George of Szeben, 61
George the Deacon, 107, 108, 155
German colonisation, 3, 14, 17, 18, 21, 163
Géza II (1141–62), 14, 78, 79
Gierke, Otto von, 71
Gleczel, Johann, 94, 172
Golden Bull of 1222, 10, 25-26
goldsmiths, 97, 106
Gotland, 8
Gozzo of Krems, 32
Gran, *see* Esztergom
Great Ravensburg Company, 112
Greczinger family, 96
Greeks, 7; *see also* Byzantium
Grenchol, chamberlain, 29
Greyf, 24, 32
grocers, 108
Groland, Hans, 95, 96, 98, 205
guilds, 50, 64, 82, 97, 120-22
Gutgesell family, 98

Győr (Raab), 8, 15, 16; Bishop, 133
Györffy, György, 32

Haiden, Henry, 104
Hailmann family, 90
Haller family, 87, 112, 174-75
Hamburg, 87
Hansa, 101
Harber family, 112, 175
Hares' Island (Margitsziget), 78, 93
Heinrich, 'Little', 106, 173
Hench, Rector, 30, 34, 35, 169
Henry the Bellmaker, 3
Hermannstadt, see Szeben
Hertlin, 94, 172
Hoffar, Johann, 84
Holy Land, 2, 93
homines regii, 66-67, 117
Horhi, 92
horses, 8
hospes, 17
Hospitallers of Budafelhéviz, 127, 128, 130, 133, 141, 158
Hunyadi period, 113-115, 124; see also, Matthias I Corvinus
Hypolitus, chamberlain, 29

al-Idrisi, 7
Iglau (Jihlava), 142, 152
Ilkusch, Martin of, 118
Imbert, Conrad, 153-4
Imhoff family, 103
impeachment, 13, 133, 146, 147
incolae, 122
inheritance law, 46, 58-9, 84, 148, 150
inquisitions, 13, 66, 128, 140
installation, see statutio
intitulatio, 49, 73, 122
introitus, 12
Isaszeg, Battle of (1265), 24
Isfahan, 8
Ishmaelites, 26
Italy, Italians, 8, 74, 91, 95, 98, 99, 104; see also, Latini
iudex curiae, see Justiciar

ius, 118, 123; ius gladii, 13, 19; ius statuendi, 20
Iváncsi family, 113
Iványi, Béla, 154

Jacob families, of Pozsony, 89, 94
Jacob of Hoya, 32
Jacob of Szepes, 137-9
Jacob von dem Pach, 98, 173
Jagiello dynasty, 116, 117; see also, Vlászló II, Louis II
Jenő, 78
Jews, 26, 75, 81-85, 100, 115-116; Jewish taxes, 82, 100, 115-6
jobag, 31; see also peasantry
Johann, Rector, 24, 32, 35-38, 90, 169-70.
Johann the Silversmith, 107
John of Luxemburg, 95
John I Zápolyai (1526–40), 112
Judge of All Jews in the Realm, 82, 84, 115, 137, 201
Judge of All the Towns, 133, 137-39
Judge of the Jews, 82
Judge of the Monies, 49, 52-3, 106
Jung, Stephen, 102
Justiciar (iudex curiae, országbíró), 84, 114, 132-39, 146

Kammerer, Ulrich, 103, 104
Kammermeister family, 103
Kantus, Johann, 55, 61
Kassa (Kaschau, Košice), 6, 17, 50, 72, 97, 123, 132, 136, 140, 143, 144, 152, 154, 157
Kelenföld, see Pest minor
Késmárk (Kežmarok), 15, 154
Keve, 8
Klausenburg, see Kolozsvár
Koler family, 103, 104
Koloman, King (1095–1116), 34
Kolozsvár (Klausenburg, Cluj), 61, 90, 94, 98, 121, 122, 137
Komárom (Komorn, Komárno), 15; county, 25, 27, 29, 131
Kopách, Dionysius de, 108, 173
Korpona, 15, 153

Košice, see *Kassa*
Kökényes-Rénold clan, 31
Kömlődy, George, *pistor semellarum,* 113, 175
Körmend, 19
Körmöcbánya (Kremnitz, Kremnica), 72, 102, 103, 143, 207
Kraft, Berchtold, 95, 98, 172
Kraft-von Locheim-Stark-Tracht-Weissenburger, merchant firm, 95
Krapundorf, 15
Kreinfeld, *see Pest minor*
Kremnitz, Kremnica, *see* Körmöcbánya
Kronstadt, *see* Brassó
Kubinyi, András, 41, 64
Kunc family, 89, 90, 94, 169-71
Kunclin, 127-29, 133, 135, 138, 141, 158, 170-71
Kurszán, prince, 2

Ladislas I, Saint (1077–1095), 9
Ladislas IV (1272–1290), 5, 29, 34-5, 42, 73, 122
Ladislas V Posthumus (1445–57), 100, 118, 158
Ladislas, Rector, 24, 34-36, 80, 169
Ladislas of Bohemia, 36, 80
Ladislas of Erd, 155
Lak, Johann Thuz de, 159
Latini, 8, 15, 18
Lawrence, son of Chamar, 94, 171
"Laws and Customs of the Seven Towns," 53, 55, 59, 121, 123, 148, 156, 157
Lemmel family, 103
Leopold, chamberlain, 27
Leuschner, Karl, 164
Leutschau, *see* Lőcse
Levoča, *see* Lőcse
lex animata, 85
libertini, 77
loans, 48, 83, 201
loca credibilia, 13, 58-9, 62-67, 74, 132, 134, 135, 138, 163
locator, 3
Lorand family, 90-92, 94, 170-72; Lorand, citizen, 30, 38, 91, 94, 170-71

Louis I (1342–82), 37, 76, 78, 99, 128, 132, 134, 136, 137
Louis II (1516–26), 50, 117
Lőcse (Leutschau, Levoča), 143, 151, 153, 154
lucrum camerae, 16
Luprechtháza, 15
Lübeck, 5, 31, 104, 142

Magdeburg, 142; Magdeburg Law, 46
Magh, Johann of, 61-2
Mályusz, Elemér, 5
Mansfeld copperfield, 102
Marczali, Henrik, 9
Margitsziget, *see* Hares' Island
Marin, chamberlain, 32
Mark of Nuremberg, 103
Markulin, chamberlain, 29
Maros, 37
Martin of Ilkusch, 118
Mary Magdalen, Church of, 39-40, 42, 108, 111
Matthias I Corvinus (1458–90), 75, 112, 159
mediatisation, 23, 118, 154
Medici, 102, 104
Megerdorfer family, 89, 90, 92, 169-70
Meixner family, 112, 174
Melamen, jewess, 84
merchants, 7-8, 40, 42, 74, 75, 94-113, 151
metals, 8, 101-104
Michael, chamberlain, 29-30
Milan, 8
mining, 17, 32, 56, 101-103, 154, 207
minters, *see* chamberlains
Mohács, Battle of (1526), 112
Mohi, Battle of (1241), 14
moneyers, *see* chamberlains
Mongols, 3, 14-18, 92, 188
Moravia, 8, 142
morgengab, 59
Moson, 35
mother-town, 134, 152-57
Mulner family, 112, 175
Munich, Henry, 103, 104
Mühlstein family, 112
Mykola, Stephen de, 113, 173-74
Mykud, Rector, 24, 25, 31, 32, 169

Nadler, Michael, 100, 104, 172-73
Nagyszakácsi, 78
Nagyszombat (Tyrnau, Trnava), 15, 19, 89,
    92, 123, 140, 143, 146, 154
Neidung family, 96
Neusohl, see Besztercebánya
Nicolas, Rector, 35, 38, 170
Nicolas of Szatmár, 29
nobility, 10, 12, 16, 25, 36, 40, 66, 74, 78, 85,
    92, 98, 99, 106, 108, 113-15, 117, 129,
    134, 138, 144
Notary, 39, 46, 54-65, 83
novum, 147, 159
Nuremberg, 47, 87, 89, 95, 96, 100-104, 111,
    112, 164
Nyitra (Neutra, Nitra), 8, 15, 19

oath of office, 72-73; see also burgher oath
Óbuda, 1, 2, 32, 42, 77-79, 143; chapter, see
    Buda Chapter
Odo de Deoghilo, 7
Ogotai Khan, 15
Onwein, Peter, 106, 173
Order of the Dragon, 163
Oroszfalva, 78
Osnabrück, 31
Otto of Bavaria, 36
Otto of Freising, 7, 9
Ottokar II of Bohemia, 32
Ottoman Turks, 112, 159
Óvár, 35
Our Blessed Lady, Church of (Matthias
    Church), 4, 40, 42, 108, 111, 118
Outer Council, 53-54
Ödenburg, see Sopron
Örkénypuszta, 26

Pach, Jacob von dem, 98, 173
palace, 99, 111, 117, 119, 139, 155, 162
Palatine (nádor), 11-13, 61, 77, 84, 85, 114,
    134, 138
Paltram of Vienna, 32
Pannonhalma, 18
Pannonia, 1
Paris, 77
Parthenopeius, Raymundus, 123

Patócsi family, 113
Pauler, Gyula, 9
Paumgartner family, 87; Hans, 42
peasantry, 11, 17, 31, 70, 74, 83, 114, 129,
    131
Pécs (Fünfkirchen), 8
Pemfflinger family, 112, 174-75
Perchin, chamberlain, 30
Pernhauser family, 90, 94, 95, 170-72
"personal presence," 113, 114, 135, 145, 146,
    154, 158, 159
Pest, 1-7, 14, 15, 18-20, 34, 37, 42, 51, 57, 61,
    75, 78-80, 93, 112, 119, 129, 136, 143,
    144; Pest county, 6, 35
Pest minor (Kreinfeld, Kelenföld), 3, 33
Peter villicus, 24, 25, 27, 28, 31, 32, 34, 35,
    169
Peter the Hermit, 8
Petermann, Rector, 24, 30, 33, 169
Pfeiffer, Gerhard, 92
"place of authentication," see, loca credibilia
Planitz, Hans, 72
platea carnificum, 97
pledge, 44, 48
plenitudo potestatis, 85
podestà, 29
Poland, 8, 101
Poll family, 98
Pozsony (Bratislava), 6, 15, 17, 20, 47-49, 53,
    56, 57, 60, 72, 83, 88, 89, 91, 93, 94, 96,
    98, 100, 101, 103, 112, 115, 123, 130,
    137, 138, 143, 151, 154, 155, 159
praescriptio, 20, 60, 65, 129, 195
praesentia regia, 10, 127, 132-40, 142, 146,
    152, 157, 161
Prefect of the Jews, 116
Prenner, Kunc, 30, 169
Preschau, Prešov, see Eperjes
Pressburg, see Pozsony
Preussel, Henry, 24-25, 31-32, 169
Privigye, 153
prorogatio, 147
Protocollum Actionale, of Pozsony, 57
protonotarius, 55

Raab, see Győr
Rabensteiner family, 90, 94, 95, 170-72

Radna, 30
Rammenstein family, 103
rape, 130
Rátold family, 32
Rauczan, Peter, 96
recaptivatio, 127
Rectors, 23-39, 86, 89, 109, 124, 161, 169-70
rector officiorum, 32
Reformatio Norimbergensis, 47
Regensburg (Ratisbon), 4, 87
Régenszenttamás, 92
Reichel, Peter, 103, 104
relatio, notarial mark, 51-52
Relković, Néda, 47
Repgow, Eike von, 47
Rév, 153
Rhineland, 95, 98
Rogerius, author of the *Miserable Lament,* 3, 15
Roman Law, 123
Rome, 8
"royal presence," *see praesentia regia*
Rozgonyi family, 94; Johann, 144
Runtinger family, 87
Rupert of the Palatinate, 104
Ruthenes, 78

Sachsenspiegel, 47
saddlers, 108
sailors, 75, 77-81, 85, 119, 136
St Benedict's-by-Gron, 93, 131
St George, *see* Thomas of St George
St George's Place, 40
St Peter, Church of, 40, 108; suburb, 4, 42
salt tax, 12, 25
"Saracens," 2, 3
Sáros county, 131
Sasad, 75
Saturday Gate, 42
"Saxons," 3
scansor, 135
Schedel, Hartmann, 111, 124
Schemnitz, *see* Selmecbánya
Schmölnitz, *see* Szomolnokbánya
Schöffenstuhl, 142-43, 152, 157, 159
Schultheiss, 14
Schürstab family, 95, 101

Schwabenspiegel, 47
Schwarzemberg, Walther von, 107
seals, 56, 61-65, 120, 197
seiger, 102
seigneurial courts and jurisdiction, 10, 12-14, 17, 70, 75, 114, 132, 141, 150
Selmecbánya (Schemnitz, Banská Štiavnica), 143, 148, 153
Sempte, 129
Seneschal, 81
serfs, *see* peasantry
Sibiu, *see* Szeben
Siebenlinder, Johann, 100, 101, 104, 151, 172
Sigismund (1387-1437), 33, 45, 53, 66, 76, 81, 99, 107, 144, 148, 149, 154, 163
Sigismund of Gemerew, 155
silversmiths, 107, 108
Simontornya, 36
Sirmium, 8, 27
slaves, 8
Smolnik, *see* Szomolnokbánya
Somogy county, 79
Sopron (Ödenburg), 6-8, 15, 17, 37, 53, 72, 83, 88, 96, 98, 112, 137, 143, 149, 154
Spain, 95
"special presence," 114, 135, 146
Stadtrecht, 6, 33, 43-66, 71, 82, 83, 86, 88, 91, 106, 118, 120, 131, 141, 144-49, 156; authorship, 45-46, 52, 58-9
statpuech, 56
statutio, 51, 66-67, 127, 139
Steinlinger, Lutz, 101, 103
Stenczel family, 112
Stephen I, Saint (1000-1038), 2, 11, 18
Stephen III (1162-72), 15, 18
Stephen V (1270-72), son of Béla IV, 27
Stralsund, 87
Strassburg, 32
Stromer family, 95, 101, 103, 104; Ulman, 89; Volfram, 95
Stuhlweissenburg, see Székesfehérvár
Summa Legum, 123
Swabia, 95; Swabian League, 163
synagogue, 82
Szamobor, 15
Szatmár (Satu Mare), 15, 152
Szeben (Sibiu, Hermannstadt), 97

Székesfehérvár, 8, 9, 15, 17, 18, 37, 131, 143,
    152, 154
Székely, György, 7
Szekfű, Gyula, 10, 155
Szentendre Island, 1
Szenterzsébet, 92
Szentpétery, Imre (the younger), 131, 132
Szepesség (Zips), 14, 153, 154
Szombathely, 7
Szomolnokbánya (Schmölnitz, Smolnik), 32,
    129
Szűcs, Jenő, 13, 14, 41, 42, 88

tabula regia iudiciaria, 114
Taksony, prince, 2
Tapolca, 4
Tarján tribe, 2, 11
Tárnok, 92
Tárnokvölgy, 6, 24
Taschental, 41
Tavernicus, Tavernical court, 55, 57, 76, 81,
    84, 85, 123, 125, 127-59, 161-62; taver-
    nici, 136
taxes, 16, 44, 53-54, 115-117, 119, 136
Telukybánya (Telkibánya), 32
"Teutons," 3
Themeskezy, Valentine, 113, 174
Thomas (Temlin) of St George, 84, 137,
    139
Tilmann family, 35, 90, 92, 169-71; Tilmann
    citizen, 38, 169-71
tithes, 41, 91, 117, 128
tolls, 12, 16, 91, 95, 96, 139
Tolna county, 35, 92
Tótfalu, 4, 41
Town Hall (Council House), 50, 59, 107
trade, 3, 7, 16, 42, 43, 48, 93, 95, 97-105, 112,
    113, 120
Transylvania, 14, 25, 30, 46, 47, 137, 146, 154
Treasury, Treasurer (royal), 54, 82, 84, 116,
    139, 151
Trencsén (Trenschin, Trenčín), 72
tributum fisci regalis, 115
tricesima, see tolls
Trnava, see Nagyszombat
Tyrnau, see Nagyszombat

udvornici, 11, 16, 77, 78, 81
Újlak, 156
Ulm, 87
Ulving family, 35, 90, 91, 94, 95, 169-71; Ulv-
    ing I, 91, 92, 94, 169-70; Ladislas Ulving,
    91; Nicolas Ulving, 91, 170
Unternehmerkonsortium, 5
urburarius, 32
usury, 83-84

Vác (Waitzen), 8, 17
Valbrecht, Johann, of Thorn, 103
Varasd, 134
Varius, Nicolas, 118
Vasvár (Eisenburg), 15
Venice, 96; see also Archynus
Verecke Pass, 14
verleger, 102
Veszprém, 8; county, 35; Bishop, 52
Vid, 78
Vienna, 8, 24, 32, 84, 91, 94, 95, 98, 100, 104,
    112; Viennese Law, 47
vinculum, 131
Visegrád, 17, 19, 93, 98, 99, 136, 140
Vitripar, Matthias, 52, 174
Viziváros, 40, 78, 80, 119
Vlászló I (1440-44), 123
Vlászló II (1490-1516), 117, 145, 159
Voevod, 137, 146
Volga Bulgarians, 2
Vorchtel, Ulrich, 104

warranty, see evictio
Weidner family, 35, 169
Welsers, 112
Weltchronik, 111
Wenceslas, notary, 61
Wendelstein family, 101, 103
Wenzel, Gusztáv, 156
Wenzel II of Bohemia, 24, 33, 36
Werbőczy, Stephen, 69-70, 159
Werner family, 34, 35; see also, Werner of
    Pest; Peter villicus; Werner, Rector; Ladis-
    las, Rector
Werner of Pest, 3, 4, 24, 34
Werner, Rector, 24, 34-36, 169

wills, 74-75
wine, 95
Wisse, Henry, 107
Worms, 77
Wroclaw (Breslau), 92

Zápolyai, John, *see* John I Zápolyai
Zeisselpüchel, 42
Zips, see Szepesség
Zólyom (Zvolen, Altsohl), 15
Zólyomlipcse (Slovenská Lupča), 19
Zsolna (Žilina, Sillein), 139, 140

Zagreb, 15, 27-31, 34, 137, 138, 140
Zala county, 79

EAST EUROPEAN MONOGRAPHS

The *East European Monographs* comprise scholarly books on the history and civilization of Eastern Europe. They are published under the editorship of Stephen Fischer-Galati, in the belief that these studies contribute substantially to the knowledge of the area and serve to stimulate scholarship and research.

1. *Political Ideas and the Enlightenment in the Romanian Principalities, 1750–1831.* By Vlad Georgescu. 1971.
2. *America, Italy and the Birth of Yugoslavia, 1917–1919.* By Dragan R. Zivjinovic. 1972.
3. *Jewish Nobles and Geniuses in Modern Hungary.* By William O. McCagg, Jr. 1972.
4. *Mixail Soloxov in Yugoslavia: Reception and Literary Impact.* By Robert F. Price. 1973.
5. *The Historical and Nationalist Thought of Nicolae Iorga.* By William O. Oldson. 1973.
6. *Guide to Polish Libraries and Archives.* By Richard C. Lewanski. 1974.
7. *Vienna Broadcasts to Slovakia, 1938–1939: A Case Study in Subversion.* By Henry Delfiner. 1974.
8. *The 1917 Revolution in Latvia.* By Andrew Ezergailis. 1974.
9. *The Ukraine in the United Nations Organization: A Study in Soviet Foreign Policy. 1944–1950.* By Konstantin Sawczuk. 1975.
10. *The Bosnian Church: A New Interpretation.* By John V. A. Fine, Jr., 1975.
11. *Intellectual and Social Developments in the Habsburg Empire from Maria Theresa to World War I.* Edited by Stanley B. Winters and Joseph Held. 1975.
12. *Ljudevit Gaj and the Illyrian Movement.* By Elinor Murray Despalatovic. 1975.
13. *Tolerance and Movements of Religious Dissent in Eastern Europe,* Edited by Bela K. Kiraly. 1975.
14. *The Parish Republic: Hlinka's Slovak People's Party, 1939–1945.* By Yeshayahu Jelinek. 1976.
15. *The Russian Annexation of Bessarabia, 1774–1828.* By George F. Jewsbury. 1976.
16. *Modern Hungarian Historiography.* By Steven Bela Vardy. 1976.
17. *Values and Community in Multi-National Yugoslavia.* By Gary K. Bertsch. 1976.
18. *The Greek Socialist Movement and the First World War: the Road to Unity.* By George B. Leon. 1976.
19. *The Radical Left in the Hungarian Revolution of 1848.* By Laszlo Deme. 1976.
20. *Hungary between Wilson and Lenin: The Hungarian Revolution of 1918–1919 and the Big Three.* By Peter Pastor. 1976.

21. *The Crises of France's East-Central European Diplomacy, 1933-1938.* By Anthony J. Komjathy. 1976.
22. *Polish Politics and National Reform, 1775-1788.* By Daniel Stone. 1976.
23. *The Habsburg Empire in World War I.* Edited by Robert A. Kann, Bela K. Kiraly, and Paula S. Fichtner. 1977.
24. *The Slovenes and Yugoslavism, 1890-1914.* By Carole Rogel. 1977.
25. *German-Hungarian Relations and the Swabian Problem.* By Thomas Spira. 1977.
26. *The Metamorphosis of a Social Class in Hungary During the Reign of Young Franz Joseph.* By Peter I. Hidas. 1977.
27. *Tax Reform in Eighteenth Century Lombardy.* By Daniel M. Klang. 1977.
28. *Tradition versus Revolution: Russia and the Balkans in 1917.* By Robert H. Johnston. 1977.
29. *Winter into Spring: The Czechoslovak Press and the Reform Movement 1963-1968.* By Frank L. Kaplan. 1977.
30. *The Catholic Church and the Soviet Government, 1939-1949.* By Dennis J. Dunn. 1977.
31. *The Hungarian Labor Service System, 1939-1945.* By Randolph L. Braham. 1977.
32. *Consciousness and History: Nationalist Critics of Greek Society 1897-1914.* By Gerasimos Augustinos. 1977.
33. *Emigration in Polish Social and Political Thought, 1870-1914.* By Benjamin P. Murdzek. 1977.
34. *Serbian Poetry and Milutin Bojic.* By Mihailo Dordevic. 1977.
35. *The Baranya Dispute: Diplomacy in the Vortex of Ideologies, 1918-1921.* By Leslie C. Tihany. 1978.
36. *The United States in Prague, 1945-1948.* By Walter Ullmann. 1978.
37. *Rush to the Alps: The Evolution of Vacationing in Switzerland.* By Paul P. Bernard. 1978.
38. *Transportation in Eastern Europe: Empirical Findings.* By Bogdan Mieczkowski. 1978.
39. *The Polish Underground State: A Guide to the Underground, 1939-1945.* By Stefan Korbonski. 1978.
40. *The Hungarian Revolution of 1956 in Retrospect.* Edited by Bela K. Kiraly and Paul Jonas. 1978.
41. *Boleslaw Limanowski (1935-1935): A Study in Socialism and Nationalism.* By Kazimiera Janina Cottam. 1978.
42. *The Lingering Shadow of Nazism: The Austrian Independent Party Movement Since 1945.* By Max E. Riedlsperger. 1978.
43. *The Catholic Church, Dissent and Nationality in Soviet Lithuania.* By V. Stanley Vardys. 1978.
44. *The Development of Parliamentary Government in Serbia.* By Alex N. Dragnich. 1978.
45. *Divide and Conquer: German Efforts to Conclude a Separate Peace, 1914-1918.* By L. L. Farrar, Jr. 1978.
46. *The Prague Slav Congress of 1848.* By Lawrence D. Orton. 1978.
47. *The Nobility and the Making of the Hussite Revolution.* By John M. Klassen. 1978.
48. *The Cultural Limits of Revolutionary Politics: Change and Continuity in Socialist Czechoslovakia.* By David W. Paul. 1979.
49. *On the Border of War and Peace: Polish Intelligence and Diplomacy in 1937-1939 and the Origins of the Ultra Secret.* By Richard A. Woytak. 1979.
50. *Bear and Foxes: The International Relations of the East European States 1965-1969.* By Ronald Haly Linden. 1979.

51. *Czechoslovakia: The Heritage of Ages Past.* Edited by Ivan Volgyes and Hans Brisch. 1979.
52. *Prime Minister Gyula Andrassy's Influence on Habsburg Foreign Policy.* By Janos Decsy. 1979.
53. *Citizens for the Fatherland: Education, Educators, and Pedagogical Ideals in Eighteenth Century Russia.* By J. L. Black. 1979.
54. *A History of the "Proletariat": The Emergence of Marxism in the Kingdom of Poland, 1870-1887.* By Norman M. Naimark. 1979.
55. *The Slovak Autonomy Movement, 1935-1939: A Study in Unrelenting Nationalism.* By Dorothea H. El Mallakh. 1979.
56. *Diplomat in Exile: Francis Pulszky's Political Activities in England, 1849-1860.* By Thomas Kabdebo. 1979.
57. *The German Struggle Against the Yugoslav Guerrillas in World War II: German Counter-Insurgency in Yugoslavia, 1941-1943.* By Paul N. Hehn. 1979.
58. *The Emergence of the Romanian National State.* By Gerald J. Bobango. 1979.
59. *Stewards of the Land: The American Farm School and Modern Greece.* By Brenda L. Marder. 1979.
60. *Roman Dmowski: Party, Tactics, Ideology, 1895-1907.* By Alvin M. Fountain, II. 1980.
61. *International and Domestic Politics in Greece During the Crimean War.* By Jon V. Kofas. 1980.
62. *Fires on the Mountain: The Macedonian Revolutionary Movement and the Kidnapping of Ellen Stone.* By Laura Beth Sherman. 1980.
63. *The Modernization of Agriculture: Rural Transformation in Hungary, 1848-1975.* Edited by Joseph Held. 1980.
64. *Britain and the War for Yugoslavia, 1940-1943.* By Mark C. Wheeler. 1980.
65. *The Turn to the Right: The Ideological Origins and Development of Ukrainian Nationalism, 1919-1929.* By Alexander J. Motyl. 1980.
66. *The Maple Leaf and the White Eagle: Canadian-Polish Relations, 1918-1978.* By Aloysius Balawyder. 1980.
67. *Antecedents of Revolution: Alexander I and the Polish Congress Kingdom, 1815-1825.* By Frank W. Thackeray. 1980.
68. *Blood Libel at Tiszaeszlar.* By Andrew Handler. 1980.
69. *Democratic Centralism in Romania: A Study of Local Communist Politics.* By Daniel N. Nelson. 1980.
70. *The Challenge of Communist Education: A Look at the German Democratic Republic.* By Margrete Siebert Klein. 1980.
71. *The Fortifications and Defense of Constantinople.* By Byron C. P. Tsangadas. 1980.
72. *Balkan Cultural Studies.* By Stavro Skendi. 1980.
73. *Studies in Ethnicity: The East European Experience in America.* Edited by Charles A. Ward, Philip Shashko, and Donald E. Pienkos. 1980.
74. *The Logic of "Normalization:" The Soviet Intervention in Czechoslovakia and the Czechoslovak Response.* By Fred Eidlin. 1980.
75. *Red Cross, Black Eagle: A Biography of Albania's American Schol.* By Joan Fultz Kontos. 1981.
76. *Nationalism in Contemporary Europe.* By Franjo Tudjman. 1981.
77. *Great Power Rivalry at the Turkish Straits: The Montreux Conference and Convention of 1936.* By Anthony R. DeLuca. 1981.
78. *Islam Under the Double Eagle: The Muslims of Bosnia and Hercegovina, 1878-1914.* By Robert J. Donia. 1981.

79. *Five Eleventh Century Hungarian Kings: Their Policies and Their Relations with Rome.* By Z. J. Kosztolnyik. 1981.

80. *Prelude to Appeasement: East European Central Diplomacy in the Early 1930's.* By Lisanne Radice. 1981.

81. *The Soviet Regime in Czechoslovakia.* By Zdenek Krystufek. 1981.

82. *School Strikes in Prussian Poland, 1901-1907: The Struggle Over Bilingual Education.* By John J. Kulczychi. 1981.

83. *Romantic Nationalism and Liberalism: Joachim Lelewel and the Polish National Idea.* By Joan S. Skurnowicz. 1981.

84. *The "Thaw" In Bulgarian Literature.* By Atanas Slavov. 1981.

85. *The Political Thought of Thomas G. Masaryk.* By Roman Szporluk. 1981.

86. *Prussian Poland in the German Empire, 1871-1900.* By Richard Blanke. 1981.

87. *The Mazepists: Ukrainian Separatism in the Early Eighteenth Century.* By Orest Subtelny. 1981.

88. *The Battle for the Marchlands: The Russo-Polish Campaign of 1920.* By Adam Zamoyski. 1981.

89. *Milovan Djilas: A Revolutionary as a Writer.* By Dennis Reinhartz. 1981.

90. *The Second Republic: The Disintegration of Post-Munich Czechoslovakia, October 1938-March 1939.* By Theodore Prochazka, Sr. 1981.

91. *Financial Relations of Greece and the Great Powers, 1832-1862.* By Jon V. Kofas. 1981.

92. *Religion and Politics: Bishop Valerian Trifa and His Times.* By Gerald J. Bobango. 1981.

93. *The Politics of Ethnicity in Eastern Europe.* Edited by George Klein and Milan J. Reban. 1981.

94. *Czech Writers and Politics.* By Alfred French. 1981.

95. *Nation and Ideology: Essays in Honor of Wayne S. Vucinich.* Edited by Ivo Banac, John G. Ackerman, and Roman Szporluk. 1981.

96. *For God and Peter the Great: The Works of Thomas Consett, 1723-1729.* Edited by James Cracraft. 1982.

97. *The Geopolitics of Leninism.* By Stanley W. Page. 1982

98. *Karel Havlicek (1821-1856): A National Liberation Leader of the Czech Renascence.* By Barbara K. Reinfeld. 1982.

99. *Were-Wolf and Vampire in Romania.* By Harry A. Senn. 1982.

100. *Ferdinand I of Austria: The Politics of Dynasticism in the Age of Reformation.* By Paula Sutter Fichtner. 1982

101. *France in Greece During World War I: A Study in the Politics of Power.* By Alexander S. Mitrakos. 1982.

102. *Authoritarian Politics in a Transitional State: Istvan Bethlen and the Unified Party in Hungary, 1919-1926.* By William M. Batkay. 1982.

103. *Romania Between East and West: Historical Essays in Memory of Constantin C. Giurescu.* Edited by Stephen Fischer-Galati, Radu R. Florescu and George R. Ursul. 1982.

104. *War and Society in East Central Europe: From Hunyadi to Rakoczi—War and Society in Late Medieval and Early Modern Hungary.* Edited by János Bak and Béla K. Király. 1982.

105. *Total War and Peace Making: A Case Study on Trianon.* Edited by Béla K. Király, Peter Pastor, and Ivan Sanders. 1982

106. *Army, Aristocracy, and Monarchy: Essays on War, Society, and Government in Austria, 1618-1780.* Edited by Wayne S. Vucinich. 1982.

107 .*The First Serbian Uprising, 1804-1813.* Edited by Wayne S. Vucinich. 1982.

108. *Propaganda and Nationalism in Wartime Russia: The Jewish Anti-Fascist Committee in the USSR, 1941-1948.* By Shimon Redich. 1982.

109. *One Step Back, Two Steps Forward: On the Language Policy of the Communist Party of Soviet Union in the National Republics.* By Michael Bruchis. 1982.

110. *Bessarabia and Bukovina: The Soviet-Romanian Territorial Dispute.* by Nicholas Dima. 1982

111. *Greek-Soviet Relations, 1917-1941.* By Andrew L. Zapantis. 1982.

112. *National Minorities in Romania: Change in Transylvania.* By Elemer Illyes. 1982.

113. *Dunarea Noastra: Romania, the Great Powers, and the Danube Question, 1914-1921.* by Richard C. Frucht. 1982.

114. *Continuity and Change in Austrian Socialism: The Eternal Quest for the Third Way.* By Melanie A. Sully. 1982

115. *Catherine II's Greek Prelate: Eugenios Voulgaris in Russia, 1771-1806.* By Stephen K. Batalden. 1982.

116. *The Union of Lublin: Polish Federalism in the Golden Age.* By Harry E. Dembkowski. 1982.

117. *Heritage and Continuity in Eastern Europe: The Transylvanian Legacy in the History of the Romanians.* By Cornelia Bodea and Virgil Candea. 1982.

118. *Contemporary Czech Cinematography: Jiri Menzel and the History of The "Closely Watched Trains".* By Josef Skvorecky. 1982.

119. *East Central Europe in World War I: From Foreign Domination to National Freedom.* By Wiktor Sukiennicki. 1982.

120. *City, Town, and Countryside in the Early Byzantine Era.* Edited by Robert L. Hohlfelder. 1982.

121. *The Byzantine State Finances in the Eighth and Ninth Centuries.* By Warren T. Treadgold. 1982.

122. *East Central European Society and War in Pre-Revolutionary Eighteenth Century.* Edited by Gunther E. Rothenberg, Bela K. Kiraly and Peter F. Sugar. 1982.

123. *Czechoslovak Policy and the Hungarian Minority, 1945-1948.* By Kalman Janics. 1982.

124. *At the Brink of War and Peace: The Tito-Stalin Split in a Historic Perspective.* Edited by Wayne S. Vucinich. 1982.

125. *The Road to Bellapais: The Turkish Cypriot Exodus to Northern Cyprus.* By Pierre Oberling. 1982.

126. *Essays on World War I: Origins and Prisoners of War.* Edited by Peter Pastor and Samuel R. Williamson, Jr. 1983.

127. *Panteleimon Kulish: A Sketch of His Life and Times.* By George S. N. Luckyj. 1983.

128. *Economic Development in the Habsburg Monarchy in the Nineteenth Century: Essays.* Edited by John Komlos. 1983.

129. *Warsaw Between the World Wars: Profile of the Capital City in a Developing Land, 1918-1939.* By Edward D. Wynot, Jr. 1983.

130. *The Lust for Power: Nationalism, Slovakia, and The Communists, 1918-1948.* By Yeshayahu Jelinek. 1983.

131. *The Tsar's Loyal Germans: The Riga German Community: Social Change and the Nationality Question, 1855-1905.* By Anders Henriksson. 1983.

132. *Society in Change: Studies in Honor of Bela K. Kiraly.* Edited by Steven Bela Vardy. 1983.

133. *Authoritariansim in Greece: The Metaxas Regime.* By Jon V. Kofas. 1983.

134. *New Hungarian Peasants: An East Central European Experience with Collectivization.* Edited by Marida Hollos and Bela C. Maday. 1983.

135. *War, Revolution, and Society in Romania: The Road to Independence.* Edited by Ilie Ceausescu. 1983.

136. *The Beginning of Cyrillic Printing, Cracow, 1491: From the Orthodox Past in Poland.* By Szczepan K. Zimmer. 1983.

137. *Effects of World War I. The Class War After the Great War: The Rise of Communist Parties in East Central Europe, 1918-1921.* Edited by Ivo Banac. 1983.

138. *Bulgaria 1878-1918. A History.* By Richard J. Crampton. 1983.

139. *T. G. Masaryk Revisited: A Cirtical Assessment.* By Hanus J. Hajek. 1983.

140. *The Cult of Power: Dictators in the Twentieth Century.* Edited by Joseph Held. 1983.

141. *Economy and Foreign Policy: The Struggle of the Great Powers for Economic Hegemony in the Danube Valley, 1919-1939.* By György Ránki. 1983.

142. *Germany, Russia, and the Balkans: Prelude to the Nazi-Soviet Non-Aggression Pact.* By Marilynn Giroux Hitchens. 1983.

143. Guestworkers in the German Reich: The Poles in Wilhelmian Germany. By Richard Charles Murphy. 1983.

144. *The Latvian Impact on the Bolshevik Revolution.* By Andrew Ezergailis. 1983.

145. *The Rise of Moscow's Power.* By Henryk Paszkiewicz. 1983.

146. *A Question of Empire: Leopold I and the War of the Spanish Succession, 1701-1705.* By Linda and Marsha Frey. 1983.

147. *Effects of World War I. The Uprooted: Hungarian Refugees and Their Impact on Hungarian Domestic Policies, 1918-1921.* By Istvan I. Mocsy. 1983.

148. *Nationalist Integration Through Socialist Planning: An Anthropological Study of a Romanian New Town.* By Steven L. Sampson. 1983.

149. *Decadence of Freedom: Jacques Riviere's Quest of Russian Mentality.* By Jean-Pierre Cap. 1983.

150. *East Central European Society in the Age of Revolutions, 1775-1856.* Edited by Béla K. Király. 1984.

151. *The Crucial Decade: East Central European Society and National Defense, 1859-1870.* Edited by Béla K. Király. 1984.

152. *The First War between Socialist States: The Hungarian Revolution of 1956 and Its Impact.* Edited by Béla K. Király, Barbara Lotze and Nandor Dreisziger. 1984.

153. *Russian Bolshevism and British Labor, 1917-1921.* By Morton H. Cowden. 1984.

154. *Feliks Dzierzynski and the SDKPIL: A Study of the Origins of Polish Communism.* By Robert Blobaum. 1984.

155. *Studies on Kosova.* Edited by Arshi Pipa and Sami Repishti. 1984.

156. *New Horizons in East-West Economic and Business Relations.* Edited by Marvin A. Jackson and James D. Woodson. 1984.

157. *Czech Nationalism in the Nineteenth Century.* By John F. N. Bradley. 1984.

158. *The Theory of the General Strike from the French Revolution to Poland.* By Phil H. Goodstein. 1984.

159. *King Zog and the Struggle for Stability in Albania.* By Bernd J. Fischer. 1984.

160. *Tradition and Avant-Garde: The Arts in Serbian Culture between the Two World Wars.* By Jelena Milojković-Djurić. 1984.

161. *The Megali Idea and the Greek Turkish War of 1897.* By Theodore G. Tatsios. 1984.

162. *The Hungarian Jewish Catastrophe: A Selected and Annotated Bibliography.* By Randolph L. Braham. 1984.

163. *Goli Otok—Island of Death [A Diary in Letters].* By Venko Markovski. 1984.

164. *Initiation and Initiative: An Exploration of the Life and Ideas of Dimitrije Mitrinovic.* By Andrew Rigby. 1984.

165. *Nations, Nationalities, Peoples: A Study of the Nationality Policies of the Communist Party in Soviet Moldavia.* By Michael Bruchis. 1984.

166. *Frederick I, The Man and His Times.* By Linda and Marsha Frey. 1984.

167. *The Effects of World War I: War Communism in Hungary.* By György Peteri. 1984.

168. *PNA: A Centennial History of the Polish National Alliance of the United States of North America.* By Donald E. Pienkos. 1984.

169. *The Slovenes of Carinthia.* By Thomas M. Barker and Andreas Moritsch. 1984.

170. *The Saga of Kosovo: Focus of Serbian-Albanian Relations.* By Alex N. Dragnich and Slavko Todorovich. 1984.

171. *Germany's International Monetary Policy and the European Monetary System.* By Hugh Kaufmann. 1985.

172. *Kiril and Methodius: Founders of Slavonic Writing.* Edited by Ivan Duichev. 1985.

173. *The United States and the Greek War for Independence, 1821-1828.* By Paul C. Pappas. 1985.

174. *Joseph Eotvos and the Modernization of Hungary, 1840-1870.* By Paul Bödy. 1985.

175. *Jewish Leadership during the Nazi Era: Patterns of Behavior in the Free World.* Edited by Randolph L. Braham. 1985.

176. *The American Mission in the Allied Control Commission for Bulgaria, 1944-1947: History and Transcripts.* Edited by Michael M. Boll. 1985.

177. *The United States, Great Britain, and the Sovietization of Hungary, 1945-1948.* By Stanley M. Max. 1985.

178. *Hunyadi: Legend and Reality.* By Joseph Held. 1985.

179. *Clio's Art in Hungary and in Hungarian-America.* By Steven Bela Vardy. 1985.

180. *Slovakia 1918-1938: Education and the Making of a Nation.* By Owen V. Johnson. 1985.

181. *Ilija Garasanin: Balkan Bismarck.* By David MacKenzie. 1985.

182. *Medieval Buda: A Study of Municipal Government and Jurisdiction in the Kingdom of Hungary.* By Martyn C. Rady. 1985.

183. *Eastern Europe in the Aftermath of Solidarity.* By Adam Bromke. 1985.

184. *Istvan Tisza: The Liberal Vision and Conservative Statecraft of a Magyar Nationalist.* By Gabor Vermes. 1985.